A WRITER'S LIFE

THE
MARGARET
LAURENCE
LECTURES

Presented by

WRITERS' TRUST
of CANADA

Library and Archives Canada Cataloguing in Publication

A writer's life : the Margaret Laurence lectures / presented by the Writers Trust of Canada.

(Margaret Laurence memorial lecture series)
ISBN 978-0-7710-8928-2

1. Authors, Canadian – 20th century – Biography. 2. Authorship – Literary
collections. I. Writers' Trust of Canada II. Series: Margaret Laurence memorial lecture series

PS8083.W75 2011   C810.9   C2010-907702-4

Published simultaneously in the United States of America by
McClelland & Stewart Ltd. P.O. Box 1030, Plattsburgh, New York 12901

Library of Congress Control Number: 2011924219

We acknowledge the financial support of the Government of Canada through the Book Publishing
Industry Development Program and that of the Government of Ontario through the Ontario
Media Development Corporation's Ontario Book Initiative. We further acknowledge the support
of the Canada Council for the Arts and the Ontario Arts Council for our publishing program.

Typeset in Perpetua
Printed and bound in Canada

This book is printed on paper that is 100% recycled,
ancient-forest friendly (100% post-consumer waste).

McClelland & Stewart Ltd.
75 Sherbourne Street
Toronto, Ontario
M5A 2P9
www.mcclelland.com

1   2   3   4   5   15   14   13   12   11

CONTENTS

INTRODUCTION

THE WRITERS' TRUST OF CANADA

Margaret Laurence referred to fellow Canadian writers as "the tribe" — a group of people collaborating for their shared survival. Writers carry out their work — a solitary occupation if there ever was one — in isolation. But this country's literature would not have bloomed over the past half-century if it weren't for the type of support offered to one another by Canadian writers — and readers. That sense of community, of mutual support, is at the heart of what the lectures in this anthology are all about.

Each year since 1987, the Writers' Trust of Canada has commissioned a senior Canadian author of stature to deliver a lecture on the topic "A Writer's Life." This anthology is a collection of the perceptive commentary and deep wisdom that the Margaret Laurence Lecturers have brought to the podium over the past twenty-five years.

It was Pierre Berton, a co-founder of the Writers' Trust, who originally proposed the creation of the Margaret Laurence Lecture series. The purpose then (as it remains now) was to have writers look retrospectively at their own lives, sharing insights into their work, the profession of writing, the growing canon of our literature, and the cultural history of our country. The series is named in honour of novelist Margaret Laurence, a co-founder of the Writers' Trust and a key figure in the emergence of Canadian literature whose work remains widely read and studied today.

While the lectures are all roughly the same length (approximately forty-five minutes), the Writers' Trust encourages each lecturer to freely interpret the phrase "A Writer's Life." Past lecturers have spoken on broad social and cultural issues (censorship, compassion, historical memory) while others were more personal, detailing their path as writers and sharing stories of their rejections, roadblocks overcome, and the good fortune that led to their success. Many have also mentioned Margaret Laurence and the role she played in their writing careers.

Delivered each year at the Writers' Union of Canada's annual general meeting, the Margaret Laurence Lectures are composed for and delivered to a roomful of writers. They are thus intimate in tone, frank, and often revealing. This anthology brings to readers, for the first time, a privileged glimpse into the conversation writers have amongst themselves.

We often have an ideal notion of where successful writers come from. The story is familiar: young and ambitious, armed with his or her own genius and little formal training, the aspiring author arrives in a metropolis and publishes a book. Fame and fortune ensue. But this collection shows how rare that tidy back-story is. Few writers spring up fully formed; instead they develop in varied, unique ways.

The contributors to this collection are some of the most prominent figures in Canadian cultural history. They helped build a rich and complex national literature. In sharing the stories of their lives, they provide a glimpse into the formation of our country's national writing community. It is often repeated, but too rarely understood, that a generation or two ago only a handful of books of any literary merit were published each year in Canada. Canadian literature was not yet taught in university courses; it was more often marginalized as an appendage to American or English literature. Now, Canadian literature is on the world stage. The growth of Canada's publishing scene from infancy to flourishing cultural sector is a story that runs through these lectures.

This collection is a collage, a diverse assembly of voices from varied backgrounds and different fields of work. The essays include Mavis Gallant on her writing apprenticeship at a Montreal newspaper; Timothy Findley on culture's devaluation to a form of entertainment; Pierre Berton on his childhood dream of becoming a chemist; Farley Mowat on why writers should speak for those who have no voice; Al Purdy on the misdirection of his youth; and Peter C. Newman on the importance of characters over statistics in non-fiction. As well, the collection includes sparkling pieces by the wry Margaret Atwood, humorous Czech dissident Josef Škvorecký, transplanted islander Alistair MacLeod, creative non-fiction maven Edna Staebler, children's author Janet Lunn, Acadian dramatist Antonine Maillet, and chronicler of the prairies Ruby Wiebe, among others.

Not every lecture delivered is included here in its original form. Tape recorders have been faulty; transcripts have been lost. Roch Carrier and Alistair MacLeod kindly agreed to our request for a re-do, and have new contributions included here. Nor was every lecture hoped for actually delivered. Sadly, illness prevented Robertson Davies and Carol Shields from being able to complete the composition of their lectures.

The Writers' Trust would like to thank the Writers' Union of Canada and its membership for hosting twenty-five incarnations of the lecture. Additional gratitude goes to McClelland & Stewart for making this anthology happen and to Merilyn Simonds, Jennifer Lambert, and Marian Hebb for crucial guidance along the way.

Founded by Margaret Atwood, Pierre Berton, Graeme Gibson, Margaret Laurence, and David Young, the Writers' Trust of Canada is, in the words of Gibson, "a great big friend for writers," delivering financial support to Canadian authors through a portfolio of literary awards and programs. A thirty-four-year-old charitable organization, the Writers' Trust relies almost exclusively on donations from the private sector to fund its activities. This support has covered the expenses of the lecture series program over the last twenty-five years and made it possible for each lecturer to receive a five-thousand-dollar honorarium. The Writers' Trust is grateful to past and present Writers' Trust supporters for ensuring that the programs like the Margaret Laurence Lecture series continue.

Canada has been interpreted to readers through the stories and poems of the writers included in this collection. The Writers' Trust is grateful to the contributors of this lecture series for turning their analysis inward, opening a lens upon "A Writer's Life," and showing us who deeply value Canadian literature what being part of "the tribe" is all about.

ABOUT

MARGARET

LAURENCE

Margaret Laurence was a novelist and short story writer and a key figure in the emergence of Canadian literature in the second half of the twentieth century. Born in Neepawa, Manitoba, in 1926, she attended United College (now the University of Winnipeg) on scholarship and graduated in 1947 with an honours degree in English. After college she worked as a reporter and wrote book reviews before moving overseas in 1949 with her husband, Jack Fergus Laurence, a civil engineer whose work took the couple to England, British Somaliland (now Somalia), and the Gold Coast (now Ghana). While living abroad, Laurence had two children, Jocelyn and David.

In 1954, she published *A Tree for Poverty*, her translation of Somali folktales and poetry. That same year, she published her first piece of fiction, the short story "Uncertain Flowering." In 1957, Laurence left Africa for Vancouver, and three years later published her first novel, *This Side Jordan*, followed in 1963 by a collection of stories, *The Tomorrow-Tamer,* and an account of her experiences in Somaliland, *The Prophet's Camel Bell*. In 1962, she separated from her husband and moved to England, where over the next decade she worked on the Manawaka cycle, five works set in the imagined prairie town of Manawaka: *The Stone Angel* (1964), *A Jest of God* (1966), *The Fire-Dwellers* (1969), *A Bird in the House* (1970), and *The Diviners* (1974). Celebrated for their memorable representation of the lives and struggles of women, these books received international acclaim and remain widely read and studied today.

Returning permanently to Canada in 1974, Laurence lived in Lakefield, Ontario, and continued to write, publishing several works of non-fiction and children's literature.

Margaret Laurence twice won the Governor General's Literary Award for Fiction, received numerous honorary degrees, and was made a Companion of the Order of Canada. Laurence helped to establish the Writers' Union of Canada and the Writers' Trust of Canada, and provided personal support and encouragement to many writers during her lifetime.

In 1986, she was diagnosed with lung cancer late in the disease's development. She died on January 5, 1987, and was buried near her childhood home in Neepawa, which is now a museum dedicated to the author.

1987

HUGH MACLENNAN

It is a very great honour you have done me in asking me to give the first of
the Margaret Laurence Lectures. Profoundly, I wish it were not so. It seems
a grim jest of God that she should be gone and I should be here, for I was
born some eighteen years before she came into the world. I came from the
extreme eastern tip of Canada before Newfoundland joined us. Margaret
was born in the dead centre some two thousand miles to the west. Both of
us were of Scottish origin, though her surname, Wemyss, indicates that she
was a scion of a prominent family from County Angus. Both of us were born
in dying small towns. Both of us went abroad before we began to write.
Both of us, in trying to discover ourselves, had first to discover some of the
historical and psychological truths of the huge, undefined nation into which
we were born.

Though I met Margaret very seldom during her lifetime, it was always like
meeting someone whose professionalism I sensed so naturally that I took it
for granted, as she, I believe, took me for granted. She had the inner generosity of a person whose life had been very difficult, and her work was at once a
deliverance from herself and a triumph within herself. Toward the end, when
apparently the whole nation held her in honour, she had to go to law to prevent a handful of self-righteous hypocrites from banning her books from the
schools of Ontario. It upset her profoundly to have to take off the gloves and
fight them in the courts, and though she won the battle, she must have suffered

some psychological damage from it, and it is quite possible that if this outrage had not occurred, she would still be alive.

In the last months of Margaret's life, when I knew she had terminal cancer, I telephoned her every second week and always found her calm, a little more husky of voice than when I first met her, but acceptant and even tranquil. She knew she had done her work and that it was good; she had rounded it off; she had gone out from the prairie small town into the great outer world, including the Horn of Africa and southern England. Then, as naturally and inevitably as a Pacific salmon swimming back to its original spawning bed, she returned and tackled the little Manitoba town where she had grown up. She re-created it under the name of Manawaka, and in so doing, like Ulysses when he returned to Ithaca, she slew quite a few demons.

The southeastern corner of Manitoba is one of the most historic regions in this entire country, and its history is much better known in Quebec than in Ontario. This is because of the early voyageurs who, over a century and a half, explored in canoes the whole nation from Montreal to the Pacific and the Mackenzie Delta, as well as the Mississippi Valley down to New Orleans. La Vérendrye, born in Trois-Rivières in 1685 – which happened to be also the birth year of Handel and Sebastian Bach – returning from service in the War of the Spanish Succession, set out for the West with a party of fifty men, including three of his own sons. He established Fort Rouge on the banks of the Red River and continued west, perhaps to a sight of the Rockies. Later, after the English Conquest of New France, the name was changed to Fort Garry, and now, of course, it is Winnipeg.

After La Vérendrye, there appeared on the plains in increasing numbers the Métis, most of them children of French fathers and Indian mothers. Colbert, the great finance minister of Louis XIV, laid it down that French settlers in America should mate with the native peoples, and this surely explains the astonishing endurance of the original voyageurs. Later on, the Scottish Highlanders of the North West Company and the HBC followed to some extent the same practice, though most of them had legitimate wives at home in Montreal. This fundamental part of the Canadian story was glossed over until very recently, but only a few days ago, at Percé in the Gaspé, President Mitterrand of France alluded to it openly, saying that many French-Canadian expressions were derived from the Indian languages.

In modern times, when at last a true Canadian literature developed, Manitoba gave us in Gabrielle Roy the finest of French-Canadian novelists, and she was a Métis from Saint-Boniface. Later on, Margaret Laurence gave us that wonderful Métis character, Jules Tonnerre. The great achievement of these two women writers was to tell hundreds of thousands of Canadians who they were.

I shall never forget a reading Margaret gave in McGill during the period I used to call "our time of troubles," when "Spock-marked" student politicians, many of them Americans, were raging against the American Empire which was committing suicide in Vietnam and involving much of the world in the general catastrophe. Margaret came into the campus like a wave of peace. She had an enormous audience of many ages, and though the acoustics were bad in the hall, she held them entirely with her. Waves of affection seemed to surge around her, and no wonder. For here was a woman of profound understanding of the human condition.

Academics have been trained for a long time to put their confidence in pure reason, and the American Republic was to a large extent founded on the theories of eighteenth-century philosophers, especially Locke, and to a lesser extent, Rousseau. Locke has a great deal to answer for. This childless philosopher asserted that the infant new to earth and sky is born with a mind which is a *tabula rasa* – a blank sheet of paper to be written on by the hand of experience. Every woman who has minded a baby understands that this is total nonsense, but sensible women were not listened to in that Age of Reason. Perhaps at last men are beginning to listen to them, the young ones at least. Writers like Margaret Laurence understood in their bones the truth of a sentence written by a great Frenchman long before the Age of Reason, which has triumphed in our time of the H-bomb and the Cold War. "*Il est bon*," wrote Malherbe, "*et plus souvent qu'on ne le pense, de savoir de n'avoir pas de l'esprit.*"

The French-Canadians and the Métis knew this truth in their bones, and that is how they managed to survive and stay sane for two centuries after the American Revolution.

I shall now leave Margaret Laurence in peace, and speak a little of my own experience as a writer in this country.

Seven and a half years ago, I finished my last novel, *Voices in Time*, and knew it would be the last novel I would ever write. It occupied some ten years of my life and it exhausted me. Becoming a great variety of characters can be a soul-bending experience. I realized that I had reached the stage when I must try to deal with the most inexplicable character I had any knowledge of: myself. Two and a half months ago I became, to my dismay, eighty years old, which is fifteen beyond the legal age described by that appalling modern expression, "a senior citizen." Two weeks ago a group of high school students from Moncton came to see me (in addition to other writers in central Canada), and a fifteen-year-old boy asked me as practical a question as I ever heard. "You're eighty years old," he said, "and that's an awful thing. What does it feel like to know that you'll soon be dead?" Now, how could anyone answer a question like that?

However, the boy had a point, and a good one. For some time now, I have been trying to write a memoir, which is a very different thing from writing a novel. In recent years I have been reading and re-reading volumes about the history of my own time, and it is worth noting that since the last war, the writers of history are far more competent, more interesting and readable, than all but a few since Thucydides.

I was born in 1907, and it was only a few years ago that I discovered that this was the most fatal date in the entire twentieth century, because it was then that the First World War became inevitable.

Years had to pass before it dawned on me that this century into which I was born, and in which I have lived and worked, written books and taught, or tried to teach, several thousand young students, has been the most agonizing for humanity of any period since the century of Saint Augustine. It came upon me just before my eightieth birthday, when I was invited to Princeton University to give the James Madison Address and to receive the James Madison Medal. As I had been dismissed from Princeton some fifty-two years ago as an irritating socialist and an incompetent scholar, this was a moving experience. Memories crowded me, and I shall share some of them with you now, if for no other reason than that the most perplexing problem in Canada's existence has always been her relationship with the United States.

I arrived in Princeton in September, 1932. In June of 1935 I left it, I thought, forever, and without prospects. In retrospect, this seems of no importance. But what surely is of immense importance – also in retrospect – is that these three years, 1932 to 1935, were the most fateful, and possibly the most fatal, in the history of Western civilization.

When I first went to the United States in the fall of 1932, the world was in the bottom black hole of the Great Depression which began with the Wall Street crash in 1929. In that year, I was in Oxford as a Rhodes Scholar, working twelve hours a day to prepare for my examinations in Honour Moderations, very tough exams which searched every nook and corner of a student's ignorance. I did not know at the time that the market had crashed, but two years later I certainly discovered what this meant for anyone my age. In 1932, only 3 per cent of Rhodes Scholars leaving Oxford were able to step into jobs, and I was not one of the 3 per cent. This was the year when the Princeton graduating class decorated the backs of their beer suits with a young man's face surrounded by a garland of barking female dogs. The message of this was "Bitched All Around," and the signature song of the Glee Club's show was "We've Got Love – And a Dime."

However wounded and confused North America was, it was not in total despair, not in any respect so desperate as were parts of Europe.

The Depression struck Europe, and Germany especially, with the combined force of a typhoon and earthquake. The savings of the German middle class had been wiped out in the early 1920s by a total inflation, but enormous financial aid from America soon revived German industry, and outwardly Germany seemed to be prospering. Now, suddenly, within a period of a few months, industry came to a virtual standstill. Millions were without jobs of any kind, and very few had any savings.

It has sometimes been said that the First Great War of our century was caused by rivalries among Queen Victoria's many grandchildren. The rivalries were certainly there, and so was the irresponsibility and so was the arrogance. But now, in retrospect, we can see that the underlying causes of that catastrophe went far deeper than the political ones; that there was a mysterious drive to self-destruction in Western civilization itself, a drive that was to culminate half a century later in the Vietnam War, the worldwide inflation produced by it among the so-called democratic states, and the self-assertions of older and previously poorer cultures.

Because I lived in Halifax as a child, and missed by two feet being killed in the great explosion of 1917, the greatest single man-made explosion before

Hiroshima, this old war is still very vivid to me. The generals, with the exception of Allenby and Pershing, were so incompetent that one marvels that such
bone-headed fools could ever have been put in command of any military body
above the company level. But the soldiers who served them were so brave and
dedicated that they seemed ready to endure anything.

> Now, God be thanked Who has matched us with His hour,
> And caught our youth, and wakened us from sleeping . . .

So sang Rupert Brooke, who died of an infection during the Gallipoli campaign in 1915. "Laughing and singing," went the legend, "they marched to the
Great Adventure" – the youth of Europe and the British Empire, ultimately to
be joined by the youth of the United States. The propaganda was atrocious
in its sadism and falsehood. One of the worst examples was the cartoon of
"The Crucified Canadian" hanging almost naked on a cross while villainous
men in German uniforms diced for his garments at the foot of the cross. This
was a poison we were all fed in those years.

As you know here, but as few Americans ever knew, Canada, Australia,
New Zealand, India, and all the minor British colonies were automatically at
war on August 4, 1914, because in those days their foreign policies were
entirely controlled in London. In 1914, Canada had a total population of only
seven and a half million souls. She suffered action deaths of sixty-six thousand
and casualties of close to two hundred thousand. If the United States had suffered proportionally, the figure would have run as high as seven hundred and
fifty thousand dead. But of course this never could have happened, for if the
United States had been at war in 1914, the whole war would have ended a year
and a half later.

Slogans, of course, abounded. Lloyd George called it "The War to End Wars."
When America entered in 1917, Woodrow Wilson's slogan was "[A War] To
Make the World Safe for Democracy." We soon learned that this holocaust
had made the world safe for nothing. The vengeful fools who broke Wilson's
heart at Versailles guaranteed that the appalling slaughter in the trenches and
at sea were only an overture to the total world war that broke out twenty-
one years later. It was an uncanny instinct that caused the people to call

November 11 "Armistice Day." With remarkable realism, Marshal Foch declared, "This is not peace. This is an armistice of twenty years." His prophecy was only a few months short of dead accuracy.

So, back to the Germany of the early '30s.

Six months before I came to Princeton, I spent my final Oxford vacation in Berlin. I had several times been in south Germany, but this was my first visit to the capital. It was appalling. In that year, the German unemployment was so universal that more than ten thousand men with doctor's degrees were begging bread from door to door. Every night, Nazis and Communists did battle in the streets of the great northern cities. The so-called Republic of Weimar was helpless and old President Hindenburg was known to have become gaga.

The first night I spent in Berlin in 1932, I was with another Oxford student, a German, and after supper we went out for one of the most informative walks I ever took. On one sidewalk of the Friedrichstrasse, there was a female prostitute at every fifteen yards and the price was two marks. On the opposite side, the prostitutes were all males. We went into a small cabaret (it was made famous many years later by Liza Minnelli in the movie called *Cabaret*) and found it another rendezvous for prostitutes. After a quick beer, we fled, but not before noting that most of the men in the joint were wearing swastikas on their sleeves. Passing a lighted bookstore, we saw that the book of the year was Hans Fallada's *Kleiner Mann, was nun?* The next year it swept the world under the title, in literal translation, *Little Man, What Now?*

My German companion muttered, "Hitler can't miss. He can't possibly miss now." I didn't take in the terrible significance of that remark, for like most non-Germans at the time I could not imagine that a man who looked like Hitler, talked like Hitler, and screamed like Hitler could possibly turn into what he became.

Anyway, I finished at Oxford, went home to my parents in Halifax, tried to get a job and failed, so my doctor-father proposed that I apply for entrance to the Princeton Graduate College.

On the train from Penn Station to Princeton Junction, I noticed that little smoke came out of the factory chimneys in New Jersey. I got a cab to the Graduate College and the town seemed beautiful and peaceful.

I was shown to my room in the Graduate College and found I was to share the bathroom with another old Oxford man whom I had met briefly before. His name was Geoffrey Bing, and thinking back on him, with some affection, I now realize that he was a portent of his time. He was marvelously witty. He looked almost Oriental, and with good reason, for he later told me that his grandfather had been a Rhenish baron who had married a lady of the famous Hungarian family of Esterházy, was later expelled from Germany, had emigrated to Indo-China where he made a small fortune furnishing white slaves to the troops of the French garrison.

Geoffrey himself had been born in Ireland. He must have been born *méchant*, for he saw the absurd side of everything and got fun out of it. After a year in Princeton he became a communist, fought in the desert battles of the Hitler War, returned to England, and befriended an African student called N'Kruma who became President, and immediately afterwards dictator, of the old Gold Coast, the name of which he changed to Ghana. He made Geoffrey his attorney general, then he went mad with megalomania, slept in a bed of solid gold, and soon afterwards was murdered by an enraged population. Geoffrey escaped, surfaced later in London, and was elected to Parliament, where his lethal wit infuriated the Conservatives. He even became respectable toward the end and was made a Queen's Counsellor before he died a few years ago.

However, a gentleman far more celebrated than Geoffrey Bing arrived in Princeton during my first year, and he was Albert Einstein. The previous year, he had lectured in Oxford, and physicists and mathematicians had assembled from all over the world to examine his latest equations. At that time they were still arguing about Einstein's theories. Some scientists thought the universe was cylindrical; some thought it was finite; more cautious ones were willing to admit that they didn't know. A headline in a London paper displayed Einstein's picture and beneath it was the caption: "WILL HE TELL US WHERE WE ARE?"

Einstein loved solitary walks, and sometimes he lost his way because his thoughts were elsewhere. One chilly afternoon I went out for a run around the Christ Church Meadows, came around a sharp bend in the tow-path, and crashed headlong into Einstein. I was aghast. But Einstein's marvellous eyes showed nothing but gentle curiosity. "Young man," he said, "can you tell me please vair am I?" Later on, in Princeton, he was to ask me the same question on two more occasions.

The title I offered in Princeton for the Madison Medal address was "A Tale of Two Countries," and I think it fits just as well at home as it did there. Never in history have two countries been more closely entwined than the United States and Canada. Never, so far as I know, has there been such a weird blending of chance and irony in the relations that grew up between these two countries.

As every Canadian knows, the first European navigator to strike North America above Florida was Jacques Cartier, and one may wonder what would have been the future on this continent if he had made his landfalls in Massachusetts or Virginia instead of Labrador, Percé, and the St. Lawrence estuary. As all Canadians know, he was stopped three times by the Lachine Rapids, but he did climb Mount Royal and saw the vast forests and the river itself curving westward on the far side. The last of his three voyages was made in 1536, and though on his return to France he wrote a description of them, nearly a century elapsed before another expedition was made to Canada from France.

Then came Champlain, first to Nova Scotia in 1605, three years later to the St. Lawrence, where he followed Cartier's route up the river, and in the year of Milton's birth he founded the City of Quebec. Immediately the ironies began to form.

Champlain's king and patron was the great Henri IV, originally a Protestant who converted to Catholicism in order to terminate the religious wars that were tearing France apart. "*Paris*," he said in a famous sentence, "*vaut bien une messe*." The Protestant Champlain followed suit because he knew he could never establish a colony in the midst of a religious war. Although a number of Champlain's team of explorers remained Protestants, there was at least no religious war in the colony.

The region now known as Quebec he called "New France," just as, a generation later, the first English colonists to the continent called their region "New England." But there was a vast difference of motive between the early French and the early English settlers. The English came for religious freedom; the French were lured on by the dream of the Northwest Passage to China.

Champlain was the first European to discover that if men were to travel in the densely forested northern country, they would have to forget about horses and even about European methods of navigation. Cartier had been stopped at the Lachine Rapids and so was he: "The water here is so swift," he wrote, "that it could not be more so . . . it is impossible to imagine one's being able to go by boat through these falls. But any one desiring to pass them, should provide himself with the canoe of the savages, which a man can easily carry."

So began, in Champlain's first tentative journey above Montreal in a birch-bark canoe, the first chapter in a long era of voyaging. For many years, the barrier of the Appalachians was to hold up the later English settlers of the original thirteen colonies, but the situation was very different for the Canadians. It was not long after the settlement that the French voyageurs in their canoes penetrated to the heart of North America. For two centuries, followed by Scottish Highlanders after the Conquest, the canoe parties threaded their way through the hinterland of North America, moving east to west and north to south. La Salle, setting out to discover the Northwest Passage, followed previous voyages of Hennepin and Cadillac and went all the way down to Mississippi to the Gulf of Mexico. Soon afterwards, Le Moyne de Bienville, who owned a seigneury across the river from Montreal, founded the city of New Orleans. Some of his descendants are living in Montreal today.

The supreme irony in the bizarre relationship between Canada and the United States came to pass in the mid-eighteenth century, when William Pitt the Elder set out to demolish French rule in North America. Louisbourg fell, then Quebec in the famous battle on the Plains of Abraham in which Montcalm and Wolfe were both killed. All French possessions in North America except the tiny islands of St. Pierre and Miquelon were ceded to Great Britain by the most ruinous king in French history, Louis xv.

Then entered a new historical factor in the person of the young George III, who was even more disastrous to Britain than Louis xv had been to France. Every American knows what he tried to do to their ancestors and knows also what his ancestors did to him. But it was not the famous Boston Tea Party that ignited the Revolution, though it certainly prepared the way for it. It was the Quebec Act of 1775, designed to keep the conquered French quiet, also to give them some rights in the land their ancestors had discovered and explored.

The ironies continue. At the beginning of the American Revolution, a small American force occupied Montreal, and Benjamin Franklin came along with the first printing press ever seen in Canada. A British counterattack sent him home in such a hurry that he left the printing press behind. It was used to print the newspaper which grew into the Montreal *Gazette*, second-oldest newspaper in the world still extant, and for two centuries one of the most conservative. Now, I'm sorry to say, it has become an oversized tabloid.

The ironies continue, and the next ones were caused by Napoleon Bonaparte. The Louisiana Purchase was the first, whereby the United States, in the presidency of Jefferson, bought Louisiana for a song without knowing what Louisiana actually was. The French-Canadians certainly knew what a good deal of it was, but they were not consulted. In the end, the United States gained from the purchase what became twelve new states besides Louisiana itself – in fact, the whole area drained by the Mississippi and Missouri rivers together with their great tributaries. No wonder that some Americans thought their country the chosen of the Lord after a deal like that. No wonder the French-Canadians, whose forebears had explored so much of that vast region, thought there was no justice in the world and put their hopes in a Roman Catholic heaven.

Now for the supreme irony of all. Henry Clay and his War Hawks, abetted by some trickery on the part of Napoleon, brought about the absurd War of 1812, in which one of the ablest of American presidents soon found himself trapped. It was the year in which Napoleon made his fatal march on Moscow. As the only area in which American troops could attack Britain was a small corner of Upper Canada, they made an invasion. They burned a village called York, now become the huge city of Toronto. But immediately afterwards, Napoleon was ruined in Russia, the British navy crossed the Atlantic, and they did what they did in Washington. A month after the war had officially ended, Andrew Jackson crushed a British force at New Orleans and matters were left, apparently, where they were. But one thing the peacemakers did accomplish. Between them, they established the Canadian-American border, and it has endured ever since. Today, relations between Americans and Canadians living along that border are more cordial, by a good deal, than were relations between New Jersey and Pennsylvania when I was student in the States.

Sometimes people ask, "What is the difference between Canada and the United States apart from the climates?" Historically and psychologically, there are very great differences. Until the long debacle in Vietnam, the Americans had never lost a war against a foreign power. But the ancestors of nearly all Canadians were losers.

The French were losers in what many Americans called "The French and Indian Wars." Then it was the turn of the United Empire Loyalists, who were forced to emigrate to Canada after the success of the Revolutionists. Next came the turn of the Highland Scotch, who were expelled from their glens to enable their chiefs to support their incompetence by turning the glens into sheep runs. Next, in the late 1840s, came the desperate Irish from the Potato Famine. Does it signify anything that a descendant of one of these who emigrated to Ontario is now President of the United States, but that a descendant of another who emigrated to Quebec is now Prime Minister of Canada, though I doubt if either of them will remain much longer in their positions? And finally, since the last World War, followed by the wars in Korea, Vietnam, and the Middle East, millions of Europeans and Asiatics, displaced persons, have come to Canada from all over the world. To a veteran like myself, Canada seems suddenly to have become an entirely different sort of country. In 1940, the population of Toronto was pretty solidly of English, Scotch, and Scotch-Irish extraction. Today, these are far outnumbered by immigrants from Italy, Quebec, China, and other Asiatic countries, as well as many from the Middle East. Swarms of Haitians have come to the province of Quebec. All this leads me to a conclusion I cannot avoid, and my early work at Princeton has drawn me to it.

In Princeton, I wrote a thesis based on the Oxyrhynchus Papyri, an enormous collection of documents, written in Greek, and preserved in the arid sands of the Egyptian Thebaid. There, the evidence of the decline and fall of the Roman Empire is spelled out in clear figures. The Roman Empire ultimately collapsed because its currency collapsed. When Augustus died in 14 A.D., the denarius of the Western Empire and the drachma of the Eastern Empire contained four grams of silver. When Hadrian died in 137 A.D., there were two grams in both. But soon afterwards, the coinage got into serious trouble. There was a century of virtual anarchy owing to vicious or incompetent emperors, and above all there were small but costly civil wars. Christianity triumphed during this confusion, but the living spirit of Christ was hard to find among its bishops. The troops hired by the emperors were mostly barbarians, and when their employers went broke, they turned on them. Alaric, a barbarian who professed to be a Christian, sacked Rome in 410 A.D. Saint Jerome had just completed his monumental translation into Latin of the Bible when this happened, and Saint Jerome recorded that when he heard this news, it seemed as though the world itself had ceased to live.

I will now venture a bold statement that I believe is fundamentally true. Whatever may be the mystery we call God, I am sure he is not a racist. For four hundred years, the white and Christian races of Europe and America have felt themselves to be the élite of history, and in a sense they were. But this century through which I have lived has seen them virtually destroying themselves.

In the first German War, France was decimated. Britain, with nearly a million dead, was brought to the verge of bankruptcy. In the second installment, France collapsed in four days; Hitler lost his gamble in Russia after appalling casualties on both sides. In the worst crisis of the Hitler War, Japan suddenly struck and that really spilled the baby out with the bath water. Churchill immediately saw that this would finish off the British Empire, and so it did. But America, with the Marshall Plan and the very shrewd statesmanship of President Truman, rescued Europe and stabilized its frontiers with Russia. Then came Vietnam, which I have heard called "Harvard's War," and apart from the social upheavals it caused among the youth of America and the entire world, it pretty well finished off the U.S. and Canadian dollars. Television has taken over the role of the old circus games in keeping the people quiet, but I must ask myself what ultimately can come of this.

When I was first in California – the year was 1939 – along the roads were signs reading ALL THE ORANGE JUICE YOU CAN DRINK FOR TEN CENTS. Yesterday in Montreal, a single large orange cost me eighty-five cents. And to go to the humblest of foods – the hot dog. In 1939, you could get one for ten cents. Yesterday, in Montreal, I bought one for $1.35 – ten cents more than the same morsel cost me a month ago. Climatic differences makes it a little easier for Americans than for us, but the trillions they are pouring out on weapons they dare not use may make their economy even leakier than ours.

Now, I would not predict that what happened to Rome is going to happen to us. We possess far more varied and sophisticated skills than the Romans ever dreamed of. Our economy could recover in a generation if there were the will and the intelligence. This was proved by America's achievement in rescuing Europe after the Hitler War.

However, of one thing there can be no doubt whatever: the rule of the so-called "White Man" is virtually over. We can see it very clearly here in Canada. Hard-working Asiatics, speaking more than two languages, are making small fortunes in small *dépanneurs* in Montreal and, I would guess, in most parts of the country. Intermarriage – or at least interbreeding – between native-born Canadians and Asiatic and black immigrants is going on apace. And the exploit that young Canadians most strongly applaud and identify with is that of Rick Hansen, the paraplegic who drove his wheelchair around the world and shortly is to marry the wonderful young woman who was his physiotherapist. I thank God that Rick comes from British Columbia – and for obvious reasons!

1 9 8 8
MAVIS GALLANT

Thank you, Graeme, Pierre. I want to thank the Writers' Development Trust and the Writers' Union for their kind invitation and for letting me say one or two things about writing.

It's a great honour to address fellow writers and a particular honour to deliver a lecture in the name of Margaret Laurence. One thing on which I think we all agree — perhaps one of the few things on which all Canadian writers do agree — is the quality and nature of her achievement. I never met her and can't talk to you about her. It was one of those things that should have happened, and didn't happen, and then it was too late. What I want to talk about is something I shall call my apprenticeship. (The reason why this lecture was announced as "The Life of the Writer" is that an announcement had to be made without too much delay and I kept changing the topic — or, rather, circling it, for the basic idea never changed.)

One's life as a writer, at my age, is to some degree what General de Gaulle, in a different context, referred to as a *vaste programme*. I have behind me thirty-eight years of fiction writing. If you add my early years of journalism, it means I have been earning my living by writing for forty-four years. When I read biographies of writers, the only chapters I find interesting are those that describe initiation and apprenticeship. I don't mean that further struggles and doubts and terrors and anxieties are negligible, but the public aspect of a writer's life once the writer has become successful, the meetings with other celebrated people, the honours and interviews, are boring to read about.

When you begin to walk as a writer, you need something strong and steady underfoot: a deep understanding of a language. In our case, it is the incomparable English language, with its solidity, its flexibility, its intrinsic poetry – qualities apparent to those who use language to its limits. What is happening to English as it becomes more and more of an international instrument is the subject of a different discourse. The wider English spreads, the thinner the uses to which it is put. I wonder, sometimes, if we wouldn't be better off as writers in some minority language, cliffhanging. But then, a shrinking language becomes an impoverished one, too; and I shall close this parenthesis before I start to flounder and to speculate about questions that can't be answered. Some of the most dismaying howlers I hear are not from people with only half an understanding of English, but – for instance – over the BBC. Just the other day, during a Parliamentary debate, a Member remarked that if the Minister of Education would only do this or that, "he would have our most fulsome support." (The Minister replied, "I'm not sure I want that kind of support.")

Is there a point where one's life as a writer begins? It seems to me to recede as one looks for it. Perhaps the start is the physical beginning, the genetic departure, the joining of cells; perhaps one's life-to-be as a writer develops with the fetus, that the vocation exists before the idea of language can emerge. I know that what I am saying is anything but scientific and most certainly not provable. I am trying to delineate the character of the born writer, the man or woman who could not easily turn to another way of life without coming to grief and frustration. I never wanted to do anything except write, or to live in any manner unconnected to writing: that was the drive, the inborn sense of direction.

I also had to earn my living. At the age of eighteen, I presented myself at the editorial offices of *The Standard*, a weekly newspaper, on St. James Street West, in Montreal. (At that time, there were four English-language newspapers in the city, three of them dailies.) I had no appointment. I didn't know you were supposed to make one. It was on a hot summer day, during the Second World War. I asked for a job. The person who received me was the Montreal painter Philip Surrey, whose title was, I think, "picture editor." (It was before television, and photo supplements were important as a source of features and news.) We stood in a doorway, talking. I had on my best clothes – a brown-and-white seersucker suit with pearl buttons, and a straw hat with a wide brim, something I thought would look good on a reporter. He was neither hot nor cold – just neutral, though slightly surprised: as a rule, no one wandered in quite that way, "off the street," as we said. I know, now, that he was not sure what to do about me. I had no background, no credentials, and no higher education – actually, neither did anyone else on the paper. You were expected to learn by working. Finally, he advised me to get some other kind of professional experience and try again at the age of twenty-one. That evening, he talked about me to his wife, Margaret Day (one of the founders of *Preview*), and, as she later told me, he kept saying, "Yes, but, you see, she's just too young." (Too young for what? I'm not sure. *The Standard* employed a nineteen-year-old feature writer, but she was an old hand who had started on the *Winnipeg Free Press* at the age of sixteen.)

Well, I did come back at twenty-one, and there happened to be a vacancy – someone had just quit to move to Toronto – and so I was taken on. Why did I want to work on a newspaper? It was so that I would be called on to write something every day, and get paid for doing it. As I've said, I needed to work for a living, and it seemed to me nothing else but journalism would do. *The Standard* published the usual kind of reporting, as well as long features and photostories with text; with luck, one could also write reviews and criticism. I had no more "qualifications" than at eighteen: I had worked here and there and at the National Film Board and had done no writing except at home, in the evening, for myself. But this was in wartime and they needed any dogsbody that could be found; they needed even women, and so women – just a few – were hired. I discovered that when they needed to fire they fired women, too – *mais passons*.

The first thing that became clear was that if I did not come up with ideas for features that were interesting to editors, as well as to me, I was going to write – well, stop! I was not going to write: I was going to produce copy. Now, there is an advantage to producing copy. If you do just enough of it, you will never in your life suffer from what the French call "the fear of the white page." Apparently, this is the fear one feels when confronted with a blank sheet of paper. If you write on the page, then, of course, it isn't white anymore, and you feel a sense of guilt, and this guilt turns into what is called "a writer's block." I've lived in France more than half my life, and so I've heard a good deal about this nonsense. Anyone harbouring a fear of the white page would not have lasted half a day on a newspaper. The page was simply a utensil. It was a convenience. And it wasn't even white; it was a dirty beige colour.

The second advantage of being forced to produce copy is that one irons out the wrinkles of grammar and syntax. Writing prose, clear, precise, becomes a second nature. But it has no other advantage that I can think of, and it contains a formidable trap: repetition. Language, the foundation stone, is ground down to gravel. I remember that at the age of twenty-six, I became aware of the trap. I noticed that I was writing feature stories about subjects I had dealt with at the age of twenty-one. Probably I looked at these subjects in a different way; perhaps I knew more, and could treat them from a wider angle of knowledge; but repetition was there, like gravel churning away in a kind of drum.

When I talk about working on a newspaper in Montreal, in the '40s, I am evoking a place and a time wholly remote. Journalism, then and now: how can I explain the gap, the distance, the evolution? It is like placing a heavy album of those breakable records — a whole opera, say — next to two compact discs. The journalism I was taught and practiced was closer to the profession as it had been taught and practiced forty years before, at the beginning of the century, than to the profession as it is now, yet another forty years later. The great change came about in the '60s and '70s. I would be unable to work in a newspaper office now. An editor would find me incompetent, ignorant. I do not understand computers, processors, screens. My own words, in green, on a screen, make no sense to me. I once read a great novel about journalism, written by a young Catalan writer — young at the end of the nineteenth century, that is — called *Servitude*. The hero is a reporter, newly hired, on his first job, exactly forty years before my time. This novel has never been translated into English. The author was — I'm going to pronounce his name in the Spanish, not the Catalan — was Joan Puig i Ferreter. In case you imagine I am fluent in Catalan — no, I am not. If I had not met the author, then an old man, I'd never have tried to read a line. (By the way, about reading Catalan: if you know French and enough Spanish, it can be done. At the top of every page, you will tell yourself, "I can't do this," but then you take a deep breath and try a word at a time, and before you know it you are swimming along.) *Servitude* is as near to autobiography as fiction can be. Its author, dead now, is one of the great figures of Catalan writing, exiled, when I knew him, for his opposition to Franco. He had been hired by a paper in Barcelona exactly at the age I was when I was taken on by *The Standard*, and he describes exactly that elation and excitement, the first days, the first desk, the typewriter, the telephone. His colleagues seem remarkable to him, not like ordinary people. He – the hero – is similar to me in background, half-orphaned, without sisters or brothers or close relations. He is on his own, entirely, as I was, then. In the Church of St. Eustache, in Paris, there is a marble plaque with an inscription to the memory of a military man of the seventeenth century, François de Chevert: WITHOUT FAMILY, WITHOUT FORTUNE, WITHOUT HELP. He became this, that, and the other. So it is with our Barcelona writer, our raw reporter. He is exhilarated by the sight, sound, and smell of the composing room, and the great printing machines – as they were in his day and still were in mine – the sound of them was like an express train. He compares it to a wild animal waking out of sleep. (And here we differ. As a Canadian, I would never compare a machine to a wild animal. I know the difference. But that is Europe – tamer, in a sense. To me, the machine kills the wildness and the animal.)

Servitude recalls the same memories, his and mine: the first time he had to work all night and came out in the street, a silent city street, and the sun rising, and that feeling one has in youth that real life is beginning, along the with the day. He missed something more thrilling, I think: the Canadian experience of having worked all night and coming out into winter, in a faint predawn light, few lights on, just some all-night neon, here and there, shining on snow. The snow was clean, untouched, for there was strict gas rationing and there were few cars. The nights, the neon, the snow have been preserved for us by the Montreal painter Philip Surrey – particularly Dorchester Street (for those of you who are from Montreal), which I had to cross as I trudged up from the newspaper office, on St. James Street, on my way home to Mackay in the empty dawn. The street was all low, brick houses; many had become small hotels. I don't object to progress and the development of cities (and who would care if I did?) but Dorchester Street, as it is now – does anyone want to paint it? The city was safe: I don't recall having felt nervous. I walked home more than once in the hour between night and dawn. There was no transport. It was too early for streetcars, and our low salaries did not encourage one to take taxis.

Why was I working that late? Perhaps because the photo section of the paper, which we called "the rotogravure," might have been changed at the last minute, and the editor-in-charge would have put on his overcoat and over-shoes and ear mufflers and woollen scarf and gone home, leaving in charge two inexperienced people, one twenty-one, the other, I think, twenty-three. We managed. And the first time I emerged from the building at dawn I felt as if I owned everything – my new profession, even the city.

And here's another experience, almost identical, Barcelona-Montreal, more than forty years apart. One day, our hero looks carefully at an older journalist, a critic he admires, and suddenly he becomes aware that this man wears the same worn suit of clothes, day after day. What does it mean? It means that he cannot afford to buy anything new. It means that his earnings have not risen with his reputation. It means that the younger man's income will never rise along with his age and increased experience – not at the same rate. And I was to have that experience, too, and to think, "This is what I wanted, but where does it take me?" When the chance of organizing a union occurs, our Barcelona reporter dives in and bangs his head; the leap comes to nothing. The same thing happened in Montreal. There was a chance of organizing a union – a branch of the Guild. I dove in, too, and banged my head, and it all came to nothing.

My apprenticeship was closer to journalism as it was practiced at the turn of the last century than to anything of the profession today. (I apologize for hammering the point. But then, if you invite a senior writer to address you, you are bound to get senior social history.) I wonder, now, if there can be a residue of experience, anything learned or discovered or rejected by me, that can be of the slightest use to a younger writer? I entered newspaper work as a presenter of facts, with few of my own opinions on view. And yet I can see now that I was always thinking as a writer of fiction. The first feature story I ever suggested was a picture story, which would depend for its effect on the vision and the technique of the photographer assigned, though I would write the text. It was as a writer, I think, that I first became interested in the daily life of a downtown urban child – a real child, not someone developed in my imagination. (The term "inner city" did not exist. As for "downtown," it was an area run down, but not left to rot, as it would be later on; and it was not particularly dangerous.) If the child chosen for the feature had been left behind in my mind, replaced by a character, his story would somehow have told itself. One of the great differences between fiction and reporting is that the author of a work of fiction has to know more than meets the eye. But this was a newspaper feature, and I could not allow myself to guess or imagine or add anything to pure description. Journalism is inflexible: you watch, you listen, you tell. It cannot be more, because "more" brings you to fancy speculation and nonsense. If you report on what might be or might have been – worse, what ought to be – you are on the messy edge of false intelligence, the blind leading the blind.

I lived in downtown Montreal, just like the urban kid – my subject. Most of the younger reporters on English-language papers lived within blocks of one another, except for those who were unable to find an apartment or still were not earning enough to afford one and had to live at home. Most of the flats were in converted stone houses. The ground floors of the old houses were just beginning to be occupied by dress shops and other stores. Many of the sloping streets were still lined with trees. Some of our neighbours worked at the CBC or in advertising agencies. There were artists, designers, musicians, people belonging to those groups that connect or interlock or lightly touch in a lively city. Between the ages of eighteen and twenty-five, about, every impulse and decision seems to draw one toward the like-minded. "Decision" is perhaps the wrong word; one is pulled by an intellectual magnet.

I was happy on those streets and in that company, in the mid-'40s. It was a wonderful time and place to be young. Montreal – yes, Montreal – was the humming centre of English-language culture. I think of it in terms of a different kind of image, something like a series of waves that broke and became flat, finally. Perhaps, where Montreal is concerned, I wanted nothing to change, and everybody to be no older than twenty-six or so. Again, perhaps I am idealizing the stone houses and shady streets, the long conversations and the visions of a long future. Soft memories or not, the streets are today arid and ugly and full of parking lots. Their mood is ugly after dark. Perhaps what I looked for, later on, in cities of Europe was the spirit of a lost Montreal.

None of us had much money. Even a good salary, so called, was small. We lived with any old furniture and second-hand books, but there was art on the walls; we knew the painters and the work was cheap. We had much to

talk about – Quebec politics, mostly, which we saw as repressive and retro-
grade. I wrote newspaper stories in the daytime and fiction early in the
morning or at night. I had a sense of space and of freedom. And now I have
to stop and ask myself if that sense of freedom was factitious, invented by
me – then and in retrospect. Have I remembered a way I wanted to live
when I was in my twenties, and did the desire just occasionally coincide with
some aspects of a reporter's life? In short, has a fiction about living spilled
across that ambiguous entity we call "real life"? I may be building an ideal
city, a lyrical downtown area – vanished, regretted, mourned by a handful
of survivors. A friend from Montreal said, the other day, "Let's face it. Those
were terrible apartments, almost slums."

At any rate, it was on one of those streets – shabby, charming, lined with
trees or utterly dilapidated; it depends on the slant of one's memory – that I had
noticed a boy of about six who seemed to spend all his time outside. It was
summer, so he had no school to go to. Perhaps both his parents worked.
Whatever the reason, he was on his own. He had fair hair; was reticent rather
than shy; his name was Johnny. Sometimes he sat on the steps of a stone house,
sometimes on the edge of the curb. He was wary of strangers and, like a soldier,
gave no information but his name. I thought it might be interesting to follow
the small pattern of his days, the miniature routine of a street kid. I never saw
the story as fiction, for my imagination did not enlarge on the evidence. In fact,
I wanted photographs to carry the substance with a minimum of text; and so
I can say, truthfully, that I was already thinking as a reporter. I had been working
only a short while, but my idea was taken up, and I had a piece of luck in the
choice of photographer, Hugh Frankel. He loved the idea and knew instinctively
how to make a child feel at ease and secure.

The photostory with my text and captions was published that summer.
It was my first professional byline. At about the same time, *Preview*, the
Montreal literary review, published two short stories about a young refugee
in Montreal. *Preview* is something of a legend now: Frank Scott was one of
the founders, P.K. Page one of the first contributors. Kit Shaw, the librarian
at *The Standard*, was married to a poet who was one of the editors; many of
the editorial and policy meetings took place in their apartment – another of
those downtown places in an old stone house. She asked me, I don't recall

why, if I wrote anything apart from newspaper stories — if I wrote poetry, for instance. I gave her two stories to read. She showed them to Frank Scott. I am certain this is how it came about, though I sometimes meet other people who say they came across the stories (one wonders how) and shepherded them into print. As a result, I had a byline in a literary review at about the same time as the first newspaper feature. I shall say that I was overjoyed, and leave it at that. As writers, you can imagine easily what I thought and felt.

I made no more attempt to publish fiction, except for one story, straight-forward and close to reporting, about a Czech émigré in Montreal, renting a furnished apartment. It was published in the magazine section of *The Standard* and read on the CBC. (Obviously, émigrés from Hitler's Europe were one of the most fascinating features to me about life in Montreal. I tried to meet as many as I could.) I do not know why, exactly, I did not try to have fiction published for another several years. I was writing, all the time. I know I thought I wasn't ready, but how much of that belief was based on fear?

I think now that I was afraid of having my work rejected. I had made up my mind that if I were to receive three refusals in a row I would give up trying. I did not want to trail through life a vocation for writing but without enough talent to justify the desire. I was the daughter of a painter — I am inclined to say "a failed painter," though he died in his early thirties, and so the word "failed" cannot apply. He thought of himself as an artist, lived like one, was so of a piece with his artist's persona that I never thought of his doing anything else. Only much later did I realize that he must have held a job of some kind, like everyone we knew. My only memories of him are as an artist — that is how strong his idea of himself must have been. It wiped out a weaker reality, prob-ably. The trouble was that he may not have had much talent.

I was always fearful that he had passed his dilemma on to me, for I resembled him in every other way. (Once, when I was about nineteen, a stranger stopped me in the street and asked if I was his sister.) Some of my reasons for holding back, for not sending my work to reviews and magazines, were, first, that I believed I was not ready and, second (though perhaps it should be first) the fear that I might discover a devastating truth: I was not a writer and never could be. It was an uneasiness that never quite left me. For many years after my work began to be published regularly, I had a repeated nightmare in which someone would tell me I had written a short story (the most recent, in the dream) in a language no one could make out.

Luckily for me, while I *was* still hesitating, I was on a newspaper, not just wondering if it could happen; so, that much was accomplished. Often when I am being interviewed, the reporter will try to make me say I wasted years of creative energy in journalism, or that I was forced to turn out dreary pieces that bored me, and that I was and have remained resentful. It is not true. From the bright June day when I was hired until the day I left, I liked what I was doing. I was not made to write anything I thought cheap or demeaning. There is another side to it, however. I was prevented from doing a great many things I thought were interesting and that I might have done well. One reason is that I was a woman. The other is the way newspapers were run, in Canada, at that time; or that particular newspaper, let us say. We kept out of political trouble, "trouble" being defined by editors' convictions and prudence and state of nerves. And then, a woman running into trouble over a question of policy would have been blamed as a woman rather than a journalist. Women had been hired because of the war and the shortage of men. I remember one editor, a former officer, and the horror he expressed when he returned from the war to find "women running all over the place." Perhaps women were pests: two of us, along with a male colleague, tried to organize a union. When I was assigned to cover a strike, I collected money for the strikers — starting with the publisher of the paper, who gave five dollars and asked no questions. (I was taken off labour stories, for all time.) I don't want to harp on the fact that women earned less than men, or on the paradox that men liked us, or seemed to, and yet did not want us around.

From the beginning, I tried to choose my own features. Unless they were political, they were seldom turned down. I chose subjects about which I was curious. It seems to me now that I moved into every corner of the city and province. My French was fluent: I had been to French school when I was small and had kept the language during my adolescence, when I lived outside Quebec and heard virtually no French at all. When I returned to Montreal, after a long detour in English-only places, I still read it easily, but my spoken vocabulary was small and my conversation halting. However, French returned surprisingly quickly and by the time I applied to work on *The Standard*, I was almost bilingual.

Much of my early fiction came straight from my newspaper assignments. The bored wives in a construction camp in northern Quebec, the war bride on a slow train to Abitibi, the angry storekeeper in the east end of Montreal were based on events and people observed. Some stories I wrote on the spot; others consisted only of notes and dialogue, which I completed years later, in Europe. I suppose the delay was due to my slowness about writing anything. I am slow to write and reluctant to call anything finished. I composed in long-hand, even as a reporter, and rewrote endlessly on the typewriter, making countless corrections, as if the most insignificant item were to be reviewed by a panel of literary critics. I shared a cubicle in the editorial room with another reporter, a woman. She used to tease me about my revisions, which she called "fussing about semicolons." "You worry about nothing," she once told me. "Nobody's ever going to bring out a book of this stuff at the end of the year."

I still ask for long deadlines. An editor who tells me, "Oh, anytime. Whenever you're ready," has handed me eternity. It isn't procrastination. I seem to lack a normal sense of time going by. The rigid deadlines of a newspaper, years ago, were compensated by the open time I gave to fiction, at home, on my own. Michel Serres, the French philosopher, teaches that a watch does not tell time except by showing the wear of age. It may mean something that I have trouble sometimes in reading a watch: I read eleven o'clock for one, or five for seven. If a stranger stops me in the street to ask the time (it happens frequently in Paris, though never in North America), my mind comes to a stop. Usually, I just hold out my wrist.

Perhaps I have always been bound to a different kind of time, less urgent, less determinate than a deadline. In fiction, time is structure. Chekhov begins a story with, "Next day they had delicious pies . . . and during the meal Nikanor, the cook, came upstairs to inquire what the guests would like for dinner."* We know that the guests were at the same table yesterday and will be there again that evening. We are not told at once who they are and why they are together, but quickly divine they are men (from the kind of conversation that ensues) and

---

* "Concerning Love," translated by Ronald Wilks; Penguin Classics. In the same story, titled "About Love," translated by Constance Garnett, the words are "At lunch next day there were very nice pies . . ."

that the host is, probably, a bachelor. It would be impossible to use the same allusive, divinatory method at the start of a newspaper story. It would irritate readers, not to speak of editors, and would seem maddeningly slow. And yet any writer of fiction can see at once that is rapid – a quick and decisive way of getting round "explanations" and moving straight to the heart of the matter. The "next day" method of presenting the past by cutting it off, acknowledging it only as a setting for the present, would be an awkward start for non-fiction of any kind. A brilliant exception, the only one that comes to mind, is the first line of "Hope Against Hope," by Nadezhda Mandelstam, the account of her life with the doomed Russian poet Osip Mandelstam: "After slapping Alexei Tolstoy in the face, M. immediately returned to Moscow." Any reader who cannot quite place Alexei Tolstoy or who may wonder where the poet was returning from has to rely on footnotes. Nadezhda has slammed the Chekhovian door, just as though she were writing fiction. After her equivalent of "Next day . . ." she proceeds in the usual chronological and historical time of autobiography. She did not know that she had written one of the most celebrated first lines of our century.

It is quite possible to write both fiction and journalism; there is no confusion of form. But I think it must be virtually impossible for a working journalist to write much fiction. The difficulty has nothing to do with style or manner or vocabulary or the stifling of imagination, but of exhaustion, mental and physical. If there are sixteen hours of the day in which to work and live, the two streams of writing easily can overflow and soak up every minute. Fatigue will force you to dam up one or the other. Which? Common sense suggests keeping free the stream that earns your living. But that may not satisfy you; not at all. I had already set myself a time limit for newspaper work: I was to be self-supporting by writing fiction at the age of thirty, or I was to forget it entirely. When a retirement pension plan was launched at *The Standard*, it scared me half to death. I was afraid of becoming cautious, losing my nerve. I asked the man in charge – his name suddenly comes back: Mark Farrell – if I could stay out. He explained that the structure of the plan had to include everyone. At about the same time I was given another push, of a different nature.

Toward the end of the '40s, I suggested a feature on a topic that I'm sure is still of interest: why are Canadian books so expensive? ("Who buys Canadian books?" said the first of the editors I approached.) The idea was accepted, once

I was made to swear and promise my piece would not be full of figures and statistics or names of writers our readers had never heard of. Among the people I went to see was John Gray of Macmillan. He was a remarkable man – civilized, tolerant – and he gave me considerable help. Occasionally after that, when he happened to come to Montreal on publishing business, he would invite me to lunch and bring me books – not just Macmillan editions, but anything he happened to like and wanted to pass along. When I told him I was twenty-seven, and had given notice, and was going to Paris – that it was now or never – he said, "I wish I were twenty-seven and going to Paris." He was the only person who did not say, "I think you're crazy," or something else along those lines. (Forty years later I read the same remark, with one word of difference, in Russell Baker's memoir of his newspaper days in Baltimore. The speaker was his editor, who said, "I wish I were twenty-seven and going to London.")

It was John Gray who gave me a collection of essays by Cyril Connolly, called *Enemies of Promise*. Most of you have read it, probably, and remember the one chapter that became famous and still is quoted – the chapter that deals with journalism as a prime enemy of promise in young writers. Connolly belonged to that leisurely breed of British authors to whom "journalism" probably meant book reviewing, and I realize only now that his idea of a writer of promise was a man. It never entered his mind that a woman could stand smack in the middle of the writing-vs.-journalism dilemma. Oddly enough, when I read his book for the first time I did not even notice his dismissal or, worse, obliteration of women. In those days we were almost invisible. Perhaps I took it for granted that a woman had to glean whatever she could from advice dispensed by a man to other men. It was only when I re-read *Enemies of Promise* just a few weeks ago, so that I could discuss it here, that one aspect of the problem became clear. The hurdle was set high for women. Budding authors, apparently, were men. Women were those dreary, hindering creatures who lured men into binding relationships or trapped them by having children. Many a writer's career had been blasted, said Connolly, by the very sight of "the perambulator in the hall." As you know, it became the most sensational of threats, used until fairly recently as a metaphor. Perhaps it will turn out to be the phrase for which he is chiefly remembered. I mention it to show how trained our minds were; I am trying hard not to say "brainwashed." For there

I was, about to drop my only means of livelihood in order to try to live as a writer, and I was accepting — unconsciously or not — a genteel, upper-class, British notion that "talent" belonged to "men."

Still, the most important factor about *Enemies of Promise* was that it had been sent to me by someone I respected, who barely knew me except as a reporter who liked to read books, and who was kind enough to believe that whatever I wanted to do could be done. Even my closest friends were taking for granted the very opposite. At the time, looking for an explanation for the difference between writing fiction and writing a feature for a newspaper, I found one in Connolly: "Journalism must obtain its full impact on first reading because it is intended for an interested and not an indifferent public. Literature is not immediately striking in its effects." Now, across several decades of reading and writing, I think it is not so. Every work of fiction makes its impact on first reading and, I think, from the first sentence. We do not begin reading a novel at page ten just because the first nine pages are not clear.

Any reader would be far more likely to close the book and forget it; whereas a blurry start to a news story might still hold a reader's attention because of the information the story is thought to contain. Once absorbed, a news piece does not require re-reading because the driving power of news itself is, "What's next?" Literature is re-read for pleasure, which is not to say, as Connolly does, that "it is not immediately striking in its effects." One of the great advantages of journalistic training is that the writer does not lose the habit of being clear from the outset; or, at least, of knowing one ought to be. On the other hand, a writer need not have been a reporter in order to compose the famous, the imperishable opening lines that have held readers for generations:

> The Mole had been working hard all the morning, spring-cleaning his little home. First with brooms, then with dusters. . . . Spring was moving in the air above and in the earth below and around him, penetrating even his dark and lowly little house with its spirit of divine discontent and longing.

> Alice was beginning to get very tired of sitting by her sister on the bank, and of having nothing to do; once or twice she had peeped into the book her sister was reading, but it had no pictures or conversations . . .

It was said that a new person had appeared on the sea-front: a lady with a little dog.

It is a truth universally acknowledged, that a single man in possession of a good fortune must be in want of a wife.

It was the best of times, it was the worst of times, it was the age of wisdom, it was the age of foolishness . . .

Well; and here I am, after forty years, arguing with a dead author, Cyril Connolly. One would never have contradicted a British author, not even in one's mind, back then. We seemed to consider everything from "over there" to be in some way "real" writing, as if everything else were counterfeit or evanescent. I suppose that our parents, born at the last decades of the nineteenth century, or just at the turn, very often in Scotland or England, had established in our earliest awareness that literature in English had only one source and one direction: it flowed to us from over there.

I know that in my twenties I put more trust in British than American writing. In much the same way, we were trained to admire British journalism, without being told there were two kinds, and that one was low, slanderous and cynically designed to attract the poorly educated and politically immature. *The Standard* bought many features from *Picture Post*, which had once enjoyed an international reputation. Many of the stories would not have been accepted from a Canadian photographer or writer, and the picture captions were of a platitude and a silliness that no Canadian would have dared try to turn in as copy. These features were handled as if they represented the highest sort of journalism. (I was rebuked for changing ice cream "comets" to "cones." I had interfered with the language of the gods.) To compound our British/American schizophrenia, we used American spelling. It produced such gems as, "The chairman of the Montreal Harbour Commission arrived at the harbor . . ."

I've mentioned attitudes to women in the '40s. If I were to speak only about that, I could call the lecture "Women: Do They Exist?" I often had to report to, or receive assignments from, the peppery editor I spoke about – the one who had been overseas with the Army and came back to find women "running around the place." He tried to ignore us. Unfortunately, we were needed. (To be fair, speaking only for myself, one felt his hostility and probably reacted to it. Years later, he told me, "You drove me nuts. You were always saying, 'Why do we have to do the piece that way? Why don't we do it this way? Why do it at all? Why can't we do something else instead?'") He began every order and assignment with the words, "Grab a cab," and then proceeded with the rest. One day he said to me, "Grab a cab," and nothing more.

I said, "Grab a cab and drive where? To do what?"

He replied, "Jesus Christ! A man would know!"

I am sure he believed it. In his view, men were divinely inspired. At any rate, they were more secure in their jobs. As the war wound down, women were fired. Those still employed hung on by their fingernails. I still wonder if some situations women had to accept would have been inflicted on men. Robert Fulford once told me that he first came across my name on a film review. He asked me why I had stopped. The answer was simple: I gave a film a bad notice and a theatre chain pulled its ads. I was taken off reviewing for all time. For a while, I wrote a weekly column of radio criticism, called "On the Air." This was before television, when radio was the important medium. It was widely read and drew a surprising amount of mail. One day I was called into the managing editor's office. He had been playing golf with the director of an advertising agency, and the subject of the column had come up. According to the agency director, "On the Air" was a stone in the shoe. I parodied commercials, poked fun at jingles.

He said to the managing editor: "How would you like it if we sponsored a column criticizing newspapers?"

"You know," the editor said, as if waking from a long dream, "I had never thought of that."

The column was dropped and never replaced. There was now nothing in *The Standard* that could offend the agency or its clients. That is what I meant by "censorship by omission." It was a side of journalism never mentioned by Cyril Connolly; perhaps he hadn't heard of it. It was journalism as it was practiced in Montreal in the late 1940s; I can guarantee that. Of course, we minded. We also took it for granted. Years later, in Toronto, I heard a theatre critic say in a radio interview, "Next thing you know, they'll be telling us to be careful about sponsors and advertising." But, the critic went on, such a thing was too absurd to consider. The world, it seemed to me, had become at once wiser and more innocent. It sounds obvious today to say that someone reviewing broadcasting could make fun of commercials; one might even consider it a duty. Forty years ago, it was a kind of *lèse-majesté*.

At the same time, I loved newspaper work. It was like a ticket to liberty, sending me all over the city and the province and sometimes to other parts of Canada. Meeting a trainload of British war brides in Halifax, accompanying their slow, puzzled journey through a rain-soaked landscape, measuring their excitement and apprehension, trying to grasp their bewilderment at a country so big and a train so slow, was one of a hundred experiences that stirred my imagination and built the reserves of memory that would feed fiction, later on.

One of the objections I have often heard to reporting as training is that it teaches one to write too quickly, without enough thought. To me, it was an advantage. I have already said that I was slow. Without a deadline, I might have spent weeks on the same piece. No amount of experience has relieved me of the stress a firm deadline can cause. I have never learned how to hurry up. Perhaps I don't see a point to hurry, except in an emergency. An emergency, on *The Standard*, would never have been confided to me. The reporter who shared my cubicle was very fast and knew at once what to say and how to say it. I admired her. We were once assigned to do something together. The result seemed to please everyone, but I avoided ever again doing something of the kind. I felt caught in a sandstorm.

I had always written, ever since I could remember – sometimes only in my head. It was joy to me to write for a living; to be writing anything. Years before I began my apprenticeship – journalism – I had a private notebook and a place to conceal it. From the time I was old enough to make my own bed, I kept it under a pillow or a mattress. I slipped it among schoolbooks. Violation of a young person's privacy seemed to be an adult's prerogative – one I have never condoned. If notebooks began to pile up and could not safely be hidden, I destroyed them. I now think it a pity, for a child's observation of things felt and said is particularly sharp and fresh. A child notices what people say and the way they say it. Perhaps because I had been to French and English schools, or because I was moved around such a lot, or because I had learned that adults never meant what they said, let alone said what they meant, I paid close attention to the spoken word, to the way words were placed in a sentence, words that betrayed whether the adult speaker was plain and direct or just engaging in ironic double-talk. I soaked up regional accents. What I see now is that if I had some of the ingredients of a writer I also had the making of a reporter. In the summer of 1939 (the very date sounds like a myth in preparation), I often heard that the coming war would change the world and nothing would be the same again. The summer we were living would be the last of its kind. It was made to sound as if life, until now, had been idyllic, made up of high standards and moral perfection. A bleak, dark, and unhealthy future lay ahead.

I began to collect mementos of 1939. I wanted a record. I got a large scrapbook and pasted into it cuttings from newspapers and magazines – not news items, but examples of the clothes people wore, the books they read, the films they saw, the songs they listened to. I was still too young to be much in restaurants, but the New York World's Fair had opened that summer and I brought back menus from some of the eating places and pasted those in, too. I collected ads for cars and furniture and saved some of those flyers grocery stores sent around, so there would be a record of food prices. I cut out and saved illustrations for magazine fiction. They showed the hairstyles and fashions of the time. I thought the world of the future would be glad to know about us. It seemed important to establish a record; and that, of course, is the essence of journalism.

At that time I lived in a small town, in Dutchess County, in upstate New York, and attended a local high school. It was farming country. Some of the kids picked up by the school bus had been up since five, doing chores and milking. They were all of early Dutch and English origin, and many had those one-syllable names like mine, which was Young, such as Crick, Tripp, Trapp, and so forth. How remote such a place was from world events, even United States policies and politics, is hardly believable today. They read no newspapers. Radio news was a distant blur full of strange names and places. We took what was known as a Current Events Class, which was held only occasionally. It was fascinating to me, but the minute any discussion strayed from America, from American affairs and transactions, the students lost interest. You must remember that these towns, which are now part of the exurbia of New York City, seemed then very far away. Most of the boys and girls in my class had never been to NewYork or to any large city, had never travelled farther than they had to for a basketball game with another school. We were about thirty miles from Poughkeepsie, but many had never been there, either – had never even seen the Hudson River.

I was different, in the sense that I had lived in cities – Montreal and New York. I had heard adults discussing the run of world affairs all my life. I do not mean that I had lived among journalists, but just ordinary, urban people who listened to the radio and read newspapers. I brought my great document, my scrapbook about the summer of 1939, to Current Events Class. I can't say that it was mocked or made fun of; the students were simply bewildered, and so was the teacher. One of the topics that had been under discussion was the Antarctic: should the U.S. seize or occupy the Antarctic and so have access to its great mineral resources? It was our teacher's idea. The Antarctic was thought to be full of coal; at least, our teacher thought so. (Believe me, please, I am not making this up.) Half the class seemed to be falling asleep; and who can blame anyone, under the circumstances? I remember one question: "Well, how are we supposed to bring this coal *from* the Antarctic?" It began to seem an immense and hopeless undertaking, the American occupation of the Antarctic – as far away as the moon seemed, then. That is what we were discussing, in the heart of Dutchess County, just after the outbreak of the Second World War. It was at that point that I introduced my research – a scrapbook full of trivia. The students, as I have said, were puzzled. Some thought I was trying to be funny. The teacher told me, kindly, that I was too old to be cutting things out of magazines, fooling around with scissors and paste. I was in my teens and easily deflated. I took the thing home and put it in the garbage incinerator. And how I wish I had it now, that record of a mythical time we still call "before the war," as if there had never been more than one.

It was a journalist's record. I have thought about it for years, and about the essential difference between the straightforward recording of one's surroundings and that other process of turning them into fiction. It depends, I think, on where the writer wants to stand, the nature and level of the ground he chooses to occupy. (When I say "he," I mean, of course, "he or she." I don't want to keep repeating the same thing.) When Harold Ross was still editor of the *New Yorker*, he was always shown the cartoon drawings they intended to use in the next issue. He would stand back (the drawing would be placed on an easel) and he would say, "Where am I?" – meaning, "Where am I in relation to the figures in the drawing?" Well, of course, he was outside. Philip Roth once said to an interviewer, "The difference between you and me is that I can put myself in someone else's place, and you can't." I should not have made that a direct quote, by the way, because I am not certain of the wording. What he was saying, in essence, to his interviewer, the journalist, was, "I can imagine being another person and you cannot."

It is a way of keeping the interviewer in his place, I suppose. I have been both in my lifetime, interviewer and interviewed. I can sit in either chair. I know how difficult it is to be one or the other, for an interview is a parody of real conversation. A reporter is perfectly capable of putting himself in someone else's shoes. If he is any good at all, he knows it is not his business to do so. He has to describe the interviewee "as seen," not from within. Anyone can imagine. A dog imagines. If you leave a dog alone in a car he imagines you'll never come back. The ability to put oneself in another person's place is not the essential difference between a journalist and a writer of fiction, but it is the difference between a writer and someone who can't write. A writer of fiction cannot address his reader with, in effect, "Look, I don't know why this man is getting on a bus. I can watch him doing it, but that's all." That is the take-it-or-leave-it declaration, which was such a blight in French fiction in the 1960s and which has, mercifully, faded away. There is an arrogance to it I find intolerable. The reader has every right to say, "Well, in that case, you don't know more than I do. Why are you writing?"

In journalism, it is not your business to speculate, without facts to sustain your guess, about this man (who is going to be getting on a bus forever, by the time I'm through with him). There is no inevitability about his acts, as there has to be if he is a character in fiction. A chain of events, of cause and effect, has to be known to you, the writer, before you can hint or describe it entirely – depending on your method of revelation.

In fiction, the piece of life that is taken in by you, then transformed and given back, like the silk in a web or the green in a leaf, contains the chain of life – the cycle and the inevitability. What you hand over to the reader is an event that could not have happened in any other way. The bus, the man, the street picked or invented, the passenger and his destination were chosen by you, but with a kind of inevitability: the scene will become imbued with a vitality of its own, but you are the cause of it and you are in control. If it were journalism, all you would be called on to do is to follow along.

I never believe it when a writer says a scene or a character ran away with him, as if it were a hysterical terrier tugging on its leash. You have noticed, as I have, how often one is asked about this by interviewers. There is a popular fancy, along with the belief that every plot line is autobiographical, that the author is somehow the slave to his own imagination. One can tell, as a reader, when a story has been altered in mid-course for an artificial reason. The failure of nerve on the part of the writer is like a blur on the page. The story has not run off with the writer: the writer has lost confidence somewhere along the way.

In journalism, whether your man boarding the bus is a poet or a spy or someone on his way to work, the most you can say is that someone saw him or sat next to him or noticed he was reading a newspaper. If the reporter tries to put himself in the man's place, see through his eyes, enter his mind – in short, submit to his fate – the result will be a diluted mixture of near-real and totally false. Fiction and non-fiction are strong currents that become weak when they are dammed up and made to blend. Even if the result is startling or scandalous, the weakness shows – frequently, nowadays, during a protracted suit for libel.

At the time when I was earning my living on a newspaper, writing (one hoped) nothing but provable incidents, without being expected to have an opinion (impossible, surely), I often thought that fiction was more truthful. It was not that the facts in themselves were lies, but that there were more facts than one was allowed to mention. The lie by omission not only was encouraged; it was enforced. We followed a line. We endorsed a political party. A poem – any poem – was more truthful than a feature hemmed in because an editor had said, "We can't publish that." There was also the inhibition that resulted from "checking it out." Checking it out did not mean making sure of one's facts. It meant making certain the political party we supported would approve. Here's an example: after the war, Canada admitted a number of Polish soldiers who, as a result of the Yalta agreement, found they had nowhere to go. They were allowed in after considerable debate and under the condition they spend their first two years working on farms. Their wages were disgracefully low, and often non-existent. For many of them, the expression "slave labour" could apply. A few of those indentured to farms in Quebec escaped and got to Montreal, where they were hidden in the attic of a Polish ex-servicemen's club. I was able to interview them after giving my word I would not disclose their place of shelter. That was where I ran into trouble: someone else on the paper was told to "check with Ottawa" (the party we supported happened to be in power) and he soon received a frantic message from the Department of Labour. No Polish workers were missing from farms, said the message, but if any Poles were found would we immediately say where they were hiding. I offer this as an example of political doublespeak. It was written more than forty years ago, but nothing seems quite so contemporary as the bland double-bind.

When I turned to fiction, hoping I could make a living at it, I had to turn my back on a way of life I found attractive, but also on a kind of thin ice I found more and more dangerous. One could not say something *only* because it was true. It had also to be suitable (to what and for whom was not always clear) and suitability was hypocrisy. I wrote only fiction for the next eighteen years, until I had enough of a foothold on that other shore and could, from time to time, go back to my starting point and write articles, essays, reviews. I would not be so naive or so disingenuous as to pretend there is no censorship in fiction. Censorship occurs every time a book is banned, for whatever reason, from a public library. It can occur — it *does* occur — in democracies. I watched in horror and amazement when, in France, during the Algerian War, whole editions of books were seized and the printers' plates destroyed. I saw how, with very few exceptions, writers and their organizations, such as they were, kept their heads down. I have long believed that the acceptance of censorship, and the shame writers must have felt, accounted for the subsequent decline in French fiction. (This is something I think; I am not saying it is provable or even true.) To this day, no French writer has ever written wholly and truthfully about the period. It is like a rotten floor plank; no one walks in that part of the room.

My own restrictions seem absurd, by comparison. I am bound by the *New Yorker*'s worry about lawsuits. Every society has its built-in threats, and North American readers have a great propensity to take offence and to try to make money out of the offence — imaginary or real. We all know that the literary coincidence exists: I once began a story with a sentence, almost word-for-word, that occurs at the beginning of a story by Heinrich Böll. I had never read his story and did not know of its existence until I came across a bilingual Penguin book of German short fiction. By that time, my story was almost in print, but I was able to change just enough so that it would not be a virtual duplicate. I have discovered that one has to be careful about names of characters. Obviously, we are not going to call everyone Ken or Mary and Smith or Jones. I have twice had to mollify American readers – one, a woman in Texas, the other a professor at a New England university – both of whom were certain I had somehow heard of them and had deliberately used their names. In the case of the professor, it was not so much that *he* objected to seeing his family's name attached to a character in fiction: it was his mother who kept writing and urging him to find out something about me, and why I had picked on them. With the lady in Texas, the exchange of letters came to nothing: she remained convinced I had heard of her. She had once published an article in a small review that I had never heard of, on a topic completely outside anything I might be drawn to read. In her case, the character's first and last names were close, though not identical, but she had discovered other similarities that worried her. I answered all her letters, aware that it was a waste of time. Once, for a story set in Paris, I had named a character Roger Perron. The *New Yorker* – I suppose it must have been its legal department – made a check on every "R. Perron" in the Paris phone book. There were two or three Rogers, one of whom, like my character, was a civil servant. I don't think that if I had let the name stand, this man would have sued: it is not French custom to sue over trifles and courts are inclined to be lenient towards authors; writers still enjoy a status of privilege in France. However, "Roger Perron, civil servant" could, had he wished to, have sued in an American court. He could have said, "I am Roger Perron. In this story, you assert that my son is too stupid to pass exams, that my wife is brainless, that as a high school student I was visiting bordellos; worse, you say that my son was a member of a fascist-sounding organization and that my father was on the extreme right of the political spectrum – in fact, that he attended the funeral of Charles Maurras, the *Action Française* leader who called the Nazi victory in 1940 'a divine surprise.' I consider all this highly damaging to my career, and I am suing you for fifty million dollars."

In order to find a name that no one could claim, I opened a dictionary, *Le Petit Robert*, and took a word, *claire-voie,* which means "latticework." I have never met anyone called Latticework, in any language; I'm still waiting.

If this seems trivial, almost a copping-out on the question of censorship, I don't mean it to be. Even a mild anxiety about the reaction of some unknown person, some casual reader who chooses to place himself or herself at the centre of the stage by pretending to be grossly offended over a petty coincidence – worse, by trying to squeeze money out of the incident – is one anxiety too many, for most of us. In France, it is the writer of fiction who most usually has the last word. But the laws governing non-fiction – biography and the like – are rather different. The private and professional lives of the subject are strongly protected. I can give you a recent example: When Brigitte Bardot was still a young actress, she tried to commit suicide. It was an incident much publicized at the time; the press was full of it. But when a book was written about her life (in fact, it was a doctoral thesis about her impact, or the impact of her image, on French society) recalling her suicide attempt, she was able to take the author and the publisher to court and to have the book seized. The reason: it was no longer news. She had stopped making pictures and it was therefore an infringement on her private life. If the author had maintained the thesis as an unpublished document, or had perhaps published it as a university press title, nothing would have come of it. But from the moment the unauthorized tale of her life was issued as a commercial proposition, she could have the law on her side.

Can a protection-of-privacy law amount to censorship? The French writer Céline is considered – even by people who think he should have been sent to jail or even shot to death – one of the great French voices, in fiction, in France, in the twentieth century. His two finest novels, *Journey to the End of Night* and *Death on the Instalment Plan*, make many admired French works seem puny and weak. He was a superb writer. He was also a notorious anti-Semite and a coward who chose to exercise his racialism when France was occupied and the Jews he insulted and slandered were in no position to talk back. Céline is a special case. His career leads one to wonder if Voltaire was right when he said that only acts, never words, count as crimes. A few years ago, writing an article about Céline, I quoted from one of his racist pamphlets.

As it happened, his widow had been able to stop the reprinting and distribution of his more violent broadsides. A book that had included only a few sentences had been seized, by law. My Céline article, collected with other pieces in *Paris Notebooks*, could not have been translated into French. Is it an example of censorship? In its way, surely, yes – particularly if you remember that Céline died unrepentant and that his opinions were not the result of some youthful wrong-headedness. In quoting a few words I was not diminishing him as a novelist, but simply trying to give a picture of the writer as a whole. They were not opinions privately expressed and repeated as gossip: they were published exactly as his fiction was published. We can argue indefinitely about Voltaire's line between thoughts and acts. (To show how absurd quasi-censorship can be, *Paris Notebooks* and the forbidden remarks can be found in Paris in English bookstores. The same book could not be on sale if it were in French.)

My first newspaper story was about a downtown child called Johnny. My last, six years later, was about another city kid, grown up now, also called Johnny – Johnny Young. Quebec in those days was governed by some laws unknown in the rest of Canada. I think the rest of the country did not care. I often meet Canadians from other provinces who tell me they knew nothing or, if they are too young to remember, have never heard of the appalling "Padlock Law." The "Padlock Law" was instituted as a way of providing immediate punishment for citizens who had the wrong books in their homes. I am talking about books containing political attitudes and opinions. There was no trial and no sentence. The offending family, its children and infants included – and, in one case I recall, a canary in a cage – were thrown into the street and the door to their home locked behind them. They were punished for their thoughts, not for their deeds. It still seems to me incredible that within my lifetime, Canadian citizens, at least in one city, had to be careful about the kind of reading matter they kept on their shelves. The men engaged in the house search, which was conducted without a warrant, were not highly literate – to say the least of it. Anything in print and between covers must have struck them as dangerous.

(Surely, you are thinking, there was nation-wide protest at this state of affairs? Surely the Montreal newspapers launched a freedom-of-opinion and human-rights campaign? I can still remember an exhausted-looking young couple with a baby, ushered into the editorial room of *The Standard* by, I think, the lawyer for some helpless and hopeless organization. He was the wrong person – too blustering, too loud. The evicted couple seemed poor, stunned, and scared to death. They had nowhere to go and nothing but the clothes they were wearing. Whether the incident was worth a story was an editorial decision. As a rule, an editor decided that it was left to the reporter to say, "I'm sorry. We've already run something along those lines," or "We don't feel it's quite the right moment," or the flat refusal: "There's nothing I can do.")

In 1950, something new was added: a law stipulating that a person convicted of any offence more than twice was to be sentenced to prison for life. And "life" meant a full lifetime, without remission or parole. A similar law existed in the United States. Gangster movies of the period made much of the "three-time loser," convicted for armed robbery or other, serious offences. In Quebec, convictions for petty crimes carried the same weight, provided they added up to three.

The first person given a life sentence under the new ruling was a Montrealer in his twenties, Johnny Young. The publicity he received made it sound almost an honour. Actually, he was a minor lawbreaker, more of a nuisance to society than a serious threat. One of his early convictions, as I remember it, had been for stealing tires and trying to sell them on the black market. "Black market" means it happened in wartime, making it, in his case, a juvenile offence. Young was barely educated and said to be not overly intelligent – though it is often hard to measure the capacity of an untrained, underdeveloped, and inarticulate mind. He knew nothing about the new law and perhaps did not understand that it had been applied retroactively. His brief notoriety must have come as a surprise. There was no legal precedent and there had been no warning – at any rate, none that could have sifted down to his street.

I knew nothing about him, had not been assigned to cover the trial, and most certainly did not look upon Johnny Young as a hero. But the idea of a life sentence as retroactive justice sounded wrong. I got a lawyer I knew to explain it to me. Had Johnny Young known about the risk he was taking in committing a third offence? No, he had not. It was a new procedure. I asked *The Standard* if I might write a feature about the man and his background.

I wondered about his trajectory, why his lifeline had sent him straight into the line of a different trajectory, that of the new law. The two editors to whom I presented my idea were all for it, although we did not see the story in the same light. For them, I was to write something along the lines of "The Making of a Habitual Criminal." *I* wanted to find out about Johnny Young's Montreal, the streets of the English-speaking poor. A sociological falsehood, current then, exists even now: in Montreal, all the poor were French-speaking and all the English-speakers were well-to-do – or, at least, comfortable. The truth was that the poverty line cut straight across culture and language. I interviewed a juvenile court judge who told me that the English-speaking poor furnished more juvenile offenders, in proportion to their numbers, than any other group. The reason? They were forgotten and out-of-place everywhere, except their own neighbourhood. (In those days no one said "poor." The euphemism was "underprivileged.")

Johnny Young came out of that minority-within-a-minority. I wanted to learn something about his particular Montreal. The idea of someone shut up for life, who had not committed a serious crime, seemed appalling. I did not say so. I was afraid my idea might be taken away from me and assigned to a male reporter, someone with a tougher outlook, unblurred by the reading and writing of fiction. Because it was my last feature assignment, because I was leaving soon, I was given plenty of time for research and writing. It had never happened before. It was to be a long piece, in two parts, to be run on consecutive Saturdays in the magazine section.

I was not allowed to interview Johnny Young. I am thankful now for the restriction. Then, I was disappointed; now, I realize that an interview might have turned the article into a profile. He could have seen it as a further chance to explain himself, in a new legal hearing, of a kind, and it would have raised a false hope of release or, at least, a new trial. I did the next best thing: went down to his part of Montreal and knocked on doors.

How much was a search for sources of fiction? A journalist's curiosity, in my experience, is no more intense than that of a writer of fiction. The difference lies in the stop signal that flashes in the mind when one is writing a piece meant to give facts – facts alone. The main character, in this case, was a man precisely described by people who had known him. I had a number of newspaper photographs of him — he could not and must not be transformed. I did not have to make a conscious effort to keep the article in focus: the stop signal was in place from my very first newspaper assignments. No one warned me to be careful, for the simple reason that the men who first hired me had no idea I ever meant also to write fiction. It was just there, like the barrier I have kept between French and English. I do not want them to overlap. If they did, I would move, without any hesitation, to a place where I was likely to hear and read and speak no language but English. I have been ready for years to face a crisis that, in fact, has never occurred.

If I look at my research on the Johnny Young story objectively I can see, quite clearly, that I must have considered this my last chance to explore yet another area of Montreal — to meet people I might never otherwise come across, enter homes I had no other excuse to visit. I had a passionate interest in my native city, but I could never have brought it, or that particular period, to life in fiction if I had not first established what I shall call the plain facts of journalism. I can still see in my mind someone I never met: the father of Johnny Young, described to me as an obese man in shirtsleeves, sitting on his front steps, eating ice cream on a hot day. His wife had died a long time ago, some said; others were not so sure, though neighbours and acquaintances agreed that the boy had been motherless and that his father was not young. The father sat on the steps, day after day, with a dog beside him. He ate ice cream cones while his child became a petty thief and then what someone called "a habitual criminal."

One of the family friends was a woman in her early twenties. She stood at an ironing board and got on with her brothers' shirts as she told me about her semi-delinquent siblings and their great pal, Johnny Young. She told me about how they had stuck up a candy store with a fake gun, but turned and ran, and how they had stolen odd things, such as alarm clocks, though not so odd if you remember that during the war alarm clocks were no longer man-ufactured, and people would pay anything for a second-hand one. They were English-speaking but there was a lost European culture somewhere — Slovak or Bohemian. In the story that evolved out of that meeting, years later, they turned themselves into Romanians. I knew Romanian émigrés in Paris. One thing blended into the other.

In a way, I still write as if I were reporting. The faces of characters, entirely imagined, or subtly altered from a living source, remain in my mind. I can see the face of the woman behind the ironing board, and I can also see the man I never met, the father of Johnny Young, on the front steps, in his shirtsleeves, eating ice cream. Journalism fed my mind and nourished my work. I am grateful to have been given an occasion to say so. Perhaps I have put more questions than I have been able to answer — I hope you are not disappointed. To sum up, where I was concerned, Cyril Connolly was hopelessly wrong. I was not crushed or in some way exploited by my apprenticeship. I worked as a journalist, and journalism worked and probably still works for me.

1989
DOROTHY LIVESAY

There were five of us, at least five. Five Canadian women who were born in Manitoba during the first three decades of this century. All of us were daughters of immigrants. As we grew up, we were part of the prairie landscape: that azure sky where clouds roamed free – the sparkling winters when huge blocks of chopped river ice, glass monuments, waited in snowy fields. How we rejoiced in the spring run-off, when brown grasses would melt into green to the song of the meadowlark. Our roots were there, in the black receptive earth. Our roots also were in the cultures of our families, for our parents had come to Manitoba from varied ethnic and linguistic backgrounds. Two of us were English-speaking Protestants – the WASPs. Another one was a French-speaking Catholic. Two were of Ukrainian Jewish extraction whose mother tongue was Yiddish. All five of us grew up either in small riverside towns or in the northern fringe of Winnipeg. We depended upon a father figure whom we loved, yet resented, and a mother figure who struggled to keep the family fed, clothed, and educated.

In point of time: If we look at the year 1909, we find Gabrielle Roy arriving on this planet in March, in Saint-Boniface. Across the Red River, Dorothy Livesay made her appearance in North Winnipeg, during an October snowstorm. 1917 brings Miriam Waddington; 1925 Margaret Laurence; and 1927 the youngest of us, Adele Wiseman. Margaret and Adele were destined to become lifelong friends.

Whatever was it that made us become writers? To begin with, there were no distractions. No radio; no TV. Film stars such as Charlie Chaplin or Mary Pickford existed, but not for us. Our parents could not afford movies, let alone a Model T Ford. Only occasionally, perhaps for a birthday, could they afford a book. In one of her Manawaka stories, Margaret Laurence has written: "[As a twelve-year-old] I was much occupied by the themes of love and death, although my experience of both had so far been gained principally from the Bible, which I read in the same way as I read Eaton's Catalogue . . . because I had to read something." It was a few years later that Adele Wiseman, also knowledgeable about Old Testament stories, was able to satisfy her craving for books by finding the North Winnipeg public library. She writes:

One hot summer day my big brother Harry and I hiked up to the library together. I was about seven or eight. It was a fair distance, a mile or so. Normally, you were allowed two fiction and two non-fiction each, but in the summer you could take out twice as many. Harry and I loaded up and, hefting, juggling, and reading all the way, we lugged home our prizes. When I finished reading my own books I read through Harry's, and he read through mine. When we had both finished all the books, it occurred to us that the Junior Library would still be open if we hurried. We gathered up our armloads and back we rushed through the bright, dusty streets to reload. What a shock it was when the librarians refused to let us take out any more books. They said it was against the rules to let children take out books more than once a day.

She writes: "I am still indignant."

My own experience of that craving for reading was somewhat different because both my parents were "newspaper people." (In those days it was considered "smart-aleck" to call oneself a journalist.) Actually my father, J.F.B. Livesay, was the news editor of a prewar news cooperative, the Western Associated Press; and my mother, who before her marriage had been editing the social page for the *Ottawa Journal*, now wrote for the *Manitoba Free Press*. She ran the women's page, in which there was a corner for children's letters. Florence Livesay was especially interested in hearing from young Indian children living in the residential schools. She awakened my interest in their lives and before I could read myself she printed stories that I had "made up." It must have been when I was four or five that I spoke out:

"I think God should tell the angels to take the children."

"Why, dear?"

"Because the angels would look after them better than the mothers do."

I never thought, of course, of suggesting that the fathers might be a part of the domestic scene and that they might try their hands at childcare.

Well, as we grew into our teens, the five of us began keeping diaries, writing poems to our friends, scribbling the plots of stories. But we all knew that as soon as we had completed high school, we would have to be on our own, earning a living. The choices were nursing, teaching, newspaper work. So how could a woman possibly become a writer? At sixteen, I wrote in my diary, "It's a man's world!" and at eighteen, when I was in my freshwoman year, the men's debating club at the University of Toronto announced a forthcoming topic: "Can women ever become writers?" The vote gave us a resounding "No!" How could we have known then that in order to become poets or novelists we would have to leave our roots, our families, and travel to another region — even to another continent? Yet this lay ahead. As Margaret put it: "You are never a stranger in your own country. That is why you have to leave!"

A central concern in the struggle of us five was how to earn a living. In the early years we had to teach, or become part-time journalists for newspapers or radio, or as Miriam Waddington and I decided, to become social workers. We used our social work experience to write poems of protest concerning the victims of the Depression in Canada and especially in Montreal. My own poem about an immigrant shot by the police was written then and there. In that context, I would like to read a stanza from Miriam's poem, titled "The Nineteen Thirties Are Over":

> These days I step out
> from the frame of my wind-
> battered house into Toronto
> city; somewhere I still
> celebrate sunlight, touch
> the rose on the grave of

Eugene Debs but I walk
carefully in this land
of sooty snow; I pass the
rich houses and double
garages and I am not really
this middle-aged professor
but someone from
Winnipeg whose bones ache
with the broken revolutions
of Europe, and even now
I am standing on the heaving
ploughed-up field
of my father's old war.

Well, we five women, we all married. Four of us had children. Three of us divorced. None of us had a faithful secretary as wife. Was this situation a part of what led us to being dubbed feminists? In the early years of marriage our husbands did support us, but they were not equally willing to give us time out for writing. In retrospect it would seem that Margaret and Gabrielle had the best deal. Margaret had a number of years supported by her husband engineer; Gabrielle eventually married a doctor. My husband died when I was fifty and my children were nearly grown up. That did give me a sense of freedom that led me to work for UNESCO, in Paris and then in Northern Rhodesia (Zambia).

Thus, in attempting to answer the question "Are we feminists?" I would have to say, rather, that we are humanists. We take a political interest in what is happening to humanity on this planet. Because we have had children, or have had the care of children, we have been concerned with all the weighty problems that arise in the lives of women and children, especially in the third world. And we wonder how our ten-year-olds today will manage to save the world when they are in charge, twenty years away. Have we prepared them for disaster – or for a fairer world? Women and men writers need to tackle these questions together, looking beyond the third world to the fourth.

In my peregrinations across Canada, I have often been asked two questions: "When did you start to write?" "What do you write about?" The first one is easy — it can be proved. I started to write poems and stories when we moved to Toronto from the prairies. At high school, aged thirteen, I had poems accepted by the *Vancouver Province* book page. When I was fifteen, I won a short story contest at school. After that, nothing could stop me. But *what* do you write about? The easiest answer is "everything." But that says nothing: I should have to put on my thinking cap. Leaving the prairie was a great wrench, but discovering an Ontario spring was breathtaking. Trees had blossoms! The woods were full of wildflowers. And later there would be cherries, and strawberries, apples, and plums. I might miss the geese, going north? The thrill of the meadowlark? Yet here in the Mississauga woods there was a bird called whip-poor-will. So what did I write about? The natural world. And how it must be saved.

Then my adolescence led me into tougher paths — how to get along with people, with friends, with parents, with teachers. Then, of loneliness, empathy, fear, and pain — all the components of love. And so I plunged into writing about people. I've never stopped — the very young and the growing older. I am sure that that is a very common process.

It took me a long time to break away from home. But I did begin with language and I did live as a student in France. It was only by being flung into the depression of the 1930s that my homecoming became a rite of passage, a struggle against my WASP background. I wrote the documentary poems "Day and Night," "The Outrider," and, after the war, "Call My People Home," the story of Pearl Harbor and the evacuation from the West Coast of the Japanese-Canadians. This was first broadcast on the CBC in 1949. I was also writing a goodly number of short stories, but there was no market for them in those slim years of struggling publishers. To be truthful, in my own case, I was only able to distance myself after my husband's death in 1959, when I was fifty years old.

We have all five been aware of our duty to the language, whether we write in French, English, or Yiddish. Our duty is to make it clear. And we all know how hard that can be.

I may sound as if I considered myself a pioneer. Actually I am a follower, because Margaret went to Africa in 1957 and I only went in 1960. Well! Margaret Wemyss Laurence was the first of us to tackle translating a foreign language into English. She had not published any book of her own when she first went abroad. She had graduated from United College, Winnipeg, at age twenty-one, in 1947.

She worked as a reporter on the *Winnipeg Citizen* doing labour news, but the following year she married Jack Laurence, a graduate from engineering. In 1949 they left for England, and then her husband got a posting to do engineering in Somalia. There, she plunged into learning the language of the Somalis so that she could discover their way of life, their myths, their poetry. In *The Prophet's Camel Bell*, it is amazing what she accomplished, translating oral poetry into written English prose. These poems are truly lovely, a gift to the world.

The result of her work was two books in English: *The Prophet's Camel Bell*, published in 1963, and *The Tomorrow-Tamer*. The Laurences' next appointment was in Ghana in 1957. The next five years gave her all the material she needed for her first novel, *This Side Jordan*. The actual writing of the novel took place in Ghana and in Vancouver when they were on leave. *This Side Jordan* was at once a classical and experimental novel wherein she, as woman, entered into the psyche of two men's lives and made their problems believable. Indeed, when I started my UNESCO tour in Northern Rhodesia, my son gave me a copy of *This Side Jordan*. I was able to lend it to my African student teachers. They were amazed at Margaret's ability to comprehend *their* side of Jordan. She stands outside looking at two different men – one an Irish imperialist, the other an educated African teacher who believes that independence must come. In *This Side Jordan*, the African Nathaniel's monologue on the riverside is as follows: "The city of strangers is your city, and the God of conquerors is your God, and strange speech is in your mouth, and you have no home."

Of the five of us, Margaret Laurence was the woman writer who made the greatest break with her past "to become a stranger." The contrast between the third world and the capitalistic exploiting world had for her an extraordinary impact. Not, as in my case, leading her to emphasize the political and economic struggle, but to explore at the moral level man's inhumanity to man. For her, this struggle was revealed through language. She has written: "One should not be too quick either to love or to hate. We were all imperialists . . . seeking a mythical kingdom and a private world."

I only remember meeting Margaret twice – once in Vancouver – was it an evening at Ethel Wilson's when the Laurences were on leave from Ghana? I felt her as being distant, as if she'd lost interest in Canada and Canadians. We met again, some years later, in Winnipeg at a conference of the Commonwealth literature organization to which we both belonged. How different she seemed. How warm and deeply concerned. As I remember it, there was one delegate from the West Indies who was telling us how he felt enriched by having learned a literature not his own. How could he write his own if he had not the rich world of Dickens in his blood? (I did not keep notes, so memory must serve.) A number of delegates resented this proposition. "No one writes a novel without having read its predecessors," said Margaret. Culture for her was a world feast. But when she came home to live in Canada and write her mature novels, *A Jest of God* and *The Diviners*, she ran into two problems. One was the disagreement she had with her publishers over her titles. *A Jest of God* became *Rachel Rachel* when it was filmed in the U.S. More serious perhaps was the change of scene. It was no longer a Manitoba prairie story but was set in New England. But what must have hit Margaret the most was the censorship that came from school teachers and librarians in Ontario. In both books she had dared to describe the sexual act. Margaret survived that one, but at what cost? Eventually, as we know, she became ill and died prematurely.

I had always thought the stories *A Bird in the House* and *The Stone Angel* were her best books (the Manawaka roots). Now I have been re-reading *This Side Jordan*. So now I can compare it with *The Diviners*. I am bound to say that *This Side Jordan* is a better constructed novel. It grips you. The parallel stories of the African, Nathaniel, and the Britisher, Johnnie, are adroitly counter-poised to give a very accurate picture of the two sides, just before emancipation. The interior monologue of each, so understanding of the quandary of both men, is admirably handled. (Remember how I gave it to my African students to read? And how they felt its authenticity?) *The Diviners* certainly is authentic, as it reveals the seamy side of prairie life, and woman's plight. But, Laurence's probe of the Scottish and Métis past seems to slow the novel down.

To my sorrow, I never met my 1909 twin, Gabrielle Roy, face to face. It was in the 1970s, while teaching at the University of Alberta, that I discovered her wonderful re-creation of motherhood as recorded in the books *Where Nests the Water Hen* and *The Road Past Altamont*. These were published after Gabrielle had left Canada and gone to France and England to study drama and playwriting. It was only when she returned to Montreal in 1939 that she began writing about Manitoba. In 1947, her greatest achievement, the novel *The Tin Flute*, won her the Prix Femina and many other honours. That novel dealt with teeming city life in Montreal; with factory life, urban poverty, struggle. And from that achievement onwards, the ideas flourished: six more novels, three of them dealing with a Manitoba childhood. Short stories also flowed from her pen, especially that jewel from her teaching life: the story of Mederic the Métis boy (published as Part Three of *Children of My Heart*). In her fascinating unfinished autobiography, *Enchantment and Sorrow*, Gabrielle had written a paragraph which illuminates my title, "To Be a Stranger." This is her statement:

> Years before I wrote that book [*Where Nests the Water Hen*], I'd already unconsciously stored away some scattered, unconnected elements of it. You could say I had them close to my heart, but wouldn't have access to them for years to come. . . . But though you'd expect having access to what's inside you to be the most natural thing in the world, it's often the most difficult.

As Margaret has said, to write it down, you have to become a stranger.

As an example of what can happen to a writer's work, let me describe this one: here is the first edition, a hardback titled *A Winnipeg Childhood*, 1972; Peguis Press, Winnipeg. Originally I began writing it as a novel based on my own family experiences. My mother, herself a writer, saw the manuscript and told me I must not publish it. It was unfair to my parents. The editor of the Ryerson Press to whom it had been submitted refused to handle it. I still believe that my mother was behind that decision. Mary Scorer, publisher of a small press, was pleased to have it, as she was making Winnipeg history her specialty. The book sold well, with sympathetic reviews. Eventually a few of the stories were used in classrooms by child study and Canadian Literature teachers. So it seemed logical to have it republished as a paperback. Miss Scorer arranged to send the plates to New Press and have them do the reprint.

Alas, it was published, but not promoted in any way. Without my knowing it or having the opportunity to buy up copies, the Toronto publisher let it be pulped. I only learned about this because two teachers of first-year English classes in Toronto wanted to use my book as a text. They were told it was out of print! I hired a lawyer who was only successful in getting me two hundred dollars – which was, the publishers said, the share of royalties that I would have received. Since the book was now truly out of print and it represented my childhood view of the world, Peguis again came to the rescue, a year ago, when I submitted the same book, but with two added stories. It is now in print as a paperback entitled *Beginnings*, distributed by Turnstone and the U of Toronto Press. Also, several of the stories have been reprinted in anthologies. In my view, this is a book of seventeen short stories, low-key and subtle, describing a child as an outsider as she views the strange adult society.

Meanwhile, my own extensive adult memoirs, *Journey with My Selves*, have been written and edited, covering adolescence and on, up to the year 1960. Just as Gabrielle Roy was unable to take her autobiography up to the present, just as the other three women writers of my generation have failed to complete their memoirs, so have I stopped. The reason, I suspect, is the same for all of us. Too many of our relatives and friends are still alive. We are too elderly now to face "the hazards of outrageous fortune." We will do better to put our efforts into trying to save what I call the Fourth World – that world of women and children in whose hands will lie the fate of this planet.

If we examine the fiction – much of it autobiographical fiction – of these five Canadian women, several themes emerge. Paramount has been concern for saving the environment. *Not* for sentimental reasons, but for the futures of our children. This theme goes hand in hand with multiculturalism. I have written elsewhere that I see this country as a five-fingered hand. For too long a time, every finger has been trying to act alone. First, we have the Maritime provinces; then the industrialized provinces of Quebec and Ontario; then the breadbasket prairie provinces; then OIL, and the mountains whose mysteries extend towards the sea. The only unifying factor seems to be the North, which covers them all. Might the North be the beginning of a hand?

For a time, it appeared, ironically, that the Second World War would unite us. Young people began travelling west-east, south-north. For a decade or so, the ancient idea of family bonding still existed. But our present decade has been one of exposure. And women's writing has revealed what has been wrong: divisiveness, hypocrisy, dishonesty, and cruelty in family lives: "I'm all right, Jill. Let's kill." Sisterhood has further to go than that. Two of our five women writers have died, too soon. Were their illnesses due to despair?

I myself went through the trauma of excessive smoking and drinking. There have been others: the murder of Pat Lowther; the suicide of Gwendolyn MacEwen. The message is a sad one.

Because of the power of film, radio, TV, video, the responsibility of the writer is greater now than ever before; we must preserve the book, for it can always be by our side. We must also preserve living drama on stage. I have in mind the plays of Tomson Highway and Michel Tremblay. There is a host of others waiting in the wings, women and men writers. So this is no time to take sides, to foment hostilities. Women and children and men will have to go on living together, seeking ways to survive on this planet.

In Canada, as I see it, there are two great causes. Anti-sexism and pro-multiculturalism. Actually, they are intertwined, because they are concerned with the future of humanity. A hundred years ago, Canadians made a martyr of a visionary, a man who was more sane than his jurors. Before they hanged him, he gave a lengthy impassioned speech proclaiming the kind of community we could create in this land. Although the people of Manitoba sent him to Ottawa as their representative, he was forced to flee Canada and become a stranger. Being himself a Métis, with Indian, Irish, and Scandinavian ancestors, he made a plea in his trial for opening the doors to all peoples. Here are his words, the words of Louis Riel:

> I will speak of the wish of my heart. . . . I say my heart will never abandon the idea of having a new Ireland in the North-West by constitutional means, inviting the Irish of the other side of the sea to come and have a share here; a new Poland in the North-West . . . a new Bavaria in the same way . . . and on the other side in Manitoba . . . I want the French Canadians to come and help us there to-day, to-morrow. . . . And on the other side of the mountains, there are Indians and . . . half-breeds, and there is a beautiful island, Vancouver, and I think the Belgians will be happy there. . . .

> The Scandinavians . . . they will have a share . . . they should have on the other side of these mountains, a new Norway, a new Denmark, and a new Sweden . . .

. . . and the Jews who are looking for a country for 1800 years . . . [we will bring them to] the other side of the mountains, while the waves of the Pacific will . . . console their hearts for the mourning of 1800 years.

The children all over this planet, the ten-year-olds today, will be eighteen-, nineteen-, twenty-year-olds. And they will have no skills, no jobs, no higher education, whatever their colour, whatever their language, whatever their citizenship.

This is the Fourth World, with only a faint light ahead and a nuclear explosion in the rear.

Did Margaret Laurence see this coming? I believe so. Not that I was near her in person. But I use her words as guides, and here they are:

There are few women and men in the service of literature, drama and art to hasten the vision. To change ourselves. [We must] break out of the tunnel or we perish.

I should like to close, not with a bang, but a whisper. One morning I awoke, recently, with a dream. Here it is:

After a bus trip I was set down in a strange country where I had been invited as guest, to be part of that nation's celebrations. In the midst of all these happily talking and singing brown-skinned people, who were wearing long colourful gowns, I lost my guides — an elderly, plump rosy-faced man, apparently — an old friend of mine — and a tall, brown-skinned man wearing horn-rimmed glasses. They set me down in an open space amongst women and children seated on the ground, eating, and talking in a strange language. My hosts vanished. Feeling the need of food, I finally stood up in hopes of finding a table. Was there a head table where I was supposed to be? No table. Then a little smiling girl drew me back to sit down near her. By her gestures I got the idea that food was to be shared as it was passed around in baskets. Then an older woman offered me a long cotton dress to wear so that I would feel part of the gathering.

There was no concert, no dancing. After a time I began to panic. Where was my purse? How was I to get home? I stood up and began to circle around, searching. Where? No one could tell me. So I wandered through fields and stooped down to squeeze through a barbed wire fence.

Finally I caught sight of my guides. The brown man immediately went off to find my purse. Then the older white man pushed me into a doorway which turned out to be the entrance to a tunnel. He gave me a flashlight and a farewell push — and behold, I was flying along as if on skates, flying along alone towards a distant circle of light.

I woke up. Now that I am awake, I can look back on these pages and note that I have stressed our similarities, not our differences. Neither have I sought to put us on a scale of accomplishment with greater or lesser creative talent. It is true that volume of production would indicate that two novelists among us have made the greatest impact on Canadian literature in English and in French, both at home and abroad. There has been room also for the story-tellers and poets. Three of us are critics and teachers, a kind of bodyguard marking out borders, inspiring students. And it is these younger women today who are writing fascinating prose and poetry all over the country who have thanked us for our struggle, our struggle for space and time: not only for a room of one's own, but a clock of one's own.

Yes! If I had time enough I could give you another lecture. It would be about the Fourth World. Because I believe that in this year, 1989, some extraordinary changes have been signalling hope. What is happening in China is happening in small pockets all over this earth. To illustrate, I will leave you with just one example. This is a news item from Mexico dated March, 1989. The girl president of the District Children's Congress stated: "Mexican children have demonstrated that they want to be a part of the country's development." She was speaking to three hundred and sixty children at the Annual Children's Congress. I believe that our Canadian school children have it in them to become a part of that Fourth World.

1990

ROCH CARRIER

On May 25, 1990, Roch Carrier delivered the Margaret Laurence Lecture at Queen's University in Kingston, Ontario. As with all the Margaret Laurence Lectures, Carrier's speech was to be taped, transcribed, and included at a later date in an anthology. However, a month later, a letter was sent to Carrier by the Executive Director of the Writers' Union. She wrote: "I regret to tell you that I have received terrible news from Queen's University. They have informed me that the taping of your speech was faulty and they cannot produce an audible tape for us."

What follows is a transcription of an interview that the Writers' Trust conducted with Carrier in October 2010 in Montreal. When the interview began and a recording device was set on the table, Carrier remarked: "It is something I learned in my life: always test the technology, no matter what it is."

———

WRITERS' TRUST: Your lecture was delivered more than twenty years ago. Do you remember any particular details?

ROCH CARRIER: There is something that happened when I gave my lecture in Kingston. It was right at the beginning. [When I lecture] I don't write my text out because for me, a written text is a written text. When you talk to people, you don't write, you don't read; you talk to them, you look at them. But I had some little notes, just some words, and I started. Not far from me there was Pierre Berton. About three minutes after I began, Pierre Berton let out a huge yawn. I took it personally. *You will not yawn again!* And I put my little words aside and I went, and that's why I don't remember anything.

WT: When did you know you wanted to be a writer?

RC: I came quite lately to the idea that there was somebody writing the stories. Because until I was fourteen years old, or something like that, the stories were just coming. People were telling stories. They were coming through comic strips. So they were there. I don't recall thinking about somebody sitting down and writing stories. Around fourteen, we were doing a lot of translation, Latin writers and Greek writers. Translating brought me to the idea that somebody did that. I understood the concept of writing and that's what I wanted to do.

Coming where I was coming from, it's great to be a writer but you have to make a living, and in my area there were no unemployed people, except the drunks. People worked. It was just normal. Fourteen was also the time I got my first brown adult working boots, new overalls, and a shovel. I shovelled gravel and that was my first job. It was election time, and in Quebec when there is an election, you build roads. So I was on a team with grown men and our job was to fill the trucks with gravel and to spread it on the road. That was tough, but it was a great experience: first, to be with those men; and second, as a kid, to try and do as much as the other men, to do your share. If you don't do it, nobody does. That was quite basic in my life: this learning that you have to do the job. So if you don't write your page in the morning, it will not happen. Nobody will do it.

WT: Can you tell me about Sainte-Justine, the village where you grew up?

RC: Sainte-Justine was small. It was a very Roman Catholic parish. The population was less than two thousand people. We were very close to the border with Maine, so the United States was something we had a lot on our mind. My dad worked on the American side. In our family we had many uncles, cousins, who were living in the States. They lived in New York, coming several times with big cars and with gold teeth in their mouth. That was very impressive. From my bedroom window, I could see, I believed, the U.S. border. When I was very small my father explained to me we had the field where we played baseball; and then there was the forest for miles and miles; and then far, far away we could see lights and that was New York City. So I don't know how many times before going to bed I would go to the window and look for the lights of New York.

WT: What would be an exciting event in Sainte-Justine?

RC: An exciting event was every day. It was something that came back to me during the summer when I saw a bunch of kids playing with branches from a tree and inventing some game and I had some kind of a flash. This is exactly what we were doing. In summertime, let's say from 8:15 in the morning, I would go knock at the door of my friend's home or they would knock at my door and then we'd go until twelve. What we were doing, I don't know. There was nothing. There were the fields, the forests, the animals, the traps. We were looking, enamoured with everything. We would sit and look at a grasshopper off the path to see what it has done. We were very bad. *What happens if we pull off the leg?* That's what we were doing. That was great. Later, when I was in Europe, I had friends that were telling me about their Sunday afternoons at home going with their parents to visit some castle, and that was so boring to me when I was thinking of my great time doing nothing in a place that there was nothing. So perhaps what I learned there was to observe. I think I learned how to look. And looking, being curious about what is, I think I still have that. And it helped me in my trade.

WT: Did you have early storytelling influences?

RC: I think I gained a lot from the older men around Sainte-Justine. They had a lot of life, but not much school. There were no books around, so people were talking a lot. The blacksmith's was where men would meet and talk. If the father was proud enough of his son, he would bring his kid to the men. So my father brought me. Listening to those conversations, people talking about their youth in the forest, the lumberjacks, and the accidents they had and the fights they had . . . that was great, great stuff.

I come from that oral tradition. My grandmother was talking about her brother who wanted to become a priest but he had some kind of problem at the seminary and he left to Cuba. And he spent his life in Cuba living in some kind of cabin where there were snakes. He came back forty years later in the wintertime, dressed in his white cotton suit from Cuba. He saw my grandmother, who he had never seen before, and he said, "Oh, you're not as pretty as your sister." So my old grandmother, she was a very old lady and she was mad at this brother. That was the stories I grew up with.

In my family, the printed material was the daily newspaper, and for me as a kid, the comic strips. Once a weekend there were comic strips. There was nothing as extraordinary as those comic strips that my mom would read me and then I would imagine. Brick Bradford in a kind of vehicle travelling to planets to old centuries . . . that was fantastic. . . . Dick Tracy, a policeman talking to his watch because there was a telephone in his watch . . . that was extraordinary. *Superman* . . . I spent afternoons in the barn trying to fly, jumping from the beam to the hay. I think my greatest reading experience in my life, and I say that now, was when they were repairing my house. My father got some money and he wanted a big house and we had a small house, so he worked and made it a big house. We had to undo the walls, and the lathing material was newspaper that was used when the house was built, meaning 1905 or something like that. On the wall when I was climbing the scaffolding, I could see comic strips from that time. Shakespeare never beat that.

WT: What was your educational experience when you were young?

RC: I went to boarding school when I was eleven. In my family there was a tradition: "We didn't go to school, but our children will get instruction." In my grandfather's family, one became a priest, and five became teachers. That was quite an accomplishment. My grandparents were proud of their children. And for me, I was the only one in my class who went past grade seven. So my father and my mother picked me to be the one who would get some education. By chance, my dad did good business and, eventually, all my young brothers and sisters got an education. My dad was working six days and a half a week.

WT: When you turned eighteen, you moved to Montreal. How did that come about?

RC: I had studied in Edmundston, New Brunswick. It was, again, at the border against Maine. We were going to Maine a lot because New Brunswick was a dry province. At that time, you could not drink alcohol in public places, but if you cross the bridge on the Madawaska River, you can have a rum and coke or a beer, according to the money you have in your pocket. There were a lot of girls there at the dancing hall, a lot of beautiful girls. And *Rock around the Clock* was being shown at the theatre.

Then, at eighteen, I'm in the Beauce, thirty miles from home, hitchhiking because I'm going to New York City. I want to become a poet. Now, I don't speak English, but my mother's uncles and cousins, my father's aunt didn't speak English when they went to New York. They found jobs. First they were cleaners. Then they became waiters. Then they had a little corner store. They became taxi drivers. Or they started a small business in their apartment. They learned English. No problem. I had learned Latin, learned Greek. English would be easy.

So I was hitchhiking on my way to New York. What do I see coming and stopping? A sports car. Low roof. Yellow. I never saw that in my life. It stops.

In French: "Where are you going?" said the driver.

"I'm going to New York," said I.

"Oh, I'm going to Montreal," said the driver. "Okay. Good night."

I shouted: "Oh, wait, wait." [He motioned me in.] I sat down in the car. Instead of going to New York, I was going to Montreal.

The man said, "So, young man, what are you off to do?"

"I want to be a poet."

"Jesus Christ! Holy Mother!" He started swearing. "Do we need poets? Jesus Christ! What we need is businessman. Jesus Christ! Jesus Christ! Get out."

He stopped. I opened the door and said, "Thank you."

"Jesus Christ! A poet? . . . Come back," he said.

That was that. We drove to Montreal. Now I don't remember exactly what happened. The car eventually started to climb [Mount Royal] and high in the mountain we stopped at a big house.

"Where are you sleeping?" the man asked.

"I don't know," I said.

"Shit. Jesus Christ! Come, come, f—ing poet." We entered into this big house. I have never seen such a big house. And the man yelled, "Laura, come and take care of the boy."

I saw this lady coming. And this is the cousin of my mother. We knew she was working in Montreal for a rich man.

"Oh, Roch," she said. "You are so nice to come and see me."

I was fed dinner and I slept in a four-poster bed. In the morning, Lauren said, "When will you leave?"

I said, "Oh, it is okay here."

"No," she said. "You will have to find a job. I will go with you."

We took a bus and went to Côte-des-Neiges. I became a wrapper: I put in bags the products people were buying at the Steinberg's grocery store.

WT: What were you doing when you were first living in Montreal?

RC: I still want to become a poet. Being very practical, I said, "Okay, I have to work. Poets, they drink a lot and they starve, but lawyers make money. Perhaps it is possible to be a lawyer and a poet." I went to the Université de Montréal Faculty of Law and I registered as a student of law. My law courses were from four to eight in the afternoon. And because I wanted to be a poet, I also registered in the Department of Literature. Early in the morning, there were courses in literature. I was rushing to take Bus #29 back to the store to wrap and then back to the university. Two months later, the dean of the law faculty called me and said there was a problem.

He explained to me, "Young man, you cannot be in the Literature Department and the Department of Law at the same time. Law is a serious business. You have to make up your mind in life. What do you want to be: a lawyer or a poet?"

This dean is so stupid, I thought. *I'll be a poet.* I got out of the law school and kept studying literature.

WT: During this time in Montreal, were you writing seriously?

RC: I was writing quite seriously. I had already published a first book of poetry when I went to university. I financed that book being a waiter in some beer joint. The poems slowly started to turn into short stories. A weekly newspaper in Montreal called *La Patrie* was publishing short stories every weekend. One of the writers was published too much to my taste. His name was Yves Thériault. He was famous in Quebec at the time. I started to send in my short stories to *La Patrie* and they were not published. They would come back, and come back, and I could not understand because in my mind many of his stories were rotten while mine were impressively good. But they kept rejecting my stories until the day, I don't know why, I signed my story "Yves

Thériault." My first story was published under the name of Thériault, and Thériault never noticed it was not his. After a while, a story under my name was suddenly accepted, and then I had stories published. Many in *La Patrie*, and then they launched *Chatelaine* magazine in French and I had a number of stories published there.

WT: Your first book of poetry was something you published yourself?

RC: It was self-published. Coming from where I come from, you try the system and if the system doesn't work, and you don't expect that the system will work, you do it yourself. It's in my culture. It was a time when people in my area, they would not trust the bank. So they would not borrow money from the bank, but from each other.

WT: Did you go to readings that other writers would give? Were there places where literary types gathered?

RC: In those days in Montreal, there were at least two or three places where young intellectuals and creators would go. My favourite one was a restaurant on Clark Avenue and Sherbrooke. A Spanish restaurant called El Cortijo. At the time, many Spanish people were coming to Montreal. They had problems with Franco so they were running away. It was not far from the Beaux-Arts school, so students were coming there. It was really a meeting place of painters, sculptors, writers, musicians, and even wrestlers. We had wresters coming. André the Giant needed two chairs to sit on. People from radio, television. Models from fashion. There was an interesting mix of people. There were some people with glory, some painters who already had a lot of visibility, but we were the young ones. It was good to be with them. There was no border. You could address them, discuss with them, tell them that they were idiots. They would insult you also, but that was just fine. We could go and have conversations with them and be with them and talk about art. That was more interesting than school.

And the other place was called La Hutte Suisse, the Swiss Hut. It was a bit more upmarket. So people had to have really made it.

WT: When you were at this beginning stage of your writing career, did you share your work with friends? Did you have a support group?

RC: We had a writing course in university. It was boring to me. I knew all that stuff. Had I not already published a booklet of poetry that Gaston Miron, an important poet of the day, liked so much that he wrote me a letter? I really did not need that course.

WT: Where did you find encouragement from? Were you self-driven?

RC: Writing was just fun to do. I was in Montreal writing my short stories. After that I went back to New Brunswick. I was a journalist. I was writing a column in *Le Madawaska*, that was a paper in Edmundston. I did some radio at CJEM Edmundston. And after New Brunswick, I went to Europe. In France, I gave myself the challenge to write one short, short story a day. It was part of what I believed should be my training. I was training as a writer and every day I had to write a short, short story. Some of them were published later.

WT: Has the publishing world changed during your lifetime?

RC: In the beginning, when we were crazy kids, we would say, "I have an idea." And they would say, "Okay. Go, go, go." Now you have to deal with lawyers who write contracts longer than your book. But there are still crazy kids around and it's such a pleasure.

WT: You set a lot of your work in the village you grew up in. Why?

RC: I wrote a lot about that place because it was there that I learned what was important, and what is still important to me. And then for me this village became a metaphor for a number of other things. But I wrote also out of the village. For example, I wrote a book that takes place in Jordan. I have a novel set in Arizona. There are some in Montreal: *They Won't Demolish Me!* I wrote short stories for children about many places in the world: *Enfants de la planète*.

WT: Do you have novels or stories that you've written that you like more than others?

RC: I will say, perhaps, *The Lament of Charlie Longsong*. It's a novel that takes place in Arizona and in Quebec City. I think it is my best writing. But I'm not the best judge. People will decide if it is worth reading or not.

WT: How do you name your characters? Some people use a phone book. Is it crucial to you to get it right?

RC: Names are very important to me. Because the name is the first indication of what a character will be. The character has to be in the name. I just undertook a project, and of course I'm spending quite a lot of time finding the right name. And when I have the right name I can say that I've unlocked my character.

WT: You often write with wit and humour about subjects that others tackle with seriousness. Why is that?

RC: I'm not trying to be funny. I'm not trying to be critical or cynical. I just try to tell a story. Telling the story is my way of listening to the story and something happens and I react . . . You see, after a life spent [doing] a lot of writing, I don't know more about it than when I began. It's the beauty of it. In writing, you're always a beginner. And is there anything more magical than beginning something?

WT: I have read comparisons made of your work with that of sixteenth-century writer Rabelais. Do you consider him an influence?

RC: Rabelais was an immense writer. I had a kind of connection with Rabelais through my grandmother. My grandmother was not an educated woman, but she was speaking French with a lot of creativity, and with a lot of words that were making my brother and I laugh because nobody knew those words. Years later, I was at the Sorbonne in Paris and we had a course on Rabelais. Suddenly I discovered that I was understanding words that nobody in the class would understand. It was just that some of those ancient words I had heard from my grandmother. She was using very old French when she was talking. So that is my connection with Rabelais.

Rabelais was a free spirit. He was a great creator of a world. Funny. Deep. With a deep philosophy on everything. By example, he was able to describe what war is about and why peace is preferable to war.

WT: Are there other writers you feel strongly about? That influenced you?

RC: There are some English writers. In school the priests didn't want us, up to a point, to learn English. Because if you learn English, you will speak English, perhaps, to some of those English girls who come for vacation, and something might happen and you might fall for them and at the end you will have an English-speaking Protestant baby. It looks like what the Parti Québécois is saying today. Only around fifteen, we started getting English lessons, beginning with Venerable Bede. Now, it's not really English, but that was really important for me.

Years ago, Graeme Gibson [and I] were at some event. I said, "Graeme, you must help me."

When I was in school we had courses on Venerable Bede and I remember something that we read through translation by the teacher, and it's a meta-phor about life. You have a bird in the dark and there is a storm, and he flies to where there is a spot with a light and that spot with a light is a window. So it gets through the window and there is a big banquet with food, music, wine, ladies, and all that. And the bird flies across the room, being attracted to the other side of the room by a dark window. And he goes through the window and he is again in the dark. And that's a metaphor for life. So that's my first lesson in English. It always stayed with me, you know, what words can do, having a message, having a philosophy, having death talking to the imagina-tion. So for me that is a very special moment of what literature can do.

So I said, "Graeme, do you know that thing?"

He said, "No. But I will research it for you."

"Okay. If you do that, if you find it, please let me know."

Days later, I got the text from Graeme Gibson. That was so precious for me to have that text. As a writer, I still from time to time go back to read Chaucer. From Chaucer, I discovered in English "April showers," and there was so much music in the rain of those words. Those writers were as impor-tant as some French writers I read later. But with French writers, I always felt they were from abroad. With Venerable Bede, even if it was a different language, I didn't feel that. But French writers, they were from another landscape. Don't ask me why I felt that way. They were not as real, like Hemingway later telling a story about fishing in the Michigan River. That was exactly what I was doing as a kid, as an adolescent going to Saint John River at the border of Maine and Quebec where we were living and fishing. That was real.

WT: What would you consider to be the best intellectual training for a would-be writer?

RC: Having a life.

WT: Do you think writers commit to writing too early without accomplishing enough experiences?

RC: I don't want to judge, but having a life, a full life, with all the contradic-tions, with all the challenges, is a good way of having something to say. Last Sunday, I was somewhere for brunch and someone told me, "Roch, I noticed that you had a lot of jobs as a writer." She was seeing a contradiction between writing and the job, something I never felt. Yes, I was sometimes managing three jobs at a time, but every day, going back to my shovelling days, there was time to put some words into the truck. Those jobs I had were just there to enrich the writing, enrich the experience. I shovelled gravel. I was a wrapper. I was a tax collector. I went into real estate. In Paris, I did some cleaning in theatres. There were a lot of jobs.

WT: Do you ever think you could be anything else but a writer?

RC: It's been a great adventure and being a writer brought me to everything else. Writing opened so many doors to me. As a young writer, I discovered in Toronto and then Western Canada that there was a group of young, naive, well-intentioned, and talented young people, and they wanted to create something like Canadian literature. That was just wonderful. In Quebec, we were feeling, *We have to do something, create something.* And then, thanks to the translation, I'm there next to Dennis Lee, Graeme Gibson, and Margaret Atwood and all those writers trying to do the same thing and being involved. That was a great feeling. And then, I was able to tour across the U.S.A., to go to Europe, having a play and reading in Paris, Brussels, and Czechoslovakia. Václav Havel, a young playwright, was at that time in jail; in protest, I translated one of his plays and it was presented in Montreal. I also had the privilege to read in a number of other countries: Australia, the United Arab Emirates. Every time, everywhere, it was a great adventure and a learning experience, like in New Zealand when I saw men coming, rolling their shirt sleeves to stand between me and the audience; [it] was explained that some days before, a speaker had been unfair to the female students, who had taken hold of him, spread caulking on him, and covered him with white feathers . . .

WT: You are admired for having a delicate touch on French-English relations and how the two cultures co-exist. How influential have political developments in Quebec been on your work?

RC: In Quebec, we have a privilege. We share a deep common experience and we can participate in the project that is Canada. . . . For me, Canada is an adventurous project for the present time. This project is to bring together all kinds of differences and understand that differences are not a problem – they are a richness. That's a wonderful project. I am very happy to be part of it.

Unlike my cousins in the Bloc Québécois, I don't feel that I am being tortured by the majority. There is a lot of room for those who want to participate. You don't have to betray anything. I like this country.

Now, sometimes I was accused of not being vocal enough against this or
against that. During my life, I was also given the privilege of serving my
country in different organizations. I learned there was a way of going to
people who were responsible for what was happening, and talking to them
about what I wanted for the people served by my organization. Writing a
manifesto would not have helped me in those days. But anyway, that's for
me. When writers were outside writing letters, or shouting, it really helped
me to get what I wanted. Writers give a powerful support to those in action
who are trying to make changes.

WT: What have you learned from becoming a writer at a point in time when
a national community of writers came together?

RC: I must say that it is amazing what was accomplished in terms of giving a
national literature to a country in some years. It has been very short. It's
during the period I was alive that a country that was without literature suddenly has a rich literature with many different voices, so that's an incredible
accomplishment. Having been a little part of that is really something. And
it's not over . . .

Now, I'm sure that your next question will be: did Pierre Berton keep
yawning? I was watching him closely: he did not yawn again, and he did not
snooze.

1991

MARIA CAMPBELL

Last September, as I was leaving my home at Gabriel's Crossing for the winter, I looked at the house and land purchased by myself and a sister in 1979 which was to serve as "The People's School."

At that time it was a dream, nurtured by the Grandmothers, that this piece of land would become the people's Banff School of Fine Arts. "The Crossing," with its seven acres and an eighty-year-old ferry house, had already hosted ten writer and theatre workshops for Aboriginal people, and as many workshops for community workers and activists.

The veranda is sagging, the windows are rotting, and one good push would take the doors right off their hinges.

It needs a new roof, and the tents donated ten years ago by northern trappers, to house the people, wouldn't see another summer.

"Grandmothers," I thought, "you've got to do something!"

In my culture you don't ask the Grandmothers for money, at least not in prayers. The Grandmothers, by the way, live in the spirit world.

However, as I looked at the house, I thought, *What the hell. I'll make an offering and explain that if the door, windows, roof, and teepees are not replaced, their vision of this school is gone in the next snowstorm.* With that, I took tobacco and prayer cloth to the lodge at the other end of the property and asked for help, reminding them that this school was "their idea." I then left for Toronto to work on a film project.

Well, you know, the Grandmothers *always* look after prayers.

Two months later, I got an unexpected contract: enough money to buy the teepees.

A few weeks later, my daughter forwarded my mail to Toronto. However, I was busy writing to a deadline, so I put the mail in the closet till the deadline was met. Then, in January, I opened the mail. Among the letters was your invitation to give the Margaret Laurence Lecture.

I want to thank you tonight for inviting me. And I would like to thank Margaret Laurence and the Grandmothers for the windows, doors, and the new roof.

Margaret was a special person in my life. I can see her up there, or wherever they are, sitting with the other grannies. Thanks to them, Gabriel's Crossing will hold its first film workshop and shoot its first major film in July. That film is the first in a series of six one-hour productions titled *Stories of the Road Allowance People*, produced by Halfbreed Productions – a partnership between an Aboriginal and a non-Aboriginal. This is a first.

I would now like to begin this lecture – no, conversation – by telling you I have never been comfortable with the title "writer." In the beginning of my journey, it was difficult, because I really tried to fit that title.

There is no word for "writer" in my language. The closest words are *Achimoo E'squauoo*, "Telling Story Women," or *Ayahtiyookun*, "Keeper of the Stories."

And for sure I didn't see myself as a Keeper of the Stories or as a Telling Story Woman.

You see, in the beginning, I didn't write a book. I put my life on paper because I had nobody to talk to and I had to talk or I would die.

The woman who put that life on paper was not Mariah Campbell. She was June, Jody, Celina, and Jessica – names she picked up here, there, and everywhere.

Emma LaRocque, a Métis poet, wrote a poem titled "Brown Sister." I remember reading it and thinking of those women – June, Jody, Celina, and Jessica . . .

I would like to share that poem with you tonight, in their memory, because, you see, in a way, they were my grandmothers – their names were there when I needed them. They gave me strength and love.

O my beautiful brown sister
your eyes are deep pools of pain
your face is prematurely lined
your Soul of Sorrow
is the Sorrow of Every Woman
Every Native
My beautiful brown sister
I know you.

I know you
you heal me
you sweep sweetgrass over
the scars of my Exile

"Swept sweetgrass over the scars of my Exile." That was what they did for me when I tried to lose myself.

Exile means to leave one's home and country. It also means — in my language — to leave the place where the spirit dwells.

When June, Jody, Celina, and Jessica put their life on paper, they opened the door for a fifteen-year-old girl, and released her from seventeen years of exile.

I was thirty-three when *Halfbreed* was published, but Mariah was fifteen years old. These women opened the door, freeing her. But the publication of their story created another kind of exile.

You see, with the word "writer" there comes a lot of baggage; expectations, real or otherwise, that June, Jody, Celina, and Jessica never had to deal with. I will try to explain that.

Maria came home in 1973 after an extensive six-week cross-Canada tour flogging her first book. Liberal Canada was feeling guilty. Wounded Knee had just happened. Everywhere, Aboriginal people were organizing and speaking out. The media and the people opened their arms to Maria.

She was easy to like — raw, vulnerable. She was the stereotype of all the things they knew Aboriginal peoples to be — especially Aboriginal women.

Jack McClelland explained all that to her prior to sending her out on the road. But she didn't understand.

"It's like a box of Tide," he said. "Packaging is important." Don't misunderstand what I am saying. I have much respect and love for Jack. He was honest with me and he tried to prepare me. I just didn't understand. Dropping the *h* from "Mariah" and using "Maria" was part of the packaging because, he said, Canadians associate "Mariah" as negative, like the black car that picks up people for jail — or worse yet, the lizard-like fish found in northern waters.

It was a hard trip over and over again explaining the difference between Halfbreeds and Indians.

No one thought in terms of Nations in those days. No one knew about government legislation. No one knew our history and no one knew Aboriginal peoples.

To Canadians, an Indian was an Indian was an Indian, and that's all. But they did like her . . . and *her* was a mess.

I remember only one thing about that tour — arriving in Toronto from Montreal and Ottawa literally holding myself together and then falling apart in my hotel room, exhausted, confused, but most of all freaked out at suddenly becoming (to white Canadians) the voice of Aboriginal people.

Fortunately, I had a friend in Toronto, an Anishinabe writer and community worker. His name is Wilfred Pelletier. I was hysterical as I tried to explain to him on the phone that I couldn't go on. He hurried over, bringing with him Willie Dunn, a singer and poet. They didn't ask me what I meant when I said I didn't know how to be an Indian or a Halfbreed. They just wrapped me in a blanket and smudged me with sweetgrass and cedar smoke — so much of it that the fire alarm went off! They then had to explain what they were doing to the two security men who rushed the door, sniffing the sweet air in the smoke-filled room. You could just tell what they were thinking.

Later that night, Wilfred gave me the braid of sweetgrass, telling me to use it whenever I felt like I was losing it. "Talk to Creation," he said. "Talk to the Grandmothers." And Willie told me never to believe what I read about myself — good or bad — because none of it was really about me anyway. "But most importantly," they said, "you can't quit. None of us can. This is a part of our liberation — like it or not. We got picked!"

Maria came home from that tour twenty pounds skinnier. She could hardly wait to get together with the support systems at home and share her experiences. However, when she called them, they were busy.

After several weeks, with no one to talk to except the media (who kept phoning for interviews on everything: street life, straight life, bad housing on reservations, feminism, Aboriginal politics, trapping, fishing, and last but not least — her next book), she went out to find friends and family.

The ones she found at home were happy to see her — but they were uncomfortable. They had nothing to talk about. They tried, but they had nothing to say to her. When she left, they hugged her.

Finally, she went to the bar, knowing the street people had never shut her out. They stood up when she arrived and formally shook her hand. Some of them kissed her. But again, there was unease. Some of them moved to other tables; others left.

She asked what was wrong. They told her she didn't belong with them anymore. One of the sisters added, "We love you and we don't want to see you in here."

She left and went to the home of an auntie, who made her tea, gave her the family gossip, and then, as she was leaving, asked her why she called herself "Maria."

How do you explain to an old lady who doesn't speak English that it was packaging, not shame about sounding Indian, that made you drop the *h* — thus removing you from the grannies you were named after?

I can't even begin to explain the isolation or loneliness I felt — never mind the incredible fear. I had reclaimed my life, but I no longer had survival skills. Maria had to develop new ones.

So I began my life as "writer." And I tried — I really did — even displacing my daughter, setting up her room as an office, with a typewriter, lots of paper . . . you know, writer's things! Never mind the fact I couldn't type.

My new life was writers, poets, editors, publishers, media, and conversation far removed from the things I was talking about. Life was now writing "the book." Everybody was working on something.

It's interesting to remember that prior to this, I didn't even know about Canadian writers. I, like many other Canadians of my generation, thought that writers were all dead or lived in England. And, in the middle of all of this, I was trying to raise four children, with very little money . . . we all know how much money writers make! And I'd also become a grandmother.

I want to backtrack a bit and just tell you about our first Christmas, 1974. I'm sure you have similar stories.

There was no money for Christmas, and only a couple of cans of soup between us and starvation.

Six-year-old Cynthia, my youngest daughter, came home for lunch and gift-wrapped the last can of soup for the poor people's basket. When my oldest daughter tried to explain to her that we were the poor people, she replied, "No, we're not . . . We're writers and we're famous!"

Later that night, we made a family decision to pool all the babysitting money and my last twenty dollars on Christmas dinner. The following morning was pretty depressing: no Christmas stockings, no gifts, only the huge ham we'd blown our money on. About four o'clock that afternoon, one of the kids asked, "Mom, how come we can't smell the ham cooking?"

Well, to make a long story short, when the ham came out of the oven and I cut it – it disintegrated! Purchased at the corner store, the only place open on Christmas Eve, it was so old and so freezer-burned, it was not edible.

So dinner was mashed potatoes, turnips, carrots, bannock, and tea. So much for being a "famous writer."

It was at this point that I became desperate. I had to write "the book" or I had to get a job. I was scared to talk to anyone. They wouldn't understand. They all talked about writer's block. No one ever talked about "posing as a writer and not writing anything." My fear was that I'd be exposed as a fraud. At least in my former lives I'd never had to worry about that.

Then one day, my daughter, Cynthia again, came home and announced that she hated Indians. "They were bad people. Stealing women and children and cutting people's hair right off!"

I marched off to blast the teacher – something it seemed I was always doing.

I came home from that meeting, sat down at my kitchen table, and wrote *People of the Buffalo* – a history of Plains Indians. This was followed by *Riel's People* – another book on the history of the Métis. These two books were motivated by the kind of history my children were learning in school about their people.

By now my grandson was four year old. One day, he asked me, "Grandma, where did we get fire?"

I'd never given any real thought to oral tradition before this. I'd never thought of my grannies' stories and writing as one and maybe the same thing.

Sure, I had talked about it in English, to my writer friends. But, inside of me, I couldn't bring the writer and the storyteller together. I just didn't see any connection between the two, because I didn't believe I was either one.

I credit my grandson for bringing me that last stretch home. You see, because of him, I went home for the first time – home to my Elders, with tobacco and offerings, and asked for a story.

It was the final step in breaking the exile, because asking for the story was a spiritual act. It was done unknowingly – true – but by doing it, I had to speak my own language in a way that was different than I had ever spoken it since I was a child.

When you go the Keepers of the Stories, you must be clean of anger, hatred. You must think in terms of *N'Wakoomacunuk* – "All My Relations." All my relations are represented by the four directions, the four colours of prayer cloth which is the offering – black, red, yellow, and white. Those directions and colours are the grandfathers and grandmothers who represent and speak for everything in Creation, including humans. They are the ones who carry our voices to Creator – Creator, who is our Mother and Father.

To come to the Elders clean means one speaks differently than when just visiting or talking politics, which, as an adult, was how I'd always come to my people. I'd never come to them humble, asking to be taught.

Little Badger and the Fire Spirit was reaching "my homeland," but I didn't recognize the landmarks. At least not then, because I was still in an English state of mind.

It was a frightening realization to know that the language manipulated me in both English and Cree and that the spirit inside of me couldn't speak because she was in a different place. I realized why I couldn't write, and when I did, it was only about pain.

That was when I learned – in my heart – what liberation means, and it was the most sacred moment in my life.

I remember the old ones telling me, "You can do it. It's easy. All you have to do is give the language a mother."

That took some doing. For the longest time I didn't know what on earth they meant. You know how you can understand something in your heart, but trying to make it connect with your mind . . .

Never mind a fifteen-year-old Maria. The old ones made me go back to the six-year-old girl.

"Homeland" has been hard work, frustration, and lots of tears. I have a granddaughter who is just learning to walk. It's the same thing. It was like seeing or finding for the first time.

So tonight, thirteen years later, I am speaking from that place – "homeland." And in a way, I feel as I did the first time I spoke to my own Elders, because many of you are my Elders, as well.

I have much respect for you. I can't begin to list what the writing and artistic community, in Canada, has given me in terms of friendship and moral support. Your books have broadened my view of the world and taken me, my family, community, and nation, to many places in the mind and imagination. But, on the other hand, I must also tell you that same writing has also been responsible for much of the pain in my home, in my community, and in my nation.

The colonizer, in first exploiting our land, then establishing a "new homeland" for himself, saw our people as weak and inferior. Realize when I say "colonizer," I do not mean the peoples for whom he opened the country – the emigrants.

To establish "homeland," his attitude of greed and disrespect of *pimatsoowin* – life – which is the most sacred of Creation, was the legacy he gave this new homeland, for the peoples whom he had already exploited, oppressed, and dehumanized in his own world.

The inhuman conditions and oppression that my people live in, in this country, are the same conditions that the new emigrants fled from in the countries of their birth. If you go back far enough, in the history of your grandfathers and grandmothers, you will find that the same conditions existed and they fought for liberation or escaped (exiled themselves) from their homeland to try to make their *pimatsoowin*, their life, healthy. Not all of them succeeded.

It is tragic that I must stand here, in my homeland, and speak to you about the same pain.

Compared to your new homeland, and I mean this country, my homeland is poor. The few material things once owned by our people, you will find in the museums of this country. We never had architecture, or works of art. The things that are visible in your world were things that were not as important as *pimatsoowin*. It was the most sacred of all.

Imagine a quiet pool of water, and you, with a small pebble in your hand. Drop the pebble in the water and you will see the original homeland of Aboriginal peoples.

The first circle is *pimatsoowin*: life, babies, inheritors. The second circle is *kaytayuk*: the old ones, teachers, keepers of knowledge and wisdom. The third circle is *E'squawuk*: women, the keepers, extension of earth, and givers of life. The fourth circle and last circle is *napawuk*: men, the protectors.

Now, see within those circles many, many circles or societies, for lack of a better word, whose purpose it was to hold wisdom and knowledge, to keep the family, the community, and the nation strong. None of the keepers ever stepped out of their circles to speak the wisdom, the knowledge, or the stories on behalf of the other, without permission and many, many years of training. To do that was unthinkable because it was the greatest disrespect for *pimatsoowin*.

The wealth of our homeland was oral tradition – voice. That tradition was the power of our community. So much so that my father, who is one of the keepers of that tradition, and whom I failed to recognize as such for many, many years, said:

My *kookoom* [grandmother] was a Keeper and a Storyteller, and so was ole *Mooshoom Peekeekoot* [*mooshoom* means grandfather]. Dat's da one dat teach me about trapping and hunting da right way. Both of dem, dey say dat da Keeper and da Storyteller, he have to listen a long time before he can tell da stories dat belongs to da peoples. Dat's true, you know, 'cause dat's where da power, he come from. Even da ones you make up yourself or da ones dat's your very own, dem too, dey belong to da peoples, and dat's what da Keeper and da Storyteller, he always have to remember. He has to be very careful when he open hees mouth, cause da Voice, hee's got work to do and hee's responsible for dat work. If hee's not responsible, da power, he can kill *pimatsoowin*.

My father was speaking about the Voice of the people.

In learning this language at the age of six, I learned to hate my homeland. In hating my homeland, I learned to hate myself to a point where I almost disappeared completely.

Today, I am home. My land and my people are beautiful and strong. Today, I recognize the landmarks. I make many mistakes; but even the mistakes are teachers and guides to a more healthy place. I am not yet a Keeper of the Stories. Perhaps I will never be. But I am a Storytelling Woman. I have earned that by being a servant to my Elders. And so, from that place, I ask you, on behalf of *pimatsoowin*, all our babies, to respect and support our struggle for voice, for liberation, and for self-determination.

In my language, *kaw tip aim so yin* means "to own yourself." Only in owning ourselves can we achieve liberation. Only in owning ourselves can we come home from exile. And owning ourselves can only be achieved if we speak for ourselves.

Our old ones say that our liberation will also be yours!

As a grandmother of my community and as a Storytelling Woman, "proud" is hardly adequate for what I feel for the Aboriginal writers and artists of "our homeland."

I thank the many friends of our people who understand what I am trying to say.

To all of you, I extend an invitation to the People's School, should you pass through our territory.

HOO — TA WOW

1992
TIMOTHY FINDLEY

Whenever I attend a Writers' Union AGM, I am reminded of one such meeting in the early '80s, which was held about forty miles from where I live. I don't drive, and my companion, Bill Whitehead, was away filming in Vancouver, and so I asked a young neighbour to get me to the key day of the meeting, and to pick me up when it was over. I was duly delivered, and at the end of the day, my young friend arrived, on time — and with his wife.

When they got there, I was standing in the hallway with Pierre Berton. I saw my friend, and beckoned him over. But he turned pale and shook his head. I went over to him and asked him if he wouldn't like to meet Pierre. "I – I – I couldn't," he said. Then he told me his wife had gone to the ladies' room, and that he'd wait outside for us.

In a moment, I saw his wife coming along the hall — and she, too, was ashen. "Are you all right?" I asked.

"Yes. No. Yes," she said — and hurried me out of the building.

Once we were all in the car, I asked them what on earth their problem was.

"That was Pierre Berton!" the young man said. "I mean, *Pierre Berton*, Tiff." It sounded almost like an accusation.

Then his wife said: "On my way to the washroom, I bumped into *Margaret Laurence*. Bumped right into her. And then, in the washroom, *Margaret Atwood* was coming out of one of the cabinets. I turned right around and left." She looked at her husband. "I still haven't gone," she said.

"Well . . ." I started to say.

"Tiff," the young man said, "you didn't tell us you knew anyone *famous!*"

Well – I have been waiting now for ten years for my young friend Len, in my presence, to have to "step outside for a breath of fresh air" – and for Anne, his wife, to be "unable to go" if she sees me. Some people sure do know how to put you in your place!

Just this past week, Margaret Laurence's beloved friend and writing companion, Adele Wiseman, died of cancer. She was sixty-four years old. I want to dedicate these words to Adele – not only for Margaret's sake, but as an acknowledgement of a maddening, inspirational, and friendly foe with whom I warred with passion and respect. Here, then, for Adele Wiseman, who has left us a masterpiece – *The Sacrifice*:

1.

It is my great honour to have been invited to deliver the Margaret Laurence Lecture for 1992. Margaret Laurence was a measure for all of us, a model for some and a mentor to others. She was also, to many of us gathered here, an honoured and beloved friend. Few can fail to envy the time in which she lived. Her unique response to being alive – so vivid in itself – is written into the body of her work and, this way, all of us have access to it.

Margaret Laurence was an incomparable companion. She spoke as she wrote – intensely focussed, often with laughter, always without pretension. She was a passionate witness of human life and one of life's most passionate practitioners. She was also one of its bravest dreamers. And that will be the subject of these words in Margaret's honour. I want to talk about dreams. I want to talk about dreamers.

The Writers' Union of Canada – of which so many of us here are members – was once a dream, and Margaret Laurence was one of its principal dreamers. Graeme Gibson. Marian Engel. Margaret Laurence. Others.

It is now just twenty years ago that Graeme Gibson began to sound out the writing community to see who might be interested in forming a union.

It was a wonderful time.

Throughout that first year, before the Union was confirmed, there was a sort of courting process. We met in people's kitchens, living rooms, and dining rooms. We sat on stoops and porches. We gathered in pubs and restaurants. We shared one another's houses. Writers flew in from Nova Scotia, Prince Edward Island, and New Brunswick – Manitoba, British Columbia, Alberta, Newfoundland. Trains brought others – and cars and trucks. Some came riding bicycles and buses. Sylvia Fraser, wearing a long white evening gown and boots, once arrived on a motorcycle, helmeted – with silver shoes slung over her shoulder. In Marian Engel's house, there was a large, dark photograph of General Booth of the Salvation Army hanging in the hall. His presence there gave us, I guess, the impetus to march – to bang our tambourines and to make a *militant* noise!

Collectively, who were we? What were we? What did we want?

We had to discover all of these things for ourselves. Now, so many years later, it is difficult perhaps to imagine, but at that time there *was* no writing community, as such. There was just the idea of it and many individual "communities" of one. Fairly quickly, it was discovered that our problems were mutual and that our needs were shared. Our publishing houses were in jeopardy. Some were being sold to offshore interests. The integrity of our cultural institutions – to say nothing of the culture itself – was seriously threatened. Well . . . *what else is new?* But in 1972, there was no one standing up, collectively, and saying *no*. Certainly, governments were not saying *no*. So this, at the outset, was one of our principal concerns.

Standard contracts. Copyright protection. Public Lending Right. Censorship problems. The importation of remaindered books and the lack of Canadian books in our education system. These were just the beginning. Our numbers grew. The community spread from coast to coast. There were, it turned out, a lot of us.

At last, we were ready, and we came here to Ottawa to found the Writers' Union of Canada. That was in November of 1973. Yesterday – or so it seems. What a great occasion it was. The late Frank Scott – a poet and lawyer, widely acknowledged as the country's leading constitutional expert – had been invited to guide us through the process of creating the Union's constitution. An Acting Chair was required and Margaret Laurence was the universal choice. It was then, at that time, that she said of us: "We are a tribe," which was, of course, the best description in the world. Writers come from anywhere and everywhere. They come in every colour and sex and – nearly – every age. They hold a myriad of cherished beliefs – and their politics are of every stripe. A tribe is not a race or a faction, but a kind. A family.

What makes us, then, a tribe?

Our dreams. And our dreaming. *Books.* Words – and ink – and the need to tell. And, the rejection slips embedded in our hearts.

Margaret Laurence did not want to be Acting Chair. Not because she was leery of the responsibility. She was perfectly capable of handling that. What she didn't want was all the standing up a Chair has to do! *The welcome. The preamble. The statement of aims.* "You will have to forgive me," she said, early on, "but I will have to sit down to do all of this." She hated public speaking with a vengeance. It was a torment to her. Whenever she was to speak, she shook. I mean – Margaret Laurence *shook*! It was visible. You could see it. You could hear it in her voice. She had to hold onto the backs of chairs and the edges of tables. At least on one occasion, she required another person to stand there with her. It was awful for her. *Dear God,* she prayed, *get me to the part where I get to sit down!* In the long run, Margaret Laurence gave up standing. In all her subsequent public speaking engagements, she was seated at a table.

Robin Phillips, the noted director, once choreographed an entire evening of public readings around the presence of Margaret Laurence's table. The event had to do with censorship, and the readings were all from censored books. There were, I guess, about a dozen readers – most of them writers, some of them actors. Margaret Laurence was the last to read and Robin Phillips had placed her table exactly where it should be – somewhat left of centre. Every writer making her entrance or making his exit had to contend with this table. *Please do not bump into the furniture!* No one did. That table, after all, is one of our tribal bonds. Every working writer must face that table every day. But that night – a night about censorship – the table took on a double meaning, because it was *Margaret's table* and no other writer in our country's history had suffered more than she had at the hands of those professional naysayers, the people who ban and censor books. When, at last, it was Margaret's turn to read, out she came onto the stage. And sat down. Immediately, everyone else stood up.

Later, an artist who was present that evening created a sculpture based on what he had seen. A number of tables — cast in bronze — are balanced on top of one another — some of them tilted like acrobats, standing on one leg, all of them piling up towards the sky. And the title of this work is *Margaret Laurence's Table*.

I see her every day. She watches me. I mean her picture. It hangs in my bedroom — a drawing of Margaret Laurence by Donna MacGregor. It is a remarkable likeness — done with pencils and ink, and a good deal of understanding. There she is — the eyes beyond the glasses, focussed — almost harsh, but not — the lips compressed — the head atilt and hunching forward — the gaze reflecting all that it has seen and taken in. *Kiddo,* she says, *you don't know the half of it!*

Yes, I do, Margaret, because you told me.

2.

This is about a writer's life and a writer's dreaming.

I live where I was born. I got here through the journeys of immigrants — Irish and Scots. So far as I'm concerned, they got me to the best place on earth. I have no desire to be elsewhere. I have no need for elsewhere. *Elsewhere* is in the mind. Of course, I have the need for travel — the need and the responsibility. But I don't want to go somewhere else and stay there forever. I want to know where I am as thoroughly and utterly as possible. I have a great passion for where I am.

It is threatened, right now, where I am. It is under a kind of siege. Sometimes, it feels as if I am alone in wanting to be here. Sometimes, it seems as if everyone around me wants to be somewhere else. America, perhaps — Never-Never Land — or the moon.

They can have the moon. The moon is dead. We killed it by standing on its face — by planting a windblown flag where there is no wind and by saying, *This moon is mine.* Talk about the death of the imagination. Talk about *appropriation.*

They can have America, too, for that matter. I mean they can have their idea of America — the good safe place — for Disney characters. As for Never-Never Land — no, thanks. I like it here. I want here. I need it.

But it's getting harder to stay in place. Not because I keep going away — but because the place keeps changing under my feet. It has become like one of those travelling backcloths on rollers they used to have in the theatre – where you walk – standing still – on a wooden treadmill while the stagehands roll the miles . . .

Miles and miles and miles – and miles of constitutional conferences. Miles and miles of Joe Clark and what's-his-name – *whosit* with the chin – miles and smiles of "All is well" and "Everything's dandy!" Miles and miles of losing my country – losing where I am.

Just the other week – while out walking – I came to a place that had been sold and there was a crowd of people standing, waiting. Out on the lawn, there was all this machinery – all this furniture – somebody's clothes and books and mementos – some kids' toys and hockey sticks and bicycles – someone's red wagon – a painting or two.

Know what it said on the sign?

AUCTION – CULTURE FOR SALE!

They are going to divvy us up, folks. They are going to subdivide us. *Subdivide and conquer.*

In biology, a culture is alive. You put it in a petri dish and watch it squirm while you alter its environment. Very often, the result of this is death – for the culture.

We once had a culture here. I mean, a *collective culture*. It was based on hope. It thrived on multiplicity. At its heart lay the belief that we were here to help one another. It set out a pattern of safety nets – of social programs created to make it possible for everyone to endure unemployment, illness, and old age. At least to endure them with dignity, while they lasted. That was the dream, at any rate, and briefly – too briefly – some of these things were indeed a part of our reality.

Susan Crean has said: "No nation can exist without culture because nations only ever exist if people think they do and believe in a common future . . ."

In the last few years, the culture that embraced these ideals has been trans-ferred to a petri dish – a petri dish at first called Meech Lake and now called Constitutional Reform. Eleven men have been watching it squirm while they altered its environment. The result of this can only be death.

Many people think that "culture" is a painting or a book – a piece of music – a way of dancing. But these are only the expressions of a culture. The culture itself is a people — and what they give to one another. Today, however, a negative environment is being manufactured — I refuse to use the word "created" in this context, because it would be demeaning to the word itself, let alone the process. A negative environment is being manufactured in which the people are being encouraged to *take* from one another — not to give. An environment where doors are being shut, not opened — and in which we are being encouraged to turn away from one another's needs and aspirations.

Part of what is being encouraged — do I mean "induced"? — in this altered environment has to do with the arts — with cultural programs and institutions. Subdivide and conquer. Subdivide and destroy. The provinces — it now seems — are to be responsible for their own cultural programs — one by one by one. The Feds, however, will continue to "maintain responsibility" for the Canada Council, the CBC, and other cultural bodies. Oh? That's interesting. Given their present record for "maintaining responsibility" for both country and culture, I think it is safe to say: *These bodies will soon be corpses.* Fascinating — the accumulation of lies . . . *Culture is not on the table!* It was. *Federal cultural responsibility will not ever be reduced to a list of institutions!* Then they hand out the lists.

Why do I suddenly hear the sound of slamming coffin lids? Just asking . . .

I keep on thinking: *It will change — it will get better.*

I keep on thinking: *We will survive this. We have to.*

I keep on thinking: *How did this happen? How did we get here?*

Out of our dreams — into these nightmares.

It's not as if people didn't try. It's not as if we didn't fight back. It's not as if we gave up. We stayed here for a reason. We stayed here to *be* here. But governments haven't listened. They have pretended to listen — and then turned back to predetermined agendas. Where *is* "here"? "Here" is nowhere, now. The backcloth is rolling on — and we can no longer identify what it depicts.

In the novel I am currently writing, a writer arrives in Canada from another country, two or three years from now. He takes a look around and, when he is asked to give his opinion of what he sees, he says:

"There is little beauty left — but much ugliness. Little wilderness — but much emptiness. No explorers — but many exploiters. There is no art — no music — no literature — but only entertainment. And there is no philosophy. This that was a living place has become a killing ground."

I wish he hadn't said that.

I wish I hadn't written it.

But what is a person to do? *Lie?*

3 .

The writer in my book is a man called Nicholas Fagan. As seems to be the norm in my writing, there is a mix of fictional characters and real people. Mr. Fagan gets his reference to entertainment as a substitute for art from a man called Arthur Miller. You can take your pick of which man is real and which is fictional. I have opted for Mr. Miller as the real person here. But still – we are all a mix of the two. And if you aren't – then I am. I couldn't live my life without my fictional self – the one who gets up every morning and looks in the mirror and says: *Oh, Tiff, how do you manage to stay so young? Why, you can't be more than thirty-five!*

The other me coughs at that point – and his eyes open – on reality. But that one brief moment in my fictional skin does a world of good. It makes me think I can do anything.

Anyway . . .

There is a passage in Arthur Miller's autobiography, *Timebends,* in which he describes another time – not unlike this time we are passing through now. He was writing of the late 1950s – the end of the Eisenhower era – an age of great wealth and of greater passivity. Miller was pondering what had become of art and of artists in that time and he wrote: "The whole [of America] seemed to be devolving into a mania for the distraction it called entertainment, a day-and-night mimicry of art that menaced nothing, redeemed nothing, and meant nothing but forgetfulness. . . ."

We cannot fail to recognize the echo of that time in this. Now we live in the Age of Indifference. It could also be called the Age of Impotence. One describes where we are; the other describes the consequence of being there.

I first read *Timebends* late in the summer prior to the last elections – the ones that gave us Brian Mulroney and George Bush. 1988. *Timebends* caused, for me, a great flood of memories – and of regret. Too clearly, we had returned, in the 1980s, to the postures and the sentiments of that earlier time. But with those elections, we were being given the opportunity to turn away from forgetfulness, and to start remembering who we are in North America and what it means to live in a privileged society. We threw that chance away, however — and now we have the consequence. We live — at last — in Never-Never Land: never offer a hand when you can withdraw it — never stand beside another person you can walk away from — never give when you can take. Never open a door when you can close it.

It was not a good time then — it is not a good time now. In the weeks just prior to the last elections, someone telephoned from the CBC. They wondered what I might have been reading through the summer, and would I like to talk about it in a series being prepared for a radio program called *Sunday Morning*?

I told them I had been reading *Timebends*. "Excellent," they said. "One writer reading about another. *Charming*."

I suppose they were hoping I would talk about Marilyn Monroe. Laurence Olivier. Yves Montand. All that stuff. They hadn't the Arthur Miller in mind that I had.

I was living then on Salt Spring Island and, when the piece was done, the telephone rang and the man from the CBC said: "Perhaps you should read it to me, just to be sure of its length, et cetera."

Its length.

Et cetera.

I read it to him, and when I had finished, there was a very long pause. *A very long pause.*

Then: "Mr. Findley?" The voice was nervous.

"Yes?"

"Do you think you could hang on for just a moment? I believe my producer should hear what you've written before I approve it."

"Certainly."

He went away. I waited.

Finally, a woman said, "Timothy Findley?"

"That's right."

"Go ahead."

My goodness — she was brisk.

I read to her.

This time, there was no waiting.

"Mr. Findley," she said. "You are not allowed to say those things on the radio. *Not now*."

"Oh," I said. "Why?"

What I had said was fairly straightforward. It was critical of both Mr. Bush and Mr. Mulroney. This was the election that would give us free trade, the invasion of Panama, the pardon of Oliver North, and the debacle of Meech Lake. Some of these events were foreseeable, others were not, but the men who would accomplish them were posing, in the meantime, as glad-handing, bright-eyed benefactors. Once elected, they would step from behind their smiles and reveal there had been a kind of disdain in the wooing. We, who were already in the process of losing our country, would have taken a giant step in the direction of that loss. A giant step in Gucci shoes. No mean feat, you should pardon the pun, given Mr. Mulroney's penchant for pussy-footing.

I drew the analogy between the 1950s in Arthur Miller's book and the time in which I would speak – times together in which our country and America had been lulled into complacency by governments with something else in mind than what we were being told. In 1959, the Cold War was at its hottest, and preparing to deliver the years of Vietnam. In America, Arthur Miller had been put on trial by the House Un-American Activities Committee because he would not give the names of communists and fellow travellers in the theatre. This had been happening to others besides Mr. Miller. One of our casualties then had been Herbert Norman – the Canadian diplomat who committed suicide while under investigation by the same committee who were trying Arthur Miller.

It so happened I had attended Miller's trials – trials about silence and being silenced and having to choose silence – each kind of silence a kind of death, if you were an artist. My memory of Arthur Miller and of the generosity of his silence was then – and remains – one of the better memories I cherish.

Miller's poise as he sat there silent, and the calmness of the interest with which he listened to the hours of testimony against him, were wonderful to behold. It was an experience both sobering and exhilarating.

Why was he there in that dreadful place in that dreadful time? Well – I suspect it was because his writings did those things that not much else was doing. They were menacing and redemptive and they urged us, above all else, to do anything but forget. Not to forget the past, not to forget the future, not to pass through the present as most of us were doing – as if it were forgettable even as we experienced it. As for redemption, Arthur Miller's plays urged us all to fulfill our promises – to return what had been stolen from human dignity.

As a writer, Arthur Miller was *there – all* there. Whole. And this meant much to me. It was what I wanted to be more than anything I could think of. But of course, I had not yet reckoned on the doing of it – and the cost. The cost, for Arthur Miller, of being whole was having to sit in that courtroom.

I wanted to say all this on the radio because it seemed to me to be a missing ingredient in the present elections – the ingredient of *wholeness* – the ingredient of *integrity* – the ingredient of *honesty*. And I knew that we had forgotten how to expect these qualities of our politicians. We were bored and cynical and inured to their lies. And watching them pass through the election process of mud-slinging, knife-throwing, and name-calling had become a sort of mania – *a mania for the distraction we called entertainment* . . . The process of democracy had been reduced to feeding that mania – and now we would pay for it.

Well, that – or something like it – is what I read over the telephone to Madame Brisk at the other end in Toronto. And she said: "You cannot say those things on the radio, Mr. Findley. Not now."

And I said, "Why?"

And she said, "Because we are in the throes of an election campaign."

"Oh," I said. "Gosh."

Dear God, this woman was treating me like an idiot.

"On the other hand," she said, "I might be able to let you do an edited version of the piece."

I remained silent.

She continued: "You would have to remove all references to President Bush and Prime Minister Mulroney."

"I beg your pardon?"

"It is our policy at the CBC that if statements are made which are detrimental to a candidate during an election campaign, the candidate must be given the opportunity for rebuttal."

I am not Arthur Miller. I did not remain poised and silent. I hit the roof.

I reminded her that Mr. Mulroney and Mr. Bush had access to every news broadcast on the CBC. And not much was said about rebuttal when *they* named names. And I said, "This is my rebuttal."

"Has the Prime Minister spoken out against you, Mr. Findley? I mean, of course, naming you."

"Hardly," I said.

"Then you are not entitled to rebuttal. Besides which, you are not a political candidate, Mr. Findley."

Thank God.

Then she said, "So. Are you willing to discuss removing the Prime Minister's name and the President's?"

"Of course not."

"In that case, we cannot broadcast your piece." Finally, she said, "I'm sorry."

Oddly, I did not believe her.

But that is neither here nor there. The thing is, I would not get to have my say, because I had wanted to name names. Arthur Miller, at his trial, did not get to have his say because he would *not* name names. Funny, isn't it — the times we live in, and the way they reflect upon one another.

Now, we have *libel chill* and *voice appropriation*. The further forward we get in time, the further back we spin in nature. It all ends up in silence.

Why?

For whom is the silence being maintained?

And *what* is being silenced?

If Salman Rushdie cannot imagine a Prophet other than the Prophet already imagined, who shall benefit? Again, I hear the sound of slamming doors.

Click-click-click.

This is the sound of something being silenced.

And silence is a form of death.

4.

This is about a writer's life and a writer's enemies.

My enemies and yours, if you write.

This is not about paranoia. This is about what happens — what has happened — is happening — and will happen again. This, too, is about silence.

The pen speaks. It has a voice. Not its own voice, I grant you, but a voice nonetheless. It has the voice I give it. But without the pen, I have no medium with which to invest my voice. Without the pen, I am silenced. Because I am a writer.

Someone keeps trying to put a cap on my pen.

In Sarnia, a seventeen-year-old schoolgirl attempted to have my novel, *The Wars*, removed from her curriculum because – and I quote – *it advocates homosexuality*.

When she was asked why she thought this, she gave as her reason a scene in which a man is gang-raped.

Advocates homosexuality. An interesting interpretation of rape.

I have to tell you that, in all honesty, I am perfectly happy to advocate homosexuality – but only for homosexuals.

It got worse. The girl, who it turned out was fronting for her parents' objections to the book, then went on to claim that *Mr. Findley and the teacher who taught the book had conspired in the advocacy of homosexuality.*

Conspired.

This, too, is interesting.

Well, the long and the short of it was, the book was done some damage – and the teacher – but both survived. I might add that homosexuality also survived.

Book-banning is a common occurrence. It happens all the time. But sometimes, the books do not survive. That, too, is a part of a writer's life.

Then we have libel chill.

I heard Robert Fulford on the radio the other week saying what a pity it was and how odd it was that journalists hadn't been more inquisitive about the Reichmanns, Olympia and York and Canary Wharf. This is to say, why had they not been more inquiring *before* the recent events that had almost brought the Reichmanns to their knees? And I yelled at the radio – *Hey, wait a minute, Bob! Just hang on there of a second, Bob! What about Elaine Dewar, Bob?*

You will recall that Elaine Dewar – a journalist – had written a book about the Reichmanns which had been suppressed before publication.

Libel chill.

Silence.

And the result of that silence — of that silencing? — a debacle that touched a lot of lives.

And then there is voice appropriation.

Well. What can I say?

I write fiction.

Fiction *is* voices.

Many voices. Thousands of them.

Millions.

The subject of voice appropriation, as it applies to fiction, is a non-starter. To begin with, writers do not *steal* voices — they *hear* them. And what I hear, I will write. *This is my job.* I am not here to purvey silence. I am the enemy of silence.

So should we all be.

Which brings me to another form of silence — and the last.

Not long ago, a friend of mine had an accident. She got in the way of a word — and it ran her down.

The word was "racist."

My friend is June Callwood.

There was a time when the word "racist" had a clear and literal meaning. It was a word of substance. It had to be. It had to have substance because it *defined* something of substance. An attitude, not an opinion. A position, not a posture. Opinions and postures can be deflated — they can be knocked to the ground with a feather. But attitudes and positions are ingrained — they are definitive. They define the whole person.

June Callwood is not a racist, either in attitude or in position. Nor in opinion. Nor in posture. But I am not here to defend June Callwood. June Callwood does not need defending. What *does* need defending is the word, "racist."

It is losing its coinage. It is losing its value. It is losing its power. And the enemies of racism and the victims of racism cannot afford the loss of one iota of the power that is required if racism is going to be rooted out and defeated.

How did all this begin?

It began when June Callwood — who is white — swore at a black woman.

Why is not important here. It is the swearing that is important. The swearing, and the colour of the players — white and black.

No one should swear at anyone. But people do. June Callwood apologized. The apology was accepted. Under normal circumstances, that would have been the end of it. But it was not. It was the beginning. The word "racist" was used. Once used, it stuck.

Let me tell you a story.

This is about Margaret Laurence. And me.

I had been concerned about an aspect of Margaret's life which I thought was doing her some harm. I made the mistake of saying so.

Margaret was enraged.

She telephoned, and stated her rage in no uncertain terms.

Boy, did I get an earful!

I heard words that night I did not know existed. It was hair-raising.

I was devastated.

When she was done, she slammed down the receiver and I could hardly breathe.

Here was this woman, you see, tearing into this man, just because he had expressed concern for her well-being – and . . .

Wait a minute.

Here was this woman tearing into this man . . .

Ah-hah!

She is a *feminist,* isn't she.

Hates men. They *all* do. So she tears into me because I'm a *man*!

And I'm gay!

Jesus Christ!

This is outrageous!

Margaret Laurence wasn't swearing at me because I was sticking my nose into her private life. She was swearing at me because I'm male – and I'm gay!

Well, I'll be damned if that doesn't make Margaret Laurence a man-hating, ball-breaking, gay-bashing bitch!

What a revelation!

Wow!

Did I get that right?

It wasn't Timothy Findley – with an "ey" – she was swearing at, but this male homosexual.

Check.

So, I guess that finally rips off the mask Margaret Laurence hid behind all those years when we thought she was a caring, principled political activist — a compassionate humanist — a giver and a maker — and a writer of moral convictions . . .

To hell with her, eh?

And June Callwood.

You know — I once heard June Callwood swear at *death*.

I guess this means she didn't like the colour of its skin.

We must end this craziness.

What is this? Are we back at McCarthyism? Back in the courtroom with Arthur Miller? Back with silence?

Stop it. Stop.

We talk about *appropriation of voice*. What about appropriation of *language*? We are writers.

Language is all we've got. If we misinterpret it, if we misdirect it, we are lost. So — what is racism?

It is the power of blame to feed on hate. It is the power of hate to feed on fear.

5.

This is about a writer with one last thing to say.

I want to end this with a beginning.

Listen:

It is raining. A child is being born. The woman giving birth is weak and ill. Her husband has gone in search of a doctor. A neighbour has come to do what she can, but when the husband returns, his wife is dead. There is, however, a child. In a month, the husband dies, from walking in the rain.

The couple had come from a small stone village in Scotland, where they'd worked for most of their lives in a cotton mill. It was the kind of life that killed. They wanted something more, and when the woman's sister — who'd gone off to Canada and married — wrote to say that life was better there, the couple saved up enough to make the journey. And so, this is the story of a dream — and of how the dream began.

The ending of those two lives, and the beginning of the other, all happened in a house near Bond Lake, Ontario. It was the birth of my grandfather, Thomas Findley. I have a photograph of his parents. It shows them both as tall and thin and hauntingly young.

When grandfather Findley was a boy, he delivered the mail on horseback. He did this near Sutton, Ontario, which is very near where I live now. He told my father that he loved that mail route, because it gave him his only chance to read. Since the horse knew the way, my grandfather sat on its back and read. Book, boy, and horse on a summer road. Bill and I drive out, now, just to see where they were.

Down near Brighton, Ontario – around the same time – there was an Irish family who sang. They had come up from the States after the American Revolution, and their whole life was music. In later years, they would make pianos. This is where my mother came from.

Books and music. Rain and roads. Pianos. Place.

I was sung to. I was given books. I was brought here by dreamers.

Their dream is not yet over.

It can't be.

Can it?

1 9 9 3
JUNE CALLWOOD

The opening sentence of Margaret Laurence's deeply spiritual classic *The Diviners* is, "The river flowed both ways." Morag, a watcher of streams, was musing on the "impossible contradiction," which she observed was nonetheless "made apparent and possible." The river metaphor, of course, represented the inconceivable but actual contradictions in Morag's life, in the life of the beloved Margaret Laurence, in all our lives. Our natures and our longings would take us in a direction of stately flow, but temporal winds play hob with the surfaces.

This past year has afforded me an opportunity to reflect on the capacity for the river of a reasonably calm life to develop astonishing eddies that suck out joy. Of late, my river, to get right to the personal, has been running in all directions. This is a baffling development. I used to find solace in the belief that serenity and grace were natural attributes of old age, and therefore all I had to do in order to get my river under control was wait to be old. I have fulfilled my part of the bargain: sure enough, I am old. The perverse fates, however, are still capable of sending a monsoon. I am struggling these days to update my rain gear.

On the other hand, there is this rich moment. I am here tonight to deliver the Margaret Laurence Memorial Lecture, standing on the stage of the National Library of Canada as the Writers' Union of Canada celebrates its twenty years of valuable existence. "The tribe," as Margaret called us, has assembled, and I am deliriously proud to belong to it. I am moved by the honour of the invitation to give this lecture commemorating Margaret

Laurence, a friend, an immensely gifted writer of heroic proportions, a shy and passionate woman, exceedingly kind and wise.

I have been a journalist for more than fifty years. The profession has shaped every aspect of my life. It isn't what I do; it is what I am. We maintain our unsteady selves in the river's turbulence by certain markers, those few familiars that hold still against the elements. Writing is a major stabilizer for many people in this theatre. We know its deep, untellable comforts, the opportunity it provides to conjure out of the confusion a phrase, a perspective, that isn't half bad and occasionally, luring us on, comes clean of the muck and really shines.

Asked why she is a writer, the incomparable Margaret Atwood recently replied, "I suppose I write for some of the same reasons I read: to live a double life; to go to places I haven't been; to examine life on earth; to come to know people in ways, and at depths, that are otherwise impossible; to be surprised. . . . I think all writers write as part of this sort of continuum: to give back something of what they themselves have received."

Tonight I wish to celebrate journalism, also known as non-fiction, and lately sumptuously costumed as "creative non-fiction."

This is not a period in world history when journalism is held in any esteem whatsoever, however adjectively decked out. Reporting on the recent leadership race in the Progressive Conservative Party was odd, and who can forget the peculiar coverage of the Gulf War, after which Stormin' Norman Schwarzkopf thanked the media for their friendly cooperation?

Journalists everywhere give us sound bites when the world needs a meal. Because so many journalists are obliged to serve the agenda of big business and the inactive social consciences of media owners, journalism has come into disrepute, like politics and evangelism. Carl Sandburg wrote, "The man in the street is fed / with lies in peace, gas in war."

And yet, and yet, journalism still stands on bedrock of the principle that it exists to serve the public good. When despotic governments wish to conceal their atrocities, they first must kill the journalists. Journalists by the nature of the profession are truth-seekers, and truth is an anathema when people in power wish to behave badly. In recent years, hundreds of journalists have been killed while attempting to report on the internal struggles in their countries to achieve justice in the face of despotism, food in the face of famine. Nick

Fillmore, who heads the Canadian Committee to Protect Journalists, did a tally for *Content* magazine last year and reported that more than three hundred journalists have been killed or have disappeared in the past ten years; attacks on journalists – physical attacks, I mean, not complaints from prime ministers – are counted at about a thousand a year. In the past year in Turkey, a country rich in human rights abuses, fifteen journalists have been killed.

Journalists, noting that life is intrinsically and immensely sad, rely on ideals to sustain them. They make audacious presumptions about the power of the pen. If torturers are exposed, they reason, decent people will rise up everywhere to condemn villains. Photojournalists and television reporters dare to hope that pictures of homeless people will result in a surge of shelter-building. If a country is informed that children are hungry, the reasoning goes, it will demand that leaders stop ordering helicopters.

This happens. Not often, but frequently enough to keep the dream alive. For certain, in the absence of any portrayal of misery in the media, the public might be lulled into the belief that the authorities have dealt adequately with suffering.

My own experience in this genre of appealing to the collective conscience has been rapturous. This does not mean that I have any evidence whatsoever in all my fifty-two years in the business that I have accomplished anything. I speak only of the pleasures of trying. As the South African Alan Paton once commented, "If you go on whether you win or lose . . . you keep your own soul." Erik Erikson observed that to be ready to die for what is true "means to grasp the only chance to have lived fully." In my case, I hasten to say, I have never risked dying – except the symbolic death of loss of income – but my life has been full. Whole-heartedness is its own reward.

Journalists are freelancers, a name that comes to us out of antiquity, belonging as it does to the medieval knights who owed allegiance to no lords, whose lances therefore were free to serve their own beliefs. Journalists can be coerced and co-opted and fooled, they can be lazy, they can spend their seed in grousing. The craft, however, has a code of honour which demands that when the emperor is naked it is not acceptable to pretend he is decked out in Calvin Kleins. In order to preserve their immortal souls, good journalists are obliged to describe the naked and warty hides of despots.

All truth-telling is inherently political, and journalists by no means are the only bearers of the torch. All artists mine themselves for seditious truth. We advance as a civilization by means of depictions of human dignity, of noble undertakings, of tenderness and love, of our moral responsibility for one another. Whether expressed in theatre or painting or poetry or novels or song, all are the voice of protest against inequity.

Journalists, however, are the most overt, and therefore the most vulnerable, of those who challenge the public enemies Gandhi defined as "untruth, injustice, and humbug."

Eduardo Galeano, the Uruguayan journalist, was in Toronto in 1981 at an international conference, the Writers and Human Rights Conference, which Rosemary Sullivan and Amnesty brilliantly put together. The theme was opposition to censorship, which when carried to its ultimate on the continuum that begins with book-banning, ends with the imprisonment and murder of writers who offend the regime. The grim feature of the conference stage was a row of empty chairs, each bearing the name of a writer in prison or missing or killed for challenging tyranny. One chair bore the name of Haroldo Conti from Argentina, who had disappeared and was believed dead.

Galeano told the conference that he had been that man's friend and that they talked a thousand times of the role of a writer who lives in a tyranny. Conti felt he was politically useless. He was ashamed that his stories, which did not explicitly denounce the Argentine dictatorship, were innocuous. Galeano wept as he spoke of his regret that he had no words of comfort for his friend, and now it was too late. "I wanted to tell him that in lighting the little fires of identity, and memory, and hope, little pieces like his are part of the forces of change in a system organized to wipe us off the face of this earth."

Albert Camus noted, "It would appear that to write a poem about spring would nowadays be serving capitalism. I am not a poet, but I should have no second thoughts about being delighted by such a poem if it were beautiful. One either serves the whole of man or one does not serve him at all."

I therefore intend no claim that journalists alone are defenders of democratic principles and justice, or that we are the only force that can prevail against the major evils of Canadian society, which are poverty, bigotry, and violence. Journalists, however, are well placed to light what Galeano called "little fires." They can cry "*J'accuse*" in a country burning with homelessness and lost youth and racism. We can and we must.

Canada indeed has a long tradition of relying on its protest journalists to relieve suffering. One of the earliest attempts occurred in 1803 with an audacious Quebec newspaper, *Le Canadien*, whose motto was "Our Language, Our Institutions, Our Laws." The editors, Messrs. Bédard, Blanchet, and Taschereau, promptly found themselves in prison – and of course were held there without trial, a quintessentially Canadian custom for responding to upstarts.

A few years later, Joseph Howe stood in a courtroom in Halifax because he had written a criticism of the fairness of judges, and the quality of justice subsequently improved. A few years after that, William Lyon Mackenzie's presses were thrown into Toronto Harbour, but Upper Canada got responsible government. A westerner, Amor de Cosmos, ran a newspaper which advocated a trans-Canada railway and the union of British Columbia with eastern Canada, both of which followed. More or less. And we should celebrate the wits, starting with Bob Edwards and his *Calgary Eye Opener* which regularly tore into the CPR. *The Eye Opener*'s front pages featured pictures of CPR derailments and collisions with such headings as "SAMPLE OF EVERYDAY TRAIN WRECK." Once Edwards ran a picture of R.B. Bennett, later Prime Minister of Canada and then the CPR's affluent lawyer, with the heading "ANOTHER CPR WRECK."

It can be argued that the voice of the American Revolution could be found in Tom Paine's pamphlets. The Solidarity movement in Poland which toppled the Berlin Wall and launched democracy in Eastern Europe was fuelled by an underground press, as was the French resistance in World War II. Charles Dickens, a journalist, turned to novels and used them as revolutionary tools to abolish, for one, child labour. Thoreau and Hemingway and Orwell began as journalists. Two journalists, Carl Bernstein and Bob Woodward, toppled Nixon.

Albert Camus, a journalist in the French underground, said that we must fight "fear and silence." He wrote, "What we must defend is dialogue and the universal communication of men. Slavery, injustice, and lies are the plagues that destroy this dialogue and forbid this communication, and that is why we must reject them."

The dialogue and universal communication of men (and women) is smothered in Canada not by placing writers in front of firing squads, but by forbidding them to espouse any cause save their own upward mobility; by firing or threatening to fire them if they become involved in their communities; by removing them from assignments when they grow noisy; by discouraging them from becoming provocative; by failing to provide investigators with access to information or time to do the job properly; by editorial judgment which decides against disturbing stories; by frightening them into self-censorship.

The interest being served by requiring journalists to distance themselves from the underbelly of hunger and despair in this country is that of the power elite. The first casualty of such isolation isn't truth; it is awareness. Efforts to prevent journalists from joining advocacy groups are as wrong-headed as the rules that require judges to be social eunuchs. It results, in both circumstances, in bad decisions. We see judges who can't comprehend the economic disadvantages of being a woman, and reporters who think that a riot in the streets is all about looting.

In *The Prairie Dog*, an excellent new publication in Regina, Gerry Sperling recently pointed out in an article on "the myth of objectivity" that reporters are supposed to avoid conflicts of interest, but owners can be directors of powerful corporations which have a very serious interest in controlling the news and discouraging inquiry.

As A.J. Liebling dryly observed, "Freedom of the press is guaranteed only to those who own one."

Journalism in the '90s must withstand intimidation and suppression on every side. Libel laws are a major silencer of journalists who would examine the dealings of powerful people. It is a fact that some libel lawyers now earn higher fees from newspapers, magazines, and books than writers do. Also, in the name of that despicable distortion called political correctness, truth and clarity are assassinated. What are future generations to make of a country that allows customs clerks to withhold books, or edits school texts so that Mama Bear does not wear an apron, or takes seriously the claim that women are at risk when convenience stores stock *Playboy*?

Franklin Delano Roosevelt in 1941 set out the four freedoms essential to the well-being of the world, and the first of these was "freedom of speech and expression — everywhere in the world." (The others, equally worth our reverence, were freedom of religion, freedom from want, and freedom from fear.)

Awareness of the interrelationship of freedom of speech and society's health is an ancient one. Domitian, emperor of Rome in about year 90, said it most succinctly: "In a free state there must be free speech." This does not mean freedom of the speech with which you agree, as Oliver Wendell Holmes pointed out early in this century. That freedom of speech is not threatened. The freedom of speech we must protect is the freedom of speech with which we explicitly, emphatically, categorically disagree. By safeguarding the freedom of loathsome, even hurtful speech, we ensure first of all that society cannot be blind to the existence of vile attitudes and heinous beliefs. When evil is forced into the underground of the deliciously forbidden, it can only flourish. Out in the open for all to see, it faces the withering test of public scrutiny and abhorrence.

As Macaulay said, "Men [and women] are never so likely to settle a question rightly as when they discuss it freely."

We are rethinking how this country works, an undertaking in which journalists will be required in the '90s to play a serious role. The assumptions of my lifetime that we Canadians are good-hearted people are being tested as we move to become the most racially disparate nation on the planet. We will not survive if we do not find the common ground. As Robert Hughes said in his splendid book *Culture of Complaint*, "In the world that is coming, if you can't navigate difference, you've had it."

The present climate of bitter clashes over racism and sexism are not moving us toward that goal. As Hughes points out, much of the hostility comes from a collision of styles. On the one hand are people who rely on logical analysis and objective thinking in order to resolve difficulties. On the other are those ruled by feelings, which puts them in the mainstream of the post-modernism cult of spreading suspicion, cynicism, and paranoia. The style of raw accusation which prevails now in universities, social services, and the women's movement diverts energy and focus from the real issues of our times, which are poverty, violence, and the suffering of children. Fanon noted that revolutionary movements fail not because the authorities are indomitable but because powerless people turn on one another.

The moral imperative of our time is to listen to one another, an exercise that isn't furthered by spot news coverage of disputes. We need to understand the anger and frustration that explodes in so many ways. Martin Luther King,

Jr. once said that a riot is the voice of the unheard. We must abolish barriers which frustrate and infuriate millions of Canadians. Joseph Conrad wrote, "We exist only in so far as we hang together." It may take a generation or two, but we cannot live without mutual trust. Journalists will be key players in that process of healing that will allow us to accomplish something wonderful – a nation of rich diversity with dignity for all.

Václav Havel said that "politics, as practical morality, as a service to truth, is essentially human and humanly measurable care for our fellow humans." So is journalism . . . "human and humanly measurable care for our fellow humans." AKA the Golden Rule. Freedom Forum, a foundation endowed by Frank E. Gannett, reported last autumn that reporters and editors are more and more dissatisfied with journalism as a profession. Only 27 per cent said they were very happy with their jobs, which is about half as many in other kinds of employment. My guess is that they are losing heart because they feel powerless. The idealism with which they entered the profession is dissolving in the political realities of the newsrooms. My prescription for their personal well-being is a renewed commitment to journalism's primary function, which is public service.

We are not in this profession to serve generals or prime ministers or multinationals, except on those electrifying occasions when they are behaving well. The propelling gene in journalism is aspiration to the public good, or else we are merely an arm of advertising.

Milan Kundera observed that journalists have a sacred right to ask anyone about anything. "The power of journalism is not based on the right to ask," he continued, "but on the right to demand an answer."

Phillip Moffit wrote in a recent edition of *Esquire*, "The idea of the common good is one of the great organizing principles of society. That's what responsible journalism is all about: providing the country with better information on which to base better, more humane decisions."

Molière wrote, "Writing is like prostitution. First you do it for the love of it; then you do it for a few friends; and, finally, you do it for money." I have progressed through those stages in reverse. Today, I am a journalist for the love of it. To be a journalist is a trust that makes me quiver with hope for myself. I'm in a line of work which has the possibility of contributing to attitudinal change, on which all improvements in society depend. I keep in mind E.B.

White's famous quip: "All writing is slanted. Writers can't be perpendicular, but they should aspire to be upright."

Standing in Margaret Laurence's river of turbulent contradictions, maintaining an upright position is a task that requires concentration and pluck; in short, we must be our best selves. What better, more zestful line of work can there be?

1994

PIERRE BERTON

There is a story told of Margaret Laurence, whose name is on this series of memorial lectures, always with a title of "A Writer's Life," and I think some of you know that story. She attended a party where she was introduced to a gentleman who identified himself as a brain surgeon. And he said "Oh, you write," to Margaret. "Well," he said, "when I retire, I'm going to take up writing." And Margaret said, "That's very good. When I retire, I am going to take up brain surgery."

Now, that joke is germane to this talk on a writer's life because I'm sure the brain surgeon never got around to writing that book, because when people say they're going to write a book when they retire, they very seldom do. It's very difficult at that age to learn to write. And I know, about Margaret, that she never took up brain surgery because, like most writers, she never retired. We don't retire. We go on until we drop. Or till the great copy editor in the sky reaches down and says, with his little pencil, "Enough!"

I've always wondered what produces a writer. Is it the genes or is it the environment? And I think it's a bit of both. Certainly, it was with me. Certainly, I had the genes. My grandfather was a famous journalist. My mother wrote. My uncle wrote for newspapers. My sister wrote juveniles. My nephew is an editor of *AsiaWeek* in Hong Kong, my niece works for CBC News, my son is an editor on the *London Free Press*.

But there was also environment. I was going to say I began writing at the age of four, but I couldn't write. Actually, I began telling stories to my little sister. The main story was about a fluffy rabbit who owned, and drove at huge speeds, a small red car. You know, just think about it, that's not a bad idea, I must get that on paper. The first sounds that I remember are the sounds of an old Remington typewriter clacking away in the next room – my mother trying to write a novel which she never sold. But she did write later on. She sold articles to *Saturday Night* and to the *Family Herald and Weekly Star,* and the *Dawson Daily News*. I was the boy on the bicycle who took down the copy every week and gave it Harold Malstrom, who put it on the linotype.

So I was used to the writing business – that was where my genes were. But my parents did not want me to be a writer. My mother said, "Oh, no, you'll never have a clean shirt." My father and my mother wanted me to be either a research chemist or a chemical engineer. To please them, and myself, I set up a lab in my basement. I had retorts and Erlenmayer flasks and Florence flasks, and I had bottles of sulfuric acid and nitric acid – the whole shmear. But looking back at it now, I realize that I was more interested in the show business aspects of chemistry. I used to hold regular chemical shows in our garage. I'd charge a nickel and about twenty people would come and I'd pick up a dollar exploding things, changing colours of liquid, pouring sulfuric acid into sugar, putting out an enormous amount of ash, I'd make an explosive with potassium chloride and sulfur and I'd put that on the streetcar tracks and have a lot of fun. But I was really more interested in newspapers.

I realize now, as a parent and a grandparent, that you should be looking to see what your kids *really* like to do, and not what their parents think they should do. I was putting out newspapers in public school, in high school, in the Boy Scouts, in the mining camps, and at Victoria College, B.C. But it wasn't until the end of the second year that I thought of becoming a newspaperman. *Why?* I asked myself. *Why are my marks in chemistry so awful?* Answer: *You spent all your time, not in the lab, but working on the college paper. Ergo: You should become a newspaperman.*

I dithered about. I remember there was some kind of rally going on – a big argument or something – and some kid said: "What are you going to be when you grow up?" I said, "I'm going to be a newspaperman!" Just like that. I'd not thought of it until that moment. But it clicked and I went home and I said to my parents, "Forget about the chemistry, I'm going to be a newspaperman." They groaned at that. "You know," my mother said, "chemists are making as much as fifty dollars a month." This was back in '39.

I actually applied for a job at the Victoria *Colonist,* and was turned down by a man named Hugh MacCallum, whom I later met, many, many years later, and he said, "Don't ever announce that I turned you down. I don't need that on my conscience." Actually, it was the only time in my life that I've ever asked anybody for a job. I've been very fortunate; all the jobs have come to me. That's the only time I asked and it's the only time I've ever been turned down. Maybe that's why I never asked again.

When I was at Victoria College, I used to read the UBC college paper. The bylines became familiar to me (one of them I married, and became very familiar). I realized that the people who got the bylines and did well always got a job downtown on one of the three Vancouver newspapers — first as a college correspondent, and later as a full-fledged reporter. So I said, *That's what* I'll *do. It's only a two-year course here in Victoria. In my third year I'll go to university and I'll work on the college paper.* And that is what I did. When I reached UBC, I discovered that a friend of mine, who was the college correspondent for the *Vancouver News-Herald,* couldn't do it anymore because his marks were too low. So I took over the job, and just squeaked through my year. That was the start of my newspaper career.

I finally went on to a permanent job at the *News-Herald.* In my college days, I had been paid twenty cents a column inch. Now I got fifty dollars a month, which was what chemists were getting, later on. I bracketed my wartime training with work on newspapers. But the enthusiasm I had for newspapers did not last. I began to feel a sense of déjà vu, because you keep repeating yourself every year. You write the Christmas story, you write the New Year's story, you write the Bible story for Easter. There was a guy who worked up in our New Westminster bureau, and every autumn he'd write the same story. "The Fraser Valley was a riot of colour today as Mother Nature dipped her brush in Jack Frost's palette," he'd write. My friend Harry Filion used to phone me every fall and say, "He's done it again! It's in there."

That was the first intimation I had that it wasn't really what I wanted to do in life. The second intimation came later. I sat across the desk from a very old man. His name was Jack McDonald. At least I thought he was old – he had white hair. He was retired and they'd given him the usual gold watch but he didn't know what to do, so he came back and they gave him a job writing the "25 and 50 Years Ago Today" column. Jack had a little bottle of rye in his desk and he used to give me a slug every once in a while. One day, the city editor came to me and said, "Look, I want you to rewrite Jack's column today, it isn't working. It's not very good. But don't tell him." So I thought, *Okay, I'll go to the morgue and I'll look up the paper twenty-five years ago and write about it.* Which I did. And there on page one was a scoop – right across the page. "Three Criminals Give In to the Vancouver Sun," by Jack McDonald. And I thought, *My God! Here I am, a young whippersnapper, rewriting the story that made him famous, because he no longer can write. I'm getting out of this business.*

I didn't ask for a job; I waited for one to come along. It came along when Scott Young came up from *Maclean's* and offered to hire me. Arthur Irwin was then editor of *Maclean's*. Arthur is the one who really made the modern *Maclean's*. But he was very careful of who he hired, and he phoned a lot of people to find out about me. He phoned his friend Fred Soward, who had tried to teach me history. Alas, I was rarely in his class. I remember what Soward said to me at the faculty tea: "Berton, I did my best to fail you, but you *just squeaked through*." I didn't tell him about his true-and-false questions, when, if you flip a coin, you've got a fifty-fifty chance, which is exactly what I got.

Irwin said to his friend Soward, "What do you think about this man, Berton?" Soward said, "He might have been a brilliant student if he hadn't spent all his time on that goddamn college paper." And Irwin said, "That's the man I want!"

The truism is that in some ways the news business is a good background for a writer, especially a non-fiction writer. It certainly helped a fiction writer, Ernest Hemingway. But there are problems with journalism, and I suffered from them. It teaches you to make fast decisions, which is great. But it also teaches you to be glib. It teaches you to use the shorthand of communication which is the cliché. To this day, I have to go through my copy after I've written everything down to try to get the clichés out of it. And thank God I've an editor who finds the rest of them. Because I miss a good many.

I was at *Maclean's* for eleven years, and it was there that I got the kind of training I needed. I was taught what research was. And I was taught that you had to have evidence for every foolish statement you made, or you didn't make it. Irwin and Ralph Allen used to write in the margins. "Evidence?" Or "Who he?" Which meant they didn't know who the hell I was writing about. That is the title of Bob Collins's recent book about his days at *Maclean's*: *Who He?*

The second thing that *Maclean's* did was to teach me about other people's writing by making me an editor. I had to put a blue pencil to hundreds and hundreds of manuscripts. You learn to write by fixing other people's work, and I found it was invaluable.

The third thing that *Maclean's* did was it made me a nationalist. I was only intending to stay in Toronto for two years. I wanted to go to the good old U.S.A. and work for *Life* magazine or the *Saturday Evening Post,* or one of the big mags. No way, after *Maclean's*! William Van Horne once said that working on the CPR would make a Canadian out of the German Kaiser. Working on *Maclean's* made me a nationalist. You couldn't help it. We were a cocky bunch. We were convinced that we were putting out the best magazine of its kind. We did not want to compete with the American magazines, and we knew that they could not compete with us on our turf. And our turf was Canada. So we knew exactly who our audience was and who it *wasn't*. And it's there I learned from people like Arthur Irwin, Ralph Allen, and the great Bruce Hutchison, who was my mentor, something about this country.

The other thing *Maclean's* did for me was they gave me the research material out of a series of articles for two books. My first book sold the magnificent total of fifteen hundred copies. That was pretty good in those days – didn't make me any money, but it *was* a book. The second one sold three thousand copies, and won me my first Governor General's Award. You see, in those days, promotional schemes of the kind we now indulge in did not exist. There was no book promotion. There were few bookstores. I remember when I was training in Brandon and I went into town to buy a book. I couldn't; there were no bookstores! There were no shopping malls to attract bookstores. There were few book pages in the newspapers: the *Globe and Mail* and I think one or two others. But there weren't really book pages worthy of the name. Nobody was writing about books. Nobody knew about books. There were no bestseller lists, no television. Books were promoted over glasses of sherry in the book-laden offices of the gentleman publisher – who wouldn't soil his hands on cheap commercialism. Some of them tended to look down on Jack McClelland because he actually *promoted* books. He was the authors' friend. At the beginning, the other book publishers tended to sneer at him, until they found that he was selling books.

Farley Mowat and I were once sent, at huge expense, to Montreal to take part in a double autographing at Morgan's. They had a table for us there and behind it were lots of our books on a kind of a library shelf. The book guy said, "There, that's your table, that's where you sign," and he walked off. Farley and I sat there, chatting away pleasantly, but a little nervous, because nobody was coming. Finally a man came along with a book by somebody else, and we signed it. And then I said to Farley, "Look, we better sign some books. You sign my books with *your* name, and I'll sign your books with *my* name." We took them all out of the shelves, we signed them all, wrongly, put them back, and walked out of the store without anybody saying goodbye. That was the situation as it existed when I began in this business.

I began writing books partly because of *Maclean's* — I had done the research — but also because I found that the CBC liked to call "authors" for panel discussions. "Best-selling author," they called us. As far as the CBC was concerned, and as far as the private station was concerned, you were an expert — a "best-selling author" even if you hadn't sold many books. So there was a little bit of extra dough to be made from panel discussions for the CBC, and we all grabbed at it.

I finally decided I had to write a book that wasn't based on early research. I had to write the best book I could. I searched around for a subject, and suddenly I thought, "Well, what the hell am I thinking about? I'm from the Klondike, my father was in the gold rush. That is the story. It's a great story and I'm going to write it." My mother said, "Why on earth would you write a story about the Klondike gold rush? Everybody knows that story." Well, everybody did in her circle, perhaps, or thought they did. But she didn't, and I didn't, and not many did until I wrote *Klondike*.

This was a complicated book — the kind I liked best, in which people move through time and space in large numbers — seeking a goal. It was a bit like a detective story doing the research. You go from one source to another to find out where the research is and you go from one person, and in this case to another, because there were people still left alive.

We had driven across the country interviewing old-timers. When my wife and I reached Seattle, somebody at the Sourdough Association said, "You know, I think that Belinda Mulroney is still alive somewhere."

Well, I gasped. Belinda Mulroney was one of the great figures of the Klondike. She was a washerwoman's daughter from Chicago who was a stewardess on the S.S. *City of Topeka* during the gold rush. She kept on going all the way to Dawson, and when she got there she had a fifty-cent piece left and she threw that in the Yukon River and said, "I won't be needing this anymore," and she didn't.

She was one of the great figures of the stampede. She ran the best saloon, the best hotel, and knew everybody. She had married the Count de Carbonneau and gone to Paris driving up to the Champs-Elysées with a coach-in-four. He wasn't the Count de Carbonneau, he was just plain Charles Carbonneau, a Champagne salesman from Montreal. It didn't matter. They called her the countess and she accepted the title gracefully.

So my wife and looked in the phone book and there we found a Mrs. C. Carbonneau. But I knew she was dead, so she couldn't be the right one. "Oh God, let's go and eat. I want a steak, I'm tired," I said. Janet said, "No. We will go down to the drugstore and we'll look in the city directory." And we went down to the drugstore, my stomach grumbling, and we looked in the city directory and there was a Mrs. C. Carbonneau living miles out of town, but with no phone. Janet got the city directory: "Let's see who lives next door," she said. I said, "Okay, phone next door and ask if Mrs. Carbonneau lives next door and ask is she the one who lived in the Klondike?" A woman answered. "I think maybe she did mention it," she said. "I can't remember." I said, "Oh, forget it. Let's go eat." And Janet said, "We're *not* going to eat. You get in a cab and go out there." And I did. It was a huge fare, I remember. Seven dollars or something like that. A lot in those days.

I knocked on the door of the little cottage and the door opened and a little wizened-up woman came out and said, "Yes?"

I said, "Are you by any chance Belinda Mulroney Carbonneau?"

"C'mon in, my friend," she answered, "we got a lot to talk about!"

It's moments like this that make writing of that kind so exciting. She was great. I never got to eat that night, but it didn't matter; I wasn't hungry anymore.

You have to be careful, of course, of oral history. We all use it. But in using oral history you must check it against other facts. I once talked to six eyewitnesses who were on the Juneau wharf on July 18, 1898 and who saw Soapy Smith shot by Frank Reid, and they all had a different version of that story. Which is why you have to mix oral history with some hard underpinning of research.

I got into TV and radio about this time. Why? Well, partly because I was on TV the fourth night it was on in Toronto. I was part of a panel show, and we were all terrified. Hundreds of people waving at us. Three cameras and coils of cable. Well, we've all gone through it. But, I thought, *Never again will I ever go into this terrible medium!* The next morning I was walking down the street and a guy came up to me and said, "I saw you on TV last night. You're the guy that writes the books." I thought, "Oh, oh; I better get used to it. Because if he remembers that and the fact that I write books, then that is the future."

Of course, the other reason I did it was for the money! I don't believe in the theory that writers do their best work starving in a garret. I think that a writer has to have security. And he gets that security by not having to worry about his mortgage. He also gets his security by doing his homework, which is the research. And then he feels good and he writes. His sense of security is always transferred to the reader. So the reader will know in an instant if the writer is insecure.

I remember Harold Town, the painter, saying to me one day on television: he said, "You know, I'm better than Picasso." I said, "Harold, you're kidding." He said, "Believe it." And after, he said, "I've got to believe it. If I didn't believe I was that good, I wouldn't be able to paint properly and everybody would know it." He said, "You've got to believe you are the best." There's something in that.

When I wrote *Klondike,* I was secure. I loved writing it. I was writing about my own part of the country. I told Jack McClelland it would sell ten thousand by Christmas and he told me, on Christmas Eve, that it had sold ten thousand. "You win!" he said.

When I do the research on a new subject, I have to ask myself, *What is this book about?* Oh sure, this book was about the Klondike gold rush. But what's it *really* about? That's the question I had to ask before I wrote the final draft, which was based on what I thought the real story was.

The real story came to me in the research. I discovered that all these guys who climbed the icy mountains and made their own boats, and went down the river and died and starved and fought their way through the rapids, and finally got to the Klondike, didn't bother to go out to the creeks to look for gold. They shambled up and down Front Street until the next steamboat came and they got on it and went home. Why? Because they'd done, really, what they set out to do: to test themselves against the elements; to prove to themselves what they could do; to learn about themselves. This Klondike story, I decided, was much more than a story of gold. It was a story about man's search for himself.

I didn't like to say this in so many words. The theme, I thought, ought to be underneath. But I knew I'd need a little quote in the book that gave a slight hint. I looked all through Bartlett and couldn't find anything and finally found this one:

"All my life," he said, "I've searched for the treasure. I have sought it in the high places, and in the narrow. I have sought it in deep jungles, and at the ends of rivers, and in dark caverns — and yet have not found it. Instead, at the end of every trail, I have found you awaiting me. And now you have become familiar to me, though I cannot say I know you well. Who are you?" And the stranger answered: "Thyself." *From an old tale.*

Which I wrote myself, of course. Made it up. It's my job to do that. I'm a writer, so I wrote it.

Now, it's interesting that *Klondike* was a successful book and won me my second Governor General's Award. It was really my first book of narrative history. I wrote fifteen other books before I wrote the next book of narrative history, which was *The National Dream*. One of them was my favourite book, *The Secret World of Og,* a children's fantasy, in which real children who watch television and read series books and love comic books and hate Pablum — they romp through this book, to the horror of librarians and to the horror of the editors. This taught me that you don't write children's books for children, you write them for librarians and children's editors. That's our real market, they kept saying. I had a little scene in which a kid paints himself green in the interests of espionage and going among some green people. And they said, "You can't do that. Every kid will want to paint himself green!" And I said, "Well, I hope so. Every boy, sometime in his life, should paint himself green." I left all that stuff in. It's still going on, as Robert Munsch knows. But it was very bad then. The conspiracy against children, I call it. *That* book was my most successful book. We've lost count of the number of copies — more than two hundred thousand.

I go to schools sometimes and I read chapters from it for the little kids in grade four, and quite often they've painted themselves green because of the book. They're painted green, and the last one I went to, even the teacher was painted green! And I thought, "I won." That's probably the only influence I've ever had in all my writing — gotten a teacher to paint herself green.

One of the reasons I couldn't write these big complicated books was because I was writing a daily column after I left *Maclean's*. (They objected to me doing television and radio, so I walked out.) I had a fail-safe — the *Star* was after me, so I took the job. The columns were very long in those days and they appeared every day. God, it's easy now, Dalton Camp does two a week: eight hundred words each. I wrote twelve hundred words every day, five days a week. I wrote 1.2 million words for the *Toronto Star,* which is the equivalent of five *Klondikes*. I get tired just thinking about it. I was also doing radio and television.

And then I wrote *The Comfortable Pew*, a tract which raised an awful fuss and made the church very mad. And then I wrote *The Smug Minority*. I read a while ago that it got the worst critical drubbing of any book ever published in Canada. Now, not many people can make that statement. And oddly, that book sold very well and made more money for McClelland & Stewart that year than any book that they had. We sold seventy thousand copies of *The Smug Minority*. But Jack McClelland, in the interests of promotion, had announced in advance that he was going to print the largest first printing of any book in history: one hundred thousand! So it didn't make one hundred thousand, it only made seventy thousand. Big deal. *Failure!* said the critics. But it was the biggest money-maker he had that year.

The wisest thing Jack ever said to me, and he said many wise things, was: "Don't ever read reviews. Measure them." He was right. Once I got an awful review — I can't remember the book — in one of the local papers, I think the *Globe*. A really slashing attack! *Oh God*, I thought, *I'm going to quit this business, who needs it?* And as I said that, I was walking down the street in my hometown,

Kleinburg, and a guy came up to me and said, "Wow, did you see that piece in the *Globe*? An eight-column headline? They mentioned your book about twelve times. You must be feeling very proud." I thought, *By George, Jack was right*.

You know, I was once invited to go to Fairbanks, Alaska, to the University of Alaska, and it was a very refreshing experience, because they treated me as a literary lion. They didn't know about *The Comfortable Pew*, they didn't know the things I'd said on radio, or written in my column, or on television. All they knew was that I'd written *Klondike*, which they revered, because it was about their part of the country. I was treated like the Ernest Hemingway of the Yukon. Very refreshing! I enjoyed it and then I jumped into the soup again as soon as I got back.

Twelve years, as I said, went by between the first narrative history and the next one, which was *The National Dream*. I was only going to write one book about the railway, but it expanded into two. I chose it because it's a very good story. It tells something about the country and because again, like the gold rush, it involves a great many people moving in a complicated way through time and space. To be able to write it, I had to quit two jobs. So I took a real gamble on these books, which I thought would sell ten thousand copies, as *Klondike* had. I quit a very lucrative television program called *Under Attack* and I quit my job at McClelland & Stewart.

Jack, in one of his weirder moments, had put me in charge of his Illustrated Books Division and then had promoted me to editor-in-chief. He didn't have a real one around, so I was called editor-in-chief. I went to him and said, "Jack, I only have two choices. I can be your editor-in-chief, or I can write a big book about the building of the Canadian Pacific Railway." And before he had a chance to decide, I said, "And I've decided to do the book about the Canadian Pacific Railway. Goodbye. It's been nice working with you."

Now, a lot of people, like my mother, when I did *Klondike*, couldn't understand why I was writing what seemed to them to be a company history. I remember Morley Callaghan said, "Why have you taken that subject? That is boring." Well, it had been boring. Harold Innis wrote the definitive history of the CPR, which made him a name because he discovered new things about the country. But the book itself is unreadable. The footnotes are longer than the text. Sometimes there's only one line of text and then there's all this little type. Holy God, who can get through that? The next book about the railways had been written by the public relations officer of the CPR. It was called *Steel of Empire,* and it wasn't a bad book. But, he was the CPR's PR, so he took a certain point of view on it.

I spent a long time on the research for these two books and I didn't write one word until I was absolutely certain that I'd done my homework. Now I had to get away to write the books. But how could I get away with these stacks of research, all bound in loose-leaf books?

So I announced to everybody that I was going to Mexico to write the books. I didn't go. To my wife's absolute horror, I had the phone taken out. Left myself totally incommunicado. Sat down and obsessively started the books. Writing from eight in the morning till midnight. I was young and healthy and energetic in those days. It was summertime, I didn't have to do radio and television. And I wrote the first draft of *The National Dream* in three weeks. I know, you can take a look at it, it's sitting at McMaster University with my papers. It's not very good. But it's on paper. The thing for me always is to get it on paper as quickly as possible.

I have to tell you that I love doing it. I couldn't wait to get to the typewriter. The story was so good. The story of the Pacific Scandal, for instance, was a wonderful story, it took two chapters in my book. I couldn't stop. It ran through my head at night and I was thinking about it all the time, which made me terrible company.

When the book came out, it got a very interesting reaction. The academics didn't understand what I was doing. Because except for Bruce Hutchison – my mentor, whose work I admired and whom I knew well – nobody in this country was writing this kind of narrative history. The well-known kind of history being written in Britain and certainly in the States by people like Barbara Tuchman, nobody had attempted it here. And the academics – they were flattering, I guess – treated it as a scholarly work, which it certainly wasn't. It had the scholarship in it, but I tried to keep that hidden so people wouldn't think it was a textbook. Some historians were very upset because I put the footnotes at the back, rather than on the same page in little, tiny type. Academics sprinkle these numbers through their books, but I wasn't going to do that. It would turn everybody off – they'd think it was a textbook. I had a line-by-line count at the back. Line 4, *source.* Line 8, *source.* You'd be surprised at the number of academics that were really upset about this because it meant they had to do some work. But I didn't care about that.

When they said there was nothing new in the book, it's all old stuff, I was baffled. I thought, *How can that be? I'm the first guy to read the diaries of the surveyors. I'm the first guy to write that John A. Macdonald rigged the Royal Commission at the time of the Pacific Scandal. That's not even in Creighton. Why do they say there's nothing new? There's all sorts of stuff that's new.* And to most people it *was* all new. It took me a long time to twig what they meant by "nothing new." What they meant was that I hadn't given them any new theories about the CPR. Any new insights. Not quite true, but I did the insights and theories under a nice sugar-coating of action. I did not have a chapter saying *Chapter Eight: New Insights.* I sprinkled it through.

You see, the academics generally wrote books for each other. I must say here that we, none of us who write this kind of history, could operate without the academics, who do wonderful work, on tiny canvases, and it's very, very important. But I was seeking a larger audience than an audience of academics. And they were thinking of themselves as the audience for this book. They weren't the audience at all. I couldn't have cared if none of them read the book.

But I've always been grateful to them and have said so from time to time when I've had a chance. Today they're a little less grudging than they used to be.

This was literary phenomenon and I was not expecting it. The books flew out of the bookstores. They took off like birds. Why? Because of the Centennial of 1967. That was only three years before the books appeared. The people were ready for it. They had been fed a strong diet of Canadianism and they wanted more. For the first time for many years in this country, people wanted to go back to their beginnings, to their roots. There was a wave of nationalism which resulted in all sorts of things in the next decade, including the formation of the Writers' Union of Canada. Also because television was going strong. The CBC's eight-part series *The National Dream* was very helpful.

Jack McClelland and I went out on a hectic promotion trip that year. Somebody phoned me in Winnipeg and said to me, "Why are you promoting these books? People buy anything you write. You could write a telephone book."

"No," I said, "I've tried that. It doesn't work."

Promotion will not sell a book. What promotion will do — and this is important — it will tell people out there that you have written the book and it will tell them what it's about and they will then decide if they want to read it. Canadian readers are very tough about this. We all do these mammoth promotion trips — the kind Margaret Atwood calls the "Kill an Author Tour" — in which you travel around and meet each other in TV stations and you all sit on the bench and the interviewer says "Next!", you know, like hogs at a slaughterhouse. And yet, after all this publicity, in which your book has been promoted by everybody, people come up to me and say, "Why didn't you write a book this year?"

So I know that you really have to keep shouting. Thanks to Elsa Franklin, demon public relations woman, Jack and I were sent out across the country to appear at a series of All Canadian Breakfasts: blueberry muffins, Winnipeg goldeye, hotcakes with maple syrup, and a drink, which she had somebody invent, called The Last Spike Cocktail. It was very powerful, and we left behind us an absolute trail of exhausted newspapermen, and the next time I came through they said, "I hope you're not serving the drinks, because you ruined the day for us and for the newspaper."

And Jack said he would never eat Winnipeg goldeye again, and I think he's stuck to that. Me, I still like it. But it was an experience that was almost claustrophobic sometimes at the autographings. I remember at Bolen's bookstore on Vancouver Island — wow, the crowd was jammed all around me, everybody holding a book and shouting, "Sign mine, sign mine, sign mine!" Later on we learned to put them in line, but we didn't in those days.

And so the next year we did a picture book too, and you know, I had four books on the bestseller list at one point. I'm kind of proud of that, I guess. Four out of ten, not bad. This is a phenomenon that's not been repeated. *The National Dream* was on the list for well over two years. *Klondike* — we did the new edition of that — came in on the coattails of *The National Dream* and *The Last Spike* and it sold another seventy thousand copies.

You're up one day and you're down the next in this business. That's being a Canadian. I kind of enjoy it, I must say. *Is it my turn to be slammed this year? Is it a good year, next year?*, you always start a year off.

I survived *The Smug Minority* only to be attacked for writing a book called *Drifting Home,* which the critics called a potboiler. I wrote it in the Algarve in Portugal over a period of about two weeks. And what a time I had! I can only write with two fingers. (I used to do it with one, and now I do two. That's real progress.) I've moved from a dreadful little Hermes Baby typewriter, which I used to carry around in my big pack in the Army – simply a dreadful typewriter that runs every line together and jams up and everything – to a Smith Corona portable, which I still use. I've got four of them because I'm terrified that I won't be able to buy any new ones or second-hand. I can only work on it. So I had this Smith Corona portable with me when I went to Portugal. I got the travel agent, in advance, to send for a machine that would change 220 volts to 110. It came down from Lisbon and was there when I arrived. I could hardly wait to get to work. I put the typewriter down and plugged the thing in, and it blew up! It blew, I tell you – flames, smoke, everywhere. I don't know how, or what happened. I'm not very good mechanically. So the real estate agent said, "It's all right, I've got a replacement." And she came rushing in with – a Hermes Baby.

I still wrote the book. People come up to say they like it. A guy came up to me yesterday and said, "You know what my favourite book is?" and I said, "I know, you're going to say *Drifting Home*." He said, "That's right." They all say that.

But most of my emphasis from then on has been on narrative history. I really like telling stories from the past with a strong research background. You know, the great bulk of my major work has been done between the ages of fifty and seventy. Well, fifty and seventy-three, because I'm doing one now. It's interesting because when I wrote *The National Dream*, I'd written nineteen books, and since *The National Dream*, I've written nineteen more and twelve of them are books of narrative history, including, I think, three of my best books: *Vimy*, *The Arctic Grail*, and *The Great Depression*.

I had wanted to write a fourth in the quartet of books about the opening of the West and Northwest which would be *The National Dream*, *The Last Spike*, *Klondike*, that would deal with the opening of the prairies, which was spurred by the Klondike gold rush and the presence of the railway. I tackled it several times and I couldn't get a handle on it so put it aside. I knew I'd write it sooner or later, but I knew I had to learn a little more about putting a book together. I wasn't ready.

There are lots of books I write now that I couldn't have written ten years ago. They are more complicated. I finally wrote *The Promised Land* and by then I had a really top research assistant who is still with me and has worked on all my major books of narrative history since *The National Dream*. Her name is Barb Sears, Barbara Sears. I couldn't work without her. She saves me at least a year on a book.

Of course, people, amateurs, think that's cheating, to use a researcher. Everybody uses them. But I've had two different interviewers shove microphones in my face as I step off an airplane and say, "Mr. Berton, one question. Who writes your books? Do you write your own books or do you have somebody do it?"

And I'm only prevented from punching them in the nose because in each case they're very attractive young women. Attractive, but dumb. Because, of course, a researcher can save your fingers and your feet. I no longer have to sit in the archives with a stack of John A. Macdonald's letters, which are written in his atrocious hand, trying to figure them out and to transcribe them with a pencil into notebooks. Now we have Xerox, we have interlibrary loan, and I have Barbara Sears. She goes to the archives and brings me back the material I want. She does not decide what's good and what's bad. She gives me the raw material, I write it, and that's how the books are produced.

So, I think, as in brain surgery, practice makes perfect. You continue to learn all your life. There are things I'm writing now that I couldn't have written ten years ago, fifteen, twenty — certainly not twenty years ago. Because you learn techniques, you learn style, and you learn all sorts of things. You learn to trust your editors. I trust mine, who save me so much. I have two. One who looks at the manuscript — just as I looked at manuscripts when I was a young editor at *Maclean's* — and then tells me what's wrong. What's dull. What needs editing, what I've left out, what the order should be. Janice Tyrwhitt, late of the *Reader's Digest*, late of *Maclean's*, later with *The Pierre Berton Show*. I've worked with her many years. She saved *Vimy* by suggesting a new opening.

I have a copy editor, who has an eagle eye for everything, who can actually tell you where to put a comma, something secretaries these days don't know. But you know, the thing about brain surgery and writing — the thing they have in common — is that they're both a learning process, I think, that never ends. In writing, of course, you don't have to show your first drafts. And in brain surgery, well . . .

I love writing. I love it! Some people tell me they don't like it. I don't believe them. Surely, if you hate it, why do it? It doesn't pay that much. Even a guy like me. No day goes by in which I don't write something. Sometimes it's on paper, sometimes in my head. People say to me, "Gee, living in Kleinburg, you come into town, that's an hour each way. How do you do it?" I say it's wonderful for a writer. I don't have a car phone, which sometimes causes me problems. I locked myself out the other day, and I didn't have a car phone to call the Motor League. But it's an asset to a writer to be able to be locked in away from the phone, away from interruptions, away from nagging people, and just think about what you're going to write. And I've done that all my life, and a lot of my writing has been done in my head so I've been able to go straight to the typewriter and put it down on paper.

I can hardly wait to get to the typewriter in the mornings, I like it so much. I really find it a marvellous vocation. It is hard on those around me. I'm very bad at parties if I'm working on a book, because I'm working on the book at the party, in my head, and I don't hear what people say. I insult all sorts of close friends by my silence. It's hard on my wife and some of my kids at home because I hide myself in my office. I have to write, and I should be out, you know, gamboling with grandchildren on my knee, which I do sometimes. But not as much as I might like to, if I were a retired brain surgeon.

The worst thing is to let go of your child – the manuscript you've worked over for two years – and you finally have to let it go. It is hard to do. I am always fiddling. They have to tear that script away from me. We used to have galley proofs, now we just have page proofs, but I fiddle with them too, always adding stuff, and the editor is saying, "Just a moment, that's expensive, you'll have to take that out." I can't help it.

Well a few years ago, I found that I couldn't walk. I could only crawl. They said it was pneumonia, but it turned out to be a pulmonary embolism. I couldn't breathe very well. I was trying to start a book called *The Promised Land* – the book that I finally got around to learning how to write. It took me eight years before I knew how to write *The Promised Land*, which was a difficult book. Again about large numbers of people moving through time and space.

But I couldn't write it because I couldn't breathe. And I was very stubborn about going to the hospital. The medication for the so-called pneumonia wasn't working and my wife finally dragged me, which is the only way I could move. There are only three stairs in our hall and I had to crawl up them, and I think that suggested to her, if not to me, that there was something wrong.

So off I went to the hospital and they gave me oxygen and they also thought I had cancer of the lymph glands, which I didn't, but I spent a night worrying about that.

You know what I was worried about? I thought, *My God, I've got all this research for* The Promised Land *and I've got to write it, but how can I write it if I die?* And I thought, *Holy God, that's the worst thing that can happen to a writer.* You spend two years and you know exactly how to write it and now you've solved this problem which has been with you for eight years. It didn't work the last time, but now you know how it's going to start, and you've got all this stuff ready, and you're in this bloody hospital and they're telling you they've got lymph cancer, or maybe something wrong with your lungs.

Well, I didn't die.

Jack McClelland came over to see me. He'd been in hospital, too, and he had a hospital thing around his wrist and he had a hell of a time getting back out again, because they thought he was escaping from York Central, when he really belonged to a totally different hospital.

So I went back from that and the next day I said to the doctor, "You've got to let me outta here, I'll feel better at home." And I did, because I got back to my typewriter. It took a little while, a bit slow at first, but I got the book done and it was published and was successful and so on.

So now I face the dilemma that so many of us face. *What's gonna happen?* Sooner or later I'm going to be halfway through a book and the Big Copywriter is going to bring his blue pencil down and say, "Out! You don't finish it."

I can't bear the thought. I've two choices. I can quit. I can say, "That's enough." I've written a lot of books – far too many. *Ah, why not just take it easy? Why not just lie in the sun, play with the grandchildren, drink the odd drink, go to see the places you want to see – the Taj Mahal and the Grand Canyon, the two places I haven't seen and want to see? Why don't you do that? You don't need to write anymore.*

But the answer, of course, is that I do. I cannot quit. I am not a brain surgeon. I have to keep writing, knowing that sooner or later, I will be halfway through something of which I'm proud, but will never get published. And that, ladies and gentlemen, is both the triumph and a tragedy of a writer's life.

Thank you.

1 9 9 5
FARLEY MOWAT

It's a pleasure to be here, if only because I hold Margaret Laurence in great affection and regard, and am happy to do what I can to help keep her memory green.

Her feelings about me at the beginning of our long friendship were somewhat ambivalent. In a letter to Al Purdy written in 1971, she expressed her reservations about me thusly:

Dear Al: Got your letter of April 20 a few days ago. Farley sounds in good form. I think you know that when I first met him, I thought he was a slob, but now, over the years, have changed my mind and find I really like him, although still somewhat on guard with him (except that well-remembered occasion at your place when Farley and I sobbed on each other's shoulders, revealing drunkenly to each other how inadequate we felt in various areas of our lives. Ah, well . . .).

Ah, well, indeed. One of the things that bothered Margaret was the arbitrary classification of writers into those who write plays, verse, and fiction, as opposed to those who write what is dismissively called non-fiction. Margaret thought this was damned nonsense. Worse, it seemed to her to be a kind of literary apartheid whereby non-fiction writers were placed outside the pale, becoming literary non-persons.

Well, tonight I find myself — one of those literary non-persons — at the sanctified head table, even if only by default. And I'm going to take advantage of my temporary elevation to the godhead to issue a *ukase* in the name of Margaret Laurence, one which I sternly adjure you to accept and obey.

From now on, that invidious characterization, *non-fiction writer*, will no longer be tolerated. From now on, its use will constitute a most serious and unforgivable breach of Political Rectitude. From now on, there will only be three categories of writers: playwrights, poets, and prose writers. The triple *p*. Long separated by arbitrary class distinctions, *all* prose writers will henceforth be united under one banner. I decree this in Margaret Laurence's name, and solemnly warn the world that her wishes in this regard are not to be ignored. The lady remains as capable as ever she was of dealing with transgressors.

Proof of her continuing ability to influence mundane affairs is not far to seek. Until last year, this prestigious lecture had always been delivered by one of the literary anointed, a novelist, poet, or playwright. No literary non-person had ever been invited to present it. It became apparent to Margaret that none ever *would* be invited. So she intervened. Last year, the lecture was to have been given by the illustrious poet Irving Layton. Alas, failing health prevented him from doing so. A substitute had to be found in a crashing hurry, and the only one who could and would take on the task was Pierre Berton — a man who stands in the very van of non-person writers.

An isolated incident? An accident of fate? I think not! Tonight, the revered novelist Robertson Davies was to have entertained and enlightened you. But scant days before the event he, too, was forced by ill health to withdraw. And who was the only pinch hitter available to fill the void? Non-person writer me!

I hope that those entrusted with the selection of future Margaret Laurence Memorial Lecturers have got the message. And I take this occasion to add an injunction of my own. Do not wait until the "senior writer" of your choice has become too senior. Such a course demonstrably has its perils. I suggest that henceforward you hedge your bets and give some of the young farts a chance.

And now I come to the subject upon which I am being paid to expound: my life as a writer.

I am a storyteller in, I hope, the ancient tradition of the saga man. That tradition is deeply implanted in my genes. My father was a storyteller *par excellence*. An example of his ability is his account of how I took my genesis. I have preserved it in my recent book, *Born Naked*. And do not look at me askance. If I can't read from my own work on an occasion such as this, and if I can't use such an occasion to promote said work, then the hell with it.

On a cloudless August day in 1950 my father boarded a Trans-Canada DC-3 at Toronto's Malton Airport. The airplane was eastbound for Montreal on a course which would take it not too high above the northern shore of Lake Ontario.

Angus Mowat was always an excitable man. On this occasion he was stimulated to effervescence. Not only was this his very first "aerial voyage," it would carry him over a coast with which he had been familiar as a small-boat sailor through most of his life.

Puffing furiously on a hand-rolled cigarette, he peered raptly through the porthole. The world of his younger years unrolled below him, and he recited aloud a litany of seamarks as these hove into view and then were swept astern: "Frenchman's Bay! . . . Peter Rock! . . . Colborne! . . . Presqu'ile!"

Near the mouth of the Murray Canal, the plane tipped a wing as it lazily changed course. By then, Angus was squirming in his seat like a birthday child. He was over home waters now and approaching Trenton, where he had been born. When the head of the Bay of Quinte opened before him, he could no longer contain himself. He began urgently calling for the stewardess.

She came at the double and a fine, buxom lass she was too, prepared to deal with whatever dire emergency might have arisen. Angus grabbed her arm and shoved her down into the window seat with, perhaps, just a touch too much fervour. She gave him the sidelong glance of a woman who knows herself to be irresistible and remonstrated gently, "Really, sir. This is hardly the time or place."

"No! No!" he cried with some asperity. "Look below, dammit! See that little island in the bay? That's Indian Island! And thirty years ago my son Farley was conceived in the lee of Indian Island in the sweetest little green canoe that ever was!"

Firmly removing his hand from her arm, the stewardess eased back into the narrow aisle. There she paused before replying evenly, "Congratulations, sir. That's quite an amazing feat . . . in any colour canoe."

Whether or not my life actually began in such aquatic circumstances – my mother denied it; she said I was conceived in the horse barns at the Canadian National Exhibition – my writing life did not begin until 1935 when we moved to Saskatoon. There were some foreshadowings, however. My words first reached the printed page in 1931, when the Windsor *Border City Star* published a letter of mine extolling the virtues of the sycamore tree. "Sicamores," I wrote, "are the rarest and beautifulest trees I have ever seen, and should be spread." I admit to having had an ulterior motive in publishing this accolade to the sycamore. A pal and I had set ourselves up as entrepreneurs, peddling sycamore seeds door to door in Windsor's residential districts, and we needed all the promotion we could get.

In 1933, the Mowat family moved to Saskatoon, where there were no sycamore trees; but my early predilection for non-human creatures continued to flower (if a predilection can be said to flower – and before an audience of professional wordsmiths it behooves me to watch my step). I became more and more involved in the lives of the Others with whom we share the planet (and generally treat abominably), and, soon after reaching Saskatoon, acquired a pair of white rats. In proper rattish style, these two soon became several dozen who pre-empted our garage.

Not everyone shared my high regard for the little rodents. Most of our neighbours believed all rats – white, black, or varicoloured – were vermin and ought to be exterminated. When rumours about our cellar tenants got around, threats were made to report us to "the Public Health." My father was annoyed at what he took to be an infringement on our privacy. I was indignant at what I regarded as rampant prejudice, if not racism, and began my first public crusade for animal rights. The following appeared in the *Victoria School Record* early in 1934.

If you were to ask me to name an interesting pet that can be kept in a small house I would immediately reply "the White Rat." This small animal has helped mankind more than we can guess. When Pasteur was attempting to find a cure for rabies the rat played perhaps the most important role of all.

It was this little creature that took the deadly injections of dried rabbit brains by which Pasteur was able to determine whether his cure was effective. . . . Most hospitals now have a room set aside for breeding White Rats for medicine. They give their lives that ours might be saved and although you could hardly call them heroic, their great service to mankind will never be forgotten.

Not only are they useful but they are very amazing as pets. They are exceedingly loving toward each other and when a male and female are separated for a few days they show ever possible affection when re-united. . . . Almost everybody who comes into contact with White Rats in a very short time becomes keenly interested and warmly affectionate toward them.

Billy Mowat

Billy, a name I chose to replace the inevitable grade-school corruption — Fartly — became my moniker during the years in Saskatoon, and it was under this sobriquet that my literary life could be truly said to have begun and come to its first fruition.

In December of 1934, a new magazine joined the ranks of Canadian periodicals. As is the Canadian way, it did so without fanfare. *Nature Lore — The Official Organ of the Beaver Club of Amateur Naturalists* came quietly upon the scene.

It will come as no surprise to learn that Billy Mowat was the editor-in-chief. He wrote an impassioned editorial for the first issue, from which I quote: "Birds and animals do not get heard enough in this country and are not treated well. The Beaver Club intends to do something about this. Every 5 cent bit contributed to this magazine will be spent on the betterment of the birds and animals of Saskatchewan. . . ."

I also wrote most of the text, although I attributed many of the pieces to my loyal tribesfolk. It was the least I could do. They fanned out all over Saskatoon in fine weather and foul, hawking copies of the magazine to all and sundry.

The public's reception astounded us. Within a week, the entire first issue, amounting to fifty copies, had sold out. The three subsequent issues, with press runs of a hundred copies each, did almost as well, earning a grand total of $25.45, which was more than many people were then being paid for a week's labour.

The articles may have been a little didactic: "Planestrius migratorius [the robin] is a prominent local insectivore"; or somewhat overblown: "The crow can talk extremely well and is as intelligent as most people." Nevertheless, the effect was to at least engender some interest in and sympathy for wild creatures amongst people who had never previously given a thought to the possibility that they might have something in common with other animals.

The several issues of *Nature Lore* (the magazine died the death when spring came and there were better things for us to do) gave me scope to develop the skills of a prose writer, but I did not neglect poetry. I was then of an age to begin having fantasies about girls with the consequent risk of growing hair on the palms of my hands. . . . Oh? Not all of you get the relevance of that remark? Too bad. You were born too late.

In any event, one of the girls I fantasized about was Muriel Pinder, the dark-haired daughter of a druggist who had done exceedingly well for himself during the Prohibition years. Muriel lived in a rococo, strawberry-pink, stucco mansion a block away and was regarded by the boys of the neighbourhood as hot stuff. Alas, she did not regard me in the same way. I wrote her this poem:

> *No bird that flies in summer skies,*
> *No mouse that lurks in sacred church,*
> *No fish that swims in river dim,*
> *No snake that crawls on sunny walls*
> *Can stir my heart the way you do*
> *With raven hair and eyes so blue.*

She returned this offering by next day's post, with her critical evaluation written across it in purple ink: "Ugh!"

As the Saskatoon years unrolled, I went through a hunting phase, but it did not last. Having taken part in the slaughter of ducks, partridge, prairie chickens, crows, rabbits, and gophers, all in the holy name of sport, I began suffering a revulsion which produced a poem indicative of the direction life as a whole, and my writing life in particular, would take.

SPORT

A flash of flame that flickers there,
A rain of lead that hisses by,
A deafening crash that rends the air,
A wreath of smoke floats in the sky.
A bark from the dog as it gallops past,
A laugh from the man who holds the gun,
The flutter of birds that seek to fly,
The words:"Good work!"when the deed is done.
A ring of feathers scattered round
A quivering pulp of flesh and bone.
A pool of blood on the autumn ground.
A life has passed to the great unknown.

My aversion to bloodletting was well developed by the time the Second World War began.

Nevertheless, in 1940 I joined the Canadian Army as a private in an infantry regiment; went overseas in 1942; served — mostly with the infantry — throughout the campaign in Italy; and ended the war as an intelligence officer in northwest Europe. I wrote quite a lot during the war itself. Partly out of outrage, horror, and despair; partly in an attempt to make light of what was hellish darkness; partly in an effort to escape from an unendurable reality.

I am going to dwell at some length on what the war meant, and did, to me. I do this for two reasons. First, because the war had such a profound influence upon my development as a writer. Second, because 1995 is the fiftieth anniversary of V-E Day, an occasion which surely deserves commemoration, and one which I am sure Margaret Laurence would wish me to make much of.

What follows is a sequence of excerpts from what I wrote while actually in the crucible.

I shall begin with part of a letter to my parents written in January of 1944 from the village of San Leonardo, on the Adriatic coast of Italy.

Last night brought a story that may or may not amuse you. It has long been an ambition of the brigade major to inveigle a dental detachment to come forward from base and attend to the toothaches which abound in the front lines. But the dental corps has such demanding needs – running water, electricity, refrigeration, heaters, and trucks converted into swanky living quarters – that they are loath to expose themselves and their equipment to the uncertain "weather" up where we live.

However, last week the BM succeeded in his machinations and two whopping big trucks full of incisors, molars, and dentists rolled into the village square where we were laagered. Our camp commandant suggested they might sleep better if they bedded down with us in the nice deep wine cellars of some of the surrounding houses, most of whose upper floors are now in a somewhat dilapidated state. The dentists would have none of that but climbed into their comfy caravan truck parked in the square in the midst of a clutch of ammunition trucks and went beddy-byes.

Along about 2300 hrs, Jerry did a stonk of the village. One shell fell in the square and set fire to a lorry loaded with 75 mm tank ammo. The dentists heard the shell land all right, and when they peered dazedly out of their daintily curtained windows they saw the flames leaping up from the burning truck. They may also have heard someone shouting that it was an ammo truck aflame.

Well, you can say what you will about dentists, they can move as fast as any of us when the mood is on them. And they know what slit trenches are *for,* even if only in an academic sense. They found one handy to their mobile home-away-from-home and popped right into it.

Shortly thereafter the tank shells began to let fly and the square became a pretty lively place. Not that we lingered to enjoy it. Everyone with any sense headed down into the *vino* cellars to wait until the fireworks were over. The poor sods of dentists were pinned down in their slit trench. No doubt there was considerable squirming and grunting in the narrow confines of their sanctuary, but they had no "better 'ole" to go to, with AP shells and hits of truck ricocheting around the square.

To shorten the story, when the explosions ceased the harassed trench dwellers were seen to emerge and stagger back to their trucks, which had been well perforated but not immobilized. There was the grind of starters, the clash of gears, then the roar of rapid acceleration as they departed down the road leading to the rear. In the morning, I sauntered over to look at the remains of the ammo lorry and happened to cast a glance into the slit trench that had saved the dental plates. It wasn't a slit trench. It was a well-used latrine trench left behind by Jerry when he skedaddled out of here a few days ago.

Some day I must have my cavity filled. But not just yet.

The light-hearted touch was part of the armour we adopted in order to stay sane. The following poem conveys some of the darker side of things. It was written after the death in action of my company commander, who had been father and brother to me.

FOR ALEX CAMPBELL. KILLED CHRISTMAS DAY, 1943, ORTONA

Who calls his name across those lonely fields
hears no voice answer for his lips are sealed
against the empty chambers of a mind
where, once, a poet's voice was wont to find
expression for its pangs and fleeting raptures.
Finds nothing now. Nor will again recapture
the beauty seen by eyes or heard by ears,
through the forgotten — and the unlived years.

Who calls to him waits endlessly in vain,
through the chill threnody of wind and rain.

Straining towards the dark, he only hears
the gentle echo of his own heart's tears.
And the shrill, mocking night alone intrudes
on the eternal vastness of his solitude.

Early in the spring of 1944, my regiment was ordered to make a "feint" attack in order to provide a diversion for an offensive farther to the west.

I wrote an account of this foredoomed action which was published in *Maclean's* a few months later. The following excerpts will, I hope, give the flavour of the whole.

As a liaison officer, I drove up to the front an hour before the show began. My driver had the most extraordinarily fluid ideas about time and space. Reduce both to a minimum as fast as possible. He came by his ideas honestly. Driving a jeep in one of the fighting regiments is no sinecure. He took me over the valley road and down the sloping stretch we called "the shooting gallery" – under enemy observation – so fast that the patient Jerry artillery spotter on the far hill hadn't time to get a single shot away. We got to the battalion headquarters observation post in record time and I told the driver to find an unoccupied slit trench and wait.

The observation post was in an isolated, shell-battered, stone farmhouse on a hill overlooking a flat, featureless plain dominated by Tolo Ridge, where the Germans were dug in.

In a ravine just back of us, six Sherman tanks began revving their engines and turning their turrets slowly from side to side, as if offering slow dissent to the query, "All set?" We couldn't see the infantry. They were up ahead in a series of gullies, lying doggo.

With a colossal cacophony the artillery opened up and the smokescreen and the barrage went in. Zero hour had struck.

The lead Sherman made good time up the road. There weren't any mines. A pioneer patrol out last night had swept right up to the forward edge of the Jerry positions. Now the dust from the barrage was blending with the thick, pillaring wall of smoke. The sound of bursting shells made a blurred, continuous thumping like the heartbeats of panic-stricken giants in the earth. The tanks seemed to move through it without noise, like toys being pulled on a string. The uneven but continuous flaming curtain of the barrage was beginning to grow ragged as the enemy artillery sent shells through the smoke, hoping to catch and shatter the attackers.

In the gullies, the companies of infantry waited, watching that appalling upheaval of ground and sky with swelling horror.

The sergeant in the lead tank hit his head on the turret and started cursing at the top of his voice. Three mortar bombs crumped savagely in front of the Sherman and they felt her shudder. The engine died and the sergeant couldn't make the driver answer. When he bent over him he saw blood. The gunner was snarling like a cat and working frantically at the hand rotating gear. The tank was suddenly very silent, then against its lifeless sides came the thudding of machine-gun bullets. The concussion as the tank's 75 was fired brought the sergeant round like a whip. "Goddamn! Goddamn!" he screamed at the gunner. "Who the hell told you to fire!"

The loader slapped another shell into the smoking breech.

People were running around in the OP like headless chickens. All the radio sets were crackling and the hubbub was like a busy morning on the stock exchange – though the words were different.

"Hello, Sunray . . . only one tank left on the right . . . two on the left . . . they're getting it from some eighty-eights."

In the gully, the infantry waited for the word to go. Enemy mortar bombs were bursting all around them now, searching, searching. A company commander was wriggling as if he had suddenly found himself lying on a nest of driver ants . . . thinking . . . "Christ, why don't the tanks get on with it . . . this fire's just bloody awful . . . why *don't* they get on with it!"

The tank troop commander had the hatch open and his head out. Fifty yards ahead, seven Germans were running madly up the slope through the twisted props of a vineyard. A burst from the Browning caught them midway in their rush and they went down. There was a wet spot here and for a moment the tank bogged, then she pulled out with a deep, stubborn roar and clambered quickly up the slope onto the objective. All the time the gunner was pulling at the lieutenant's leg, trying to get him to draw his head in.

A low, stone farmhouse a hundred yards to the left of the tank was chattering hysterically as its defenders sent streams of machine-gun bullets bouncing sharply off the armour. The lieutenant's body sagged, headless, into the tank's interior.

One section of infantry started across an open stretch at the double, all bunched up, and was straddled by four mortar shells . . . ! The rest of the platoon passed through them and only one man paused to glance at the human wreckage. A bullet took him just below the left arm, punching up through his neck.

The fire grew heavier as the whole enemy front began concentrating on the naked infantry, whom they could now clearly see. Overhead, shells from our twenty-five pounders and mediums kept up a continuous overtone of whines and whistles that blended into one throbbing flight of terrible wings. The attacking infantry could see no enemy. But a corporal let go a burst from his tommy gun into the air. For a moment it made all the men around him feel good. Then suddenly they were going back, running, stumbling, crawling, running.

In the ravine, their company commander clapped on the earphones and spoke to the CO. "We'll try again, sir! We'll try it again," he said. He was almost crying. The remnants of his company huddled under the lip of the gulley, breathing very fast and shallow, not looking at each other.

The commanding officer stood at the OP window and there were things in his face it is not good to see. The smell of phosphorous fumes and of burnt explosives was drifting back so thickly that at times it was hard to breathe. The noise was less, though.

Back in the gulley, one or two men were smoking as they crouched below the crest, almost oblivious now to the stray mortar bombs that lit near them. Most of the wounded were already on their way to the regimental aid post in the deep ravine. The lieutenant in command of this little group sat by the radio set with his hand held out in front of him. He seemed fascinated by the way it was shaking.

Like a play that has run overtime, the great noise of battle ceased. It did not fade; it stopped. I honked on the jeep's horn and after a moment my driver came up the slope towards me, munching a chocolate bar and stuffing a pocket detective novel into his blouse. "Pretty hot, eh?" he said as we started back. "Yeah," I answered, "hot," and we rolled noisily over the bridge.

One of the stratagems I used to maintain a degree of sanity was to write verse for a bestiary which, I told myself, I would some day publish. This sort of thing:

The carrion crow, I've heard it said,
Lives on the entrails of the dead.
It loves to gorge on rotting bowel,
Which spoils it . . . as a table fowl.

Or in a somewhat lighter vein:

The double-crested cormorants
Sport twin cerebral ornaments.
The female sings in high soprano
When not engaged in making guano.
In winter she lies doromant.

Sex was seldom far from our escape fantasies.

The Earthworm is bisexual.
He's he, but also she.
Though this may seem a happy state
It's not quite trouble-free.

For one end is the female end,
The other is the male,
And so the Earthworm seldom knows
Just where to find its tail.

Protection from things that go *whump* in the night was a preoccupation.

The shy and self-effacing Mole
Is happiest when in a hole.
Moles seldom to the surface come.
They aren't so dumb!

Literature offered another avenue of escape.

A poet named E. Allan Poe
Kept a raven that talked like a crow.
It quoth, "Nevermore,
You mad son-of-a-whore!"
Which, for Poe, was le mot à propos.

And, of course, our thoughts often turned to food.

When dining on a Mouse or Rabbit,
Owls have the most disgusting habit
of glutching hair and bones and all,
which forms an undigested ball.
So, after Owl has had his sup,
he turns his head and brings it up.

Perhaps it's staying out so late
that make the Owl regurgitate.

And even then I was making mock of my betters.

"Pigeons on the grass, alas!"
is a poem by Gertrude Stein.

"The Yak is out of whack, alack!"
is mine.

Wherever we went, whatever we did during those long months that stretched into years, we were never in sanctuary. Even on our rare leaves far from the front, the war could and did catch up with us. I wrote this piece after a leave in Naples.

We sat on the terrace of the "Orange Grove Club" and looked out over the ethereal blue of the Tyrrhenian Sea. . . . Beneath our feet the bay lay quiescent. Along the curve of the shoreline, towards Sorrento, glaring white buildings with red and garish roofs clustered on the foreshore close to the brilliant sea as if in flight from the gargantuan threat of Vesuvius smoking thinly above the grey line of mountains behind them.

It was very hot, but up on the crest of the ridge, suspended over the teeming, stinking cesspool of the city, we were touched by gusty little breezes that came, high-flying, from the snow-capped peaks beyond Cassino.

Frank slumped in an ornate wicker chair, a glass in his hand full of a sticky concoction composed of equal parts of gin and ice cream. He looked out towards the purple loom of the island called Die and said, "My mother used to tell me that joke – 'See Naples – and Die!'"

"Hell!" I said. "I'd sooner Siena and suffer."

He turned his head lazily, eyed me for a moment and replied, "Mowat, it's too goddamn bad Jerry didn't put a Teller mine under your jeep. You don't deserve to live."

The afternoon was passing very pleasantly. The drinks were lousy but they were at least cool. The conversation was sparse and aimless. Best of all, the war was five hundred miles away.

I sprawled back in my chair and peered up into the blue dome, thinking how much it resembled summer skies over the prairies. I thought that if I looked hard enough, I might even see a red-tailed hawk soaring ponderously in great lazy circles. Suddenly I did see something. In the shining expanse of emptiness, there had appeared a tiny cloud, a puffball of a cloud, a foolish little white cotton dab that seemed ridiculous in that majestic cone of space.

At the same moment, my ears caught the dull "woof" of a shell-burst and I was instantly flat on my belly on the marble terrace. I got quickly up and sat in the chair again, wiping the dust from my knees and feeling foolish. "It's those goddamn reflexes," I said. "They double-cross you every bloody time . . ."

Frank was leaning forward, his head cocked sideways like a terrier. Then I too heard the faint irregular beat of engines, muted but menacing, penetrating the dull moan of the city's noise as the whine of a fly penetrates the sultry murmur of a crowded school room.

Next moment there was bedlam beneath us. Sirens on ships, hooters on destroyers, sirens on buildings, cluster after cluster of ack-ack guns all joined their angry and indignant voices in a shattering cacophony. The sky became speckled with the little cotton dabs and the wump, wump, wump of the bursts came back to us as something felt rather than heard.

"My God, my God!" Frank yelled. "Caught our silly buggers napping for sure! Oh Jerry, you smart sneaking bastard!"

Right out of the eye of the sun, an evenly spaced string of twelve tiny silver beads appeared and began to sink gently towards the sea. A destroyer had slipped her cable and was dashing across the fairway in the bay below, belching greasy black billows from her twin funnels as she laid a smoke-screen. Along the docks and from every high point around the harbour, other massive pillars of smoke began to rise.

The heavy whack of the 3.7 flak guns became a thunderous tattoo that came to us through the solid rock under our feet and set the glasses on the table tinkling. Interspersed amongst their basses was the slow regular hiccup of Bofors guns . . . and I could follow the red globes of their tracer rising effortlessly into the sky as if by some act of levitation.

Then, clear and evil through the vast bellowing of the guns, came a new sound. A high-pitched, unnatural whine that sent every nerve in my body into a twitching desire to flee. . . .

Over the mouth of the harbour, the glittering beads had miraculously expanded into the smooth and efficient forms of aircraft hurtling seaward. The bellowing of the big guns was now almost drowned in a crackling roar as hundreds of smaller cannon and machine guns joined in.

The leading aircraft began to flatten out over a rift in the artificial cloud that now cloaked the bay, and I plainly saw the bulbous shape of a single big bomb as it sank away from the plane's belly and slid gracefully downward in a slowly lengthening curve.

Before the crunch of the explosion reached us, the plane had crossed the harbour and was climbing steeply under the cliff on which we stood. We stared down at it and saw the simple black cross against the greenish drab of the fuselage.

"He's smoking!" Frank yelled, but I too had already seen the fine spume of white vapour that bled outward from behind the cockpit.

The wounded machine lurched convulsively away from the cliffs, side-slipped and then swung back towards the granite wall. Time seemed to freeze and fragile wings to hang suspended in a passing caress with earth, and so close below us that we could see the round helmeted head of the pilot clearly under the dome of the cockpit.

I remember thinking, "Why doesn't he fall?" and then there was a livid flash of orange flame and a slow rain of fire sinking down towards the foot of the cliff.

A few minutes later, the sirens began to sound the all-clear and a waiter came casually into view in the centre of the terrace. I raised my glass of gin to my lips and drank it down at a gulp, shuddering slightly at the oily, rancid flavour.

And the words flashed unbidden through my head. "See Naples, and die!"

The Second World War was bad enough, God knows, but there are many kinds of warfare, and I am afraid the worst kind of all is being waged now, in our time.

We are now engaged in the most significant conflict ever to involve the human species. It is not the struggle between capitalism and communism, or between any other set of "isms." It is not the contest between affluent societies and impoverished ones.

It is the conflict between those who possess the means and the will to exploit the living world to destruction, and those who are banding together in a desperate and last-ditch attempt to prevent the New Juggernaut from trashing our small planet.

If the right side wins, this combat may become known to future generations as the Crusade that Rescued the Earth. If the wrong side wins . . . there may well *be* no future human generations.

After the Second World War, most of which I spent trying not to be killed by my fellow men – an experience that, incidentally, gave me considerable empathy with wild animals trying not to be killed by men – I went to the Arctic as a student biologist to study caribou and wolves.

One evening in the Barrenlands, when the sun hovered above the horizon's lip, I sat beside an Inuk and watched a spectacle so overwhelming as to be transcendental.

Below us, on the undulating darkness of the immeasurable tundra plains, a hundred thousand caribou were moving – a tide of life flowing out of the dim south to engulf the world, submerging it so that it seemed to sink beneath a living sea. The very air was heavy with the breath of life. There was a sound as of the earth breathing and moving. It was as if the inanimate crust of rock below us had been imbued with the essential spark.

This experience, together with others over the next several years shared with wolves, caribou, Aboriginals, tug-boat skippers, fishermen, and peoples of natural adversity, brought me to a *conscious* awareness of just how far modern men have distanced themselves from the world that gave us birth, and which still nurtures all other living beings indivisibly linked together, and to us.

I remembered one of Rudyard Kipling's stories in which Baloo, a wise old bear, tells the human child, Mowgli (who has been adopted into the jungle world by wolves), "We be of one blood, ye and I." I had felt that this was true when I read it at the age of eight or nine. Now I knew it to be true, and thereafter I became more and more anxious to bridge the abyss that yawned between.

When the 1960s began, I was living in the remote Newfoundland outport of Burgeo.

During the early spring of 1967, a seventy-foot, female fin whale became trapped in a saltwater lagoon close to the settlement. By the time I heard about her plight, she had become the target of a dozen or so rifle-wielding men shooting steel- jacketed bullets into her for sport. Two or three of us came to her defence, hoping eventually to free her.

In the end, we could not save her. The bullet wounds, which in my ignorance I had thought might have meant no more to her than flea bites, gave rise to massive and virulent infections from which, one night, she died. And finally I had to accept and learn to live with the sure knowledge that I was a member of the most lethal, murderous, and unnatural species ever to run riot on earth. Thereafter, only one course was open to me. I had to become a full-fledged member of the conspiracy to save the planet.

Since 1967, I have served that cause. Alas, I am not an organization man, so could only do what I have always done best. I worked as a writer. In that role I have written several books and scores of shorter pieces in defence of nature, and in explanation of man's true place in nature. I have tried to be a spokesman for the other beings who have no voice in how we treat them.

I have not been entirely ignored by humankind. I have been called a liar in the House of Commons by a minister of the Crown. I have been sued by Canada's largest consortium of hunters – the Canadian Wildlife Federation. I have even been denied entry to the ultimate citadel of the Masters – the United States of America – because some of the environmental causes I have espoused are considered subversive there.

In 1984, I made what I think may have been my most significant contribution – a book called *Sea of Slaughter*. It details five centuries of human destruction of life on the Atlantic seaboard. Its epilogue sums up what I believe to be the truth about the works of modern man – and the future of life on earth.

I sit at the window of my home beside the Atlantic Ocean. Having led me through so many dark and bloody chronicles, this book comes to its end . . . and leaves me with a terrible and unavoidable conclusion.

The living world is dying in my time.

I look out over the unquiet waters, south to the convergence of sea and sky beyond which the North Atlantic heaves against the eastern seaboard of the continent. And in my mind's eye I see it as it was before our coming.

Pod after pod of spouting whales, the great ones together with the lesser kinds, surge through waters everywhere a-ripple with living tides of fishes. Wheeling multitudes of gannets, kittiwakes, and others such becloud the sky. The stony finger marking the end of the long beach below me is clustered with resting seals. The beach flickers with a restless drift of shorebirds as thick as blowing sand. In the bight of the bay, whose bottom is a metropolis of clams, mussels, and lobsters, the heads of a massive concourse of walrus emerge amongst floating islands of eider ducks. Their tusks gleam like lambent flames.

Then I behold the world as it is now. In all that vast expanse of sea and sky and fringing land, one gull soars in lonely flight – a single, drifting mote of life upon an enormous and an empty stage.

When our forebears commenced their exploitation of this continent they believed its animate resources were infinite and inexhaustible. The vulnerability of the living fabric which clothed the New World – the intricacy and fragility of its all-too-finite parts – was beyond their comprehension. So it can at least be said in their defence that they were mostly ignorant of the inevitable results of their dreadful depredations.

We who are alive today can claim no such exculpation for our biocidal sins and their dire consequences. Modern man now has every opportunity to be aware of the complexity and interrelationships of the living world. If ignorance is to serve now as an excuse, then it can only be willful, murderous ignorance.

The hideous results of five centuries of death-dealing on this continent are not to be gainsaid; but there are some indications that we may at last be developing the will, and the conscience, to look beyond our own immediate gratifications and desires. Belatedly, some part of mankind is trying to rejoin the community of living beings from which we have for so long a time been alienating ourselves – and of which we have for so long a time been the mortal enemy.

Evidence of such a return to sanity is not yet to be looked for in the attitudes and actions of the exploiters who dominate the human world. Rather, the emerging signs of sanity are to be seen in individuals who, revolted by the frightful excesses to which we have subjected animate creation, are beginning to reject the killer beast which man has truly become.

Banding together with ever-increasing potency, they are challenging the self-granted licence of the vested interests to continue plundering and savaging the living world for policy, profit, and for pleasure. Although they are being furiously opposed by the old order, they may be slowly gaining ground.

It is to this new-found resolution to reassert our indivisibility with life, to recognize the obligations incumbent upon us as the most powerful and deadly species ever to exist, and to begin making amends for the havoc we have wrought, that my own hopes for a renewal and continuance of life on earth now turn. If we – and I include all of you here present – persevere in this new way, we may succeed in making man humane . . . at last.

1 9 9 6

W.O. MITCHELL

We writers are travellers – all travelling through time, from the time that we were born till the time we reach a common destination that all mortals have. As a boy on the prairies, I was filled with a feeling of sad loneliness in the fall when long wavering skeins of geese drifted high over our town, their two-note plaint floating down as we stood with face upturned to sky. I was being left behind, passed by. That same feeling visited me as I stood on the Weyburn depot platform and the porters lifted their steps to put them back into their Pullman coaches and the train released a sigh from beneath itself, then pulled away for such exotic places as Minneapolis – St. Paul – Duluth. Then finally Florida. For at the age of twelve I had contracted TB from drinking the raw milk from my Uncle Jim's farm south of Weyburn. For this reason, on a doctor's advice, my mother was taking me down to St. Petersburg, where I spent four years of my adolescence.

In writing, there is an element of search – not pursuing anything quite so tangible as gas or oil or their by-products – but the search is an intense and continuing one, and it takes a writer through many strata of human nature. Oil and the artist's truth are where you find them. Perhaps the writer's work is more closely allied to the work of the refiner. He separates and he combines until he has what he seeks. Any artist, but particularly a writer, uses the raw material of people – feelings delicate and passion vivid – wishes and fears – hopes and disappointments – sadnesses and happinesses – nobilities and intolerances. A writer looks for and finds bits of people and experience – a nose, an earlobe, fragments of youth and age, the way people walk or talk, eat, sleep, make love or make hate. And from these autobiographical bits of truth the writer creates his story. Every single bit is the truth, but the whole thing is a more meaningful and dramatic lie – a magic lie. Many people who are not writers do this simply for the fun of it. They're called gossips. It makes up the sort of occupation that would attract any curious, undisciplined, and lazy man – or woman. I suppose we're all three. But writing is a search which involves a selection, a separation, and then a combining again into a poem or story or novel or play which explores larger, universal truths.

Like many Canadians, I have had a foot in both cultures north and south of the forty-ninth parallel. Between the ages of thirteen and seventeen, south – very south – the Gulf of Mexico. During those years, my sense of being Canadian became incandescent. Yet my sense of similarity also vivid. Both nations belong in the same cultural bag, for both are New World societies. Because of this, both of us have to pay a higher loneliness price than Old World humans do. White Canadians and Americans, relatively speaking, have a shallow and recent past; for us, our part of the earth's skin is really – still – both wild and tame. A New World child has no medieval cathedrals with soaring Gothic arches to awe and to comfort him with ancestor echo. We do not unearth Roman baths and walls and roads. Because it was Western, my generation, north or south of the border, was the newest of all. American or Canadian, we were the first whites to be born and stained in childhood by the prairie or the foothill or the mountain or the seashore West. It is difficult to be much newer than that – and therefore historically lonelier.

However, Minnesota or North Dakota or Montana or Manitoba or Saskatchewan or Alberta grass is older than Roman cobblestone. Our grass-hoppers probably go back to John the Baptist's locusts. The peaks of the Three Sisters in the Rockies are older than the Egyptian pyramids.

I am not sure what culture is, but I do know that it has a geographic dimension and that during the early litmus years of childhood, it stains. The year I was twelve, I developed a tubercular wrist and was taken out of school for almost a year. It was as though – every day between nine and four – some great blackboard eraser had wiped all the kids off all the streets but missed me. In our town of Weyburn – or the province of Saskatchewan, or Canada, or the world – I was the only kid left alive. Nobody kicking a road apple down the street. No little girls playing hopscotch or jacks. No lisping hiss of a skipping rope. All streets – wiped bare.

I would walk to the end of the street and out over the prairie with the clickety grasshoppers bunging in arcs ahead of me and I could hear the hum and twang of the wind in the great prairie harp of telephone wires. I remember looking down at the dried husk of a dead gopher crawling with ants and flies and undertaker beetles. Standing there with the total thrust of prairie sun on my vulnerable head, I guess I learned – at a very young age – that I was mortal. I *could* die – end of Billy Mitchell. And the humming, living prairie whole did not give one good goddamn about it. But my mother did, my grandmother, my brothers, Fin, Ike, Hodder, Fat – quite likely they did.

I guess the time you learn you're going to die is the time you really understand you are human. So – I must have learned that, too, at the same time.

Unfortunately, ever since the Industrial Revolution, only those things which can be weighed, measured, calibrated, priced are valued. Forget silly things – the song of a meadow lark, the great harp of telephone wires in a Western wind, the faint mucous trail of a snail on a leaf, the hiccuping sound of a diving board, the pale honey scent of wolf willow by an August river bank – all the things savoured and valued in childhood. Let's not take the arts too seriously. When I attended university here, I did not. I had acted lead in the senior play at St. Petersburg Senior High. My dear mentor in Public Speaking and Drama, Miss Emily Murray, wanted me to go on to the Yale Drama School; my mother, a nurse who worshipped doctors, did *not*. I enrolled in Medicine. The TB, which had metastasized to put my right wrist in an aluminum crate with leather straps till Florida sun healed it up, exploded again in my second year. I lost all my labs; end of medical career.

I switched to arts, became a Lodge boy majoring in philosophy. Rupert Lodge was an internationally celebrated Socratic Scholar who made us all Platonists. My aborted medical career had been a wonderful disaster, for it led to my discovery that there is artistic logic as well as logic logic, the logic which is the thematic foundation for play, poem, and novel structure. This logic, which causes a work's final meaning destination, is not limited by the logic of *this* and next *this*.

I must apologize to Rupert wherever he is now, for about thirty years ago I realized that I was no longer a Platonist dedicated to the world of the one. Actually, my older son, home from his first year in university, smartened me up. He said, "Dad, you aren't a Platonist."

"Oh . . . what am I?"

"Existentialist."

"What the hell is that?"

"Absolutes balanced with the world of the many."

Till he brought it up, I had never heard of existentialism. He sold me on this new school of fluid philosophy which melds both materialism and idealism, the worlds of the one and the many. So, too, do the illusions of art. Not for Rupert Lodge, though; he would have labelled existentialism a euphemism for pragmatic dualism. In his book on Socrates, he had compared a pragmatist to a frog that hopped off the river bank from which he had clear and true vision of the whole to immerse himself in the obscurity of the water. Up and down, out and in, again and again. In time, I suspect I would have made the philosophical switch without my son's nudging me.

The practice of all the arts is acrobatic. Not much difference between being a high-wire walker, a trapeze artist. No guarantee each time that you won't lose your balance and fall. Like most artists, I have had spotters. Several. My first had been in high school: Miss Emily. Then Rupert Lodge here at the University of Manitoba. And years later at the University of Alberta, Professor F.M. Salter. During the first two years of writing *Who Has Seen the Wind* he was there to catch me. I owe them all.

It was during those years with Salter that I accidentally made my greatest discovery. At some point I stopped typing and leaned back to remember – not to write. Unbidden, my father, who had died when I was seven, came back to me. I remembered his reciting "In Flanders Fields" – "The Flag" – "Mr. Dooley Says" – "When Father Rode the Goat" – I also remember standing with him in front of the upstairs toilet. We called it "crossing streams." Of course Mother never knew about it.

Each spring the McLaughlin seven-passenger car would come down off the blocks. Mother would take me and my brothers out to the cemetery just south of town, where we would play tag, making sure we cleared the graves, not setting a foot down on the earth mound over mortal remains. On our second or third first spring Sunday visit, there was a gopher hole right in front of the gravestone that hadn't been there the fall before. I was outraged. The gopher popped up and squeaked. He had no damn right to trespass on my dad's grave! I looked up to my mother, saw the prairie wind had laid a long dark lock of her hair across the side of her face, where tears were streaming down her cheeks.

More and more often I found myself travelling back into my stored past to find someone I had loved or hated, dramatic incidents, sights, sounds, feelings, smells. I wrote them down in detail. It wasn't writing; it was finding. When I would touch base with Salter almost weekly, I would give them to him to read. In a way it was an imposition, for I was not enrolled in his creative writing class. We often met in his backyard after he had put aside the lawnmower or the hoe – or in his living room or office at the university. At the end of almost six months, in one of our meetings he said, "Bill, this stuff you've been show-ing me is autobiographical chaos. You've got to start behaving. I've been going over all of it to see if there's any possible literary order suggested."

He pulled the great pile of papers across his desk. With Scotch tape tabs he had singled out page parts. "Let's consider these." We went through them all one by one. The first had been the time Ike Parsons and Jack Andrews and I had discovered the pigeon nest in the loft of an abandoned barn out on the prairie. One of the eggs had just hatched out. I took the baby chick home with me, cuddled it in a handkerchief on my bedside table. Three days later it was dead. Next came the time my mother let me have a fox terrier puppy I named Tom – her suggestion because she had always regretted she had not named one of her four sons Tom. He existed just two years till the day that the Snelgrove's Bakery wagon rolled over him. Then there was the two-headed calf in Stinchcombe's Livery Stable and veterinary building. I saw it the same day Mackenzie King visited our town and spoke to all the Haig School students. I ran home and shouted the exciting news to my mother and Grandma and Aunt Josie: "I've seen everything: the Prime Minister of Canada and a two-headed calf!" Next came the day of my father's funeral in our living room with the open casket in front of our fireplace. There was the birth of my youngest brother, Dickie, when I was four. The death of my grandmother.

Salter shoved the papers aside. "Do you notice anything promising in the way of a novel?"

"I don't know."

"Consider. First there's the just-born baby pigeon . . . then its death. Then there's the puppy, then he dies. Your father's funeral, the two-headed calf, your brother's birth, your grandmother's death. Get it?"

"No."

"Birth, then death, then birth, then death?"

"I don't know."

"It's a clear pattern. Could suggest a possible novel."

"Still don't get it. No plot."

"Forget plot. Think symphony."

"Whaaat?!"

"Alternating high and low notes."

"Sheeyit! I was born tone-deaf!"

"There are notes of vulgarity too. Look, Bill, all art is one and indivisible." Whatever that meant. "Take a run at it."

I did. The result five years later was my first published novel: *Who Has Seen the Wind*. How I owe that man and the others — but especially him. In time I came to understand what he meant when he said, "All art is one and indivisible." He persuaded me to forget law study and become a teacher. After I got my certificate I taught officially as a high school principal for only two years. But ever since then, I have helped writing protégés as a teacher and as an Artist-in-Residence in five different universities and at the Banff School of Fine Arts. I had no choice — I had to discharge my gratitude debt to Miss Emily and Lodge and Salter. It had been one hell of a creative breakthrough Salter had given me. Many of us in what Margaret Laurence referred to as "the tribe" have been helping first writers. Is any experience more satisfying than seeing their success?

Death and solitude justify art, which draws human aliens together in the mortal family, uniting them against the heart of darkness. Humans must comfort each other, defend each other against the terror of being human. Thus the dictum of Conrad (another existentialist), "We exist only in so far as we hang together — woe to the stragglers." Humans must comfort one another, defend each other against the terror of being human. There is a civilized accountability to others. The coyote, the jackrabbit, the badger, the killdeer, the weasel, the undertaker beetle, do not have that accountability. As a child I never did run across an artistic gopher or weasel or badger – though I'm not so certain about dragonflies or meadowlarks. Coyotes and ants are quite political. The wolf is very much aware of territorial imperative.

The novelist Wallace Stegner, who was a prairie boy till he was fourteen in Eastend, Saskatchewan, has said in his book *Wolf Willow* that the prairie creates poets. I agree – all that land and all that sky do make poets. Prairie certainly teaches early that to be human means to be conscious of self – and separation from the rest of the living whole. "Human" therefore equals "lonely." Stegner used the word "poet" in the sense of its Greek origin – "maker." All artists make or create and the result is an important ingredient in the recipe for culture, for those bridges and patterns which connect us, which create human "solidarity." Humans are the only animals who make poems, plays, novels; the only animals who paint, dance, sing, sculpt, compose. Artists, philosophers, historians know that man is a finite, warm sack of vulnerability. And because of this knowledge, they do have an unfair advantage over politicians – generals – and quarterbacks – and CEOs. Art is the only thing that man does for its own sake, that does not involve an adversary relationship. There are no winners over losers, no victors over vanquished, no toreador over bull. Readers are creative partners. As they read they have explosions of recognition from their own experience – somebody they have loved or hated, sensuous fragments, insights. Instead of relying entirely on what is written, they contribute from their own unique past, thereby making the fictional illusion all the more vivid and meaningful. Creative partners to artists, who look and wonder at a painting or a play or a ballet, who listen to a symphony – or even an opera – do not take anything from the artist. The book is not taken from the author. Both partner and artist win – through shared pity and terror, compassion and empathy, laughter and tears.

The writer explores and reveals bridges and patterns to the human community. They are fragile and they can be destroyed. They are only man-made. They are not divine, or absolute; they are life patterns, which grow like life and which change in a living manner. Man has grown them out of his generation-after-generation flow to defeat the heart of darkness. Exploring these patterns and bridges is of particular importance to our young. Our vulnerable young.

Many years ago, Socrates said that the unexamined life was not worth living. Now, there's an old prairie expression that says much the same thing: "Don't you eat that there stuff, Elmer. It's bull shit." But humans do not live by reason and common sense alone — neither the simply intellectual life nor the purely utilitarian life is the whole answer. We must have *artistic* life as well. Over a hundred and seventy years ago, Shelley wrote, "We have more moral, political, and historical wisdom than we know how to reduce into practice. There is no want of knowledge respecting what is wise and best in morals, government, and political economy. We want the poetry of life. Poets are the unacknowledged legislators of the world."

Shelley's warning — that our utilitarian culture has eaten more than it can digest — is even more relevant today. Which means that our culture is in even more need of the shared gift of the writer, the "poetry of life."

1 9 9 7
EDNA STAEBLER

I consider it a great honour to have been asked to give the Margaret Laurence Memorial Lecture. Some of you – perhaps many of you – have written more and better than I have, and you may be wondering why I have been chosen to speak to you today. Well, if you look around the room you'll see that I am the oldest person in it, and that's no doubt the real reason I'm standing here. If you feel slighted, be assured that in time your turn will come.

In 1906, I was born in a house two blocks from the public library in Berlin, Ontario (now Kitchener). My parents didn't read fairy stories to me in bed because we had gas lights downstairs, but not up, and my two younger sisters and I always went to bed in the dark.

As soon as I could read, I went two or three times a week to the library, where I chose my own books and somehow missed *Robinson Crusoe* and *Alice in Wonderland*. I read about Jimmy Skunk, the little cousins who lived around the world, mild mysteries, and adventures. My mother bought us *The Books of Knowledge*, a condensed literary set, and *The Harvard Classics* – which I never read.

After I passed my entrance exams and was allowed to borrow books from the adult library, I read all Alexandre Dumas and romantic English novels. (I knew of no Canadian ones until Hugh MacLennan wrote *Barometer Rising*.)

When I was sixteen, I wrote very cautiously in a journal, though nothing exciting happened to me; Kitchener and my dates seemed very dull. I was much happier and uninhibited when I went away to the University of Toronto.

I told friends I wanted to be a writer and they agreed that I should be. In my first year, I was on the staff of the *Varsity* but wrote only one piece – about girls drinking buttermilk in the Women's Union.

The Great Depression had started when I graduated in '29. I went home and lived with my family. Away from the stimulating environment of the university, I was often depressed. I worried that I'd never get a job, or be married, and I had to start wearing glasses. Every day I wrote miserable entries in my journal and one short story that I sent to *True Confessions* and got back with a rejection slip.

In the new year, I was taken on by the *Kitchener Record* at ten dollars a week. I wanted to be a reporter, of course, but they put me in the circulation department, where I had to take the money the newsboys collected, add it up, and get a balance. I never did get one. The head of the department kept muttering, "What's the good of a university education if you can't add nickels and dimes?"

When a school friend told me she was earning seventeen hundred dollars a year as a high school teacher, I enrolled at the Ontario College of Education, then taught for a year at Ingersoll Collegiate. In the fall, my father died, and I managed his manufacturing business until it was sold.

Next year, I was married to Keith Staebler and had to learn how to cook. One day, I made gorgeous dumplings; next time, when I'd invited my in-laws for dinner and wanted to show off, the dumplings dissolved in a mush. I learned to knit and sew my own clothes; I designed and watched the building of our house. I made frilly curtains for all the windows, braided a large living-room rug, hooked a mat. I went to meetings and parties and dances, acted in Little Theatre plays, lobbied to get women on public boards, did interviewing for the Gallup Poll so I could meet people outside my own social group, and found out that those in the lower income bracket were more interesting than those in the stereotyped middle where I was.

I read hundreds of books: novels, plays, biographies, and books about writing: Virginia Woolf, Mary Webb, Arthur Koestler, T.S. Eliot. Some of them expressed thoughts I'd had and I wondered, *Why didn't I write that?* And all the time I felt guilty as hell because I wasn't trying.

I wrote a couple of one-act plays that won contests, but most of the time I just woozled around, not knowing what to write about. Many people came into my life and a lot of things happened, but I lacked the confidence and the skill to tell about them. I knew no writers; there were no local colleges or universities where writing was taught.

When World War II started, my popular, talented, party-loving husband had a nervous breakdown. When the war ended, he was manic depressive, alcoholic, and having three sessions a week with a psychoanalyst – for fifteen years. I became deeply introspective and wrote my problems in my journal.

In the summer of '45, I visited my sister in Halifax and had a chance to drive 'round the Cabot Trail with a couple of her friends. Because they couldn't get accommodation in the posh Keltic Lodge, they turned around to go home. I didn't want to go with them. They left me in a bleak fishing village, where I found a room in the house of two spinsters and their senile mother. They gave me fried mackerel, old boiled potatoes, and turnip for dinner.

I walked up a hill to a point of land where I saw a white lighthouse. I sat in its shadow and looked past the wharves at the village – a strange collection of grey shingled fishing shacks and little wooden houses painted white, yellow, green, and faded brown; each with a gable pointed towards the bay, a wind-tilted little barn, and an outhouse. There were no hydro or telephone lines. I decided to leave Neil's Harbour as soon as I could find a way out of it.

I moved to the wharf and watched the fishermen land the day's catch of swordfish; I walked along the seaside road where the people I met said, "Good evening," and a male voice behind me murmured, "Hello, dear."

Next day, the fascination of the sea breaking on rocks and the promise of swordfishing kept me from leaving. Each day that followed, I said, "Tomorrow, tomorrow, tomorrow I'll leave." But one day I went out with the men in a snapper boat; on another I hitchhiked over the mountains to Cheticamp; every day I swam in the saltwater pond; I square-danced one night on the platform in front of the Orange Lodge Hall. I listened to the friendly people who spoke to me in their Newfoundland dialect and became so engrossed that I no longer worried about my problems at home. I stopped being introspective.

One evening, a fisherman I often talked to said, "You really loikes it 'ere, don't you?"

"I love it," I said, "I don't want to leave it."

"We men was sayin' t'other day, 'Seems just loike you be one of us.'" I turned my head to hide my grateful tears.

After I'd stayed two weeks in the village, I woke one morning and said to myself, *THIS IS IT! At last I have something to write about. I'm going to write a book about Neil's Harbour. It must have an interesting history, shipwrecks, treasure, I must learn about the different kinds of fishing.*

I stayed one more week and asked questions, took two hundred pages of notes.

I went home and started to work — and to realize that I didn't know a damn thing about writing. I couldn't just use a lot of adjectives and similes to make my reader experience what I felt as I watched the ever changing sea, the children who played on its shores, the conversations of the fishermen and their women.

Every day I sat in a corner of the chesterfield and wrote what I could remember. I was completely immersed and amazed at what seemed almost total recall. It would be time to make dinner on Friday afternoon, but I was in Neil's Harbour on a Tuesday morning watching a starfish in a shallow cove.

My mother kept saying, "Why waste your time? You can't be a writer, you have to have talent."

Then Dr. John D. Robins came into my life. Author of *The Incomplete Anglers* and head of the English Department and the library of Victoria College, U of T, he came to speak to the K-W Women's Canadian Club when I was president of it. I told him what I was trying to do, and whenever we could meet we talked about writing. He read what I'd written and wrote me encouraging letters. He said my book must be better than good and he knew I could do it.

Though I'd filled thousands of pages with typing, my husband said, "You're not a writer until you've had something published," and a neighbour said, "Put up or shut up."

I spent weeks writing a twenty-four-page story about my day's swordfishing and took it to *Maclean's* magazine. Scott Young bought it. Drastically cut, it was published in 1948.

W.O. Mitchell, then fiction editor of *Maclean's,* came to speak to the Canadian Club; he asked me to drop in to his office when I came to Toronto. When I appeared in his doorway, he was talking to his wife on the phone and said, "Merna, Edna Staebler has just come in, I'm bringing her home for the weekend." Wow! I went to Holt Renfrew's and bought a pair of pyjamas.

Bill took me to meet Pierre Berton, the new articles editor. Bill said, "This is the girl who wrote the swordfishing piece that was number one in the July issue. She lives in Mennonite country and I think she could write a piece for us about the horse and buggy people."

"Would you be interested?" Pierre asked me.

I told him I'd thought I might write about them someday, but I was working on a book about Neil's Harbour. After some discussion, Pierre said, "This would be a definite assignment. Send us an outline."

When we got out of his office, Bill said, "Edna, you've just been given an assignment by the leading magazine in Canada, on the strength of having written one piece. You don't say, 'I'm working on a book,' you get at it."

I went to the general store in St. Jacobs and asked the owner if she knew an Old Order family that might let me live with them and write about their strange, secret ways. I drove to the farm and persuaded the mother and daughter to let me stay. The husband, in the barn, agreed. He said, "You think you'll find out all about us but we'll find out just as much about you." I stayed with them for a week, living their way of life, and we all had a wonderful time. "You got a lot of Mennonite in you yet," the man said, and I hoped he meant I had some of their simplicity, their enthusiasm and independence.

Three weeks later when I sent in my story, Pierre returned it for a few minor changes. "Get everything in this paragraph into one sentence, but don't lose any of it," he wrote. I was lucky in having Pierre as my editor. He said because of my distinctive rhythm and style, no editor could change my work without having it show. Because I had to make my own fixes, he taught me much that I needed to know.

My Mennonite story won the Women's Press Club award of two hundred dollars, *Maclean's* sent me a huge box of flowers, I had to have my picture taken for the Canadian Press, strangers congratulated me. My mother said, "Of course you're not a real writer or it wouldn't take you so long." My husband said he only got his picture in the paper if he paid for an ad.

Scott Young called and told me I should join the Canadian Authors and go to their conference in London. I was thrilled. I was a Canadian author at last.

In the fall — before the award was announced — I spent two weeks in Saint Pierre—Miquelon and from there sailed to Newfoundland in a little coastal steamer carrying cattle. On the trip back to Halifax, the captain was drunk; the chef, wielding a straight razor, held three deckhands hostage in the wheelhouse; there was a fire in the engine room; and we were struck by the worst storm the crew had ever experienced. I was seasick. It took me three months to write the Saint Pierre story; the rest of the adventure was never recorded – but I often told it.

Maclean's sent me to Donnacona, Quebec, to go on a canal barge through the inland waterway to New York. Two of the crew were drowned in the Hudson River while I helplessly watched them disappear. I called *Maclean's* and asked if I should come home. They said, "Stay there and get your story."

Between *Maclean's* trips, I kept rewriting my Neil's Harbour book. In '47, '49, and '51, I returned to the village. The spinsters had found me a place to stay in the shingle house of a fisherman whose wife had had fourteen children with only seven still at home. The rest came to the kitchen every day to visit with their wives or husbands and children. I was accepted as one of the family. I sat on the wood box beside the large iron cookstove and listened and loved every minute that would enrich my book with the colourful language and stories I heard. Though based on fact, my book was not factual, but nor was it fiction. "Creative non-fiction," Dr. Robins called it. I changed the names of the people to give me greater freedom in writing their conversations. Because I never used a tape recorder and made notes only after I'd heard someone talk, I had to visualize and think myself into the person I wrote about as carefully and honestly as I could so there could be no denying or hurt feelings.

In my magazine work, Pierre said if I was so concerned about hurting people's feelings, I'd end up not being an honest reporter, but after living with families, they trusted me and I knew if I thought deeply enough, I should be able to show them and quote them so truthfully that when they read what I'd written they would say, "That's right, that's how it was, that's what I said."

One day, a friend who had written for *Maclean's* said to me, "I don't know why you take so long to do research. I just make a list of questions, ask for the answers, and write my story."

I couldn't be satisfied with that. I had to let people happen to me. Asking prepared questions presupposed answers, left no space for surprises and all those delightful things I learned when I came to know and love people. I never saw my friend's byline in *Maclean's* again, but she wrote books.

After five years of work on Cape Breton Harbour, I had filled a large carton with numerous drafts. I sent the manuscript to an *Atlantic Monthly* world competition for non-fiction and they congratulated me on its being a semi-finalist.

Bill Mitchell wanted me to submit it to Macmillan; his publisher, John Gray, took me to the King Edward Hotel for lunch. He told me the book was beautifully written, was sure to be published eventually, but in 1950 Canada was not yet ready for regional literature and the book would lose money.

Jack McClelland wanted me to introduce a love interest: girl goes to Cape Breton, falls for a fisherman: should she or shouldn't she? I said, "*No way*." Lippincott's asked me to come to New York to discuss publication; they wanted conflict – girl all screwed up goes to the village and comes home straightened out. Ryerson's editor, Lorne Pierce, said the book was too happy, people in fishing villages live squalid lives full of tragedy and I'd shown none of that.

I put the book in my filing cabinet for twenty-two years and thought of it as my writing apprenticeship. *Maclean's* kept enticing me to do more assignments. They sent me to Alberta, where I stayed in a Hutterite colony, ate boiled duck in the communal dining room, and slept under a goose-feather comforter in a bedroom with Katie and Annie Kleinsasser.

I wrote a piece for *Maclean's* about the great food I'd eaten when I lived with the Mennonites, one about Kitchener-Waterloo, and the farmers' markets.

In 1954, Keith announced that he was going with a friend to Florida to lie on a beach and drink beer. That was my chance to realize a lifelong dream of travelling in Europe. All the people I talked to said I must go on a tour as everyone did. I thought it would be too restricting. I sailed from New York on the Queen Elizabeth with no reservations ahead.

For three months, I wandered and marvelled: eight days in Paris, three weeks in Spain, the southern French coast, Italy, Switzerland, Austria, Germany, Holland, Belgium, and a month in England, Scotland, and Wales.

When I came home, I was asked by clubs and church groups to tell about my adventures. People said, "You must write a book." I said, "No. When I was in Europe I was constantly asked about Canada, and I wanted to write only about my own country."

I stayed on an Iroquois reservation. Enchanted by the imaginative stories the old chiefs told me, I came away with one hundred and sixty pages of notes. I wrote a history of Electrohome for the company, a piece about the Old Order Amish, one about Isle-aux-Coudres in the St. Lawrence River, and a deprived Negro community in Nova Scotia. Every piece I wrote had a personal story that was never written.

During fallow periods in my magazine writing, I edited a carton of my sister Ruby's letters. I showed them to Jack McClelland, but he said letters didn't sell and he wouldn't even publish Stephen Leacock's. I put Ruby's away in my filing cabinet.

In the winter of '60 to '61, while Keith was in an alcoholic rehab centre, I stayed in Neil's Harbour and wrote a story for *Chatelaine*. When I came home, I was told my college friend and confidant had persuaded my husband to marry her! She had been divorced with little alimony. I'd invited her and her two children to visit us at Sunfish. They stayed for three months. I got her a job and Keith drove her to work every day.

Divorces at that time weren't common. There was much talk and uncertainty. John Clare said, "Edna, you're a darn good writer, but don't count on making a living at it." I had nightmares of standing on a windy street corner, waiting for a bus to take me to a nine-to-five job. It was a helluva year. I wrote my misery in my journal. For the first time in my life, I was completely responsible for myself. I could no longer blame delay in my writing on Keith's binges. I'd been married twenty-eight years, had never lived alone, never paid household bills. At fifty-six, I thought I was old and probably couldn't make it on my own. But I had to.

The house and cottage were in my name. I would be getting enough alimony to live on if I was thrifty. I sold our townhouse for twelve thousand dollars, winterized the cottage, and wondered if the wooded hills at the end of Sunfish Lake would be the extent of my horizon.

Friends came to see me. Pierre and Janet and their six children and Pierre's mother came several times in a summer. So did other *Maclean's* editors, Sheila Burnford, and a male admirer. I was never lonely; I had two cats and a phone. There was always something to watch on the lake: ducks, geese, herons, small birds at the feeders, raccoons, squirrels, deer, the changing sky and the water. I was never bored.

I kept writing for *Maclean's* and *Chatelaine*. They had paid me one hundred and fifty dollars for my first story. Many pieces and twenty years later, I'd reached a peak of three hundred dollars. I always had to ask for an increase. In '87, when *Saturday Night* asked me to write about my involvement in the Great Cookie War, the editor apologized because they could pay me only three thousand dollars. The piece won a Canadian National Magazine Award and every year since there has been a fee for a movie option.

The most encouraging thing I can tell writers who come to me for advice is that I was sixty when my first book was published. For Canada's Centennial year, the k-w University Women's Club asked if I'd let them publish a book of my pieces about the local area. *Sauerkraut and Enterprise* sold ten thousand copies that year and Jack McClelland asked to reissue it.

Whenever the Bertons came to Sunfish, I cooked schnippled bean salad, schnitz pie, and other things I'd learned from Bevvy Martin. Janet would always say, "Why don't you write a cookbook?"

In 1966, I got a letter from Ryerson Press asking me to write a book on Mennonite cooking! I didn't think I knew enough, but I might as well try it.

The little handwritten cookbook that Bevvy loaned me had only lists of ingredients. I had to interpret "a pinch of this" and "a handful of that." My version was strictly personal: the book has almost as much writing as it has recipes. I called myself a culinary fraud.

Two years after I started, I delivered the manuscript to Ryerson. The editor assigned to it knew less about cookbooks than I did. She objected to the subject of a chapter I called "The Cities Built on Schmecks Appeal." "Too suggestive," she said. The book's title would be *Mennonite and Country Cooking*, she told me; the salesmen objected to my suggestion of *Food that Really Schmecks*. They were going to give the book a brown cover but changed it when I told them the only brown I associated with Mennonites were gravy and manure.

The book was an instant success. Edith Fowke called it folk literature. I got hundreds of fan letters. "Dear Edna," they said, "I love your cookbook and feel as though you are my friend. I like to read it in bed at night." Was I to blame for Canada's declining birthrate?

Four publishers wanted me to write another cookbook. Jack McClelland said, "Let's have another look at your Neil's Harbour book." By that time, the

Cabot Trail had been paved and half a million tourists were driving around Cape Breton. Jack read the book, said he would publish it but it would be more saleable if it were under two hundred pages. I worked willingly for a year on another revision. Experience had taught me a lot about writing and cutting since I'd put the book in a drawer.

But I had other problems. Sometimes I heard Neil's Harbour people use four-letter words that I never heard at home. Though used as functional words, not expletives, I wondered if I dared record them. Would my *Schmecks* fans object? After long pondering, I quoted a questionable word when I wrote about a young woman.

Molly sat on the cribbing of an old dock with her nine small children playing around her. She pulled her gum out of her mouth and folded it in again. Little Philip called, "Molly, here comes Lizzie Deaver."

"Whoi so she do," Molly greeted her friend with pleasure.

Lizzie, a stout young woman with a front tooth missing, kept covering her mouth with her hand. "I might go down to Sydney this fall," she said, "does you good to git away."

"Yes, it does," Molly agreed, "some toime Oi'd loike to leave keeds behind and go away for a whole week."

"Where to?" I asked.

Molly's eyes were full of dreams. "Oi'd loike to go to Ingonish and stay at the Keltic Lodge where the Goverman General was to."

Lizzie gasped, "Oh Molly, not with all them swells?"

"Whoi not?" Molly pulled out her gum. "They's only people, pisses same as we."

"Yes, but they pays twenty dollars a day just for what they eats," Lizzie said.

"Moi Gohd, ye'd have to eat a lot to git twenty dollars worth into ye, wouldn't ye now? What could they feed 'em would be worth twenty dollars?"

"Ain't got nothin' there we ain't got here, has they?"

Molly said, "Holy jumpin' Cheesus, Oi'd loike to go and foind out."

When I thought I had done my best with the book, Jennifer Glossop, an M&S editor, spent a whole day with me at Sunfish going over a long list of questions and suggestions to discuss with me. For three months after that, I did another revision and was thrilled with the way the book became truly creative.

Cape Breton Harbour was published in June, '72, given great reviews but no promotion at all except an interview with a man who flew over Toronto every morning in a helicopter and gave weather reports. Marketed only in Ontario and Nova Scotia, the book sold out two printings. Jack said he'd never let it be out of stock, but when Avie Bennett took over he dropped it.

McGraw-Hill's publisher said it was a classic and should never die. He reissued it in '90 but kept it a secret. Two years later he left the company, the book was remaindered, and I bought all the copies. What could I do with thirty-eight heavy cartons of books? I sent five hundred copies to Neil's Harbour High School, sold half of the rest to a bookstore in Tavistock, and some to Waterloo stores.

My Old Order Mennonite friend, Eva Bauman, said she'd like to sell them. One day in my car we drove to the little stores where the Mennonite farmers go shopping: in Wallenstein, Yatton, Conestogo, St. Clements. Eva did all the talking; she told the storekeepers that the book was really interesting and clean. That morning she sold ninety-eight books, and since then has sold several hundred at the farmers' market where she sells her maple syrup.

I made some new friends. Margaret Laurence stayed overnight with me when she was Writer-in-Residence at U of T and came to Waterloo to speak to the University Women's Club. She was very nervous about reading her fifteen-minute-long speech (the Club had expected an hour). We returned to the program convenor's house where we'd had dinner and were offered a liqueur. Margaret said, "Make mine a double Scotch."

At my house, we talked until four in the morning; Margaret's husband had asked her for a divorce so he could marry a Dutch woman who spoke little English, and Margaret thought that might be good because she couldn't upstage him.

Margaret came to Sunfish whenever she could, and when she left Elm Cottage in England and bought a cabin on the Otonabee River I visited her there. She was on the board of the Canada Council and wanted me to apply for a grant for *Cape Breton Harbour*. A grant seems to give books prestige – but I'd paid my own way to Neil's Harbour and didn't think I should ask for money that some writers really needed.

In 1975, when the Writers' Union was formed and had its first conference in Ottawa, Margaret insisted that I be there. It was a great experience for me. Besides learning a lot, I met writers I'd heard of and made friends of a few. Claire and Farley Mowat, Sylvia Fraser, Rudy Wiebe, Marian Engel, Harold Horwood. All but the Mowats have visited me at Sunfish.

Harold didn't think I should write another cookbook. He said, "If you do you'll be known as a cookbook writer, and you are a creative writer."

I had a lot of good recipes and anecdotes that weren't used in *Schmecks*. I thought I'd got the hang of writing a cookbook and a second one would be easy. But then I was afraid that people who had paid $6.95 for the first one might be disappointed if the second wasn't as good, and reviewers would say, "She did it once but she couldn't do it again."

I tried recipes and worked on *More Schmecks* intermittently for six years. When it was published in '79, it sold more copies than any other M&S book that year. I was sent on a coast-to-coast tour; I did hundreds of interviews and autographings. People who came to buy the book told me the philosophy and simplicity of *Schmecks* had changed their lives! I stopped feeling guilty about having written it instead of a novel which might have been mediocre and sold only two hundred copies. My *Schmecks* books made it possible for me to tell my lawyer I no longer needed alimony from my ex-husband.

From the time I first met him, Jack McClelland said that someday he'd publish my magazine articles. The book was called *Whatever Happened to Maggie* and later, when reissued by McGraw-Hill, *Places I've Been and People I've Known*. It met the same fate as *Cape Breton Harbour*.

Jack came to Sunfish and persuaded me to write a third cookbook. When *More Schmecks* was published, there were fifty-two pages left over because the girl who did the page count had forgotten to count the spaces. That was a good start for *Schmecks Appeal*, which was written in a year.

A few days after I returned from a trip to New Zealand, a lawyer from Toronto came to see me about the Great Cookie War between Procter & Gamble and Nabisco. More lawyers came from New York, Ottawa, and Washington. I was warned to have nothing to do with them, but I was curious and enjoyed our conversations when they took me to the best restaurants for dinner.

When the media discovered my involvement, there were pieces in the papers. *Morningside* paid me to come to Toronto to talk to Peter Gzowski; a reporter from the *Wall Street Journal* spent half a day at Sunfish; radio stations called me for interviews from Buffalo, Toronto, Memphis, Saskatoon, and San Diego, where the program was syndicated to twenty-nine countries around the world. A TV crew came to my cottage from the K-W station; *the fifth estate* filmed a session at Sunfish; the *Ontario Lawyer's Weekly* had a two-page spread; *Harper's* and *Forbes* business magazines in New York had long talks with me on the phone. *Saturday Night* asked me to write my story. The Ottawa lawyer took me and my niece to New York, where we stayed in a luxury suite in the Waldorf Towers, had a stretch limo and chauffeur at our disposal, and were entertained in the best restaurants and theatres. There was a dramatic homecoming; the Cookie War was settled out of court because of my cooperation, they told me.

In '90 and '91, I wrote a series of twelve little *Schmecks Appeal* books that were poorly marketed.

In '95, *Haven't Any News: Ruby's Letters from the Fifties* was published by Wilfrid Laurier University Press. After being in my filing cabinet for forty years, they had become social history and were much more interesting than when Jack turned them down. In the *Globe and Mail*, Margaret Laurence's daughter Jocelyn wrote a sparkling review. "Ruby burbles on about everything and nothing – her new clothes (never enough), her endless plans to make money (a worm farm was one), her attempts to draw and paint (look at it from a distance, she advises), the menopause (life is strange for we girls) – but thanks to the honesty and dancing energy of her writing, the account that emerges of the daily life of a fifties housewife in small-town Ontario manages to be funny, touching, and, most surprising of all, totally compelling."

I'd like to tell you about my sessions with all the photographers who have come to Sunfish to take pictures for magazine articles and TV crews who came for a whole day with vanloads of equipment to produce a half-hour profile or interview.

But I want to talk about my award – not awards that have been given to me, but one that I give every year for creative non-fiction, to bring encouragement and recognition to an unestablished Canadian writer. It must be a first or second book, have a Canadian location or significance, first-hand research, well-crafted interpretative writing, the writer's personal discovery or experience, and creative use of language or approach to the subject matter. It is administered by Wilfrid Laurier University.

Two of the winners were from Vancouver Island, Susan Mayse and Liza Potvin; then Marie Wadden from St. John's, Newfoundland; Linda Johns from Antigonish, Nova Scotia for *Sharing a Robin's Life*. Linda is an artist as well as a writer, and recently Laurier had an exhibition of her dynamic paintings and sculptures. Three of the winners live in Ottawa: Elizabeth Hay, Denise Chong for *The Concubine's Children,* and George Blackburn, the 1995 winner for his five-hundred-page book, *The Guns of Normandy*. At a meeting of the judges I said, "Do you think an eighty-year-old man is a beginning writer?" A few months later *The Guns of Victory* arrived, and this fall M&S will publish his third book!

As soon as I get home from here, I'll start reading three cartons of books that have been sent to Laurier for next year's three-thousand-dollar award.

Because I've lived so long, I could talk for hours about my life as a writer. So many wonderful people and things have happened to me. I'm constantly grateful. I love living at Sunfish Lake with my cat and all the friends and strangers who call on me there. I keep writing in my journal every morning in bed; I don't know why, but I seem to be compelled to record.

My great regret is that I haven't yet written some of the books that are in my head. Pierre is still waiting to read about Fred, Philip, and George, and a young woman who had many adventures in Canada and abroad. Professors at both Waterloo universities keep urging me to write memoirs. At the University of Guelph, with my literary papers, there is a carton of loose leaves from eighty years of my journal, and copies of letters I wrote to lovers and friends. The last time I was on *Morningside*, Peter talked about books I should write. I said, "Peter, I'm not immortal." And he said, "Edna, how do you know?"

Finally now, I'll read from my favourite of my twenty-one books.

Tonight as I sat on a fence rail with the sea moving near me . . . Old John Clipper came limping along with his cane, his cap rakishly on one side of his head. "You always writin', ain't you?" he said. "Must be noice to write."

He looked wistfully at my notebook. "Never could figure out how people done it." He examined a page. "All them little marks got meanin' to 'em, ain't they?" he said. "Hit's a funny thing," he raised his cap and scratched his scalp, "first they's in your haid, then you puts 'em on paper, someone else sees 'em and if they can read they gits 'em in their haid. That way anybody can git the same thing you got." Old John nodded, limped away slowly, then turned to call back to me, "Guess people needs be awful perticler what they writes."

1998
AL PURDY

I grew up in a small town, Trenton, Ontario, on the Bay of Quinte. Across the road from the red brick house in which my mother and I lived (my father had died when I was two years old), there was a pumpmaker's workshop. In a dark cave of slapping pulleys that smelled like a cedar forest, he made wooden pumps for farmers' wells. Farther down the street was a blacksmith's workshop. And in winter the nearby Trent River became a highway for sledloads of ice, great blocks of it, hauled by jingling draft horses from Quinte, stored and preserved with sawdust to await the housewives' summer.

In winter I played pickup hockey on river and bay. Sometimes at night in zero weather I listened to ice splitting beneath my feet from the cold, the sound like a memory of the last ice age.

At Trenton Collegiate I wrote poems and played football. A poor student, I read books in classroom when I should have been doing schoolwork; and my poems were worse than any I have seen since. Bliss Carman was the principal influence, and it took years to break myself of the deadly rhyme and iambic habits. I failed grade ten exams, but stayed in school another year to play football, and spent the next two years doing very little. My mother, of course, worried about me.

In the spring of 1936, at age seventeen, I was bored enough with Trenton to start hitchhiking west to Vancouver. My ostensible object was to get a job on a fishing boat, seiner or gillnetter, earn a lot of money, and gradually the problems of being young would solve themselves.

My mother objected to this western jaunt, but felt helpless to do anything about it. I left Trenton with a full quota of equipment, money inside the rubber ankle patch of running shoes, extra shorts, razor and shaving cream, also a hunting knife; an assortment of mostly useless stuff, considering the mode of travel. That first day in early June, I got as far west as Toronto, then north to Barrie, sleeping in a bandstand beside Lake Simcoe. At midnight the local cops roused me, not ungently, escorting me to the hoosegow, where I spent the rest of the night. In Sudbury, a used car lot provided sleeping accommodations.

At Sault Ste. Marie, a serious problem: no more highway. The Trans-Canada was then in process of construction. It ended at a small village called Searchmont, in the middle of the northern wilderness. Searchmont was also a water stop for freight trains heading northwest (this was before the advent of diesel engines). Around midnight I boarded a flat car (in railway terms, a gondola) that had previously carried coal, curled up in a corner, and went to sleep. Sometime in the night it began to rain. Waking up in the grey morning found me miserably wet and cold, despite a waterproof windbreaker. I had no idea where I was. All around were silent rows of boxcars, a slow drizzle of rain still falling. (Later on I found out the place was called Hawk Junction, a divisional point where trains changed engines.)

I climbed down from the flat car with canvas duffle bag, wet and uncomfortable, resolved to escape the rain. A closed boxcar nearby seemed a likely shelter, but it had a thin strip of metal encircling the door mechanism. I cut it off with my hunting knife and yanked at the closed door. It refused to budge. I yanked and tugged some more, without result. The train just lay there quiescent, although I expected it would soon be continuing its western journey. But there were no empty boxcars, no shelter from the rain. Discouraged, I went back to my empty flat car, deciding to wait there till something happened.

A railway cop happened. He appeared above the car's low railing, in glistening slicker, beckoning to me resignedly. "Come along with me." I was locked up in what appeared to be a conductor's caboose, the last car on a freight train. The side door was padlocked on the outside, windows broken but secured with heavy strips of iron. By this time my mental condition could be described as disturbed without any exaggeration.

The cop reappeared around noon. He escorted me across the tracks to a small frame house, where I sat down to lunch with his wife and daughter. This reassured me. Obviously a guest of the family, I thought my offence couldn't be a very serious one. Back at the prison caboose (my hunting knife confiscated), I asked my host about the legal penalties for my crime. He glanced at me quizzically. "Ripping the seal off a boxcar, you could get two years."

I was terrified. Jail was a disgrace as well as imprisonment; besides, what would my mother say?

I explored that caboose from end to end, blood pounding in my head and hands trembling. It had served as a jail before now and probably would again. The wooden door that opened inside rattled when I yanked at the doorknob. Half an hour must have gone by while I cudgeled my brain for escape ideas.

The door's hinge keys were outside, and therefore not removable. But the door latch released enough to open it a fraction before the outside hasp and padlock brought it to a stop. I ran my fingers upward along the narrow springy opening between upper door and sill, squeezing them through, and clasped around the door. Holding onto the door near the top, I swung myself off the floor until my feet were opposite my hands, and hung there like a six-foot clothespin. I yanked and hauled at that door until the top of it bent inward under my fingers. There was a ripping sound, and quite abruptly I was flat on my back.

The screws had torn out of the wood, releasing the outside hasp and padlock. I stayed on the floor, breathless and scared, hoping no one had heard the noise. And the boy who was not exactly me, but wasn't not-me either, peered out into brilliant sunlight.

Early Sunday afternoon, not a sound in the small railway town. No blue uniforms in sight, nothing but rows of brick-red boxcars marching off backward and forward. I dropped onto the cinders, hoisting the nearly empty duffle bag over my shoulder, and started to walk. But no more freight trains and railways cops for me. I was heading back to Sault Ste. Marie, one hundred sixty-five miles south.

I slunk along close to the boxcars, ready to duck between them if anything moved. People must be avoided; anyone catching a glimpse of me would report a gangling youngster with a suspicious manner to the police. But after a mile or so of boxcars, a few scattered houses, then a railway bridge over a wide river, I felt more comfortable.

South of the bridge, I began to think about food, something to eat later. I took a chance, knocked on the door of an isolated house, asked if I could buy some sandwiches. The housewife made me up a big package, and seemed surprised when I gave her a dollar.

The railway cop's estimate of my jail sentence began to din in my ears again: two years locked up somewhere. I held a conference with myself, deciding to follow the railway tracks from a distance of thirty or forty feet inside the bush, thus avoiding possible observers. But after an hour of traversing the forest's spongy floor, I headed back for the tracks again. They weren't there. And I couldn't find them. Without knowing it, I'd wandered deep into the bush, and hadn't the least idea how to get out. Everything, everywhere looked exactly the same.

I was lost, and it was the most terrifying experience in my life up to that point. I started to run, mindlessly, as if being pursued, scratching my hands on bushes, breath whistling in my throat. No longer able to even think, hot and sweating, I ran uphill and down, splashing through shallow creeks, scarcely noticing them, mind gone completely blank.

That race through the Algoma bush was impossible to sustain. Panting, legs buckling under me, I collapsed to the ground, tears streaming from my eyes, sweat pouring from my face . . . That night I slept with my body curled around a hillside tree, in a nearly fetal position. And woke to look round in horror at the bad dream of the forest. And pissed while still lying on my side.

That day, I made a strong effort to be rational, to walk in only one direction, and return to the railway tracks. I heard yard engines shunting back and forth at the divisional yards, but the sound seemed to come from nowhere and everywhere. A rotting structure of logs, which I took to be an old hunting camp, was encountered three times; I had been walking in circles. Once I thought I saw a bear, a hunched dark figure slipping between the trees.

I began to think of God, a possible someone in whom I had never fully believed, but whose non-existence was equally impossible to disbelieve. On the second day of being lost, I was still terrified but able to keep it under control and avoid complete despair. And I prayed, with a fervency entirely outside my character, knowing it was extremely probable that my bones would remain in the bush.

It began to rain. Not heavily, but with a persistence that after a few hours amounted to a downpour. I wore a waterproof windbreaker, but my pants were soaked. The June air was brisk, though not extremely cold. I stood under a tree, watching a silver mist that enveloped the landscape. My mind was dull, thought difficult. I couldn't stay on any subject more than a few moments.

Staring at the dark grey sky, trying to find a brighter spot with the sun behind it, hence some idea of the direction I was taking or not taking. I climbed trees several times, but it was hard to find one that reached high enough over the forest ceiling. Then a thought formed in my head: two sides of an equilateral triangle, the river and the railway tracks: they were two-thirds of a triangle. High school geometry was some use after all.

Exactly how I did it is now beyond memory. I kept sighting on trees, and any other possible landmark in order to walk in one direction. My pace had increased again until I was almost running, and I had to slow down before exhaustion.

After only an hour or so, I burst through some bushes and nearly drowned myself in the wide deep river; then I followed the river back to the railway tracks. So simple. When a train stopped to pick up some fishermen, I was hiding behind the trees, and thought, *To hell with cops.* I rode behind the coal car, apparently unobserved, all the way into Sault Ste. Marie; then headed for a steam bath to boil the shivering ache from my bones.

A lifetime often feels like a century of instants. For three years in the mornings of summer, I rode the trains west. Memories of the shape and configurations of the country underlie all my succeeding recollections. There are mountains in the mind that resemble the B.C. mountains. And standing halfway up the sky near Field, B.C., looking down on a dozen branches of the moonlit Kicking Horse River in late summer when I was working for the CP Railway helping to clear a landslide, and the silver river landscape suddenly replaced everything else.

And riding the trains at night across the dark prairie, perspective reversed itself, and small towns seemed to be moving and the train standing still: the towns passed us like moving ships on the dark prairie, blazing with lights.

I spent nearly six wartime years in the RCAF. I quote Pierre Trudeau, who quoted someone else whose name I forget: those six years were "the best of times and the worst of times." I hated every minute of it, but oddly enough I like to remember bits and pieces of that old chronology.

I met my wife, Eurithe, during the earliest days of my Air Force stint. And after a disciplinarian training course in Ottawa, I was promoted to Acting Corporal, then Acting Sergeant in charge of the guard at Picton RCAF base. This guard was entirely composed of future air crew awaiting openings at their training schools. After just a few weeks at Picton I was brought up on charge of dereliction of duty (I was asleep when supposed to be awake) before a squadron leader at Trenton Air Base. It seemed the Hitler war effort was about to go down the drain because of the abject failure of Acting Sergeant A. Purdy.

Hatless and standing at rigid attention, flanked by an armed guard, I stood quaking, awaiting my condign punishment. And the gold braid slowly raised its head; from its mouth issued the voice of Moses on the mountain: "Reduced in rank to Acting Corporal."

Lo and behold, it was so.

As Corporal of the Guard, I encountered fame in the person of John Gillespie Magee, an American air crew candidate in the RCAF. He'd written a poem called "High Flight," which received more than a modicum of media attention. I made a point of meeting him, and shyly let it be known that I wrote poems too. He was then an Aircraftman Second Class, lowest of the low, but probably about to become an officer, as designated by the white flashing of his wedge hat. Whereas I would remain a corporal forever (but even that supposition was wrong).

Magee was young, slender, quite handsome I thought, wearing a small moustache. Under those circumstances it was impossible that we should be more than passing acquaintances. But I've often thought about the opening lines of his poem:

> O I have slipped the surly bonds of earth
> And danced the sky on laughter-silvered wings . . .

In the summer of '41, my superiors decided that I might make a pilot myself, or navigator or tail gunner, given proper training. I took the medical twice, and both times my blood pressure shot up as high as an eagle can spit. I was excited at the idea of hobnobbing with Billy Bishop and the Red Knight of Germany's ghost. Sadly, the realization was brought home to me: *Shit, now I'll never be able to slip the surly bonds of earth.*

All that summer I'd been going out with Eurithe, but only intermittently. A couple of other girls were also among those present. I pursued all of them, earnestly and hopefully, without success except for smooching in parked cars. Then Eurithe left town, having procured a job as waitress in Niagara Falls. Absence did make the heart grow fonder: bright lights flickered over my Ford coupe, smote me in both torso and nether regions: I was in love, or a reasonable facsimile thereof. I drove to Niagara Falls on a forty-eight-hour pass, talked and smooched some more. And slept in a nearby farmer's field.

When Eurithe returned next weekend to her home in Belleville, I was Corporal of the Guard that night and couldn't escape my bounden duty. It preyed on my mind. Just a word from the lady would ease my inner hunger. I drove the guard panel truck to Belleville, nine miles away, wearing full regalia of webbing and sidearms. Nobody stopped me at the station gate or said: "Nay, Corporal Purdy, thou mayest not desert thine assigned post – even now at this fateful moment, sixteen German saboteurs are crawling through the grass at Trenton Air Base's outer periphery." Nobody said that.

Ann Street, Belleville, around 1 a.m. I threw small stones at her window, shouted in my softest baritone whisper. She came. And bliss was that night to be alive.

There were repercussions, of course. I can't remember all the charges brought against me, but they were multiple. The guard unit's Officer Commanding had been a school teacher before the war. His face remained entirely expressionless while speaking; and from what I'd heard of him previously, no flicker of intelligence was ever known to have touched his countenance.

This time I was knocked down to LAC, which is the rank of Leading Aircraftman. I didn't lead long. Successive demotions brought me down even lower. It's hard to imagine what depths I might have plumbed if the war hadn't ended first. Weeks later, when I was finally allowed off the air base, I encountered a very drunken civilian. He looked at me sneeringly, despising all uniforms. I saluted him.

After the war came several years in a Belleville taxi business. Then Eurithe and I returned to Vancouver. In 1950, I was the lowest paid employee of Vancouver Bedding on Clark Drive. I wrapped mattresses and box springs, and piled them higher than my head. When orders came, I slid them down a hardwood chute to the shipper one floor below.

There were several machines in that factory, each requiring different techniques to operate, each with a different personality. Personality? Well, it seemed to me they did possess such human characteristics. The roll-edge machine consisted of a waist-high table and a hunchback grey machine that clattered around the table on steel rails. The operator inserted a mattress edge into the machine's jaws with an ice pick; a big needle stitched the roll-edge, closing steel jaws narrowly missing the operator's fingers.

I learned to run that machine during noon break, given hints by Doug Kaye, a recent employee. And I walked backwards all day long, pursued by a hunchback machine that nipped my fingers occasionally while I dreamed poems.

Doug Kaye had come to Vancouver Bedding a few months after my own arrival. A slightly built man, ex-seaman in the merchant marine, seemingly very calm and self-possessed, he had introduced a union into Restmore Mattress, and hence became very unpopular with that concern.

Curt Lang was a precocious sixteen-year-old I met at a science-fiction fan club gathering; and Curt could talk the pants off an argumentative theologian. Doug Kaye had some pretensions to culture; he was taking violin lessons. The three of us met on weekends, with two wives in attendance (Curt hadn't achieved one at his age); we talked, played records, drank beer sometimes, and pretended to be intellectuals.

Also among friends of this period were Steve McIntyre, Alex LaFortune, Wayne Thompson, and Raymond Hull. McIntyre owned a used bookstore, smoked continual cigarettes, dispensed behind-the-counter beer to his friends, and talked great literature when in the mood. He was regarded as something of an oracle by his listeners. Alex LaFortune was a blonde Toronto poet who had hitchhiked to Vancouver. Wayne Thompson was a part-time book scout; Ray Hull, a dour ex-Englishman who eventually joined typewriters with a UBC prof to write a book called *The Peter Principle*.

On one memorable occasion, McIntyre's literary lectures and personal opinions had a strong effect on me. Perched on a high stool behind the counter and partly concealed by wispy clouds of cigarette smoke, he said, "Purdy, you ain't read nothin' yet." This unflattering judgment festered in my head a few days, then sent me to the Vancouver Public Library in search of Thomas Mann, Dostoevsky, Proust, Virginia Woolf, and several others. As a result, I still have literary indigestion at times.

This was the mix of personalities with whom I interrelated during those Vancouver years, and who provided some of the stimulus and chemicals whereby my mind turned itself inside out. And the question still haunts me slightly: *Why me?* Despite knowing some of the reasons, I still wonder why the doggerel I wrote changed to a different kind of doggerel. And more pretentiously, why did the African australopithecines, the human precursors, change and become *Homo erectus* and finally *Homo sapiens?* And there I was, reading Dylan Thomas on the interurban going to work in the morning, keeping my eyes peeled in case any attractive female might be noticing my cultural proclivities.

As well, I was reading W.B. Yeats, Eliot, Oliver St. John Gogarty (what a name), Ezra Pound, and above all D.H. Lawrence. Except Lawrence kinda snuck up on me a few years later. I was imitating everybody I admired, and getting a helluva kick out of it. But under all the pretension and literary doubletalk, I knew my stuff was mediocre, even though I concealed this hurting knowledge deep inside under several self-protective layers of psyche. You can't fool yourself about that; at least I couldn't.

At the mattress factory, I progressed from wrapping table to roll-edge, filler (for cheaper mattresses), tape-edge, and tufting machines, with consequent hikes in the weekly stipend. If Doug Kaye hadn't talked me into the idea of installing a union into the factory (he didn't have the seniority if he did it himself, and would've been fired), I might have ended up factory manager. However, that's extremely unlikely.

After the union got going, I became shop steward, then recording secretary of the Vancouver Upholsterer's Union, when they discovered I could read. But after a few weeks of both those duties I decided I was working much too hard, and quit both jobs. And like Doug Kaye, I was now extremely unpopular with management because of the union. So I quit that job too, and went to Europe.

On the way there I stopped in Montreal, and slept on Irving Layton's studio couch in the living room. Sissy-Boo and Maxie, the two Layton kids, kept hitting me up for dimes, then quarters.

I escaped them, and sailed for Liverpool on the liner *Ascania*. In Paris a friend of Curt's joined us. We spent our first evening in the City of Light discussing possible philosophic or sanitary uses of the strange object in the bathroom, which the management called a bidet. Later I found these odd ceramic creatures all over Europe, and thus capable of procreation.

We moved to Montreal after my return, having previously scraped acquaintance with Frank Scott, Ron Everson, Louis Dudek, etc. in that city. My first play had been produced in Toronto a year before, and I settled down to write some more. Eurithe got herself a secretarial job with the CP Railway in order to support me, as was her bounden duty.

We stayed in Montreal two years; then my sixty-year-old mother began having some health problems. Eurithe and I moved back to Trenton, Ontario to see if we could be of any help. But there were slightly uncomfortable feelings in someone else's house, so we made a big decision: we decided to build our own house.

A couple of weeks were spent driving all over the Trenton-Belleville area, searching for a reasonably priced building lot. We found one on Roblin Lake in Prince Edward County. Our total wealth then was about twelve hundred dollars, the proceeds from a couple of play sales to CBC and Eurithe's CPR savings. The price of the lot was eight hundred dollars, on which the down payment was three hundred dollars, leaving us nine hundred dollars for living expenses, building materials, and gas for the old red Chevy.

Away from Montreal, our combined incomes amounted to virtually nothing. A trickle of money came our way from my reading of other people's radio plays for CBC producers (five bucks for each play is a "trickle"). Then we got lucky. The federal building in Belleville was being torn down, the demolition providing us with used lumber, wallboard, and hardwood flooring at reasonable prices.

Both of us were babes-in-the-woods where house-building was concerned. I could saw a board and pound a nail; Eurithe about the same. We bought concrete blocks for the foundation (imperfect ones called "seconds"), poured concrete for the "footing" (twenty feet by thirty in the days before metrics), and disagreed about nearly everything. Plans for the A-frame house came from one of those *House Beautiful* magazines, adapted and enlarged to suit our own needs.

All summer and fall of 1957, we worked at the house. Four-foot walls supported A-frame roof rafters, which soared seventeen feet above the floor. Those rafters gave me a lot of trouble, sawing them at the right angle in order to have two of them meet and join like lovers. And later, I felt like a retarded mountain goat while climbing that hair-raising roof.

During the first winter, our new-old house had only tarpaper-covered wallboard for siding. Heating was supplied by a nearly worn-out cookstove, its fuel scrap lumber and some precious hardwood blocks. The chimney was a stovepipe which exited from the wall of our tiny flat-roofed kitchen. During really cold nights we had to set the alarm clock for every three hours in order to wake up and stoke the stove: water would freeze a few feet away from it. And we huddled in bed, hugging each other for warmth.

House lighting was three oil lamps, and you needed all three to read a book. I chopped holes in the lake ice for water: in March the ice was more than three feet thick. Standing above those funnel-shaped holes with axe in hand, stripped to the waist in zero weather but dripping sweat, I had as much sense of my own identity as I've ever had before or since. It was like a name moving in my blood.

When our money ran out in 1958, those were the "bad times" of our lives. I worked at whatever jobs I could find: gathering old iron for sale to the Belleville junkyard; selling grounder apples in north Hastings County; both of us toiling at Mountainview Canning Factory; doing just about anything to raise a few bucks. A couple of times I can remember a neighbour giving us road-killed rabbits.

On one occasion, Eurithe and I with our twelve-year-old son rummaged the nearby Mountainview RCAF garbage dump for anything useful – and nearly everything was. We found large quantities of discarded Air Force emergency rations in little tinfoil envelopes, powdered eggs and milk, dehydrated fruit, and other perfectly edible stuff. (I had spent nearly six years in the RCAF and never eaten this kind of thing before.) We picked up boxes made of quarter-inch plywood, and partly-used cans of red and black paint. The boxes were disassembled, fitted onto the living room floor, then painted like a checkerboard in red and black. Our artwork now reposes quietly under hardwood flooring that came originally from a Belleville high school gymnasium.

My mother died in 1958. Speaking with the United Church minister before the funeral service, I'd been unwise enough to mention that I wasn't a very religious person. At the funeral chapel with my relatives in attendance, the sonuvabitch preached his eulogy for my mother directly at my own ears, a tirade condemning atheists and unbelievers. I raged at him silently.

My mother's strong impression for years was that her only son was a spend-thrift, and would waste her money in riotous living. Therefore, her last will and testament left her money in the permanent keeping of the Victoria & Grey Trust Company of Belleville. In case of need, I was to receive an allowance for medical expenses (this was before Medicare). I convinced her to change that will, but after she died the trust company was obdurate and would not relin-quish the money.

The Trenton lawyer I'd secured was a complete flop, and could do nothing. After nearly five years I asked Frank Scott in Montreal for the name of a good lawyer. Scott proposed Andrew Brewin of Toronto. Brewin, of course NDP, then entered federal politics and was elected. He delegated Ian Scott, a young man in his office, to take over. Scott and I attended a hearing before a Belleville judge; he ruled in my favour. The will was probated: Eurithe and I breathed more freely.

Years later, I was at the Ontario Legislative Buildings in Toronto to receive an award. Ian Scott, then Attorney General of Ontario, was also present. We ran into each other, and he said, "Do you remember me?" I said, "Hell, yes. You saved my life." Well, he did, almost.

It seems I have always written poems. They reflect and refract and some-times even distort my thinking. Writing them is an addiction for me, just as much as marijuana or any other drug. The constants in my life have been my wife — and writing poems. And there is such pleasure in knowing other people, the infinite variety of human character. Also such impure delighted pleasure from delving into unknown places in your own mind. How surprising is what you may find there! It's a journey and a search when you arrive, a gift from yourself to yourself.

In Vancouver in the early 1950s, when I was about thirty-two or thirty-three, there was one moment when I came close to realizing that I'd been writing drivel most of my life. I say "close to realizing"; but not quite. If I had known exactly how good I was not, the knowledge might have been too much for me to endure about myself. But I did know I wasn't as good as I had thought myself previously; and had entirely misjudged both myself and the world around me. As a result of this half-awareness, I started to change, being very much aware of myself changing. In other words, there was one luminous moment . . .

In the Christian Bible, I think there is one passage where St. Paul or some other disciple of Christ was on the road to Damascus and had a revelation. Now, I am not in the least religious; in fact, I haven't even bothered trying to find the relevant passage. But the parallel seems obvious to me: there was one luminous moment when everything became different.

Perhaps this memory from the past is a legacy from the time when I was a pimpled adolescent, and was reading the Bible for the obviously sexual passages. But that's all right, for it doesn't really matter, and makes the parallel both real and fictional in my mind. However, the reasons why I was changing do seem important to me, for the process has continued into my old age. Many of us have felt that same moment in themselves, and don't know why. I didn't either. Maybe the people I met in Vancouver were my personal reason. Perhaps Steve McIntyre and his under-the-counter beer. Maybe John Gillespie Magee, who "slipped the surly bonds of earth," and died in the last great war.

Anyway, it's what I wait for still, the luminous moment. It's what we're all waiting for.

I am delighted to have been asked to give this lecture in honour of Margaret Laurence. We had three important things in common, she and I: gender, profession, and provenance — we both grew up on the prairie. I met her only once, at a Writers' Development Trust dinner where unfortunately we had no chance to talk. I admired her greatly. She wrote both well and very well, and she had something to say — something immensely valuable for women, and immensely valuable for men. What higher praise can I give?

But to address "A Writer's Life" — the title given me for my talk tonight — is, for various reasons, far from easy. To begin with, although I have been writing since I was a child, it is only within the last year or so that I have owned to the title of "writer." It was the day the surveyor for the city directory came to the door. To her inquiry as to my profession, I said, "Housewife." "Why didn't you say you were a writer?" my husband asked. "Well, you know how doubtful I feel about my own work. It makes me uneasy claiming to be a writer." He gave me a sharp look and said, "She didn't ask you to say you were a *good* writer."

At that moment I realized that, good or bad, I was, in fact, a writer, and that I had been for perhaps sixty-five years. Even so, I still have difficulties. The word "writer" surely means "one who writes." And I have spent most of my life not writing. Also, I am far from sure that I am the perpetrator of my own work. By that I don't mean I plagiarize — consciously, at least. But I do feel, as many writers do, that I am a vehicle, a channel for something that writes through me — badly sometimes, better at others. I cannot write if "it" does not write me. I remember many years ago bumping into an old friend. "What are you writing?" he asked. "I'm not writing," I replied. "You mean you have given up poetry?" "No, poetry has given up me." "Are you telling me that you are not the master?" he asked. "Nor mistress," I replied. And that is still true with poetry. Less true with prose. I think I could guess the poets who would disagree with me.

So much for the "writer" side of the title. But "life" . . . How do I tackle "life"? The fact is, we live not one life but many, and this creature that answers to my name is not single, not simple, but multiple – a crowd. As well, the mind's eye is far from an accurate glass. When I recall my teenage years, I see myself as solitary against the dun-colored prairie where, from June to September, we pitched our tents and camped, swam in the muddy waters of the Elbow River, and rode our horses into the foothills. My memory of the locale is accurate. But was my youthful figure so isolated? I think not. My parents encouraged children to be both seen and heard, and I recall no short-age of friends. Yet my essential self, the self concerned with rhythms and beats, was solitary and seldom shown until, summer ended, I returned to the city and the one friend who shared my interest in the arts.

We heard Debussy's *La Mer* in our heads as we cycled to school, pulled anguished faces at each other as her mother sang "Trees," and spent hours poring over art books in the Calgary Public Library. There was not a wide selection, but because we had no idea of what could be available, it never occurred to us that we were deprived. Epstein's break with realism – contrasted with the high romanticism of the Pre-Raphaelites – set up a curious counterpoint.

I remember the near-spell laid upon me by the reproduction of Dante Gabriel Rossetti's *How They Met Themselves* – a painting of a young couple in a wood face to face with their clones; and the shock of recognition when I read his "Sudden Light," with its lines:

> *I have been here before*
> *But when or how I cannot tell . . .*

Is there a built-in apparatus that selects whatever one needs for one's own particular nourishment and development? Or is this as naive a question as that of the child who wanted to know why the kitten's eyes were exactly behind those two little slits in its face?

I am grateful to have grown up in an age when Grimm, Andersen, Perrault, and the *Arabian Nights* were not considered too frightening for children. These tales must have laid a basis for my continuing acceptance of worlds other than this immediately tangible one – worlds where anything is possible – where one can defy gravity, become invisible, pass through brick walls. What appear as surrealist images in my work may stem from listening to such tales, and from my subsequent belief in the possible infiltration into our three-dimensional world of our brothers, the gods. The content of folklore may well be metaphysics.

Talking to a young man at a party one night, when I said it was time I went home, he asked, "How do you plan to go?"

"Oh, dematerialize and then teleport myself," I replied.

"But *you* can't say that," he exclaimed, "you belong to a generation of rationalists."

So much for labels.

I am reminded of a story in which an old lady was going from London to Edinburgh by train with her turtle. On a previous trip with her dog, she had had to buy a dog ticket. When she approached the ticket seller, she asked if she would have to buy a dog ticket for her turtle. "Oh, no, Ma'am," he replied. "Dogs is dogs and cats is dogs and rabbits is dogs. A squirrel in a cage is parrots. But turtles is insects and we don't charge for those."

But to get back to adolescence, when my conscious interest in poetry began. I see myself as a body of land struggling to emerge from an infinite surround of ocean. A sleeping land that moved about in its sleep.

> heave me
> lift me
> out of this undreamed
> amorphous mound
> where who knows who lies sleeping
> my me I
> hidden

unbidden still

undead unborn

utterly unimaged even

leaven me

In these lines from a poem written many years later, I was trying to recapture something of the feeling of that period. (Trying to recapture? Is that what I really mean? It is not the way poems are made — not mine, at any rate. How, then, since we are on the subject, are poems made? With me they start, not so much from thoughts or emotions, as from a given line or rhythm, occasionally a form. How they go on — or don't! — is another matter.)

I am sure that nobody, least of all myself, knew that while I played basketball and tennis, passed exams and wrote poems, I was — as it were — underwater, asleep; or that my real business, the serious work I was intent upon — albeit subliminally — was that of awakening, surfacing, presenting my small sea-drenched island to the sun. For what purpose? Stonecrop? Vegetable marrow? A grove of palms? How could I foresee the use I would put it to?

This struggle to emerge continues still and will continue, I imagine, as long as I do. But whereas now, the thought of emergence is relatively conscious, in adolescence it was undefined. The poetry, of course, was part of the struggle. The rhythms and beats, the inexpressible longings, the love poems — oh, to whom? — were all part of the "upward anguish"; while the good serve at tennis, when I achieved it, or the high mark in algebra, occurred in the world of my daylight self.

Looking back at that period of my life from this vantage point, I would say that the right hemisphere of my brain — the dreaming, intuitive, creative hemisphere — was battling with a system of education intent upon developing the rational, logical, lineal left.

Calgary, in the years I grew up, was a sportsman's town. Many of my parents' friends were ranchers who came to town on horseback. One friend of my mother's, impeccably habited, and mounted side-saddle, would arrive for afternoon tea with a gift of a live chicken struggling in a burlap bag. It wasn't until many years later in Mexico that I received a similar gift — this time presented by the mother of a girl who worked for us and whom we had saved from a ruptured appendix. The mother had travelled countless miles by crowded bus, with her laying hen and her *setesima*. A *setesima* is a seven-month baby. The fact that a premature child can survive in primitive conditions is so extraordinary that its very presence confers good luck on all who encounter it. I was ill in bed at the time, and before I knew what had happened I found the broody hen, the baby and I were all snuggled down between the sheets.

But to go back. The Calgary of the late '20s and early '30s seemed hardly conducive to fostering artists, yet it produced the painter Maxwell Bates. His parents and mine were friends and spent many winter evenings wood-carving, taking their designs from art nouveau magazines. Within my home circle, as with the prairie landscape, shapes and their relation to space were an unspoken part of my life. As I wrote much later, thinking of the prairie:

> *One's self the centre of a boundless circle*
> *So balanced in its horizontal plane*
> *And sensitively tuned that one's least move*
> *Could fractionally tip it east, north, south.*
> *Westward, in undulations of beige turf*
> *The fugal foothills changed their rhythms, rose*
> *To break in fire and snow. My Hindu Kush.*

One was indeed smacked by infinity's vast hand.

Adolescence, that great releaser of hormones, must also be blamed for masses of bad poems. Mine were mainly about suffering. As I think of it now, I had little to suffer about except, I suppose, the turbulence that goes with one's teens. Unlike many of my writing friends, I had no reason to complain about my parents. They both came from families that had produced artists and writers and they, themselves, were artists *manqués*. They encouraged me, urged me to send poems to whatever magazines might print them. When I actually had a poem accepted, I took immediate refuge in my initials, P.K., for fear that my school friends would recognize me. It has been suggested that I chose initials to hide my gender. Not true. At that point I was far too unobservant and unworldly to have taken in that most published writers were men – a fact that only crashed through to me much later. But I did know that writing poetry simply wasn't done! Eating with your knife was preferable.

At seventeen, my schooling behind me, I had no intention of going on to university. I was not a student. Curiously, almost no literature had fired my imagination. But that is not entirely the case. Did I not give a speech in grade nine about Ernest Thompson Seton's animal stories? And do I not vaguely remember poems by Pauline Johnson, Marjorie Pickthall, and Drummond? All of them in subject matter no less foreign to me than Keats's "Ode to a Nightingale" and nowhere near as full of wonder as those "magic casements opening on the foam" or Coleridge's "caverns measureless to man." It was not that I had read nothing – I had read omnivorously, Gene Stratton-Porter, Hugh Walpole, Charles Morgan, endless historical romances – but I had no idea of the flavor of contemporary writing until I found myself in England with a membership in Boots's remarkable library system. There I stumbled, blind, upon Virginia Woolf. She was my first great literary discovery, and I was totally unprepared for her. I opened *The Waves* and read without drawing breath:

> "I see a ring," said Bernard, "hanging about me. It quivers and hangs in a loop of light."
>
> "I see a slab of pale yellow," said Susan, "spreading away until it meets a purple stripe."
>
> "I hear a sound," said Rhoda, "cheep, chirp; cheep chirp; going up and down."
>
> "I see a globe," said Neville, "hanging down in a drop against the enormous flanks of some hill."
>
> "I see a crimson tassel," said Jenny, "twisted with gold threads."
>
> "I hear something stamping," said Louis. "A great beast's foot is chained. It stamps and stamps and stamps."

This marvellously rhythmic prose turned my heart to water. I burst into tears. And I fell in love with words.

I also discovered Edith Sitwell: "Jane, Jane, tall as a crane, the morning light creaks down again." *Creaks!* It was as if I had found a friend. I am sure we all are born synaesthetic, but we learn to keep quiet about it. Adults tell us it is not possible. But here was an adult, a published adult, who clearly knew of it too. I had, of course, not yet read Rimbaud.

Nor had I discovered Eliot or Auden or Yeats or Pound. Clearly, I was retarded. Compared with what travelling young people see and hear today when they go abroad, I was an ignoramus. But during that seminal twelve months, I actually saw Epstein's *Rima* in Hyde Park and his *Ecce Homo* on exhibition in the Leicester Gallery.

I was a romantic, of course. How could I have been anything else? If the prairies – aided by Zane Grey's novels – had not made me one, Russian ballet would have. And my writing style, if style it was, was hopelessly romantic. Starting in grade school, I wrote narrative poems. My earliest, about Napoleon, was in fact, an epic. It began:

> *Napoleon, as a boy, we're told*
> *Was ever noble, ever bold.*
> *And this short poem will show to you*
> *What a young boy can really do.*

I tried my hand at free verse. I acquired a book on prosody and wrote triolets, sonnets, villanelles – about love, requited and un-.

When I returned to Canada a year later, I had had one poem published in the London *Observer*, had lost my heart to Russian Ballet, George Bernard Shaw, and modern art. I was more eyes than brains, a dreamer rather than a planner, and my future stretched before me – blank.

My family had moved from Alberta to New Brunswick. There, I joined them, astonished to find that this, too, was Canada. New Brunswick gave me the excitement of a creative community. I met poets, potters, painters, theatre people – Kay Smith, the Deichmanns, Miller Brittain, Jack Humphrey. I wrote masses of bad verse, and a youthful novel, *The Sun and the Moon*. It was about a girl who turned into a tree. Of *course* one can become a tree. Daphne did; and Baucis and Philemon and all Phaeton's grieving sisters. The manuscript went the usual rounds of publishers and ended up at Macmillan in Toronto. They offered to publish it as soon as the wartime paper shortage ended. I was ecstatic! I wrote plays for children's theatre, and even acted myself, having come back from England stage-struck and unfocussed. Did I want to write or act?

I immersed myself in Ibsen. *Peer Gynt* and *An Enemy of the People* represented the poles of my interests — the imaginative/symbolic on the one hand, and social criticism on the other — interests which, when I emerged from a protective family into the more sophisticated and contemporary world of Montreal, polarized around Jung and Marx. I had neither a Jungian analysis nor did I become a Marxist, but the great continents of myth and seas of dream, uncovered and explored by Jung, and the Marxist vision of a world in which all men and women are privileged, could not help but stir me. Perhaps utopia *was* possible — personally and communally — the one through individuation, the other through politics.

I arrived in Montreal from the Maritimes early in World War II. The whole idea of going off alone to a strange city was totally foreign to my friends. But I knew there was another world. I had already tasted it.

I rented a room in a boarding house and wrote every morning from nine to twelve, just like a real writer — living on a minute allowance given me by my father. But it was not long before I realized that if independence was what I wanted, I had better not accept financial help from home. So, ill-equipped as I was, I found a job in an office that handled blueprints and specifications for small arms.

This was wartime — a time of rationing, and grief. My poems about offices were written at this period — poems about stenographers and typists. It was not my first job — I had worked in a department store in Saint John, New Brunswick and already had an idea of how abused unorganized workers could be. Much of my poetry reflected these ideas — poems of social criticism, often expressed in the images of dream. I suppose it was as close as I ever came to polemics.

A few months after I arrived in Montreal, the long arm of chance introduced me to the young English poet Patrick Anderson. He invited me to attend a meeting of a recently formed literary group — the *Preview* group — which was planning to produce a small magazine — although "This is not a magazine," ran the first editorial. And indeed, it was not; it was a handful of mimeographed pages held together by a staple. You should remember, you who have grown up in an age with the Canada Council and a proliferation of little magazines, that in the early '40s, throughout the entire country, only two magazines regularly published poetry; the poets themselves were just emerging from their closets, and World War II was raging on in Europe.

The first *Preview* meeting I attended was at F.R. Scott's house. Present were Scott Anderson, Bruce Ruddick, Neufville Shaw, and Margaret Day, plus a few partners and friends – all strangers to me but for Anderson, briefly met. I had been asked to bring some poems with me, and they were passed around and read in solemnity and silence. Never had any poetry seemed as bad in my eyes as mine at that moment. Finally, Scott said, "Bones! My God, here's a girl who writes about bones. You can't write about bones anymore." After such silence, it seemed the kindest remark I had ever heard. Nothing further was said about my work, so I presumed there would be no return engagement. But as the meeting broke up, Anderson said, "Miss Page" – a formal fellow was Patrick – "our next meeting will be held on . . ." and he gave me a date and place. And so I became a member of the *Preview* group.

It was a heady time for me and, set on fire by Patrick's imagery, coupled with the whole experience of living in a large bilingual city and working in wartime offices, I could barely keep myself in enough paper to get everything down – poetry and prose. Nor could I take in the rush of ideas I was exposed to.

Having come from a military family where politics were never discussed, I now found myself in the thick of discussions on both local and international politics. With Anderson a communist and Scott a socialist, I had an early lesson in the differences between the two.

Meanwhile, I was reading – Tolstoy, Dostoevsky, Gogol, to say nothing of Eliot, Yeats, and Pound. The second phase of my education had begun. I made just enough money to keep myself modestly, and I became friends with a number of writers and painters – A.J.M. Smith, A.M. Klein, Jon Smith, Goodridge Roberts – all of whom, in their various ways, contributed to quickening my eye and my ear.

There was never, I think, an issue of *Preview* that I didn't contribute to. I published regularly in *Contemporary Verse*, occasionally in John Sutherland's *New Statement*, and, during Earle Birney's editorship, in *The Canadian Poetry Magazine*. I had work accepted also by *Poetry: A Magazine of Verse*, in Chicago. Caught up in this new world, I had completely forgotten that *The Sun and the*

Moon was on a back burner at Macmillan's until the day I received a telegram saying they were all set to publish. Only too eager to see the book in print when I had written it, I now had serious misgivings. In doubt as to what to do, I asked a friend. He said that as I had written it in good faith, I should go ahead, using a pseudonym if that made me feel better. And so I did. *The Sun and the Moon* by Judith Cape came out in 1944 to little acclaim. But like all events, it had a ripple effect: the first being the book's republication in 1973 when I claimed it as my own; the second when it was dramatized by Peter Haworth and produced by Don Mowat on CBC radio.

My first book of poems, *As Ten As Twenty*, was published in 1946 by The Ryerson Press. At that time, Ryerson was almost our only publisher interested in poetry. Looking back, I find it astonishing that they accepted my slim forty-three-page manuscript consisting of random poems. Sequences of poems – a commonplace today – were uncommon then. It may be that the Canada Council, by asking grant applicants for project outlines, began the trend.

At about this time, I got a job with the National Film Board as a writer for filmstrips. I had no great dreams of writing for film, although I think I had a natural instinct for letting the visuals do the talking. The wide variety of subjects I had to tackle filled in many gaps in my education, and I gained a certain confidence that I could – after a fashion – write for a living. I wrote the script and commentary for an animated film, sponsored by the Department of Health. It was about teeth. Entitled *Teeth Are to Keep*, it won an award at Cannes. My finest hour!

In 1954, my second book of poems, *The Metal and the Flower*, appeared. It was the seventh in the Indian File series begun by Jack McClelland – a series title that would be unacceptable today! It was well-received wherever books *were* received in those days – the *Canadian Forum*, perhaps – and it won a Governor General's Award. We were in Australia when the award was announced, and in the circles where I moved, which were mainly diplomatic, few people knew I wrote. One acquaintance, after reading the book, looked at me in astonishment and said, "I shall never again know what you are thinking." She must have been more of a fiction writer than I, because it had never occurred to me that I knew *her* thoughts. The remark has made me wonder if perhaps that is the reason I had never felt completely comfortable with fiction.

During our years in Australia, I wrote poetry – in the main placeless, as my poetry is apt to be – and intermittent notes about a country that fascinated and appalled me. I read Australian literature with curiosity but without admiration. Their novels informed, but failed to engage me; their poetry was still Georgian. I must remind you that this was in the '50s, and things have changed radically since then. Pre-computer, pre-TV, the world did not have the simultaneity it has today, and time lags were very apparent.

I was intrigued by Aboriginal bark drawings – as I still am. Because they arise out of ceremonial and belief, rather than neurosis or loss, they seem closer in spirit to early European religious paintings than to the work of contemporary artists. For some mysterious reason, they are personal to me – all that stipple, and cross-hatching.

I was fascinated by the Southern Hemisphere: the Southern Cross in the night sky, kangaroos pogo-sticking across the outback; koala bears snoring in the eucalypts; and actually in our garden, multi-coloured parrots, wrens as blue as Brazilian blue butterflies, and a bird with the scream of a madwoman. I have always been a nature buff. Small wonder I was enthralled.

If Australia fascinated me, Brazil, where we went next, fascinated me still more. Here the butterflies were as blue as Australian blue wrens! It was also my first immersion in the baroque – its architecture, its vegetation, its people. I fell in love with it totally. But it took away my tongue. I had no matching vocabulary. It was painful for me to be unable to write, but by some alchemy the pen that had written, began to draw. I drew everything I saw. Drew in a way I would be unable to draw today, and eased the pain of writers' block – or what I thought of as writers' block. Actually, I *was* writing – almost daily – but because it was not poetry, it didn't feel like writing. What I produced – very often with a marmoset on my shoulder examining my hair for nits – were voluminous notes to be published later by Lester & Orpen Dennys as *Brazilian Journal*.

During our time in Brazil, and in Mexico, which followed, drawing and painting obsessed me. In Mexico, I had the good luck to meet the surrealist painter Leonora Carrington, who taught me how to use egg tempera. I taught myself to lay gold leaf. Not easy! The least breath while handling the delicate foil will send it flying, and what you see in your hand, if you are quick enough to catch it, looks like nothing more than a crushed clothes moth. *Or volador,* the Spanish call it – flying gold. It is well named. I kept a journal once again, parts of which have appeared in magazines, and it has been my intention to consolidate it and make a book of it, but it *does* feel like the past, and the older I grow, the more I want to live in the present.

In 1967, McClelland & Stewart published a book of new and selected poems: *Cry Ararat!* – a poor title for a non-biblical age, and frequently referred to – I might add! – as *Cry a Rat*. Beautifully designed by Stan Bevington, it includes the first of my black-and-white drawings to appear in book form. It was my re-emergence after years abroad.

In response to proddings from George Woodcock, I wrote two essays in which I attempted to explain my reactions to northern North America after roughly ten years in a Latin culture. In one, I say, "The culture shock of home-coming after many years abroad is even greater, I think, than the culture shock of entering a new country. One returns different, to a different place, misled by the belief that neither has changed."

An obvious and radical change was in the poetry scene. Ryerson, McClelland & Stewart, and Oxford were publishing more poetry; a number of small pub-lishing houses had sprung up; poets had multiplied; and poetry readings had begun – an unheard-of activity! This astonishing change was undoubtedly thanks to the CBC, which provided a stage for Canadian writers, and to the Canada Council, which had not existed when we left Canada early in the '50s.

I soon realized that if I were to be part of this scene, I, too, would have to give readings. My first – at the invitation of Al Purdy when he was Writer-in-Residence at Simon Fraser – was to Sandra Djwa's English class. I was terrified in advance, but as with many other things in my life, once I had taken the plunge, not only was I unafraid, but I actually enjoyed it. I did a small tour in B.C. with Margaret Atwood – a young star; a winter Maritime tour that took me to P.E.I. by a ferry that doubled as icebreaker; and a tour of England with Earle Birney and Michael Ondaatje. I loved the chance to meet fellow poets, talk to students, and make new friends. On the debit side, I was disappointed that the academe I had so greatly respected – partly, I suppose, because I had not been to university – was often inflexible and doctrinaire.

During this period, Margaret Atwood collected my youthful novel, together with some of my early short fiction, and published *The Sun and the Moon and*

Other Fictions, the first of Anansi's Found Books. The following year, believing rightly that if my work were in hardcover only, it would never appear on a university curriculum, she edited a paperback, *Poems Selected and New*. The whole philosophy of hard versus soft covers, an interesting subject, has changed greatly in my lifetime, but this is not the place to go into it.

In the '70s, I edited a book of short poems, *To Say the Least: Canadian Poets from A-Z*, which, if read consecutively from beginning to end, is a poem in itself. What inspired me was listening to my mother as an old lady reciting reams of Shakespeare, Wordsworth, and Tennyson. It gave her great pleasure. I thought how deprived we are today by not having been made to learn poetry by heart. And how, with our shortened attention spans, we could probably only memorize poems as brief as F.R. Scott's "Is":

> *Is*
> *is not*
> *the end of Was*
> *or start of Will Be*
> *Is*
> *is*
> *Is.*

Or Eldon Grier's

> *I am almost asleep*
> *with your poems on my chest,*
>
> *Apollinaire*
>
> *I am almost asleep,*
> *but I feel a transfusion of fine little letters*
> *dripping slantwise into my side.*

Or my poem, "Truce":

My enemy in a purple hat
looks suddenly like a plum
and I am dumb with wonder
at the thought
of feuding with a fruit.

Because I was devoting more time to it, the pace of my literary life was quickening. I taught for three summers at Jerry Lampert's Writers' Workshop in Toronto – terrified once again. What did I know, that could possibly be useful to anyone?

I wrote a long short story, "Unless the Eye Catch Fire," based on a dream. Or was it? Some of it was. It is a story about an ordinary woman who suddenly sees her world transformed. At the same time, barely noticeably at first, the temperature is increasing. The story appeared as a prose centrepiece to a book of poems, *Evening Dance of the Grey Flies*, published in the fall of 1981. Since then it has been performed as a one-woman show by Joy Coghill, and is currently in production as a movie. *Evening Dance . . .* arrived in my hands from Oxford the day our local paper ran a story with a *New York Times* byline that began, "Strong new evidence that carbon dioxide pollution is causing a potentially dangerous warming of the earth's climate . . ." etc., etc. My short story was written in the late '70s, before any talk of global warming had reached the press. I am not trying to suggest that I have prophetic powers. I haven't. But it does make me ask myself something about dreams. What are they? Where do they originate? Surely they are not merely the garbage pails of our lives, as some psychologists would suggest. I suspect that all of us here know the qualitative differences between dreams. Some are patently rubbish. But the others . . . ? How can one help but wonder? Are they perhaps an escape hatch to a higher realm?

Those people in a circle on the sand
are dark against its gold
turn like a wheel
revolving in a horizontal plane
whose axis – do I dream it? –
vertical

invisible

immeasurably tall

rotates a starry spool.

So begins a poem based entirely on dream.

The '80s diversified me. Murray Adaskin, commissioned by the Victoria Symphony Orchestra to compose a musical score for children based on "The Musicians of Bremen," asked me to write the text. The story, as I read it, is about team spirit and the triumph of art. The beauty of folk/fairy tales is that — like poems, or like *anything*, come right down to it — what you see in them is what is in them for you. I try to tell students this — and so run counter to the prevailing analytical methods of teaching.

That year I also put together a selected poems, *The Glass Air*. It had as its cover an egg-tempera painting by me and contained drawings and two essays. In 1991, reprinted as *The Glass Air: Poems Selected and New*, it included a convocation address, given at Simon Fraser, and written in verse. I had watched ruthless developers mindlessly destroying our rainforest, I had heard a voice saying, "It doesn't matter what you do as long as you serve your planet," and I was split about the role of the artist. In such an extreme situation, should the artist become an activist, or should he/she believe absolutely in the redemptive power of art? Or better still, embrace both? Towards the end of my address, I say:

> *But to get back to art, for there my heart is,*
> *there — beyond materiality,*
> *beyond the buy-and-sell, beyond the want*
> *embedded in us, and beyond desire —*
> *resides the magic greed has cancelled out.*
> *If well but give it time, a work of art*
> *'can rap and knock and enter in our souls'*
> *and re-align us — all our molecules —*
> *and make us whole again. A work of art*
> *could, 'had we but world enough and time,'*
> *portray for us — all Paradise apart —*
> *'face (we) had/before the world was made'* . . .

Still in the '80s, encouraged by George Woodcock and Michael Ondaatje, I began work on a period piece based on the notes I made in Brazil. Perhaps this is the moment to say that more than thirty years earlier I had married Arthur Irwin — a man with a formidable reputation as an editor. I had seen strong men blench beneath his editorial gaze and had, as a result, rarely asked his advice about my work. By 1987, I must have felt brave, for I enlisted his help with *Brazilian Journal*. It was one of the exceptionally happy periods of our life. He worked on the manuscript, section by section, and passed his comments on to me. I acted upon them or not — almost invariably the former — and was astonished to discover that a good editor is one who actually makes you more yourself.

At about that time, I was asked by Don Mowat to write a poem for radio about Sibelius. I was far from sure I could write to order in this way. But I borrowed or bought all Sibelius's recorded music, read what little the library could provide about his life, and was drawn into reading "The Kalevala" — creation myth and Norse saga — parts of which he had used as texts for his songs. Its form and scope were a revelation to me. I flooded the house with his music, and finally, not without surprise, wrote a half-hour piece for two voices entitled "I – Sphinx." It was performed on CBC radio with a young Finnish composer in the role of Sibelius and me as narrator.

We live in Victoria, my husband and I. But Arthur's roots are in Ontario, and so for many summers we travelled east to cottage country where fourteen grandchildren learned to swim and handle boats and get to know the family face. One summer, I began making up a fairy story about a poor boy who lived in a land-locked kingdom. Day after day the story grew. It was criticized by the sophisticated members of my juvenile audience, who *knew* that love at first sight is impossible, and animals don't talk, but despite their derision, I finished what was finally published as *A Flask of Sea Water*. A sequel, *The Goat that Flew*, followed. Having grown up on fairy tales, it was not unnatural for me to write them. I agree with Joseph Campbell that they are "the picture language of the soul."

In the 1990s, I encountered the *glosa,* a form used by the court poets in medieval Spain. Fourteen *glosas* later, I published *Hologram*. Since then, Stan Dragland has edited my collected poems, *The Hidden Room*, and Francesca Valente translated a selection of my work into Italian in a book entitled *Compass Rose*.

I could go on, but the speech I had thought would be a creed, a philosophy, or an aesthetic has turned into a laundry list. Let me try to save it.

I have never belonged to a school. I have been in love with, but not wedded to, form. I believe with Graves that the theme chooses the poet; with Salvador Dali, that to gaze is to think; and with Goethe that "Beauty is the manifestation of secret laws of nature which, were it not for their being revealed through beauty, would have remained unknown forever."

I suspect that metre is a brain-altering drug – one we ignore at our peril. Just consider what we know, but take for granted: that iambic is the lub-dub of the heart, and iambic pentameter that lub-dub repeated five times – roughly the number of heartbeats to a breath. It is difficult for me to believe this is accidental.

I believe art has two functions: a lower and a higher. The lower is invaluable. It shows us ourselves – Picasso's *Guernica*, for example. The higher – more valuable still in my view – gives us glimpses of another order. If I may quote from my poem "Poor Bird":

> *in the glass of a wave a painted fish*
> *like a work of art across his sight*
> *reminds him of something he doesn't know*
> *that he has been seeking his whole long life –*

Where do I go from here? I have no idea. The journey is without maps. But when I glance back, as I have tonight, to where I have been, I know that the life of the artist is a most privileged life and I would have chosen no other way.

PETER C. NEWMAN

Good evening. I want first of all to thank Pierre Berton for introducing me. He has been not only a friend but a mentor, my most significant role model. And I want to ask Pierre a question because my next book is going to be my autobiography and I want to mention something that happened between us to make sure I've got it right. After I finished my Diefenbaker book, I started a book on the CPR. The railroad's commissioned history was titled *Empire of Steel*, describing the ribbons of steel that had been thrown across the country. My book was to have been called *Steal of Empire*, because that's what the CPR did – steal an empire through government land grants, in return for building the railway. So I phoned Pierre and told him. "No, you can't do that," he said, "I'm doing the CPR," as he later did in that magnificent two-volume history of the National Dream. I said, "Okay, but I want to do the Hudson's Bay Company." We sort of divided Canadian history, and it worked out well for both of us.

One reason I'm so glad to be here is that this lecture is named after Margaret Laurence. She was very proud of being a professional writer, and hated people who didn't respect her craft. She was once at a reception in Montreal when this elderly gentleman came up and, gushing all over her, said: "I've read all your books. They're wonderful. I'm a brain surgeon and as soon as I retire I'm going to start writing, just like you." Margaret leaped at this guy, grabbed him by the elbows and said, "Now, isn't that a coincidence. When I retire I'm going to become a brain surgeon!" True story.

Now, I've never given a formal lecture before. Most of the lecturers in this series have been literary personages, a status that I dare not claim. I am the Arnold Schwarzenegger of CanLit. My field is Creative Non-fiction, whatever that is. The easiest way to define this art form is that it's like Canada. We say we're Canadian because we're not American. Well, Creative Non-fiction is neither journalism nor fiction, but something in between. It uses fictional techniques but is hemmed in by facts.

What fuels Creative Non-fiction is that we are competing for our readers' time. There are so many other ways readers expend their leisure. We must give them good reasons to spend their time with us, to read our articles and books. Non-fiction writers in the past have been able to get away with thinking, "Well, I'm passing on valuable information and that's why readers will take the time to read what I write." But in this age of television, computers, and the Internet, that's no longer true. At the same time as you inform readers, you must entertain them. And that's Creative Non-fiction. You must appeal not only to the mind of the reader but to his or her emotions.

My mantra in Creative Non-fiction has always been:
- to paint is to see;
- to compose is to hear;
- to write is to *feel* — not only think, but *feel*.

The kind of prose I'm talking about comes not only from the head, but from the heart and from the gut. You must establish an emotional link with your readers.

The subtle ideal that I strive for in my writings was best expressed by James Thurber, a satirist who was also a cartoonist for *The New Yorker*. There is a famous drawing of his where two men are dueling with swords and one of them is better at it and cuts his opponent's head off. It's such a subtle thrust that the head stays on his body. "Come on, let's keep dueling," he says. "What's your problem?"

The other duelist quietly suggests, "Try sneezing."

That's the subtlety I aim for — that my literary thrusts be so subtle that my subjects don't realize their heads have been cut off.

My other objective is taken from Barbara Tuchman, my favourite historian, the author of *The Guns of August*, *The March of Folly*, *The Proud Tower*, and so many other great books. Asked about her literary approach, she replied that in her mind she pictures herself as one of Kipling's itinerant storytellers in ancient India. They used to visit distant villages and in the evenings sit around camp-fires and tell stories. As the nights grew darker, they would pass around a rice bowl. A good storyteller, able to hold his listeners' attention, would get plenty to eat — if he lost his audience, he would go hungry. I feel just as urgent a con-nection with my readers.

THE WRITER'S LIFE

I believe that a writer's life is the best life — and that writing books is the summit of our craft. Nothing is more exhilarating than creating a book, a permanent record; the whole is always greater than its parts.

I've always loved writing in English because it's not my mother tongue. I'm still at the stage — and always will be — of experimenting with how this won-derful and flexible language can be used. It's ideal for the vagaries of Creative Non-fiction.

To me, the most exciting element of writing is cadence — its inner music. Ideally, sentences, paragraphs, pages flow so seamlessly that they can be sung. It's difficult to define, but you know when you've reached that state of grace, because the cadence of your prose will capture and entrance your readers. To endow prose with magic, cadence is everything.

Here is an example of cadence from one of my books. The most admirable characters in my trilogy on the Hudson's Bay Company were the voyageurs, its lowest-ranking employees, called *engagés*, who paddled the birch-bark canoes into the fur country from Montreal and back again. This involved unimaginable toil that cracked their backs and ruptured their intestines but never broke their spirits:

No smear of their sweat or echo of their lives reaches out to us, yet in their time they were cockleshell heroes on seas of sweet water. Unsung, unlet-tered, and uncouth, the early fur trade voyageurs first gave substance to the unformed notion of Canada as a transcontinental state. The traditional post-card pastiche of slap-happy buffoons with sly moustaches and scarlet sashes, bellowing dirty *chansons* about pliant maidens, that was *not* who they were. Their eighteen-hour paddling days were more wretched than most men then or now could survive. They were in fact galley slaves, their only reward being the defiant pride in their courage and endurance; they could boast of their exploits to no one but themselves.

They thus had to concoct their own sustaining myths. No voyageur ever reported meeting a small bear, a tame moose, or a wolf that wasn't snarling with blood lust. Running through mosquito clouds along boggy portages with 180 pounds or more on their shoulders, strong-arming four tons of cargo through icy rapids while, as one trader told it, "not only hanging on by their hands and feet but by their eyebrows," the canoemen cherished these small daily victories, which became grist for the self-justifying legends that kept them going.

The tally of hardship was most clearly visible at the steepest of the killing portages – the plain wooden crosses, sometimes thirty in a group, marking the spot where drowning, stroke, heart attacks, or strangulated hernia finally claimed their victims. Out in that witches' brew of a wilderness, they outran their souls and maimed their bodies and nobody, nobody was there to salute them or mark their passage.

The writing life is the best life and the worst life. Every time you publish a book, you go into the boxing ring to defend your title. You're mostly fighting yourself, because you have to do better than last time, refine your voice, improve your cadence, garner better reviews; whatever.

Writing is the loneliest of all the creative arts – just you and your computer. I add a third party. I never write anything without music pulsating through my earphones. I write accompanied by big band jazz: Stan Kenton, Woody Herman, and Buddy Rich, played loudly enough to endow me with its energy, and above all, through its time signatures, rhythmic patterns to empower my cadence. The exuberance of the music is catching.

By the way, book reviewers in this country are butchers. They review authors instead of books. We have no literary critics worthy of that title, only butchers – and maladroit ones at that. But the future is brighter. On some new Internet sites, authors can review their own books. That's a trend I heartily endorse.

I notice that the Writers' Union of Canada has a first line contest, so I'd like to enter my most recent volume. I was trying to signal the irreverence that characterizes the latest of my literary efforts, *Titans: How the New Canadian Establishment Seized Power*, so I started the book off describing an Establishment party in Toronto's tony Rosedale district. The first sentence reads as follows: "'Sorry,' smirks the hostess who has just refused me a drink of water, 'we never serve the stuff, fish fuck in it.'"

I had a big fight with my publisher about that opening, but she finally agreed. Later in the same chapter, one guest asks another: "Do you believe in sex before marriage?" Her friend shrugs and replies, "Well, not if it holds up the ceremony."

As mentioned, my technique is to tell stories. To illustrate the contemporary trend of economic globalization, instead of citing statistics, I wrote the following:

As editor-in-chief of the *Toronto Star* in the 1970s, I was very much in tune with that paper's passionately held nationalism and regularly attacked the multinationals who were gobbling up Canadian companies. That made my office a regular port of call for the slyly genuflecting Genghis Khans anxious to de-fang the *Star*'s not-very-effective sting. Knowing that I had been one of the founders of the Committee for an Independent Canada, dedicated to stopping foreign investors from taking over this country's most valuable assets, the heads of the marauding multinationals would call on me to try and persuade the *Star* they were doing the right thing.

My favourite gentleman caller was an American cowboy capitalist named Joseph Culliman III, then head of Philip Morris, who was taking a run at one of the larger Canadian breweries, Carling O'Keefe. A John Wayne clone, Joseph Culliman III was an over-sized Texan who looked as if he made love with his boots on, and kept excusing his frequent lapses into obscenity with the winking admonition, "Pardon my French."

"I'm telling you, buddy," he told me man-to-man, "we're going to make a lot of beer, lot of money, and lot of jobs, you know, the whole guacamole." When I inquired in my deferential Canadian way whether he was planning to retain Carling's Canadian board of directors, he broke up. I could tell he had been waiting for that obvious question all the way from Laredo or Cheyenne or wherever he had come riding in from. He moseyed over, leaned over my desk, and gave me his best shot. "Listen up," he said . . . and I still remember that proud gotcha look in his eye, "WE'RE GOING NATIVE ON THIS DEAL!"

So there it was, the end of the Canadian dream. We had been reduced to tokens in our own country and it took a Texan wearing spurs to make that clear to me.

The point I'm trying to make is that Creative Non-fiction is a bit like a novel. I transformed Joseph Culliman III into a character instead of a statistic. That same fierce disregard for a nation's soul personified by Culliman is what ultimately separates Canada's Titans from the rest of us. They are the most successful and the most cynical of this country's citizens because they have reduced the idea of Canada to a flag of convenience, or occasionally inconvenience. The once-proud maple leaf flag is used or discarded like a Zeller's apron. As Canada's economy becomes part of a homogenized global marketplace, the Titans will remain Canadian in one sense only: their passports.

A WRITER'S CAREER

Let me briefly recap my writing career. My first important book was *Renegade in Power*, published in 1963. It broke the mould of Canadian political writing because up to then there had been mainly two kinds of political books: radical tracts claiming that all politicians should be put to the guillotine (which actually wasn't that bad an idea), and commissioned books which friends of retired politicians had financed.

Instead, I wrote about politics the way it is actually played out. I tried to portray the Canadian political scene as a spectator sport, which of course it is.

For example, this is a fragment of my coverage of the 1965 election which was John Diefenbaker's last national campaign, and the last anywhere fought from the back of a train. I was on that train. At the time, books describing elections were filled with statistics and official quotes from party leaders, basically stuff that was not very interesting and highly perishable. I tried to create a mood instead of just passing on facts — to be a story*teller* instead of a story repeater:

The election waged by John Diefenbaker in the fall of 1965 was not a campaign. It was a guerilla war, fought along a four-thousand-mile front in treacherous circumstances with unreliable troops and intriguing generals. Victory was impossible. Success would be measured by survival.

The Diefenbaker campaign transcended ideology. Even more than winning the election, The Chief, as everyone called him, seemed obsessed by his self-imposed mission of trying to hold back the mechanized urban society threatening to engulf his world. From the campaign's beginning, Diefenbaker refused to read the portents and omens of his defeat. It was as if he had decided to transform himself into the incarnation of the Canada he knew. He thus became a figment of his own imagination, a politician for whom nothing was impossible because he saw himself personifying a national dream that no longer existed.

Diefenbaker had to lose but the odds didn't seem fair. While his opponent, Liberal Leader Lester Pearson, was firing salvos of press releases from his private ministerial jet, Diefenbaker was jolting into small towns at twenty-minute intervals on a punishing coast-to-coast railway tour. An air of timelessness hung over the Diefenbaker campaign train as he whistle-stopped his way across the country. There was little sensation of progress or reality. The landscape on which the Diefenbaker train moved seemed like a sequence of Krieghoff tableaux run through an IMAX lens. At Matapédia in Quebec, only five off-duty trainmen and three stray dogs turned out to meet The Chief. At Amqui, the Conservative leader was introduced to a Monsieur Legree, who in turn presented the young man beside him as his son: "*C'est mon fils.*" Diefenbaker smiled, shook his hand, and said, "*Bonjour, Monsieur Mon fils.*"

It wasn't until the Diefenbaker train was being pulled into the rural way-stations of southern Alberta that the campaign began to pick up. The signs that dotted most station platforms, sometimes printed, sometimes scrawled on fences, read: HE CARED ENOUGH TO COME.

Nothing else mattered. Diefenbaker cared and had come. Pearson had not come and, by implication, didn't care. Out of his passion for these awkward and shattering small truths came Diefenbaker's rapport with the people of these small, flat Prairie towns slanting across time. Here he could feel again the only role he had ever played well, the champion of society's downtrodden, assaulting the nation's various Establishments. He soaked up the mood of rural Canada and gave it off like a hot, swift fire that burns away the scrub of a hide-bound life. The Diefenbaker train went tumbling through the night of time, the press car filled with the noise of tapping typewriters, the tinkling of beer glasses, and the slap of cards. In his private car, Diefenbaker dictated and signed three hundred letters a day, mostly to well-wishers along the route. Between whistle stops, particularly late in the day, fatigue would dissolve his face into deep crevices like the starved topography of some rugged mountain range. Occasionally, he would relax by taking off his clothes and stomping around his private car in a bathrobe, hunching his shoulders like a prize fighter flexing for the big bout.

The leader had been given a canary from a supporter in Richmond Hill, Ontario, and Diefenbaker spent hours trying to coax the bird to sing, as if its song would be an omen of good fortune. The bird never uttered a sound. But on the morning of November 6, between Saskatoon and Prince Albert, the railway steward imitated a canary whistle and Diefenbaker, who thought it was the real thing, got very excited. No one ever told him the truth.

The Prairies became a land to flee across — every town, every village a destination. When would these place names — Yarbo, Watrous, Wadena, Morris, Maple Leaf, Taber, Gull Lake, Champion — ever again appear in reports of Canadian election campaigns? At Fort Macleod, seventy-eight-year-old Norman Greer confided to the Chief, "Heck, I wouldn't vote for them Liberals, they want to give away Crow's Nest Mountain to Quebec." At Morris, local musicians serenaded him with a wavering version of "The Thunder" and reporters couldn't file their copy because the telegrapher was playing the drums. As the train pulled out, the brave little aggregation struck up "God Be With You Till We Meet Again." And John Diefenbaker cried. At Swift Current, two dozen blue-gowned ladies in the back of a Mac truck broke into "Land of Hope and Glory." Somewhere along the route, an old man sat by the tracks in the twilight holding up a sign that read: JOHN, YOU'LL NEVER DIE.

Renegade in Power became Canada's first major political bestseller, topping a quarter of a million copies. Diefenbaker himself, asked what he thought of the book, would typically reply: "I haven't read it, but there are sixteen mistakes in the first chapter."

I went out to cover Diefenbaker's final campaign in his Prince Albert riding, only months before he died. He was very old, shaking with Parkinson's and quite unwell, but the political blood was still pumping through his narrowing veins. I respected him and didn't want to get him excited. So I would go to the Legion Halls, where he mostly spoke, and I'd sit right in the back where I thought he couldn't see me. But one time he spotted me and stopped his speech. He pointed at me, his forefinger quivering, and declaimed: "There's that hireling of Liberalism who writes pseudo-biographies for monetary gain!" Only the last part was true.

I wrote six books on Canadian politics and enlivened my reportage with off-the-cuff politicians' quotes, not from speeches or position papers, but what they actually said in moments of what might be described as "loose thought." Charlie Van Horne, a New Brunswick Conservative, once proclaimed: "To shoot off your face is one thing, but to put your shoulders to the wheel, that's a horse of a different colour." A Liberal cabinet minister got himself all wound up in his own rhetoric and, in a visionary aside, declared: "I see before me the footsteps of the hand of destiny." A Commons committee chairman, talking to his caucus, advised: "Let's get our heads together and see if we can come up with something concrete." My favourite was the NDP-er, urging the government to action, who shouted across the floor: "It's time to grab the bull by the tail and look the situation straight in the face!"

Just as a footnote, such murder of the language is not peculiar to Canada. During the Gulf War, former U.S. Vice-President Dan Quayle and George Bush (the older, smarter one) were in the Oval Office, when the President complained that the war with Iraq wasn't going very well and told Quayle: "You know, Dan, we're going to have to impose an air embargo." Quayle got very excited and replied: "You can't do that, George. How will the people breathe?"

Incidentally, Ronald Reagan, when he was president, got it into his head that trees cause pollution and nobody could talk him out of it. During one of his campaigns, when the presidential entourage was driving past a small college in northern California, the students, who had heard of his peculiar conviction, put this huge sign on a big oak tree in front of the campus so that Reagan could see it as he went by. The sign on the oak tree's gnarled trunk read: CUT ME DOWN BEFORE I KILL AGAIN.

I should probably pay homage to Joe Clark while I'm talking politics. My definitive judgment of Mr. Clark is that he'll never set the world on fire, except by accident. I also like a quote by Brian Mulroney, who once said: "I'm not denying anything I didn't say." I wrote about Mulroney, at the time he was in office, that even when some of his cabinet ministers admitted they'd lied, nobody believed them. Mulroney's was the only government ever to over-throw a country.

His great problem was that he wanted so badly to be liked; he didn't under-stand that prime ministers must be respected, not loved, and never stopped trying to ingratiate himself. It reminded me of the French philosopher François-Marie Voltaire when he was on his death bed. "*Monsieur Voltaire,*" somebody said, "would you like to renounce the devil?" Voltaire looked very surprised and said, "No, no, this is no time to make new enemies . . ."

For some reason, that aspect of Brian Mulroney's flawed stewardship reminded me of Grace Slick, the legendary rock singer. At a San Francisco concert when she was severely hung over, she complained to the audience: "You know, it's very hard to sing and vomit at the same time."

One of the problems central Canadian politicians have in this country is what to do about the West. They feel comfortable only with governing that part of the country they can see from the top of the CN Tower on a clear day – and I'm not so sure about it being a clear day.

What to do about western Canada – how to satisfy the aspirations of people who live past the lee shore of the Humber River – has always eluded them. When Jim Coutts was chief of staff to Prime Minister Pierre Trudeau, the Liberals kept losing votes in western Canada, so the two of them concocted a scheme that Coutts would fly to Calgary, go to one of the city's rougher cock-tail bars, and yell out, "Trudeau is a horse's ass!" The theory was that people would come and tell him why they agreed. He could then return to Ottawa and explain to Trudeau why he was so unpopular. Coutts put on a cowboy outfit, went to the most macho Calgary bar he could find, and yelled out, "Trudeau is a horse's ass!" Somebody immediately hit him. Now, this really surprised him because he thought everybody would agree. When he came to, he asked the fellow who had hit him, "Is this Trudeau country?"

The guy looked him up and down, and shot back: "No, this is horse country."

My books are full of stories like that — and worse. Once again, I'm making the point that you must entertain people as you inform them.

MOVING ON TO BUSINESS:

One of my next efforts after the political books was a controversial volume about the Bronfman family. There had never been an honest book about the Bronfman Dynasty because nobody could get the facts about their bootlegging days. At the time, I was editor of *Maclean's*, and Seagrams, the Bronfman-owned liquor company, was our largest advertiser. So I couldn't really publish anything unless I had incontrovertible proof, and even then, it was difficult. My publisher, Jack McClelland, had hired an ace lawyer named Doug Laidlaw who examined me as if I were a witness in court. Everything I wrote had to be supported by documents. This was very difficult because the Bronfmans had effectively hushed up their beginnings as bootleggers across the Prairies. Then I got lucky.

There was a commissioner of the RCMP called Clifford Harvison, and his widow, hearing that I was doing this book on the Bronfmans, gave me her late husband's police files. Harvison had been a corporal during the Depression on the Prairies and had tried to get a conviction of the Bronfmans but couldn't because they had bribed local judges. I had his correspondence, his police reports, and you couldn't argue with that kind of evidence. Secondly, I was very fortunate that these were *Canadian* bootleggers. Unlike their American cousins who, when they had a fight, shot each other, Canadian bootleggers went to court. I found the court records, and in some of the old people's homes at Oxbow and Estevan, I discovered some of the original drivers who had actually driven the booze cars across the border for the Bronfmans during their bootlegging days. So I had the evidence.

My manuscript was kept under lock and key, but we sent one copy to the Book-of-the-Month Club because we wanted them to take it. What none of us realized was that the Bronfmans then owned the Book-of-the-Month Club. So of course they got a copy and we were summoned, Jack McClelland and I, to the fifty-fifth floor of the TD Centre in downtown Toronto. Now, most people think that the building has fifty-four floors —that's what it advertises — but actually there's a fifty-fifth, which at that time was the private hangout of the Bronfmans.

There was a little table set up in the middle of a large, bare room. Charles Bronfman and Leo Kolber, who was his hatchet man, were on one side of the table, Jack McClelland and I on the other. Jack was in one of his comatose financial phases, with his company in grave danger of going under, which was pretty routine for Jack. Anyway, he was there to defend my book, and so was I.

The first thing that happened was that Leo Kolber, who not only was a hatchet man but looked like a hatchet man and talked like a hatchet man, got up from his chair and sternly announced to McClelland, "Jack, if you publish this book, we'll buy out your company."

McClelland leaped over the table, exclaiming, "Leo, would you really do that?" And that was the end of that little caper.

But they did get back at me. After the book was published and they couldn't sue me because my facts were accurate, one of the Bronfman minions, a Seagram's Vice-President named Michael McCormick, sued me on very strange grounds. Since he had been the right-hand man to Sam Bronfman, I had interviewed him, and he had told me some great anecdotes about Sam, right into my tape recorder. He later claimed that I had stolen these stories — even though he had freely volunteered them. The whole thing was just a nuisance maneuver to soak up my money, time, and energy, which it did. Anyway, the Bronfman book broke sales records in Canada and became a main Fortune Book Club selection in the United States.

Then I did a book on Conrad Black. When Conrad moved back from Montreal to Toronto in his late twenties, he had done nothing except written his master's thesis on Maurice Duplessis, which was very good. I introduced him to Jack McClelland, who published it as a book. That started a friendship. What I asked Black to do, because I could tell that he was going to amount to something (at the time he had a minor job with a small brokerage named Draper Dolby), was that at the end of every month he would spend private time with me and I could debrief him on what he had done during the previous thirty days. Out of four years of those conversations — during which he took over Argus, which was then the biggest capital pool in Canada — came my book. It was the first serious study about him; he was only thirty-five years old when it came out. He was a real person then and answered questions honestly. He had yet to become a personage or a metaphor; he told me the unvarnished truth, the last time that he did to any writer.

Now, of course, he and Barbara Amiel are royalty. When they travel, cooks and butlers precede them to assure their every comfort. My favourite comment about Conrad was made in 1997, when the Moderator of the United Church cast doubt on the divinity of Jesus Christ. His was strictly a theological argument, but *Double Exposure*, then CTV's comedy team, picked up the cue. "Great news," they announced, "Conrad is back in the running." Terry Aislin, the Montreal *Gazette* cartoonist, caught Black perfectly, when he showed him talking to himself: "So at a very early age I had to make a decision: Do I really want to be prime minister? Shit no, I thought, I'd much rather be powerful." I once tried to describe the colour of his eyes, and he said they were hazel, but I couldn't tell and kept looking at him. It finally occurred to me that they're the same colour as you see looking down a gun barrel. Anyway, in the end he sued me for something I wrote, but it didn't go anywhere.

TURNING TO HISTORY:

I then spent a decade writing the history of the Hudson's Bay Company. These were four volumes. Penguin had signed me up, and there was a leak at the Frankfurt Book Fair that I had received a five-hundred-thousand-dollar advance. That was true, and I was, of course, immediately excommunicated by Canada's literary community. This wasn't nearly as extravagant as it sounded. It covered ten years and four books, which amounted to fifty thousand dollars a year, before taxes and research expenses, which is what junior history professors earn.

At its height, the HBC owned one-thirteenth of the earth's land surface. It defined not only Canadian geography – because in 1870 it sold its western holdings to Ottawa, thus forming Canada – but it also defined the Canadian character. The HBC occupied a thousand forts. They weren't really forts; they were company towns. And when you live in a company town, you defer to the authority of the company – and it was that deference to authority which characterized Canada's frontier and thus marked the Canadian character. This was very different from the American frontier, where there was a genuine Wild West, where men and women didn't defer to authority, they challenged it. They had sixty-nine Indian wars; we didn't have any. By that I don't mean that the HBC didn't exploit the Indians. They did. But it was a commercial transaction, and the Hudson's Bay Company even had an unofficial slogan: "Never shoot your customers."

The HBC had a nasty reputation in the West. People made fun of their initials because all of what later became western Canada belonged to the HBC. Indians claimed the letters HBC really stood for "the Hungry Belly Company," while Indian women claimed, with good reason, that the initials signified "the Horny Boys Club," and people in Edmonton said it stands for "Here Before Calgary." Others thought "HBC" really summed up the Company's long history, as in: "Here Before Christ."

In their hunt for profit, the HBC did some very strange things. They sold ice during the California Gold Rush, towing icebergs down the Pacific coast. During World War I, they operated a merchant fleet of three hundred ships, even sank two submarines, and supplied the Allied Armies in France and Belgium.

One of the dominant traits of the company was its Scottishness. I remember interviewing Joe Links, who was the official furrier to the Queen of England and was the first Jew to be named a director of the Hudson's Bay Company. When I asked him whether this created difficulties for him on the board, he laughed, "No, no, being the first Jew wasn't a problem – the problem was that I was the first Englishman!" The Bay men were Scottish to their core. Dick Murray, who was the managing director of the Hudson's Bay Company in Canada, used to leave his car at parking meters and when he came back from shopping, if there was still ten minutes on the meter, he would sit in his vehicle to make sure he got his money's worth.

George Simpson, the greatest of the HBC governors, inspected his empire from the back of an express canoe, accompanied by a bagpiper. I found one report by a Cree, who had heard the pipes, describing the novel experience to his chief: "One white man was dressed like a woman in a skirt of funny colour, he had whiskers growing from his belt and fancy leggings. He carried a black swan which had many legs with ribbons tied to them. The swan's body he put under his arm upside down, then he put its head in his mouth and bit it.

At the same time he pinched its neck with his fingers and squeezed the body under his arm until it made a terrible noise." A fair description.

The Hudson's Bay Archives, on which much of my book was based – although I also did about a thousand interviews – consists of sixty-eight tons of documents housed in their own building in Winnipeg. It's one of the best-documented institutions next to the Vatican. I always remember the exhilarating moment when I was reading the journal entry of James Isham, who was at York Factory in 1730. He writes about the "swarms of mosquitos that had visited this place like a plague" – and finding a mosquito carcass bloated with English blood squashed right into the page of his journal.

THE ESTABLISHMENT EXAMINED

When I moved to Toronto to become editor-in-chief of the *Toronto Star* and later of *Maclean's*, I couldn't write about national politics anymore because I wasn't in Ottawa, where most of the action took place. I discovered very quickly that there was another form of government in Canada, consisting of about a thousand men – yes, and I'm sorry to say, very few women – who acted as if they were the country's real government. I'm talking of course about the corporate elite who wield most of the power that counts in Canadian society. Jim Eayrs, the University of Toronto political scientist, once wrote that "corporate power is not tangential to Canadian society; *it is Canadian society*." That was the group I called The Canadian Establishment, and I've written half a dozen volumes on its evolution. Now, the Establishment is not some woolly writer's device or invention; it exists and has run this country since the end of World War II. It is the hidden hand behind the hidden hand that organizes who gets what and how much – if and when things get done or vetoed.

If you want to visualize the Establishment, think of the Olympic symbol and its overlapping circles, because that's how the Establishment works. There are circles of influence around capital pools as well as powerful individuals – and they overlap. It's that overlap that makes it an Establishment, because there are people common to all these groupings.

Is it a conspiracy? Not really. It doesn't need to be, because its members don't need to conspire. They think alike anyway. That's what makes them an

Establishment. They form a psychological entity, share habits of thought and action, common sets of values, beliefs and enemies. They touch and greet each other on a wide spectrum of commonality. It's as if they spent most of their waking hours on one giant conference call.

People think that it's easy for me to see these people and that they willingly talk to me. Well, most of them don't want to talk to me at all – and I don't blame them. I'll give you one example. When I did my first Establishment book, there was an underground rumour on Bay Street that there had been a coup d'état in the Canadian Imperial Bank of Commerce boardroom, which had never happened before. Indeed, Neil McKinnon, the venerable and authoritarian chairman and CEO of the bank, had been displaced overnight. I had to find out why. I knew there was a big story there, but it happened at the board of directors' level and of course directors are sworn to secrecy. They couldn't tell me what had happened, even if they wanted to, which they didn't. I had just enough information to know that it was true and a few second-hand quotes. I did something I'd never done before or since. I drank a bottle of wine and wrote a draft chapter on the putsch. What I didn't know, I made up. I then sent it to Neil McKinnon with a note that this was the draft of my chapter about what happened to him, and that maybe we should talk. I sent it down by courier, and about an hour later my phone rang. It was Neil McKinnon. "Let's have dinner tonight," he abruptly told me.

I went to his condo overlooking Upper Canada College, a lavish, serene space, as tidy as his desk at the bank. We had dinner and talked about the weather and the stock market, just chattered away. Finally, he said, "I'm going to walk my dog. Why don't you wait for me in the library?"

So I went in the library and there, on a large table, were the board minutes of the Canadian Imperial Bank of Commerce – everything, all the facts. I had a tape recorder with me because I had expected to interview McKinnon, so I just read the minutes into it. When McKinnon came back he didn't say anything, and I didn't say anything. But as he was helping me with my coat, he looked me straight in the eye and said: "Do you use this technique very often?"

Over the years I have learned to subscribe to Gore Vidal's dictum that "anyone who doesn't feel paranoid about power is not in full possession of the facts."

Some people suggest that I'm a member of the Canadian Establishment. I am not. I'm very much an outsider looking in. I think of myself as a court jester. In Shakespeare's plays, a court jester is an interesting character because he's in the court but not of the court. He reports to the court what the people are saying, and reports to the people what's happening at the court, all disguised as quips and fables, which is what I try to do.

My favourite review of my Establishment books was in *Time* magazine. They praised the inside information I had been able to garner and concluded their review this way: "Newman's books read as if he was invited into the Establishment homes. Once." Which is pretty accurate.

I want to stress that I write only tangentially about money. I write about power, which is much more interesting. I write about the kind of power that moves markets. This is real clout; the might of the mighty.

One of the accusations made against my Establishment books, and it's quite accurate, is that there aren't enough women in them. It's sad but true that women don't yet have that kind of power in Canada, very few do. One of my favourite powerful women is Sheila Whittaker, who runs a very large electronic data systems company in Canada. I asked her when there was going to be true equality, and she gave me this wonderful answer: "There will be true equality," she said, "when there are as many incompetent women in positions of power as there are now incompetent men."

The main point I made in *Titans* is that the old Establishment was a club and the new Establishment is a network. My book defines those networks. They're like telephone exchanges: people plug in and out depending on what deal they're doing. Members of this new Establishment are not just different people, but different *kinds* of people. It doesn't matter anymore who your father was, what clubs you belong to, or what private school you attended. All that matters is what you've done. You can now achieve your way into the Establishment. Canada has in many ways become a meritocracy, and that's good news.

These people live as much for fun as for money. They believe implicitly that it's never too late to have a happy childhood and that you should die young as late as possible.

They are seriously rich as well as genuinely powerful. Here is one example of how they spend their money. Peter Nygard of Winnipeg, who is a leading fashion manufacturer, has built a home in the Bahamas on his own atoll, and I'm the only journalist ever to have been there. This was how I described his holiday hangout in *Titans*:

A mixture of vanity and fun, Peter Nygard is showing me his new home. What do you call a structure that spreads over four acres, its habitable area covering 100,000 square feet [twice as large as Bill Gates' house in Seattle]? How do you describe a residence that requires guests to drive electric cars to their bedrooms, located somewhere in its suburban extremities?

In Nygard's case, what you call this architectural monstrosity is a temple. It's a place to worship his outsized personality; a shrine to his success as one of Canada's largest manufacturers of ladies' quality garments; a cathedral for a man whose appetite . . . knows no bounds. . . .

[Nygard's] athletic six-foot, three-inch body is crammed into a pink silk shirt, a pair of fashionable short pants, and label running shoes. He watches for my reaction as I stumble around his acreage, at first trying hard not to laugh, but gradually realizing that while a place like this is strictly Looney Tunes . . . it is a lavish labour of love that has taken him a decade of planning and work, plus an estimated twelve million dollars to put together.

"Is this," I ask, exhausted from hiking across his living room, "is this the world's largest house?"

"No," he acknowledges, "Buckingham Palace will always be bigger." *Right*.

"Actually," Nygard goes on, "it's sort of wrong to call my place a house. It's more like a resort."

Actually the place sort of gallops to infinity; it's a series of interconnecting pods that house his entourage and fourteen guests, plus professional-sized tennis, volleyball, and basketball courts that can be transformed into covered runways for fashion shows. The dominant motif is sensual curves and secret places from which to watch a sunset. . . . There are bending roadways everywhere to carry the narrow-gauge electric cars that interconnect the sprawling structure's outlying regions. (I can visualize some exhausted guest, roused from deep slumber by a call of nature, complaining, "Damn it, now I gotta drive to the bathroom.")

"I'm trying to go back to nature," Nygard insists. "It's as if Robinson Crusoe had a found a huge shipwreck and built himself a home."

Well, not exactly. As far as I remember, Robinson Crusoe's wilderness bedroom didn't have a mirrored ceiling. I also doubt whether that primitive castaway could relax, as Nygard does, in an exquisitely carved stone sauna built for twenty-five of his best naked friends. Chances are that Crusoe couldn't avail himself of a double-storey, treehouse office, accessible only by cable car. . . . Nygard's idea of a social conscience is his pledge to turn part of his property into a retirement home for aging circus animals.

When I ask him about who built his tropical dream, he becomes surprisingly defensive. "I'm the best bloody crane operator on site, lifting those 7,000-pound palm trees," he boasts. "I run the biggest crane here."

Then he grows very quiet. "When we first came over from Finland to Canada in 1952, I was ten," he recalls, "and our family lived in a converted coal bin in Deloraine, a small town in the southwest corner of Manitoba."

Nygard pauses, and for a moment the mask slips: "I didn't have a crane when I was a little boy," he confesses, sounding very much like a little boy. "I didn't have a choo-choo train or a treehouse either. But I've got a big crane now."

One of the ways that people like Nygard achieve legitimacy, if that's the right word, is by giving money away. Philanthropy is a very important activity because it endows them with a patina of class. My chapter on philanthropy starts with Billy Graham. I had been hired by *Time* magazine to cover Billy Graham's first Canadian crusade, which was in Toronto during the late 1950s. This was my report:

Back when television evangelists had private sex lives and Billy Graham was still a prime newsmaker, he decided to launch one of his revival crusades in Canada. . . . My evangelism has its limits, but I had always thought of Graham as being superior to the righteous opportunists who pollute the Sunday morning airwaves.

It isn't hard to tell the good Bible-thumpers from the bad. The voices of those who are in it strictly for the money seldom come from deep inside them. Theirs is the nasal twang of insincerity as they singsong their way through sermons, bellowing *Jaysus!* or *Ahmen!* whenever they lose their place. Their body language screams for attention (remember the Jimmy Swaggart crouch?) as they prowl the stage – hollerin', stompin', prayin'.

Not Graham. When I interviewed him, the man's deep voice and sub-dued grace were impressive. I figured that his burning eyes reflected either deep religious conviction or not enough sleep. Being the representative, however temporary, of a major U.S. newsmagazine, allowed me access to his entourage. When I visited him backstage at the close of the first night's activities, the Graham people were a gloomy lot.

The Canadian National Exhibition Coliseum, which they had turned into a makeshift place of worship for the occasion, was still reverberating with the echoes of Graham's sermon. More converts for Christ had come forward than at any other first night of the Graham crusade. I had watched in awe as ordinarily reticent Canadians ambled towards the dais, displaying the appropriate symptoms of loose-limbed ecstasy. But when it came around to collection time, the crowd responded with nickels and dimes instead of the more substantial contributions Graham was accustomed to Stateside. Since I happened to be the only Canadian behind the curtains, Graham came over and asked me what the trouble was.

"Billy," I said, "this is Canada. Before you ask for money, make it clear you'll issue tax receipts. Even when they're saving their souls, Canadians want to be damn sure it's deductible."

"Bless you, brother," a couple of Graham operatives mumbled, and the next evening, after the appropriate announcement . . . oh Lord, how the money rolled in.

Another chapter deals with the exclusive Establishment clubs. They were once essential, validating institutions. But no longer. Typical of the change was this incident at the Mount Royal Club in Montreal in 1993. Red Wilson, then the CEO of BCE, Canada's largest company, sponsored a black-tie dinner with a star speaker, Marvin Shanken, the editor and publisher of *Cigar*

Aficionado, which is the international glossy magazine devoted to the pleasures of cigar smoking:

> The guest of honour at the dinner was Ray Hnatyshyn, then Governor General of Canada. That's an office the Brooklyn-based magazine editor had never imagined existed. He didn't know how to deal with it and kept addressing Hnatyshyn as "Your Admirable," instead of "Your Excellency." But things ran pretty smoothly until the question period. The room was filled with the aroma of forty-five smokers exhaling the luxurious fumes of their smelly habit, when one member harrumphed and asked which cigar to smoke at various times of the day. Marvin stood up and went through the liturgy of how people are usually advised to have a small, thin one in the morning and work themselves up to a fat, full-flavoured cigar after dinner. But looking straight at the Governor General of Canada, Marvin said he didn't believe in any of that. "Personally, Your Admirable," he said, "I light up one big motherfucker at 7:30 in the morning, and that keeps me in orbit all day."

Thus died the Canadian Establishment.

WAVING FAREWELL TO CANADA

I want to end by talking not about writing or about my books, but about my country. We are in big trouble. So much of Canada, so much of what we believe in, so much of what we've achieved is being taken over by outsiders that we are becoming squatters on our own land. I believe that quantitative takeovers in the corporate and cultural sectors eventually add up to a qualitative change in the country, because fewer and fewer decisions that count are made by Canadians in their own interest. We have lost control and are losing our country.

For years, we sought validation from the United States. "I bought it on Fifth Avenue." "I studied at Harvard." "I beat the tables at Vegas." "I got my tan in Palm Springs." These were the meaningful accolades. We were the country cousins of the empire to the south of us and understood perfectly what Anthony Burgess meant when he wrote that John Kenneth Galbraith and Marshall McLuhan were the two greatest Canadians the United States has produced.

We believed wrongly that Canada was born without ever having been conceived, that we were in effect a residual state with no economic logic or the fulfillment of any manifest destiny — that we just sort of simmered up, an incongruous mixture of legacies from foreign wars and mercantile extravagances left out to dry in the long wash of history.

That isn't true. All you have to do is read Pierre Berton's books to know that it isn't true. But so many Canadians still believe it. I remember interviewing a man called Jacques Maisonrouge, the head of world trade for IBM, and I was talking to him about the Canadian border, asking how IBM handles it. His eyes kept glazing over and finally he said, "Look, to us, borders are meaningless. Borders are like the equator, just a line on maps. They don't mean anything." I was quite angry at the time, but he was right, at least in terms of the mercantile theology of the twenty-first century.

I contend that we are in some ways our worst enemies, that we thrive on making the worst of a bad situation by underestimating our own worth. The conquest of any nation takes place not on battlefields or in boardrooms, but in the hearts of its people and in the minds of its leaders. Conquest requires surrender. The U.S. takeover of Canada owes less to American strength than to Canadian weakness. Led by a timid and opportunistic Establishment, we have allowed ourselves to believe that there's something lacking in us that the Americans might provide. So we took the chance that the invading Yanks would supply those qualities and signed a free trade agreement. I have no particular quarrel with free trade, but I have a lot of problems with that agreement because it gave away not only our water and energy, but control over too many of our remaining cultural institutions, which is all we have left.

"What is a borderless world?" Eric Kierans, one of my favourite political philosophers, demanded, then answered his own question. "It's a world emptied of every value and principle except one: accumulation." In this context, it is essential to remember that the Americans treat culture as a commodity; it is in fact their most profitable export. To us, culture is who we are and why we're here; it's not negotiable, or shouldn't be.

The progress of our disappearing sovereignty is easy to chart. There are six steps:

- A FREE TRADE AREA, which is what we signed in 1989, eliminated tariffs with the U.S.A.;
- A CUSTOMS UNION, which was NAFTA, signed in 1994, is a free trade area plus the adoption of common external tariff against a third country, Mexico;
- A COMMON MARKET, which would be the next step, is a customs union plus a pledge by member countries for the free movement of labour and capital;
- AN ECONOMIC UNION is a common market plus a pledge by member countries to integrate all of their economic (not just trade) policies;
- ECONOMIC INTEGRATION is an economic union plus the unification of monetary, fiscal, and social policies, which is what's happening in Europe.
- This is only one step away from POLITICAL UNION, which means that member countries abandon their independence.

That evolution is not some vague theory. It's how countries disappear — and we are well launched along that voyage of no return.

THE SEARCH FOR IDENTITY

Charles-Louis Montesquieu, the eighteenth-century French savant, once commented that Frenchmen never discuss their wives, in case the listener knows more about the subject than they do. But we never tire of speculating about the Canadian Identity. We seem to be constantly telling ourselves that Canada has reached its threshold, the point at which the bell curve of fulfilled national aspirations begins its inevitable downturn.

That's not true. Here is the United Nations telling us year after year that we're the best place to live in the world, and yet we dismiss that notion out of hand, although it is based on objective statistics of what a happy life is. It doesn't mean we're perfect, but compared to other countries, this is the place to be.

Let's begin to appreciate what we have. It's time to sing some songs of praise of ourselves.

We have trouble defining ourselves. Stu Keate, former publisher of the *Vancouver Sun*, once said that Canada is the vichyssoise of nations: it's cold, half French, and difficult to stir. Some people seem to believe that the Precambrian Shield is a birth control device, yet symbolizes our territorial integrity; holding on to our northern turf remains our strongest claim to identity. All men and women are sons and daughters of their landscapes, but nowhere is this more true than in Canada, where the dominant gene of nationhood has been possession of the land itself. We laid claim to this large land by planting settlements on the shoulders of our shores, the elbows of our rivers, and the laps of our mountains.

I have never believed that Quebec would abandon Canada, even when it looked as if it might. I spend most of my time travelling this country, and I've always found that there exists a quiver of common intent holding, determined to hold, us together. Unlike the Americans, we don't shout about it, we don't sing about it, we don't wave flags about it, we don't set off firecrackers about it – but the feeling is there.

Canada was built on dreams as well as appetites. This country was put together not by bloodlines, kin, or tradition, but by waves of newcomers who arrived dreaming big dreams. I came here from Europe when I was ten years old. I didn't know a soul. I couldn't speak a word of English. Now I'm being attacked by the *Globe and Mail*. What a great country!

Being Canadian is not a nationality; it's a condition. If somebody says they're Swedish or Japanese, it's a fact. When somebody says they're Canadian, it's a condition, because there's so much left of our potential to fulfill. It's an act of faith.

What we've got here is a daily miracle of a country. Ever since 1867, we have lived out successfully the dictum that a nation is a body of people who have done great things together. We have, and we will again.

What it consists of, this Canadianism of ours, is a kind of pride that we are here, that we have survived for more than a century with an unfriendly climate, a harsh political environment, and a dominant giant to our south. We may be a nation in trouble, but this is our home. The great principles of individual and collective freedom are practiced here as in few other lands. Anyone who believes that's too rosy a picture should go to any other country on earth and look back at Canada. Whichever country they're in is bound to have more serious problems than ours.

Too often, as a nation and as individuals, we decry what we lack instead of celebrating what we have. Yet to most of the world, Canada seems blessed with the mandate of heaven.

I was in Richibucto, New Brunswick once, covering an election, and when a journalist goes to a place he's never been, he looks for somebody who's been around for a while. I saw this fisherman standing at the dock, puffing his pipe, and I went up to him. Just to start a conversation, I said, "Have you lived here all your life?"

His answer reflected the kind of quiet optimism I feel about Canada's future, because when I asked him whether he had lived there all his life, he replied, "No, not yet."

I had a brief and pleasant correspondence recently with Carol Shields, in which I informed her that I was both awed and honoured to be stepping into her very large shoes – metaphorically speaking – and I recounted to her a recent speech anxiety dream. I was here, on this stage, and when I looked at my notes they were blank; I was in fear that I was going to have to invent words, to make something up.

I suppose the symbolism stems from the dread of the blank page from which we all occasionally suffer. Either that, or the fear of naked exposure suggested by the topic of "A Writer's Life" – though perhaps my anxiety was provoked by my history of wrong-footing myself at these conventions of writers. Despite whatever respect I may have gained before a larger audience, I am considered by my own community of creators as a source of amusement, if not pity.

My résumé of calamities at AGMs of the Writers' Union include the following:

One chipped tooth suffered when I played the gallant fool, trying to change a flat tire on Marilyn Bowering's rent-a-car.

A week of temporary near-blindness – this was in the years of my vanity, when I wore contact lenses – the result of have soaked them in the cleaning solution before wearing them through dinner.

And one time I lost my return air ticket, somewhere in the bowels of the Queen's University campus.

So do not be surprised if I step off the edge of this stage tonight into the lap of Penny Dickens.

Given the title of this series, I thought I should speak of some of the unvarnished edges of a writer's life — particularly so because I have a captive audience of fellow writers. Margaret Laurence once referred to her fellow members of this odd profession as a tribe, and it takes some bravery to quarrel with her, but art — and Margaret Laurence knew that well — is a task for loners, and it is only at occasional celebrations such as this that we writers come together. (Unless one has the misfortune to live in Toronto.)

Yet she is right in that there is a sharing in spirit, a sharing in the satisfaction of giving voice to the muse within. There is also a sharing in the pain of freeing that voice, and what I propose to talk about are some of the more stressful aspects of that collective experience. Those of you who are members of the Writers' Union will relate to much of what I will say. As to those here who are yet unpublished, I can only hope that by the end of my talk I will have discouraged all but the most reckless and obsessive from taking up this career.

My first inkling that a writer's life was not a constant gala came when I was flown to Toronto to be presented with the Seal Prize. Though McClelland & Stewart did not consider me worthy of a first-class ticket, alcoholic drinks in those days were free in the steerage compartment, and I was in a celebratory mood.

On arrival in the city, I was spirited into a hotel salon by a horde of publicists whose task was to groom me for a press conference the next day. I needed grooming. Determined not to look like a stuffy lawyer, I was in jeans, and had grown my hair below the shoulder. Everyone else was in suits, the men with ties. Unlike me, they were relatively sober.

I was immediately subjected to a grilling into my background: they knew little about me and I suspect they had anticipated some slick manicured trial lawyer. The head publicist finally crept away to the phone to confer with Jack McClelland, and I overheard her say, "Well, I guess he looks all right, but he's a little West Coast."

That was my first intimation that an author's task was not only to write but to sell. You are not told when you sign away two years of your creative sweat that you are expected to earn your small pittance in royalties by going on a publicity tour. The publisher, of course, dreads camera-shy wallflowers or those who, in the current newspeak, are cosmetically disadvantaged.

As an aside, a major British publisher has just confessed to the long-standing practice of preferring the beautiful face to the beautiful book. Several weeks ago, I read with resigned cynicism a piece in the *Guardian Weekly*, and this is the lead paragraph:

Agents and publishers in London last month confirmed what embittered old stagers have long suspected: literary success is now as much about looks as the quality of your books. Whether a new author is seen as gorgeous or not has become a key criterion in deciding whether a book gets the kind of marketing push that will give it a chance of selling. With publishers no longer giving literary authors the luxury of three or four books to find a readership, a culture of hyping photogenic young things has gripped the industry.

The article recounted a debate at the London Book Fair at which a publishing director bluntly owned up to this long-standing practice. He went so far as to say the author of *Corelli's Mandolin* would have found success earlier if he had not been short, fat, and bald.

I guess I was chosen to be the photogenic young thing of 1979, and since it is the custom of publishers to withhold all manner of secrets, they offered no advice about how to deal with the booby-traps waiting to be sprung. These tours are not only tests of stamina, but of sanity; the worst years are the early ones, when you are trying to convince the public you're not a lucky one-shot wonder.

There are not many authors who could not contribute, from their experiences, a chapter to a horror novel. I think the one I would write would be set in Winnipeg, where, several years ago, I was hyping *Platinum Blues*, a story about a stolen love song.

I found myself on one of those TV shows where they shuffle people from green room to studio, live on camera, for their five minutes of local glory. The host was sweating under his toupee and seemed otherwise distracted. Clearly he was not aware that the wrong guest had been deposited on the seat beside him, and he began asking me questions about how to care for the family dog. Apparently he thought I was the veterinarian who was still waiting in the green room.

There are rare, sweet occasions when you are dealing with professionals – Michael Enright or Vicki Gabereau – but a more typical episode, one I think many of us can relate to, might be this: You take a forty-dollar cab ride to a radio station somewhere out in East Scarborough, because your publicist can't take you there; she has John Updike in tow, or Martin Amis. As you introduce yourself to the receptionist, you look with trepidation at the station motto: "88 FM: All Country All Day." You know immediately that whoever will be taping the interview has not read a book in the last twelve years, particularly yours.

You realize who you really are. You are not a writer. You are fill. You are Canadian content.

And you wait. Station personnel scurry about, they engage in desperate whispered conversations, and you worry that they forgot to slot you. Can you come back tomorrow, they ask. You have to explain that tomorrow you're in Edmonton.

Someone finally races in with a tape recorder, a breathless cherry-cheeked apprentice who apologizes because she's only read half of the first chapter. At least she's honest. I get a kick out of those interviewers who fake it – they can't bring themselves to admit they haven't read the book, but they're eager to have you sign it so they can give it to their aunt for Christmas because she likes to read occasionally.

Or there's the graduate student at the local university station who is determined to deconstruct your novel, asks questions you can't comprehend, snidely demands to know whether popular fiction has intrinsic cultural merit, then proceeds to give away the entire plot. Your only comfort is knowing the station has an audience rating of .01 per cent.

And then there are the so-called hotline shows . . . where no one phones in. You're staring at the host's telephone console, praying that one of those lights will start blinking before the commercial ends, and when someone finally does call in, he's complaining about the sewer rates in Burlington or wants to know your views on animal testing.

You fly into Saskatoon for an anticipated full schedule and the publicist greets you with, "It's not a heavy day," and of the two interviews scheduled, one has to be cancelled because the host of *Good Morning Saskatoon* is still in detox.

So the publicist fills with visits to bookstores, and you wander into Chapters to sign a bunch of your books, and the acne-faced floor manager apologizes because they didn't order enough and they're all gone. You're reminded of a remark by Calvin Trillin: "The shelf life of the modern hardback writer is somewhere between the milk and the yoghurt." When you finally find the town's last surviving independent bookstore, there are lots of books but no customers, and you spend half an hour commiserating with the owner because the superstores are driving her bankrupt.

Another aspect of the writer's life of which I was unaware in my early naiveté is that we must read aloud to people. We usually do that in libraries. You earn a little side money doing this, and can usually cadge a free dinner. Often, if the library staff is on its toes, you get a good audience.

But there are disasters. You make your way to the Inglenook Public Library and find two people waiting for you and one is the town drunk looking for a place to stay warm and the other is your only fan, who has brought in half a dozen books to sign and you can't look him in the eye.

Remember the first time you read from your latest book, and stumbled over a misprint that had escaped proofreading? I found one in *Trial of Passion*, and my listeners wondered why I stopped in mid-sentence and said, "Shit."

I've been compiling a list of the questions most commonly asked at these events.

"How do you arrange your working day?" This is from the earnest young mother who has two children in tow, the kids who shuffled and whined throughout your reading.

"How do you get a publisher? How do you get an agent?" You feel forced to explain. Normally you can't get a publisher unless you have an agent. And you can't get an agent unless have a publisher. They stare at you blankly, trying to absorb this conundrum.

"What is your working routine?" You don't want to boast about your steely self-discipline because that will only depress the questioner – he harbours literary ambitions, you faintly remember him from a writers' workshop.

You explain sternly that in this trade there is no time clock to punch; you must exert a will of iron. You recount how you leave for your writing studio promptly at ten every day, imbued with determination. But you can't help but notice that the weather is fair; for a change it's not raining, so perhaps a walk in the woods might invigorate the mind, and the field mushrooms are out and perhaps one should gather some for dinner.

I came upon a wonderful phrase by the German physicist, Helmholtz, who said that great ideas come not at the worktable or when the mind is fatigued. The best ideas, he said, "come particularly readily during the slow ascent of wooded hills on a sunny day."

Many among the unenlightened do not have a proper appreciation that doing nothing is actually part of a writer's work. Robert Penn Warren describes as a kind of discipline taking pencil and paper and going out and sitting under a tree. Discipline resides, he said, in "the willingness to waste time, to know you *have* to waste a lot of time."

Indeed, William Faulkner is said to have divorced his first wife because she could not understand that when he appeared to be staring idly out the window, he was actually hard at work.

Ultimately, after a couple of hours of this kind of hard discipline, you take your bag of mushrooms to your studio and sit down to keyboard and monitor. But first you have to turn on CBC FM and listen to the news, and that's followed by the Brahms second symphony, and it would be insulting to the master not to listen. And in the meantime, of course, there's that unfinished chess game on the computer that might just sharpen the mind – to be followed by a few rounds of computer bridge. I have yet to fall prey to Internet addiction only because I have banned it from my studio.

Suddenly you realize that yet another hour has passed, and you sense within the first tremblings of panic disorder, and you finally bring up the chapter you've been working on, and you begin to read, to edit, to compose – and then just as suddenly it's seven o'clock and you're late for dinner and in deep shit and you race to the house, forgetting your bag of mushrooms.

Art may be a jealous mistress, but it is nothing as compared to the wrath of a wife who is about to be late for a meeting of the Pender Island Fall Fair Committee.

Here's a question we all like: "How much money do you make?" Or you get this one: "Do you have any control over what goes into your dust jacket?" She wants to say: "That picture makes you look younger than you really are; they must retouch those old photos." This is the one I fear the most: "Mr. Deverell, I wonder if you'd have a moment later to look at something."

This is the gentleman who pulls you aside over the cookies and coffee — he has never actually read one of your books, but he has written his own eight-hundred-page saga, about his struggles with the corrupt courts, about his wife's lying allegations of abuse — and he wants to know if you could put a word in with your publisher.

Louis Dudek once remarked that fame is the privilege of being pestered by strangers. Or you might prefer the definition by the Calgary iconoclast Bob Edwards: "Fame, from a literary point of view, consists in having people know you have written a lot of stuff they haven't read."

Sometimes you give readings in stores, but that's usually done jointly with, say, the former NHL star who's just had a ghostwriter churn out his auto-biography, and he has fifty people in his line for signings, and you have three. Sometimes you read in schools. Can there by anything more deflating than sitting in front of a group of shuffling teenagers who are waiting for the bell to ring?

Another question commonly asked: "Do you draw on real people for your characters?" This is an awkward one, given the laws of libel, but all fiction writers must admit to a little such plagiarism, mostly of friends, occasionally of enemies. My bête noire when I was in practice was a conniving prosecutor, a charter member of the Old Boys' Club and a foul-tongued master of locker-room humour. Ultimately, of course, he became a judge. He has passed on to an even higher court, so I may freely tell this story.

I sought to wreak revenge on him for his various misdeeds by portraying him in one of my early novels. This I did with fearless precision, and I was somewhat alarmed when this particular high court judge approached me one day in the Vancouver courthouse. He told me he thought my latest was my best and that all my characters rang true. It's odd how some people cannot recognize themselves in the mirror.

Not all characters come, of course, from life, except as patchwork figures made of scraps of reality, but sometimes they take on a life of their own. Or, to be more exact, they enter the life of the writer. I have been known to become the characters I create, to the dismay of those around me, who must endure the tedium of listening to me recite like a Buddhist guru or a depressed eco-neurotic jungle guide – that's this fall's book. My latest incarnation, in my work in progress, is a neurotic psychiatrist who is himself undergoing analysis. People avoid me because I am constantly analyzing their dreams.

Here's a twist on that theme: sometimes another person enters the life of the writer. Six weeks ago, I learned I have an impostor. This is the email that arrived:

Dear William Deverell,

I was wondering if you could do me a huge favour. Send me a signed photograph of yourself. The reason I ask is complicated. When my uncle died two years ago, my Auntie went mad suddenly for dating agencies, alcohol, and holidays abroad. A month ago she found a boyfriend named Ray Duval who claims to be Canadian and writes under the pseudonym William Deverell. On meeting me he handed me a copy of your paperback *Mindfield* and said, "This is one of mine." He also showed me a poem of very, very poor quality. I am a young Welsh author who had my first novel published at the age of twenty-one and I knew instantly that the works were by different people. Hence my search for the real you. When I found your website I confronted him with a printout and he now claims he and his publishing company, Mandarin Paperbacks, will sue you for copyright infringement. My aunt in her lonely foolishness believes him hook, line, and sinker. For my own sanity please send me some identification, autographed.

Since the message arrived shortly after April Fool's Day, I played with the thought that I was the target of a Machiavellian practical joke, but no, various researches have established that this young woman exists, as does her gullible and doubtless sweet auntie. I have sent proof that I am the real me.

Let me turn to another question commonly asked: "How did you become a writer?" Allow me a few minutes to make answer.

I never wanted to be a lawyer. All my life, I have harboured only one secret shameful fantasy, and I am living it. I have found early proof of this fantasy while in the process of assembling my archives for the University of Saskatchewan, my alma mater. I came upon a mouse-nibbled scrapbook deeply buried in a trunk. It was a sporadic attempt at a diary, and it swept me back to those years of middle teens.

Carol Shields once remarked, "There are chapters in every life which are seldom read, and certainly not aloud," but let me risk reading an early chapter of mine.

Listen to the voice of this angst-ridden yet swaggering adolescent. First entry, April 24, 1954: "I am feeling very dispirited today, so I decided to start a diary. A funny thing about this diary is that I hope it will be read by posterity. Someday I may shock the world into noticing me. I hope to be a great writer." Forgive him, for such splendid arrogance is the province of youth. The great writer goes on: "I'm dispirited because I'm afraid I'm falling in love with a girl. I wouldn't mind that very much, except that the girl seems to be quite bored with me."

Entry a few days later: "Ruth is babysitting. I tried to phone her. But I botched it. I can't speak on the phone to girls. I had wanted to go to *The Cruel Sea* with her. No dice. I think she is giving me a gentle hint to stay away. Warner and Frier are going to see *I the Jury*. I pity their intellects. It's about 7:30 now. I'll go to *The Cruel Sea* by myself, I guess."

Home was Regina. I grew up in the tough end of town, the north side, attended an institution called Scott Collegiate. My reflections on school: "We are going to be tested on some poetry, Browning and Shelley. How can someone be tested on something he loves? I'm goddamn sick of school. What a waste of time and energy."

A week later: "It's Saturday. I've been neglecting my diary. Nothing is happening. Finished reading *To Have and Have Not*. Ruth refused another date."

On the next page, the diary takes on a staccato tone: "I begin to have regrets about diary. It is ridiculous. Passed Ruth on the street today. She was with a girlfriend. She said, 'Hi.' I said, 'Hi, Ruth.' Warner is trying to convince me to be bold with her, but I can't."

Following that: "Went to an art gallery today. Student paintings. Some are all right. One of Ruth's was there. I was prejudiced and thought it was good, but my unbiased opinion is that it stinks."

Here's our young hopeful getting into politics: "Most interesting thing of this week is our coming election at school. I plan to start a political party to run candidates for the eight posts."

May 26, 1954: "Reaction sets in. I worked my heart and brain out for a bunch of dull dolts to get elected."

A cry of anguish: "It was I who conceived of forming a political party. It was I who convinced Eleanor to run. It was work to keep her going. It was I who convinced Frier to run. That was harder. It was I who brought Mitchell in with us, despite objections. It was I who got Lois Fritzler to run, perhaps our only safe candidate. It was I who got some expensive bristle board from Service Printers. I hate appeasement, so I walked out."

Entry the next day: "Eleanor lost the election by one vote. They're having a recount. Delva, Mitchell, and possibly Emily would have won if I had been allowed to manage their campaigns. I voted for Frier and that's all."

Here's my final entry — July 24: "I had stored my diary away. Just a while ago I opened it to glean over old memories. It makes me sound like a psychopathic freak. My mind sounds unbalanced. I'd like to go out with a girl tonight."

I made another stab at a diary a year or so later: "Now I am seventeen years, two months old, and I believe I should recap my literary career."

It was, I'm afraid, a pitiful career, consisting solely of having won, in public school, a citywide essay contest with an auspicious reward — the promise of publication. A children's magazine, *OWL* or *Chickadee*, one of those, would publish anything I would care to write.

This was the beginning of a case of writer's block that could almost be classed as pathological. I couldn't do it. I was overwhelmed by a fear of failure that continued to haunt me through my teens and early adulthood. Occasionally, during my years as a journalist, I tried my hand at fiction, but my trials were imperfect, incomplete, and what I produced I had not the courage to send anywhere.

This fear of failure drove me to the law. I shelved my dream of writing, stuffed it in a closet where I wouldn't have to face its steely glare. That dream collected dust for decades. Though I suppressed it, I was tortured by it, haunted by the whisperings of a forsaken muse.

But an internal pressure was building, fuelled by a fear that I might live out the rest of my life plagued by the guilt of never having tried. I was at that fearsome age of thirty-nine, so this was the classic archetypal midlife crisis. When I announced to my partners that I was taking a sabbatical from practice to write a novel, I could hear them muttering: "His mind is gone."

I don't think I have ever fully thanked Tekla for encouraging me to do this, to run off to the solitude of the Gulf Islands while she strove in the city as a counselling psychologist, homemaker, and mother of two teenagers, and it was with great trepidation that I walked out of the closet, dusted off the dream, and took it to Pender Island along with an old upright Remington, a box of blank paper, a three-volume Webster's dictionary, a first edition of *Fowler's Modern English Usage*, and that slim masterpiece by Strunk and White called *The Elements of Style*.

You all remember E.B. White's jaunty foreword, his reminiscence about his mentor, Professor Strunk:

> "Omit needless words!" cries the author . . . and into that imperative Will Strunk really put his heart and soul. In the days when I was sitting in his class, he omitted so many needless words . . . that he often seemed in the position of having shortchanged himself – a man left with nothing more to say yet with time to fill. . . . [He] got out of this predicament by a simple trick: he uttered every sentence three times. . . . "Omit needless words! Omit needless words! Omit needless words!"

My difficulty was that I had no words to omit. Nor would plot or character come. My intention had been to write a *serious* novel – God forbid I would lower myself to popular fiction – but all I managed to squeeze out were a few dribbles of descriptive prose. I stared at that Remington, memorized every bolt and spindle, began talking to it. I hiked, I biked, I scuba dived, I hung around with the locals at the bar. Weeks passed, months dragged by. Had I lost the use of the right side of my brain? Had too many years of exercising the left side, unravelling the quirky logic of the law, caused it to atrophy?

But I was to learn that the root of my problem lay elsewhere: I had been brought up by a literary father, brilliant and self-taught. A journalist, a voracious reader of classics who had learned German so that he might read Goethe and Schiller without the impediment of translation. He quoted Shakespeare on occasions appropriate or not, recited Keats and Shelley when in his cups – which regrettably was not an uncommon condition – and regularly insisted that I would be better off reading *Moby Dick* than *The Lone Ranger*.

My mother, for her part, devoured mystery novels, and she would simply, with her usual grace, shrug off Bob's withering denunciations of formulaic fiction.

Secretly, he wrote – stories that he mailed off to the *New Yorker* but that never saw the light of print. He showed me such a piece once, and with all the cool superiority of the teenage snob I was, I praised it insufficiently, and I don't think he wrote after that, and I have ever since carried the burden of my impertinence.

Even his last words to me, by long distance from Saskatoon, as he lay dying of cancer, were borrowed from a literary master: "The reports of my death are greatly exaggerated." But they soon turned out not to be, and I flew to Saskatoon too late. He had known I was writing a novel. He had had a dream: me, his son, buried in piles of paper.

If that was his dream, I was determined to make it mine.

As of that time, I was still suffering under the grinding weight of my writer's block, despite several blind forays into a self-conscious CanLit style that I assumed was demanded by the industry. But suddenly I underwent a catharsis. It was this: I had been afraid to write because of my father, afraid to follow in the footsteps of his failures, but also cowed by something larger, the sense that I would disappoint him if I did not follow the true and noble path – produce a work that would attract that adjective he most admired: "literary."

Despite my sadness at his death, now I was unchained: I was free to junk earlier efforts. I had been a criminal lawyer, I had defended the innocent and the guilty and prosecuted the vilest murderers. I knew something of the underbelly of my city, Vancouver; I knew something of the pompous theatre of the courtroom. I was nearing forty, and I was determined to break into print with both guns blazing. I would write a thriller.

I found justification from G.K. Chesterton: "Literature is a luxury; fiction is a necessity." But Hilaire Belloc may have better described my purpose: "When I am dead, I hope it may be said: His sins were scarlet, but his books were read."

Suddenly it was as if a dam had been breached, and I was drowning in a torrent of my own words. I was startled and awed, and I found myself muttering to my typewriter, "My God, Remington, I think I can write." I suddenly had a concept, a story. I had twisted characters and twisted plot. *Needles* would have a psychopathic killer seeking vengeance against a prosecutor.

As an anecdote, the germ of this plot was to be found in a murder trial I prosecuted, a thrill killing with macabre literary nuances. The accused had found himself absorbed in a thriller by Lawrence Sanders called *The First Deadly Sin*, in which a psychotic murderer seeks orgiastic pleasure through his deeds. As a sick form of plagiarism, the defendant had copied the crime. As he was being led away after being sentenced to a life of imprisonment, he slowed by my table and said in a low voice: "Someday I'm going to get you."

I later learned he escaped. So upon occasions like this, I always tend to look about to ensure he is not lurking among the audience.

Though I had some sense of foreordination that *Needles* would be published, I wasn't cocksure, and I will tell a guilty secret as to how I ensured my manuscript would not perish at the bottom of a sea of entries for the Seal Prize. One of my partners at the time – she is now Madam Justice Nancy Morrison – was a close friend of the late Judy LaMarsh, whose political memoirs had just been published by McClelland & Stewart. I forever honour Ms. LaMarsh's memory for personally handing the manuscript – we're talking about six hundred pages here, by the way – to Jack McClelland.

It was later reduced to half of that, a painful surgical process in the manner of limbs being amputated.

Jack McClelland is one of my heroes, a great showman, and not above employing the most disreputable devices to ensure a book might achieve the notoriety that boosts sales. Everyone hates lawyers, he warned me, especially critics, and they will utterly despise a lawyer who won fifty thousand dollars for his first book. So he devised an idea that was bound to inflame this animosity.

I became aware of it only when I looked one morning at the front page of the *Vancouver Sun*. The zipper – the human interest item at the bottom of the page – began thus:

Bill Deverell's Toronto publisher is needling book reviewers across the country to make sure they get the point about the Vancouver lawyer-author's new novel, *Needles*. The book is a courtroom drama set against the background of the Vancouver heroin trade, so in an effort to promote it, McClelland & Stewart mailed hypodermic syringes to the media. Complete with attached hollow needles, several hundred of the disposable syringes have been mailed to book editors across the country.

"You're kidding," was Deverell's reaction when the *Sun* told him about the promotion. "Anything in them?" he asked.

But the one-time *Sun* reporter knows a good headline when he sees one.

"The needle is part of the hype," he said.

My first inkling that Jack's publicity coup was to cause undesirable fallout came with the book's first review, also in the *Sun*. It began by quoting a section of the Criminal Code of Canada: "'Any publication the dominant characteristic of which is the undue exploitation of sex or of sex . . . and crime, horror, cruelty, and violence shall be deemed to be obscene.'"

The reviewer proceeded as follows:

The author of this unwholesome collage of sex, crime, horror, and violence is a Vancouver lawyer with considerable experience in criminal law. He should know that a decade ago, before decency was outmoded, his book would have risked prosecution under Canada's obscenity laws. Today, in our permissive society, the book wins a literary prize. It is a thoroughly nasty book. . . .

None of his characters, including police officers and lawyers, has any redeeming quality. The single exception is a judge. Lawyer Deverell prudently avoids sticking it to the judiciary.

I have since made up for that oversight.

I take comfort from Malcolm Lowry. In a letter following publication of *Under the Volcano*, he wrote, "The sales in Canada have been two copies, and my sole recognition here is an unfavourable squib in the *Vancouver Sun*."

My second novel, *High Crimes*, was about an audacious gang of Newfoundland drug smugglers, and was frankly fact-based. My reputation was not much enhanced by a Canadian Press review which was reprinted in dozens of newspapers. The lead paragraph read simply, "William Deverell is back on drugs." That made for easy work for the writers of the headings, and invariably they read as follows: "William Deverell is Back on Drugs." "Deverell Back on Drugs." "Award-winner Deverell is Back on Drugs." Ken McGoogan interviewed me for the *Calgary Herald*, but couldn't escape the temptation, though he offered a twist: "Lawyer Still on Drugs, Vows to Quit."

My more recent books may show no evidence that I have beaten the habit, but they do suggest I have been trying to escape from the chains of the criminal genre — I'm still haunted by childhood literary abuse, but it is no easy task to escape a life of crime. Or to write — if I may dare call it — bloodless prose. When I finally produced a book without a murder, it won two crime fiction prizes. I haven't killed anyone since, but the genre won't let me free from its clutches.

To the extent that my current creation, the neurotic psychiatrist, has subsumed me, I have found myself voraciously poring through psychiatric texts, seeking, as he does, to understand the artistic impulse. As the novel begins, my protagonist has just been abandoned by his long-term partner, a visual artist, and he is struggling to grasp the artistic impulses that drive her.

So I thought that for the remainder of my time here, I would share some of my research into the artistic urge, that itch to create from which we all suffer.

First, the good news: a comprehensive study of artistic creators at Berkeley inspired the authors of a popular psychology text to list these traits that were found to characterize creators:

1. Independence of thought, not interested in activities that demand conformity, not easily influenced by social pressure.

2. Tendency to be less dogmatic in their view of life than those rated as not creative.

3. Willingness to recognize their own irrational impulses.

4. Preference for complexity and novelty. (One researcher hypothesized that this reflects a desire to create order where none appears.)

5. A good sense of humour.

6. High emphasis on aesthetic values.

The conclusion drawn by these investigators seems both natural and agreeable: because creative persons are more flexible, they face fewer obstacles to problem-solving. In their next breath, however, the authors of this text go on to pop the balloons of conceit:

The reader may now be wondering why we have not listed intelligence as the prime characteristic of creative individuals. . . .

Beyond a certain level there is little correlation between scores on stand-ard intelligence tests and creativity. Some of the most intelligent persons are rated lowest on creativity. Among artists such as sculptors and painters the correlation between quality of work and . . . intelligence is zero, or slightly negative.

I have checked out this study, and I am able to assure you that writers scored somewhat better.

I would add a further quality which has been amply demonstrated to me during my twenty-one years of pleasant association with members of this Union. Not only are most writers less dogmatic and conformist, they tend to have a high social conscience, and many, I am happy to say, can be counted on to be in the front ranks of opposition to a society which marginalizes its artists, who oppose the new world order in which culture, health, and environment are held hostage to the marketplace, who share an ideal with those who stood outside the barricades of Seattle and Quebec.

One cannot write without a conscience.

But are we also diseased? There exists a school of thought that writers suffer a compulsive disorder that forces us to the page. Juvenal, in *The Satires*, put it bluntly two millennia ago: "Many suffer from the incurable disease of writing, and it becomes chronic in their sick minds." That brief thesis has sur-vived the centuries, and we still speak, in the words of Henry James, of "the madness of art."

That great explorer of the undiscovered self, Carl Jung, was once called upon to address a convocation of German poets, and he chose as his theme "the divine frenzy of the artist," which he says "comes perilously close to a pathological state." He reassures us, you will be relieved to know, that "only when its mani-festations are frequent and disturbing is it a symptom of illness."

Jung speaks of art forcing itself upon the author: ". . . his hand is seized, his pen writes things that his mind contemplates with amazement. . . . While his unconscious mind stands amazed and empty before this phenomenon, he is overwhelmed by a flood of thoughts and images which he never intended to create and which his own will could not have brought into being . . ." In a poetic phrase, he calls these images "bridges thrown out towards an unseen shore."

He advises us to think of the creative process as an alien impulse, "a living thing implanted in the human psyche which can harness the ego to its purpose."

So there you have it. We are led by an alien impulse. Like characters from speculative fiction, we are walking about with living implants in our psyches. To be fair, he was writing primarily of poets here.

The biographies of great artists, Jung said, "make it abundantly clear that the creative urge is often so imperious that it battens on their humanity and yokes everything to the service of the work, even at the cost of health and ordinary human happiness."

Sigmund Freud offers an even more dour analysis: he would regard us not only as slightly ill, but dreadfully unhappy. This is from a piece called "Creative Writers and Daydreaming": "The creative writer does the same as a child at play. He creates a world of fantasy which he takes very seriously, that is, which he invests with large amounts of emotion — while separating it sharply from reality." And he goes on to say, with utter confidence: "We may lay it down that a happy person never fantasizes, only an unsatisfied one. The motive forces of fantasies are unsatisfied wishes and every fantasy is the fulfilment of a wish."

But he is not finished shattering any smug self-images we may hold: we daydreamers are overcome with shame and guilt. "The daydreamer carefully conceals his fantasies from other people because he feels he has reasons for being ashamed of them. Such fantasies, when we learn them, repel us or at least leave us cold."

Still, Freud finds hope for the creative writer, whose personal daydreams, he says, can induce great pleasure. "How the writer accomplishes this is his innermost secret; the essential *ars poetica* lies in the technique of overcoming the feelings of repulsion in us."

How, you may ask, do we overcome this repulsion? "We can guess two of the methods. . . . The writer softens the character of his egoistic daydreams by altering and disguising it, and he bribes us by the . . . aesthetic yield of pleasure which he offers us in the presentation of his fantasies."

Freud makes the process sound utterly conniving, and I wouldn't doubt he was in one of his sour moods when he composed this. Maybe he had just got a bad review.

But Freud refrains from portraying us entirely as beyond salvation. We writers have a useful therapeutic role to play: "[The] enjoyment of an imaginary work proceeds from a liberation of tension in our minds. It may even be that not a little of this effect is due to the writer's enabling us . . . to enjoy our own daydreams without self-reproach or shame."

Dr. Otto Rank was an early follower of Freud, but he ultimately took a divergent and possibly risky path. He devised the concept that male creators are motivated by jealousy of female procreation.

The great psychiatrists don't offer a cure for what ails us. Sigmund Freud: "The nature of artistic achievement is inaccessible to us. Science can do nothing toward elucidation of the artistic gift." When asked to publish his theories on sexuality, he himself replied as an artist might: "If the theory of sexuality comes, I will listen to it."

Carl Jung: "What then can analytic psychology contribute to the mystery of artistic creation? . . . Since nobody can penetrate to the heart of nature, you will not expect psychology to do the impossible and offer a valid explanation for the secret of creativity."

Though he tenders a theory that art comes as eruptions from the collective unconscious, he joins Freud in abandoning us to a mystery that must fascinate us all.

And while studies have shown that creative artists rank in the upper 15 per cent of the population in psychopathology – we score high particularly in the hysterical and paranoic disorders – we also rank in the upper levels of ego strength. As one observer put it, we are both sicker and healthier than those with less artistic bent.

But let me not leave the topic without quoting some sunnier observations from proponents of self-actualization: "The mainspring of creativity," says Carl Rogers, "[is] curative. . . . Man's tendency to actualize himself, to become his potentialities . . . is evident in all organic and human life." Maslow speaks of the "peak experiences" particularly enjoyed by artists. Rollo May tells us we are characterized by an intensity of awareness, a heightened consciousness.

On that more reassuring tone, I should conclude, because I note the bar is about to open, and I sense, particularly among my fellow writers, a stirring and a thirst. In thanking the Writers' Union and the Writers' Trust of Canada, I can think of no better exit line than this quote from a magazine piece written forty years ago by Hugh Garner: "A short time ago, Morley Callaghan and I were talking typical writers' talk — about our current work, critics, publishers. . . . Before we parted, Callaghan said, 'Being a Canadian writer is tough, isn't it?' I answered, 'Well, it sure beats working in a pickle factory.'"

2002

JANET LUNN

Thank you to the Writers' Trust of Canada. While it's more than a little unnerving, it's a very great honour to be asked to give the Margaret Laurence Memorial Lecture.

My memories of Margaret Laurence are few, but they're good ones. I knew her first through her books. Many years ago, I had an ongoing argument about Canadian literature with a librarian in a small Ontario village. Bessie Webster had been in her library for forty years and she had never become a fan of Canadian literature. I was, and we used to argue strenuously and at great length. Finally, I bought the library a copy of *The Stone Angel*. The very next morning, Bessie called me on the phone. "Alright," she said, "you win. Would you like to go shopping for Canadian novels with me?"

Years later, after I had joined the Writers' Union, I knew Margaret slightly — at the distance that I felt fit my status as the author of three little-known books. More years later, I had lunch one day with her and a mutual friend at her house in Lakefield. She was then, as she always was, a warm and gracious woman.

She was also a great storyteller. It is this that makes me particularly pleased to be giving this speech honouring her memory. I've called my speech "For the Love of Story."

When I visit schools to talk about my books, children often ask me, "If you weren't a writer, what do you think you would be?" All I can ever think to answer is, "Beats me."

I loved writing long before I started doing it, long before I could even imagine doing it, long before I realized I *was* doing it. And at the heart of my life as a writer – of my entire life, in fact – is a love for story.

I heard my first stories from my sister Martha. We snuggled together in the big armchair by the living room stove while she read to me. I was probably about three. Martha is four years older than I am and she was already in school. Slowly and laboriously, she read me Old Testament tales from our book of Bible stories for children and fairy tales from her school reader: *Rapunzel, The Goose Girl, The Twelve Dancing Princesses*. I was enthralled.

"Once upon a time . . ." The words would no sooner leave my sister's lips than I would be in the story, living it with the spell-struck princess or the goose girl. Those stories settled forever into the marrow of my psyche. And not only those particular stories: story, itself. It invaded my life – and it invaded the landscape where I lived.

When I was two years old, our family went to live in an eighteenth-century farmhouse, a mile and a half outside the village of Norwich, on the Connecticut River in Vermont. The house belonged to my divorced grandmother who was a businesswoman in New York. She'd bought it to retire to. It was 1931. My father was an engineer out of work, and we lived there through the years of the Depression.

We were a middle-class German-American family – all my forebears are German, except for a pair of Jewish great-grandparents. Almost all of my immigrant ancestors came to the U.S. in the 1830s and '40s, but they and all their descendants, until our time, lived in German communities in or near New York City. And so both my parents spoke German. Mine is the first generation that doesn't.

These very urban New York parents had a hard time in rural Vermont. But they made the best of it. While my mother dealt with farm animals and vegetable patches, wood stoves and freezing water pipes, my father sold cars and found a variety of small jobs that added up to an income. As an adult, I know what those years must have been like for them, but I didn't know it then – and those years were such a gift to us children.

We were three girls then (I have a brother, but he wasn't born until I was eight). We all fell under the spell of the Vermont countryside. It was a paradise of hills and woods and rushing water, of trailing arbutus blooming under the last snow in spring, of white winters and summers heavy with wild berries and the scent of roses.

We only had each other until we started school, and the brook just behind our house and the meadows on the hill above it marked the boundaries of our world. I remember hot summer afternoons, lying in the meadow, dreaming, and others, standing with my sister Ann in the ripples the brook made as it glided over the stones. We would dare each other not to move when the minnows nibbled our toes. In winter we would lie on that same spot on our stomachs and clear a place with our snow-crusted mittens so we could watch the minnows darting around below the ice.

I have read essays on the subject of mythology that argue persuasively that the creatures of European folk and fairy tales do not belong in North America. For the most part, I believe that's true. In fact, I wrote an entire novel predicated on this conviction. But it isn't always true. Children make their way through their world, happily picking and choosing whatever fits into it. Certainly, I never found castle ghosts or creatures born of mist or bog in the sunlit hills and streams of Vermont. But I knew that the ones I found in the Scandinavian stories of Selma Lagerlöf and Elsa Beskow could be there, the elves and brownies and trolls and gnomes, the creatures of clear, northern light. They lurked behind the high rocks. They scurried down the hills and slid along the shadows made by winter snow drifts. They were as real to me as our two horses, our cow, our pig, and our ducks and chickens.

There was, too, the ever present past. My sister Martha did more than read me fairy tales. She told me stories of savage battles that were fought in our brook between the early Vermont settlers and the native Abenakis (she would always lower her voice and say, "And the water was thick with blood"). She told me there was an Abenaki baby buried under the huge pine tree that tow-ered over my bedroom window. It was sadness for the dead baby that made the tree sigh so mournfully. I believed every word. And why not? Our brook's name was Blood Brook and that tree did sigh endlessly.

Then, when I was old enough to go to school and our class went tramping through the old village graveyard on Memorial Day, I discovered that that old graveyard was full of people named Blood. As for the pine tree, when it had to be cut down about forty years ago, there were no tiny bones among its roots, nor was there any sign that there had ever been any. All the same, the scenes I saw as I listened to those tales are still as real in my memory as the brook and the tree they were told about.

But the past that lingered in our community was that of the forebears of the families descended from the eighteenth-century pioneers. That past was as near as yesterday's memories. When I listened to the stories at gatherings in kitchens, or in the Grange or the church hall, most of the time I couldn't tell whether they were about our old neighbours or about their ancestors with the same names. They were told in a way that made it impossible. The past was always there, nudging the present. It was just beyond a barrier that was not quite imperceptible. You could almost reach out and touch it. I longed to go into that past. I dreamed myself into it. I have written fictional characters into it.

Teachers have thanked me for writing historical novels in order to teach history to children in an interesting way. I don't. I don't write historical novels to teach anything. I write them because some small, stubborn part of me still feels that, if I am quick enough, or wily enough, one day I will find my way through that time barrier.

Stories. Eventually I learned to read for myself and, like every writer I've ever known, I was, straightaway, a voracious and a compulsive reader. Ours was not a book-loving family. I never saw my mother read a book that wasn't a cookbook. She was much too restless to sit down long enough to read. My mother was a wonder. She was incredibly energetic, she was volatile, and she had a mind that knew no logic. It worked in swoops and swirls and figure eights and I found it mysterious, even as a child.

My father had a very logical mind. I think of my father's mind as being like a piece of graph paper, squared off and unbendable. He was a solid, very conservative thinker. He was not much of a reader, either.

Neither of our parents ever read to us except that, every Christmas Eve, Dad read Dickens's *A Christmas Carol*. And neither of them encouraged my predilection for reading. (I can still hear my mother's voice: "Janet, put that book down and go outside and get some fresh air!") Years later, my father wasn't entirely happy about my writing, either. After I'd published my first book, he took me aside and told me that I could lose my husband by spending so much time writing books.

I slid into making stories without even realizing I was doing it. Daydreaming. Aren't all fiction writers daydreamers? Alas for me, daydreaming was considered the eighth deadly sin by my parents and my teachers. I was always in trouble for indulging in it. I daydreamed for the reasons most people do, to feel better about the painful realities of life, but, every bit as often, to make stories or to burrow more deeply into the books I was reading so that I could create sequels. I had no idea that I was practicing to be a writer. But, of course, I was. I worked my inventions over until they felt right. I was tireless. I checked every detail of every setting. I tried the dialogue again and again until it sounded real – and like the good descendant of all those Germans that I am, I carefully added the *he said*s, *she said*s, and *they said*s.

But I never once thought of those daydreams as stories. Stories were what you found in books. Ordinary people like me did not write books. The names on the spines of the books I read – Louisa May Alcott, Frances Hodgson Burnett, Lucy Maud Montgomery – were names belonging to unreal, mythical people, not ordinary people you could actually know or be.

I had friends – sisters, Audrey and Marguerite Frost – who were Robert Frost's grandchildren. This meant absolutely nothing to me. But they had an aunt, Eleanor Frances Lattimore, who had written books for children that were in our library. And one of them was about Audrey and Marguerite and their cat Ulysses. It was called *The Clever Cat* and I was given a copy of it for my ninth birthday, the year it was published. I had the kind of reverence for that book that a votary has for vials of water from the Ganges or bits of wood purported to be from the true cross. I still have that book and I swear it still exudes a faint aura of the sacred.

I created an Eleanor Frances Lattimore in my mind, a creation which, no doubt, would have startled the original. I never met the original and I have no idea what she looked like. But my Eleanor Lattimore was beautiful. She had soft, white hair piled high on her head and a beatific smile on her face. She was a bit plump, she was always dressed in a sort of generic historical costume, and she vaguely resembled the picture of Martha Washington in the book the library had about American presidents and their wives.

No, the notion that I might become a writer never even suggested itself to me: not then, not all through school or university. There was nothing in the environment of my growing years that might have offered that suggestion. No Eleanor Frances Lattimores came to our four-room schoolhouse in Norwich to talk about books or the people who wrote them, and we did not write stories in school. Nor did I write the plays some of us put on in Janice Reynolds's garage. I was shy and timid and my daydreams were much too private.

We left the Connecticut River country when I was ten. All these years later, I still feel the echo of the heartache I felt. It wasn't that my entire childhood was an idyll. I don't think anyone's childhood is that. But the hills that rise steeply from the western shore of the Connecticut River had become the country of my heart. No place I have lived since has held me so powerfully (although the low-lying country at the edge of Lake Ontario where I lived for thirty-one years has come a close second).

We moved in 1939. The U.S. didn't enter the Second World War until 1941, but the Americans were building planes, warships, and weapons, and there were jobs for engineers again. My father found one in New York City and we lived in the outlying suburbs.

I graduated from high school in 1946 and was set to go to Bryn Mawr College in Pennsylvania, where I'd been offered a scholarship in English. But, when I wrote the college entrance exams, I failed Chemistry. (That place in the human brain where numbers are computed is missing in my case.) It was a dreadful shock when the college not only took away my scholarship, but would no longer have me as a student. The day the letter came to tell me this, I cried all afternoon, my mother got into the sherry, my brother and sisters tiptoed around us with great care, and my father started looking for other possibilities. He found Queen's University in Kingston, Ontario, Canada. Our Canadian next-door neighbours suggested it. Now there was an exotic notion to brighten the gloom!

The registrar at Queen's wrote to say that I'd have to have grade thirteen. My resourceful father checked out the World Almanac and found Ottawa University. The Oblate Fathers who ran the university didn't accept women, but they had an affiliated college that did. The college turned out to be the Notre Dame Convent School in Ottawa and I went there.

I don't think I'll ever forget the day I arrived in Ottawa. My father and I flew up from New York. We got rooms at the Lord Elgin hotel, registered me at the convent school, and went out walking. It was a warm, soft September evening and we wandered for quite a while in awe. The castle-like Chateau Laurier, the Old World–looking Parliament buildings, the canal, the river, the space – the whole city seemed to be not quite of this world. We finally came to roost on a bench behind the Parliament buildings to watch the sun set along the river. Then the carillon began to ring. That was the grace note. I was captivated.

I was a very young seventeen and I took to boarding school life as only a girl who'd steeped herself in girls' school stories could do – and I did manage to get through upper school math. That fall, I went to Queen's to study psychology. I was defeated by graphs and white rats and B.F. Skinner. I changed to English and history. My ambition to become a serious student of English or history – or anything – was defeated by a very good-looking ex-airman with a wicked sense of humour. He sat behind me in Professor Alexander's class in Middle English. This was 1947. The veterans were just back from the Second World War and Richard Lunn was one of them. We were married a year later.

Richard got a job as a reporter for the *Kingston Whig Standard*. I started having babies. And I was reviewing books for the paper. When the older babies became small children eager for bedtime stories, I asked the editor of the paper if I could review the children's books. He was some surprised. It had obviously never occurred to him to review those books. Nobody in Canada, outside of library publications, reviewed children's books. I got the job.

It was a casual decision that turned out to be among the most important of my life, although I didn't realize this at the time. What I did realize was that I was rediscovering the joy of reading books written for children. Maurice Sendak was new on the scene in the 1950s and so were both E.B. and T.H. White, Rosemary Sutcliff, Philippa Pearce, and Mary Norton. I took great delight in the inventive plots of books like *Charlotte's Web, Tom's Midnight Garden*, and *The Borrowers* – and something more than that.

Children read differently than adults. Adults tend to read first with head, then with heart. Children read with every part of themselves at once. As Graham Greene said once, "No one ever reads again with that intensity with which he reads at the age of ten." And so children's books tend to be more of a piece. While I wasn't about to give up reading the subtler, more complex, more leisurely novels for adults, I was revelling in the simple, spare, understated writing that's found in the best children's books. It touched something in me that has always been touched by essential forms of expression: myths, fairy tales, traditional folk music, line drawing, poetry.

I was hooked. I not only read all the new books that came to the paper every month, I read again all my own childhood favourites. Then I reached back into history to read every children's book I could find that had ever been published in – or translated into – the English language, plus all the critical books and essays that touched on the entire field of children's literature.

Richard got a job at the *Toronto Star* and we moved to Toronto. The book editor there let me have the children's books as well as a whole special section at Christmas time. I had a fine time gathering books from publishers – and building a library for my own children (none of which I relinquished to them when they left home). I was filled with missionary zeal. I persuaded a couple of magazines and a CBC radio program to take my reviews. I gave talks on children's books to Home and School Associations, I gave lectures at summer school to school-library student teachers. Finally, I had read and dissected so many books that, almost in spite of myself, I started writing.

My first efforts were stories for children's magazines and they were pretty embarrassing. I remember labouring long and lovingly over a story about a dear little witch who wasn't very good at her job. When I think about some of the splendid books I was reading and how much I'd always loved the Grimm Brothers' collections of fairy tales, *The Secret Garden*, and the stories of Louisa Alcott, I have to wonder in which carefully concealed corner of my psyche I found the impulse to write precious stories like that. There were others just as bad.

I sent them out to magazines. Back they came. Over and over again. Is there a writer who doesn't know that game? Then one day I got a twenty-five-dollar cheque from *The Family Herald* in Montreal for a story that took up two inches in a very small box at the foot of their children's page. I was so carried away by the excitement of having sold that story that when the repair man came to fix my grandmother's old electrified treadle sewing machine, I let him talk me into buying a new one on time. And that's not the whole story. That man wasn't gone long when the Encyclopedia Britannica salesman showed up. I signed up with him, too. That afternoon, I knew that soon, very soon, I was going to be earning real money. The euphoria faded at about the time Richard came home from work that evening. I knew, then, that I'd better sell a lot more stories – fast.

It took a lot more stories – and years – before I was making any money at all, but I did sell a few. And it had finally gotten through to me that my mentors were – had to be – the authors of the books I loved best. I'd never had any encouragement to write and no mentors but the authors of those books and, gradually, I was realizing just how important they were to my writing. I found myself reading my treasured old books once again, not with a child's eye nor with a critic's eye but with a student-writer's eye.

I once heard the painter Robert Motherwell being interviewed on the radio. He talked about the painters he admired and the painters who sent him home to paint. I realized that I was finding this with the books I read. There were writers whose stories I admired. There were writers whose stories I picked apart, chapter by chapter, sentence by sentence, almost word by word, to see how they were put together. And there were writers I read simply because they sent me racing to the typewriter. That's still true.

Then, in 1968, I published my first book, the one that got my father worrying about my marriage. I was forty by this time, and at the centre of a growing family – the oldest of our five kids was in his late teens and the youngest was ten. And they all had friends who had friends, all of whom seemed to be living in our house. My life was a juggling act. It was, often, more than I could cope with. I was greedy, I wanted it all, but time to write always had to be stolen. And always the stolen time came in frustratingly small scraps: an hour here while babies napped, fifteen minutes there while they were with the kids next door, a blissful half-day on a Saturday or Sunday when their father took them all off to the park and, later, whole working days while they were all in school and proper mothers were pushing vacuum cleaners through their houses – or baking prize-winning pies.

The thing with writing, of course, is that it won't be confined to those stolen times. It's like yeast dough, it crawls out of its bowl and sneaks across the floor at you; it's like the dog who chases after you when you thought you'd locked him in the yard on your way out to get the groceries.

I would find myself stirring soup with one hand and writing dialogue with the other, jumping up from the dinner table because the disparate fragments of plot that just wouldn't work had suddenly come together. I'd stop in the middle of reading a bedtime story because something in it made me see that the protagonist in my story had the wrong name or should be two years older than I had thought. I beat my stories into the cake batter and the cake batter into my stories. I made not only my husband, but my kids act as sounding boards for every word I wrote, and every word I wrote had an echo of them in it. (My son John remembers squeezing himself into the family laundry basket full of clothes that never got ironed while I read to him.) There are discernable bits of my life in all my stories, as well as the lives of my parents, my siblings, my husband, my children, and my friends.

I now had two books published and we moved from Toronto to Prince Edward County on Lake Ontario. The second book was a history of Prince Edward, Richard's home county. Because he was a journalist, the County Council had asked him to write the book as a 1967 centennial project. We wrote it together. This, I might add, is not a great exercise for a husband and wife to engage in.

During the research for the history, we had come across an old Loyalist farmhouse. It hadn't been lived in for years. It had no furnace, no plumbing, and a leaking roof, but it had an original fireplace and bake oven in its kitchen and it was on a small bay. Richard was willing to settle for anything that would get him home to his county. The old fireplace, the bake oven, and the bay were all I needed. Then, when we discovered that the house had a resident ghost, all the kids wanted to live there, too. So we moved.

I wrote a book set in the house with the ghost as one of the characters. I sent it to the U.S. publisher of my first book. In my blissful ignorance, I was sure that once you'd had a book published, you would never again have any trouble publishing anything you wrote. The manuscript came back to me – not as fast as those early stories had done, but fast enough. It had a long, friendly letter accompanying it with criticisms and suggestions, but it was very definitely a rejection. I was crushed. When I could finally bring myself to re-read the manuscript, I knew the editor was right but I didn't know what to do with it, so I shoved it into the back of my filing cabinet. I wrote and published a picture-book story and a collection of Canadian hero tales but not another novel.

It was 1970. The arts were coming alive in Canada. It's hard now to remember a time when opera in Toronto was performed in the old Maple Leaf Gardens, there was no National Arts Centre in Ottawa, and music concerts in most towns were a few chairs gathered around a record player in the public library. There were few bookstores (and none of the giant chains, either, of course) and there was very little publishing in this country. Then came the Canada Council for the Arts and with it grants for writers and publishers and support for organizations like the Canadian Children's Book Centre. With this kind of encouragement, hopeful writers for children were beginning to send manuscripts to publishers who, of course, had no editors who understood – or even liked – children's books. Clarke, Irwin & Company, one of Canada's pioneer book publishers (now long gone), decided to hire a children's editor and I got the job.

What a new wrinkle this was in my life! Manuscripts were coming in. I was meeting other writers for children. We editors talked book talk at lunch in the restaurant across the street (when my house was full of teenagers who, in those days, weren't talking to anyone over thirty). I stayed at Clarke, Irwin for two and a half years, got into a fight with my boss over the subject matter of a book, and quit.

At the same time, my children were finishing school and leaving home in rapid succession. Richard was now teaching at Ryerson (then Polytechnic Institute, now University) in Toronto. He was home weekends and for three months in the summer. My rejected manuscript about our house and its ghost had been nagging at me almost from the moment I'd put it away. Now, at last, I was free to get back to it. But I couldn't. I couldn't touch it. While I had often questioned my ability to do it, raising children had always felt like an essential and rewarding job. But that job had grown up and gone away. I was honourably retired. I could write stories with a clear conscience. And it felt like an acutely selfish thing to be doing. I felt as though I should be out delivering Meals on Wheels or pushing gift carts around in the local hospital, the things my farm neighbours did when their children grew up. But I wanted to write. But I couldn't write. I couldn't even go near my workroom. I became seriously depressed.

Rescue came in a form I could never have anticipated. I met an elderly British scholar/mythologist/children's writer named Katherine Briggs. She was in Toronto to give a lecture at the Osborne Collection of Antiquarian Children's Books. The editor at her British publisher's was a friend of mine, and she had asked me to take Dr. Briggs to lunch and entertain her. Well! I listened, Katherine Briggs entertained.

She was entertaining before she even opened her mouth. She was a woman of just above medium height with short, wavy, white hair, very blue eyes, and a commanding presence. I can't remember what kind of dress or suit she had on but I remember her bright purple shoes, her bright purple cloak, and her bright purple hat. The shoes were suede and had buckles, the cloak was voluminous, and the hat was a sort of wide-brimmed cavalier affair without the plume. I was impressed. We had lunch and then she said, "Now, my dear, where shall we go where we can talk?" So we spent an afternoon in the members' lounge of the Royal Ontario Museum telling stories and drinking gin. We both drank gin, but Dr. Briggs told most of the stories — and dispensed wisdom.

When I confessed to her how selfish I had come to feel about writing stories, she told me a story that snapped me out of my depression and made the rest of my writing life possible. She told me that, during the Second World War, she'd helped staff a tea kiosk in London during the Blitz. She said that the firefighters would come in towards dawn. Their faces would be grim and grimy, and they would be so weary they could hardly reach across the counter for their mugs of tea. After a minute or two, one or another of them would always say, "Give us a story, Kate."

At once, everything about the importance of storytelling I'd been trying to get across to myself fell into place. I went home that day with a cheerful heart, and I have never been bothered by that demon again. There were others.

During the writing of the history of Prince Edward County, I had become very attached both to the people who lived there and to their history. What's more, researching that history had brought a revelation. Prince Edward was settled by the Loyalist refugees from the American Revolution. I had pledged allegiance to the flag of the United States every single morning of my twelve years in American schools. I'd studied American history for all but two of those years — a lot of it about that revolution, its glorious patriots and its dirty traitors. Now, I discovered that the dirty traitors, the Loyalists, were the heroes, the good guys in Canada.

I had become a Canadian, not by conviction but because I couldn't seem to grasp the mathematical formulae needed for the study of chemistry, and because I had fallen for the nifty fellow sitting behind me in an English class at university.

Conviction had soon followed. My fondness for this country that had begun on my first evening in Ottawa had grown until I was like a convert to a religion or political party. There was a time when I practically buttonholed people on the street to tell them what a great country this was. I had come to feel more at home here than I had anywhere since leaving Vermont. I'd read Susanna Moodie and Catharine Parr Traill, Hugh MacLennan, Morley Callaghan – I'd read everyone from Sam Slick to Frederick Philip Grove. I'd taken out Canadian citizenship. I canvassed for a political party. I wanted to belong here. I wanted to belong to this country the way my husband did. I spent years working at saying *caffee* instead of *cawffee*, *ooranges* instead of *aaranges*, and *hoose* instead of *hause*. To no avail.

At one point in her novel *The Four-Gated City,* Doris Lessing says that once you've left one country, you've left them all. I think she's right. After writing the history of Prince Edward County, I finally had to admit to myself that, no matter how my twigs and branches might wave in the Great White North, my roots were deeply imbedded in that rocky New England soil south of the border. I didn't – couldn't – entirely belong in either place. I was never really going to belong anywhere.

Much as we belonged to the countryside, we were strangers in that Vermont community. (The people there couldn't even pronounce our name, Swoboda.) I never felt at home in suburban New York, and here I was, an immigrant in Canada with no hope of ever belonging the way my husband did. I couldn't even be as Canadian as my children. That longing to belong has informed my life and almost everything I've written.

When I started writing again, I went back to the book about my house and the ghost that haunted it. With my newfound confidence, I let my imagination travel where it wanted to go. And away it went, back in time to the American Civil War with a child who, like me, belonged everywhere and nowhere. While the story, which I called *The Root Cellar*, is not autobiographical in its plot or its characters, it is emotionally autobiographical. I realized, when I'd finished writing it, that I'd gone step by step on the journey my heroine had taken and I'd made a kind of peace with myself about having been always an immigrant.

As well, I had come to care deeply for the Lake Ontario country where I was living — and where I'd set so much of my story. Another demon dealt with.

Another thing the writing of this book did for me was to help me see myself as a writer. A couple of years earlier, during the time I hadn't been able to write anything, I'd gotten the invitation Margaret Laurence had sent to every writer in the country to join the newly formed Writers' Union of Canada. There was no way I could have brought myself to join a union of writers with the stature of Margaret Laurence, Margaret Atwood, Pierre Berton, or Alice Munro. I was a housewife who reviewed children's books and had written one book. One small book.

In the intervening years, I had published two more small books and I was finishing this novel. I got up my nerve and joined the union. I still didn't feel like a full-fledged writer but, surprisingly, I felt as though I belonged with those who were. It was almost a shock to find out that there were other people who understood about the compulsion to write, who suffered the same agonies when stories wouldn't come right and the same mourning periods when stories were finished. It was a gift I had never expected.

I did know, by this time, however, that I was a writer for children. C.S. Lewis insisted that no one writes well for children who isn't still, at least partly, a child him- or herself. When I first read that, I had been reviewing children's books for some time and I thoroughly agreed with him. I saw this in writers like E.B. White, Mary Norton, and Lewis himself. But I had also just published my first book and I wasn't at all sure I had enough of this quality to make me ever succeed as a writer for children. One day I confessed this fear to Peter Martin, who was my publisher. Peter stared at me in absolute astonishment. Then he burst out laughing. "You're the only eight-year-old I know with a thirty-five-year-old vocabulary," he said.

At first I wasn't sure how I should take this, but I decided, finally, that however it was meant, it was true. I have never managed even the semblance of sophistication. I am still astonished by the world and everything in it. The fact is, I have never even quite gotten used to myself.

As well, I had no sooner ceased to be an actual child than I started working with children. During my teen years, I earned my pocket money babysitting. My great contribution to the Second World War effort was volunteering at the local hospital as what is now called a "candy striper." I used to pedal my bike furiously on my day to work so I could get there first and sign up for pediatrics. I always wanted children. I married young and had all five children in a space of time that worried my mother, outraged my mother-in-law, and sent my husband to the surgeon. I like kids.

Wrapping your life around children puts you in a funny place in our world, though. A child psychiatrist I saw being interviewed on TV recently pointed out that ours is not "exactly a child-centred society." I've known this for years. But it still irritates me when I get asked, "Why do you write for children?" – or more bluntly, "When are you going to write a real book?" No one ever asks me why I write history or historical fiction, but interviewers, teachers, kids, quite a few writers for adults, and, sometimes, even friends still ask me why I write for children. In fact, the only people who never do are other children's writers and children's librarians.

The answer is that all the stories I feel compelled to tell are for children – or teenagers. At one time I thought I would write fiction for adults, but it wasn't for me. What sustains a writer through the hard, agonizing, sometimes tedious hours, weeks, months, years of writing a book is the compulsion to get said whatever drove him or her to it in the first place. That compulsion never leaves me when I'm writing a story for kids. The excitement that comes with being taken by a new story idea may dwindle and even completely disappear through the miserable times when the story won't come together or a character won't emerge into the light or the right word or phrase lurks just beyond the crack in the door to my subconscious, but the compulsion to tell the story? Never.

Sheree Fitch said in a talk she gave in Ottawa a few months ago that, for her, writing for children means "staying in a safe place." I'm not at all sure that children's stories are all that much safer than adults' stories, except that they have more conclusive endings than most adults' stories and stick closer to Aristotle's definition of drama. And children's books do not deal in irony or despair.

Perhaps this is what makes them feel safer. Whatever the truth of that may be, it isn't the safety that entices me; it's that *frisson* I feel as I start off on a new adventure with a set of characters I have only just met. I know where the adventure starts and I know where it's headed, but, try though I may to map the whole of it, it gets away from me. I have discovered that I am a true combination of my mother and my father. The part of me that's my father carefully maps out a story from start to finish. Then the part of me that's my mother takes over, and there goes the map. They battle for the upper hand, back and forth, back and forth in a sort of uneasy counterpoint, until the adventurers finally come to rest on the last page.

I'm addicted to the journey, the actual writing process. It's awful, it's wonderful, I feel driven all the time I'm writing, but I'm never completely happy when I'm not in the middle of a story. My husband once told me, crossly, "When you're not writing a book, you're doing your damndest to make a story out of your life, and not always a good one, either." So I keep writing.

My life story is about love affairs with places, with people, and with words. In it there have been so many good friends, so many rich experiences, and so much fun. I now have a seventy-three-year old vocabulary and I'm quite content to know that I am still eight years old, still amazed by life, and can still so easily cross that thin line between this three-dimensional world and the other one where time gone by is lodged and stories happen. One of these days I may have to drift off into whatever brain fog is currently afflicting the aged. I can only hope, if that happens, that I will have found myself, once again, in the hills where the brook runs clear and the wind sighs in the big pine tree. But not yet.

I'm like a small boy I once knew, a neighbour when my children were growing up. He was a dawdler. One morning, his exasperated father shouted up the stairs, "Gregory, have you made your bed yet?"

Greg shouted back, indignantly, "I can't make it, I'm still in it."

That's how I feel about this writer's life: I'm still in it — and I'm still loving it. Thank you.

On May 23, 2003, Alistair MacLeod delivered the Margaret Laurence Lecture at Library and Archives Canada in Ottawa. Similar to Roch Carrier in his 1990 lecture, MacLeod chose to speak without the aid of a written text; also similar to Carrier's lecture, a recording device malfunctioned and the lecture was never taped. The following text, written by MacLeod in 2010, is a reconstruction of what was said that day.

—

This lecture is entitled "The Writer's Life: Geography as Inspiration." I'd like to talk a little bit first about geography and then about how it affects a writer's life and how it has affected many great works of literature. (The geography doesn't have to be positive.) I may also talk a little bit about my own personal relationship with geography; perhaps how it helped to make me who I am, even in ways over which I had no control.

All writers, as all people, come from a specific place in a specific time. As children, we are born into a specific geography. When we look through whatever windows (openings?) there are, we see what is before us. We may see the ocean, we may see forests, we may see icebergs, we may see sand, we may see herders following their flocks of sheep and goats, we may see looming apartment towers. We eat whatever is given to us. We may eat codfish, we may eat porridge, we may eat blubber, we may eat French fries from McDonald's, we may eat Kraft Dinner, we may eat tortillas. We may subsist on milk and cheese from our family's animal herds. In our early years we eat whatever is given to us and in the years before choice, we seldom complain. (We may also experience certain dietary rules and regulations – "We don't eat that," "We refrain from eating such and such on certain days or for certain periods" – based on the religion of our geography.)

Our first acquaintance with language comes from our parents or caregivers. We imitate their words, their accent, their dialect. The naming of things (nouns) comes from their geography: what they see before them and around them. (These are mountains, this is a camel, this is a kayak, this is a crocodile, this is a crow.) Occupations are often dictated by geography. People who live by the ocean may seek their sustenance from it. People who live on the pampas may become gauchos. People who live in West Virginia or Kentucky may seek employment in coal mines because there is nothing else. Mountain climbers and mountain guides come from regions where there are mountains. (Sherpas don't come from downtown Ottawa.) Hockey players rarely come from Patagonia. Hockey players rarely come from Kenya, but many marathoners do. People who live in certain geographies develop different immune systems, different lung capacities; pigmentation differs. Geography very often dictates who we are and what we do.

There is also, in addition to mountains and deserts and oceans (physical geography), political geography, religious geography, racial geography, gender geography, tribal geography, and on and on. If you are a certain colour or religion, you had best not go into a certain neighbourhood, or be found on a certain side of the wall, be it a physical, historical, or psychological wall. If you come from a certain tribe, you had best not be found in an area dominated by another. You had best not apply for a job there or maybe even try to apply for a passport. If you are from the South of Sudan, be careful of those from the North – if from the North, best not be found alone amidst those from the South. If you are from a certain caste in India: "Do not go there – do not even try." If you are a young woman in a country such as Afghanistan and you do not choose to wear a burka, be warned. If you are a young woman in an area controlled by the Taliban and you choose to read or write, be careful – you may have acid thrown in your face, you may be stoned, you may be killed. And this is real.

These are the various geographies into which people are born. You may be born into a home in which certain food is eaten and certain political and/or religious attitudes are expressed and the ocean or the wind is in your face all of the time and you may hate it. And probably, in Canada, when you are seventeen, you may say, *I am going to get out of outport Newfoundland, or rural Quebec, or the Ottawa Valley, or interlake Manitoba, and I am never going back there because I dislike it so much*. But you will always carry within you what happened in your original place. You will always be affected one way or the other by the kind of geography which helped to make you what you are. And it may be positive as well as negative. If there are people trying to get out of Cape Breton, there are others trying to get back. In parts of the world, if you don't like your geography, you can move. In other parts of the world, movement is difficult, if not bordering on the impossible.

It has been said that people write about what worries them. If "worry" is too strong a word, one might say that people write about what they "think" about. And people worry/think about different things depending on their geography. Everybody in Canada (with the possible exception of those in Victoria or Vancouver) worries about winter. Most Canadians in November, or earlier, are running around doing all kinds of pre-winter things: getting antifreeze, winter tires; checking their furnaces; putting plastic on their windows; buying mitts and gloves, and shovels and salt; putting insulation around their pipes. Why are they doing this? Because if they do not, winter will cause them great discomfort or even kill them. Canada has no comfortable South. Nobody in New Orleans or Miami or San Juan or Acapulco engages in any of the above activities. Winter will not kill them, but perhaps some other regional particularity will.

In countries as vast as Canada and the United States, the geography varies and so do the worries. (In the United States, there is a strong difference between those who live in the geographies of Montana and North Dakota and those who live in Louisiana or southern Alabama.)

In Cape Breton, where I grew up, members of my family were engaged in coal mining. In times of labour unrest, the initials UMW (United Mine Workers) resonated through the atmosphere. (Would the UMW support the strike or not? Was the UMW's headquarters in Pennsylvania too far away to be interested in Cape Breton? etc.)

People near the ocean think and worry a lot about DFO (the Department of Fisheries and Oceans). DFO regulates fish quotas, the seal hunt, the length of fishing seasons, the mesh sizes of nets, the number of lobster traps, the establishment of marine zones, etc.

Where I live now, in Windsor, Ontario, the major industry is the manufacture of automobiles. In addition to the decisions made by the manufacturers, the input of the CAW (Canadian Auto Workers Union) looms large in most manufacturing decisions.

Yet, if one were to go to the Prairies and shout "UMW!" or "DFO!" or "CAW!", with the exception of a few specialized locations, the shouts would fall largely on disinterested ears. The "worries" of such an area would focus instead on the decisions of the Wheat Board, the price of oil, the Hog Marketing Board, the perils of the softwood lumber industry, the fear of mad cow disease, etc. In a country the size of Canada, the concerns are often regionally specific. Yet nationally, all Canadians, presumably, love their children, don't wish to be murdered in their beds, yearn for financial security, and hope for the healing power of love.

Canada, we are told, is 4,726 miles in width. It consists of different settlements with different histories, different attitudes, and yes, different worries. It would be impossible to write the "great Canadian novel" because such vastness contains so many differences. The Inuit are supposed to have their twenty-seven words for snow. If this is so, it is because they are in it all the time. (The Bedouin in the desert probably don't even have one word for snow – but, perhaps, many words for sand and its movements.) The people of Quebec have been in their landscape for as long, in some cases, as twelve or thirteen generations. They are largely of one racial stock, one language, one religion, and they have been in a certain climate for a long, long time. "My country is a country of winter," as Gilles Vigneault says. They are distinct. The people of Newfoundland are largely the descendants of West Country English or Irish ancestors. They represent 96 per cent of their province's population. 40 per cent of the population of New Brunswick is still classified as rural. In the western provinces, many of the people are descended from "all the little Europes," as the poet Peter Christensen tells us, and, of course, the Aboriginal peoples have been here since "time immemorial." Yet over one half of the population of Toronto, Canada's largest city, was not born in Canada. These latter see the images of Toronto, largely urban, but they also carry within them images from their original homelands; from Bosnia, Sri Lanka, Tanzania, Somalia, Pakistan, etc. Generally they have not been in a kayak or participated in an Alberta cattle drive.

The writing that comes out of the regions generally reflects the images of the region. In the early English/Scottish ballads, all of their early comparisons come from the images provided by geography. These are primitive but generally accurate: "hair as black as the raven's wing"; "nut-brown ale"; "milk-white skin"; "sharp as the thorn." (They never say "white as a polar bear" because they have never seen a polar bear!)

Language and imagery generally grow out of the region's landscape and concerns. In the United States, the imagery of Cormac McCarthy, Larry McMurtry, and, sometimes, Annie Proulx often consists of sagebrush, windmills, dry riverbeds, horses. It is very different from the imagery of Simon and Garfunkel or that of Woody Allen – imagery based largely on New York City, featuring Central Park, neon lights, etc. In the same manner, the imagery of W.O. Mitchell and Guy Vanderhaeghe is quite different from that of David Adams Richards or Donna Morrissey.

I think my point is that literature often comes from places where the various kinds of geographies have an effect upon the central characters. Such works could not come from anyplace else. The work of James Joyce could only come out of the Ireland of its time. It couldn't come out of New York or London or Calcutta. *Wuthering Heights* could only come out of those Yorkshire moors – with those birds, those plants, that wind, snow, and isolation. It could not come from London or Cambridge or Oxford. Chinua Achebe's *Things Fall Apart* could only come out of a certain African milieu. Pre-Apartheid South African literature uses the particular imagery of its landscape as it reflects on apartheid (its major "worry" or idea). In *Oedipus Rex* by Sophocles, we encounter the "super-smart" man living amidst the various geographies of his home. Here are the mountains, the sheep, the shepherds, the plagues, the riddles, the prophecies, the oracles, the power struggles.

In the literary culture of such a recent country as the United States, great differences exist, depending on the various kinds of geographies explored by individual authors. In the early stories of F. Scott Fitzgerald, there are boys trying to get into their chosen fraternities at Princeton. They worry about having the right kind of white trousers and about denying their more humble Midwest geography. But in the landscape of Flannery O'Connor or, generally, in William Faulkner, the worries are much different. No one, in these worlds, is going to Princeton; and certainly no one in the writings of Richard Wright, the anguished black writer who explored the brutalities of his time, is Princeton bound. Yet all of these authors and their characters are American, trying to live out the dramas of their lives in the landscapes given to them.

The American short story writer Raymond Carver once said that it was the writer's job to bring the news. By that he meant that the writer's task was to tell the larger world what it was like to live in a certain place at a certain time. This is why fictional works are often more informative than historical documents. Fictional works contain characters and thus have a human dimension. "This is what it was like to be a child in nineteenth-century England," the great writers of that time tell us. "This is what it was like to be a little boy," Dickens tells us in *David Copperfield* and *Great Expectations*. "This is what it was like to be a little girl," George Eliot tells us in *The Mill on the Floss*.

"These were the issues and this was the geography along the Mississippi," Mark Twain tells us in *Huckleberry Finn*, written in 1884. "This is what it was like to be a certain kind of boy in rural Nova Scotia during the 1940s," Ernest Buckler tells us in *The Mountain and the Valley*. "This is what it was like to be a certain kind of young girl in southwestern Ontario," Alice Munro repeatedly informs us. No one is encouraging these girls "to be the best they can be," but rather the question is, "Who do you think you are?" "This is what it was like to be in love in Quebec at a certain time," we are told in *Maria Chapdelaine* and *Kamouraska*. "This was life on certain streets in Montreal," says Mordecai Richler, ". . . and life on the Prairies," say Sinclair Ross and Margaret Laurence.

Enduring literature, such as that found in the titles above, deals with characters living out their destinies in certain geographies. The same things, the same specifics, would not happen to them if they lived somewhere else. (A black man born in southern Alabama would not face the same situations as a black man born in Nairobi, where almost everyone is black.) Geography matters.

In a country as vast as Canada, our strongest voices seem to emerge from the regions and the landscapes and the worries endemic to specific geographies.

It has probably always been so, as I have tried to illustrate. One could draw a literary map depicting "the Atlantic voices"; "the Quebec voices"; perhaps the urban (Toronto?) and rural Ontario voices; "the Prairie voices"; "the B.C. voices"; and, hopefully, with more to come, "the voices of the North." There is nothing in this that is narrowly exclusive. Certainly one may love his or her husband or wife without hating everyone else.

Yet out of these specific places comes the literature of Canada. It is often specific to its geography, but the best of it is universal in its scope and in what it has to say. Specific geography inspires the author so that he or she might say something universal to the larger world. I think that is what the English poet William Blake, that most universal of men, meant by "seeing the world in a grain of sand" and "eternity in an hour."

Thank you very much.

2 0 0 4
AUDREY THOMAS

We were sitting around one evening at Moskowitz's down on the Lower East Side in New York. It must have been during Prohibition days because we were drinking turnip wine.

An intense-looking pale blackhaired young fellow comes over from another table, plunks himself down in the seat opposite, and announces that he is a high school senior. He gives me a black look through his glasses.

"I've been watching you all evening."

"God forbid."

"What I want to know is why don't you act like a writer?"

"How ought a writer to act?"

"You know just as well as I do how a writer ought to act."

I tried to ease him off. "Suppose I did know," I answered as mildly as I could, "how do you know I'd want to act like a writer?"

He glared at me through his glasses. He was groping for words. He got to his feet. "Let me tell you one thing," he spluttered all out of breath, "meeting you sure is a disappointment."

— John Dos Passos

When Deborah Windsor called to ask if would like to give the Margaret Laurence Lecture this year, a dear friend was helping with the final packing-up for my annual winter removal to Victoria. He said, "For years, for as long as

I've known you, you have wanted a separate writing studio, and now you have one. Perhaps you could begin by talking about that. Or you could put a table on the stage – if there is a stage – and show it covered with books and papers."

"Books and papers on chairs as well," I said, "on every surface, even the floor, although that is changing now that the writing shed is finished."

"What about a picture of the writing shed?" he said.

I liked the idea of some visuals, and I remembered a wonderful play I saw last year in London, a play called *Pretending to Be Me*, about the poet Philip Larkin. Tom Courtenay played Larkin, or rather, for two hours he *became* Larkin, standing there amidst piles of packing boxes (he had been forced out of the place where he had lived for the past thirty years) and telling us his thoughts about life, poetry, other poets (he called Ted Hughes "the Hulk"). All he had unpacked was a kettle for tea, a mug, a whiskey bottle, his old gramophone – the kind where you actually lifted the arm to set the needle down – and a few records. Larkin was a serious jazz fan and even wrote a book about jazz; every so often Courtenay would put on a record and behind his voice we would hear the haunted voice of Billie Holiday or Armstrong's "The Lonesome Road."

And so, although I have brought no music – I thought about it, beginning with "Mairzy Doats and Dozy Doats," perhaps, moving through some of the hymns I sang in the Junior Choir, past "That Old Black Magic," "Blue Suede Shoes," Flanders and Swann, Peggy Lee, Miles Davis, The Beatles, Leonard Cohen, and on and on and on. Decided against that; in the end (can't leave out West African music, Greek music, can't leave out all those classical gentlemen), there would have been nothing but music. Not a bad thing, but I'm supposed to deliver a lecture. I have compromised with a few props and a few slides, which might help you to form an idea of what my "writing life" is like today. What you will see for the next minute or two are pictures of the new studio (I like the word "shed" better, but it is rather grand for a shed), the rocks and trees of North Galiano, the government dock where I watch the sunset and where a few years ago I watched the Hale-Bopp comet night after night as it streaked across the sky and tried to imagine what such a sight would have meant to our ancestors whose world was controlled by gods who had to be placated with prayers and offerings and sacrifices.

[*Editor's note: At this point in the lecture, Thomas presented a slideshow of personal photos.*]

So now you have seen where I ended up, where I am today, but this is not where I began:

I was born in Binghamton, New York, a small city which specialized in light industry; it was connected to two other similar towns, Johnson City and Endicott. Together, the Triple Cities, as they were called, produced Ansco film, Link Trainers (for aviation), shoes, and furniture, not to mention the presence of IBM in Endicott, where my Grandfather Corbett was head of the Mechanical Engineering Department. A few years ago, I was listening to a computer person on the CBC. He was talking about the new voice-activated word processors and the interviewer asked him if they were really any good. He said that you had to get the computer used to your voice and this took a while, even if you spoke slowly. For instance, every so often his computer would print "ENDICOTT" in capital letters, instead of the word he'd said.

"'Endicott'?" said the interviewer. "What does that mean?"

"I have no idea," he said. Well, of course I had to write in and explain about growing up with the IBM plant right next door in Endicott, New York. I said I suspected it was like E.T. calling home.

At one time, in Binghamton, there had been a cigar factory where a woman worked who had been the champion cigar-roller in America. She would have loved Wallace Stevens's poem "The Emperor of Ice Cream":

> Call the roller of big cigars
> The muscular one, and bid him whip . . .

although Stevens seemed to see cigar-rollers as men.

Binghamton itself was a city of about eighty thousand people when I was growing up. Two rivers ran through it, the Chenango and the Susquehanna, so to get downtown, where the department stores were, where the movies were shown at the Strand, the Riviera, and the Capitol, you had to walk over a bridge. Because of this, people said they were going *overtown*, not *downtown*. About once a month, when my sister and I were in elementary school, our widowed grandfather took us over the bridge to see the latest Bob Hope and Bing Crosby "Road" movie and after that we went to the Ritz Tea Room, where the hostess, in a black dress which set off her blonde upsweep, greeted my grandfather by name and led us to a good table. I always chose a "French pastry" because it seemed appropriate in such a place. My mother did not approve of these outings – she thought the "Road" movies were too risqué for young children. We never told her how Grandpa flirted with Helen, the tea room hostess, and told us, with a wink, to call him "Uncle Larry." Up at his summer camp, Grandpa also had some amazing drinking glasses with pictures of pretty girls stamped on them. If you filled a glass with water and then drank, the girl's dress came off and there she was in her undies. You can imagine what my mother thought of this! My mother thought her father was "too highly sexed," but I think it was all talk; I think he loved one woman, and when she died he never wanted anyone else. He told me he had seen my grandma sitting on a porch swing, in Brooklyn, when she was sixteen. (She was the friend of one of his four sisters.) He told her mother he would come back and marry her in three years, and he did.

By special dispensation from the Superintendent of Schools, I was allowed to start school before my fifth birthday. My sister was already in school, and I think I drove my mother nuts. She said I begged to go, but I don't remember doing so. I was small and shy and spent most of my early school years daydreaming or staring out the window, having finished the reader on the day it was handed out. I wasn't crazy about school but when we learned to write, in grade two, I loved the long wooden penholders in those bright primary colours and the inkwells, which the monitors filled up with "washable blue" every Monday. However, if you pressed too hard with your steel nib, the point went right into the paper and left a blot. (My efforts at perfect penmanship were never displayed with a gold star on Parents' Night.) It is almost impossible to remember what it was like, not being able to read. I think I got a taste of it in Latakia, Syria, walking around with a friend, trying to make sense of the shop signs and street signs. It all looked like decorations; how could these be *real words*? We needed to get back to our freighter, having flagged down a fish boat, which, in exchange for my friend's hat, agreed to take us into the port. Now it was two days later, and we would have been left behind if we hadn't met up with the local Singer Sewing Machine representative, who took us to his shop, fed us tea and sweetmeats while women in black came and went, buying a single needle, a spool of black thread. There were blue hands painted on the outside walls. He wrote out instructions for us to hand to the guards at the port, insisted on sending his driver with us, and we were eventually taken out to the ship (which was a mile out) by a boatload of traders.

When I thanked our Singer Sewing Machine friend for all his help, he shrugged and said, "Well, why not, I'm Syrious." I love mistakes like that. Outside Latakia, at the famous site called Ras Shamra, the guide who showed us around said that people were buried in large earthenware jars. They were buried, he said, knees to chest, "in the fatal position."

A Nigerian dentist in London told me he wanted his children to be "absolutely fluid" in English.

My oldest grandson, then aged four, stared out at the rain and told me it was a "drismal" day. I myself, maybe seven years old, saw something in the evening paper (we really weren't supposed to look at it until my mother removed anything she considered "unsuitable") about a child "mole taster" who was on the loose. As I had a small, rather pretty mole on my neck, I was terrified, turned the collars of my blouses up for weeks.

I don't mind not understanding a language. In Japan, where the poet Robert Bringhurst and I had been sent to talk about Canadian Literature, I tended, most of the time, to just let the language flow over me, like standing under a waterfall, like listening to music. I had taken a few weeks of polite Japanese at a local high school, but that was all. Robert could read it. He told me our subway stop was called Dream Mountain.

In Greece, where I spent an entire year – mostly in Crete, but I went up to Athens for the winter – I took Greek lessons at the American-Hellenic Institute and went wandering around the city reading signs. I never became *fluid*, but when I went back to Crete in the summer, I too could sit on a straight-backed chair with the women on my street and chat a little, join in hurling insults at the watermelon man who had years ago done something stupid and unforgivable. The street was so small it had no name: I called it "*Odos Anonymous*." In the evenings, the priest in his black robe and stovepipe hat leaned in the window of the only house that had a television set.

"Humph," said my neighbours. "He is lazy, that priest. He cannot get up in the mornings; his old mother rings the bells."

I can still hear the rusty braying of the donkeys, the sound of the women's looms, can see the thick afternoon light pour down the whitewashed walls.

In Athens a bus stop was a *stasis*. One left the cinema by the *exodus*. Most fascinating of all were the little green trucks that raced across the city, they had cardboard signs in their windows that said "*Μεταφορά*" – metaphor. They were transfer vans taking goods or parcels from one place to another. And isn't that exactly what a metaphor does? All the world's a stage.

"Roast lamp" was on the menu of one of the little *tavernas* in Crete.

Language, then, and travels: two of my obsessions. Have I told you that from the time I was in grade three, when I had the measles and chickenpox, one right after the other, I wore glasses? (And glasses were horrible in those days. There was not the incredible choice of today and they certainly weren't chic, either, for girls or boys. They came in one style and two colours: pink for girls, blue for boys.) I think that people who are very short-sighted tend to compromise by listening quite carefully to what people say. I know I love the visual world and am told I am quite a visual writer; if I could have one transforming wish, I would wish for 20/20 eyesight. Did you know that optometrists have special eye charts for people who play bridge, for musicians? I expect that soon they will have them for people who stare at computers all day long. Dos Passos had congenital myopia and we all know James Joyce was blind as a bat.

Television tires my eyes; radio doesn't. We all listened to the radio when I was growing up, especially on the weekends: *The Lucky Strike Hit Parade*, with its slogan, "L.S.M.F.T.," "Lucky Strike Means Fine Tobacco" (later, the bad boys in the high school changed that to "Loose Sweaters Mean Floppy Tits"); *Amos 'n' Andy*; *Lux Radio Theater*; *The Shadow*, although I never quite trusted that The Shadow was on the side of good, what with his sinister laugh and the fact that in our town he was brought to us by the Blue Coal Company. After school, we listened to *Jack Armstrong, the All-American Boy* (not forgetting Betty, his sidekick); *Captain Midnight*; *The Lone Ranger*. We had one radio, a table model in a walnut case. I loved the dial with its cat's-eye glow and all those tubes in the back. Sometimes my sister and I were allowed to take it upstairs at night, where we scared ourselves silly listening to *Suspense* and *Inner Sanctum* and holding hands across our beds.

When we came to Canada, the first thing we bought, after groceries, was a little radio. It was turquoise and white and we had it for years, until someone took it off the kitchen table and put it on top of the fridge in an impromptu

poker game. It fell off and smashed to bits, or "smithereens" as my mother
would have said. (We didn't get along very well, my mother and I, but I miss
her language: "highfalutin," "lollygag," "hooligan," "smithereens," "get-up."
"You're not going out the door in that get-up!") I remember listening to *Stories
with John Drainie* in the afternoons and vowing that someday I would have one
of my stories on the radio. Thanks to Robert Weaver and Don Mowat and
John Juliani, I had not only stories, but also many plays produced on the CBC.
And last year my novel, *Isobel Gunn,* was on *Between the Covers*, the wonderful
voice of actor Duncan Fraser really bringing the narrator, Magnus, to life.

*But were you always writing? When did you begin? You've mentioned the pretty colours
of the penholders, you've mentioned ink, but this is the first time you've mentioned anything about writing. Were you writing all this time?* Well, yes – and no. I started
writing poetry in elementary school, but it is what I would call *dishonest writing*: poems written to please adults and, hopefully, to win prizes. One of them
did – a *Scholastic* magazine regional prize – for the county but not the state. I
can't remember what it was about, but I received a pin and a cheque for fifteen
dollars, which I promptly spent on a pair of saddle shoes. You would think I would
remember the poem, but I don't. This is probably because I knew in my heart I
was a fake. I could hardly write about my quarrelsome parents, all that yelling, or
the bill collectors or the plaster on the living room ceiling falling down and nearly
killing the dog. I never even talked about such things. Why would I write about
them? So – romantic poems with titles like "Autumn," "The Unknown Soldier,"
"The Gold Star Mother Bakes a Cake"; that's how it all began. My progress was
slow; my early work was neither astonishing nor precocious; it was just plain
bad. Oh, and doggerel limericks, those were fun. I can remember one of those:

> There once was a fellow named Farrell
> Whose life was in terrible peril.
> He fell in with some rogues, who took all but his brogues
> And had to walk home in a barrel.

Both my father and my grandfather were great kidders and it's only recently
I've come to realize how much I owe them in that direction. My father used
to sing a song which began, "Oh the bulldog on the bank and the bullfrog in

the pond" and went on in a nonsensical fashion, ending, "Be careful of that monkey wrench, your father was a nut." He liked Vaudeville and lamented its demise, loved Laurel and Hardy. He sometimes broke up sentences to make a perfectly ordinary statement seem silly: "What's that in the road — a head?" "What are we having for dinner — Mother?" Drove us to New York City once, even though he was a terrible driver, so we could all see the Rockettes and the show at Radio City Music Hall. My father once confessed he wished I were a drum majorette or something showy like that.

My grandfather liked joke shops and humour of a crude kind. There was a small box which looked like a book, labelled "Gone with the Wind." Open it up and inside was a tiny pan of beans. I've already told you about the girls and their disappearing dresses on the drinking glasses. Sometimes when we went for a ride with him in the summer, up at his camp in the Adirondacks, he'd say, "Well, we're off like a bride's nightie." It took me years to understand why my mother always said "Dad!" in a horrified tone.

I used to memorize the Burma-Shave signs on our way up to camp and sometimes made up rhymes of my own:

> Be careful now
> And don't get funny
> Remember, birds, these signs cost money.
> BURMA-SHAVE

These days, I think up cartoons or the captions for cartoons. (I can't draw.) The "Swiss Army Wife" with many arms, holding a baby, a frying pan, a telephone, car keys, a bag of groceries, etc. A flock of Canada geese high in the sky, the last one holding a banner that says "Honk if you love Jesus." And after I went to Australia in 1990, I imagined a picture of the Ken doll standing flipping burgers on a barbeque: "Ken and Barbie." I like the words in dictionaries that say "o.o.o.," "of obscure origin" — little linguistic orphans — or "obs.": not "obscene," but "obsolete." I like phrase books with their useful phrases: "Where is," "How much," "Too much," "I have a pain in my _____."

Oh, even a two-year-old knows the wonderful power of words: "No," "Won't," "Mine."

Larkin, too, liked squibs and limericks, although his are often nasty. Here's one from January 1954 called "Love":

> *Not love you? Dear, I'd pay ten quid for you:*
> *Five down and five when I got rid of you.*

(And yet he could write something as beautiful as his poem on the Arundel tomb.)

In the outhouse during the war there was, in addition to the Sears catalogue, a corncob in a glass box with a little sign underneath, IN CASE OF EMERGENCY, BREAK GLASS, and toilet paper with caricatures of Hitler, Hirohito, and Mussolini: WIPE OUT THE AXIS, it said. Nailed to the door was a sign from the gas station: IS THIS TRIP NECESSARY?

There is a story, probably apocryphal, about me standing on the beach below my grandfather's summer place (my grandmother wasn't well and someone had said, "Take that child down to the beach"). I was told I was too noisy to stay in the house and must play quietly with my sand pail and shovel for an hour so that Grandma could get some rest. Apparently I was furious, raised my infant arms, and yelled, "All right, all right, you win. But some day I'm going to Yurrup."

This sounds too sophisticated for a three-year-old, but I did know about "Yurrup" thanks to my grandparents' stereopticon, which my sister and I were allowed to play with on rainy afternoons, if we were very careful. Do you know what a stereopticon is? Two pictures of the same thing were taken at slightly different angles – Notre Dame, say, or Buckingham Palace – then printed side by side on the same card. You looked through a thing shaped like a snorkelling mask and pressed a wooden crosspiece holding the picture until suddenly, what you were looking at became three-dimensional and thrillingly real. I was often confused about life, especially the world of adults, and thanks to the stereopticon and its magical cards, I got it into my head that if I could get to Europe, things would become clear. (Many years later, I used the stereopticon in a story called "Natural History.")

My grandfather's camp was very important to me; we went there every summer from the time I was a baby until I was eighteen and he was forced to sell it. It didn't seem to matter that we had no other kids to play with when we were up there – or it didn't matter until we were well into our teens, but then we discovered the Saturday night square dances at the Fish and Game Club, an old wooden building within walking distance. The camp was only about a hundred and fifty miles from Binghamton and we left home the day after school got out (my father was a high school teacher), returning the day before Labour Day. Only a hundred and fifty miles, but another world: one where my parents didn't dare quarrel, where we could run down the path and across the beach into the water any time we liked. Where we woke up to the smell of wood smoke and went to sleep to the sound of the frogs in the creek that led to the lake. We even had our own rowboat and later on, when we were bigger, a big double-oared boat, which we skimmed across the lake chanting, "We must, we must, we must increase our bust." We never wore shoes, except on Saturdays when we went into Speculator, New York, to get the weekly groceries and the newspapers. (It was in Speculator that I saw the front-page photo of the mushroom cloud over Hiroshima.) We stopped at the general store which had a soda fountain. I always ordered the same thing – a sarsaparilla ice cream soda, because I liked the name. It didn't taste very different from root beer, but it sounded much more exotic. The store also sold postcards, some of them scenic and some the sort you find at English seaside resorts (an operating theatre and the doctor saying, "Nurse, nurse, I told you to remove his *spectacles*"). When I was old enough to have an allowance, I saved up and bought a small pillow stuffed with balsam needles; it said, I PINE FOR YOU AND BALSAM.

The first summer we stayed in town, I knew I had to get a job. I was on a big scholarship to a college in Massachusetts, but it wasn't enough, and besides, I had to start saving for Europe. I looked in the paper and the only possibility seemed to be a part-time job demonstrating hairbrushes in one of the three department stores. "Young lady with excellent head of hair and good diction needed," etc., etc., etc. I felt I was tailor-made for the job and who knew, it might lead to bigger things. Unfortunately, I overslept, and the job was gone by the time I made my way to the personnel office on the fifth floor. They had nothing else part-time, so I headed over to the State Employment Office to see if they had some position I could fill. I should say at this point that I had no marketable skills at all. This was long before girls could work on road crews holding up a "Slow" sign or engage in anything seen to be unfeminine. There were lifeguard jobs, but I have never been a good swimmer, never quite got the hang of the Australian crawl. Worst of all, I had vowed I would never learn to type, even though my mother said this was foolishness. She was a cracker-jack shorthand typist and had trained in New York at Katharine Gibbs. At this point in my life, she was secretary to the Jury Commissioner in our town, a good civil service job, but I had got it into my head that I would never get out of Binghamton if I learned to type. I still don't type, although I can hunt and peck well enough to send an email or write something short like a book review. I write my novels and stories on lined yellow paper.

I am probably one of the last of the longhand prose writers, a dying breed. At the Dickens House last year, I tried writing with a quill pen such as he used. My God, how did he do it? I couldn't even write my name without big blobs of ink decorating the paper. I have it easy with my Pilot Hi-Tecpoint V7 fine-point pens, which I buy by the box. My cheerful typist, Carole Robertson, lives in Montreal, just below a street with the charming name of Souvenir. She has been my typist for fifteen years, and to me, when I pop what I hope is a close-to-final draft into one of those red-and-white Express envelopes, it's like sending the children to camp. For a week or two, I am free.

But let's go back to my eighteen-year-old self, her hair shining from the Breck shampoo of the night before, her summer dress pretty yet demure enough to demonstrate hairbrushes in the Ladies' Department of a department store, waiting anxiously as the woman behind the desk at the employment office looks through her card file.

"Nothing, I'm afraid."

"Not even a chambermaid?"

I had been a chambermaid for a month at a small resort not too far from my grandfather's camp the summer before. I didn't like it much, but the money was helpful and sometimes people who stayed a few days left a nice tip (especially when their kid had thrown up all over the mattress, things like that). There was only one respectable hotel in our town — the Arlington, down by the station — but they didn't want temporary help.

"There is one job," the woman said, hesitating, "two if you can find a friend to go with you."

"Where is it? I'll take it."

"The Hill."

My sister was away — it's strange that I can't remember what she was up to that summer — but a friend of hers, whose father was a doctor, said she'd be willing to try it, so we drove up together, borrowing her brother's old convertible, a little anxious but pretty sure we could manage.

The Hill was the state insane asylum. Joan quit after two days; I worked there all summer, for three years.

I never said a word to my parents about what it was really like. My father hated talk of illness of any kind, but my mother must have known; her sister had been in there briefly after a nervous breakdown, and one of my grandfather's sisters had been put in there, again briefly, to prevent her marrying a man her father didn't approve of. We all pretended I was just some kind of candy striper, those nice girls at the regular hospital who found a chair for your visitor or a vase for your bouquet. I never told them that on the first day, when the director of the building took me up in the elevator (which worked with a key) and unlocked the door to Ward 88 with another key, the staff nurse said, when we were introduced, "Good. We need you. Welcome to the Shit Ward."

By the end of my time on The Hill, I had worked not only on 88 and 93 (geriatric wards), but the Shock Ward (both insulin and ECT), the ambulatory wards, the O.R. Every ward but the Violent Ward. I got up in the morning, took a bus overtown, changed to a bus that would take me close to The Hill, and walked the rest of the way. I wore a white cap with a grey band and a bunch of keys on a rope around my waist. I was the only girl from the West Side who worked there. Most of the nurses (male and female) and orderlies were from the East Side and had names with lots of consonants next to each other. The nurses were great — in many ways they were the beginning of my social education. The only bad thing they did was teach me to smoke. From them, I learned about abortions and the dangers of; I learned words like "vulva" and "vagina" and "testicle" — words never said aloud when I was growing up. Even words like "cunt." Sometimes, when we came out of the elevator and headed over to the dining room for a stodgy lunch (shepherd's pie, cottage pudding), one of the fellows from the male ward would call out, "Hey, Koneckny, lend us the Princess for a quick fuck." Oh, this was long before "fuck" was used as it is today, as a verbal tic. Every other flicking word is "fuck."

The minute I changed into my summer dress, turned in my keys, and walked down to the bus, I put it all out of my mind. None of this had anything to do with me.

When I returned to college in September, my friends would say, "How was your summer?"

I would say, "Fine."

My bank balance grew and grew and in my third year I finally got to "Yurrup," spending a year at St. Andrew's University in Scotland with my best friend.

We sailed from Boston on the Furness Withy ship the *Nova Scotia,* the smallest passenger ship to cross the Atlantic. There was some kind of strike on at Boston Harbor. Our steamer trunks, labelled NOT WANTED ON VOYAGE, went into the hold, but we were asked to carry our cabin luggage up the gangplank ourselves. A photographer from the *Boston Globe* asked if I would mind doing that again, and so back down I went and up again, twice, before he got it right. I still have that photo somewhere of this strange-looking girl in a pageboy and high heels, smiling a strained smile. Her slip is showing, or as we used to whisper to another girl, "It's snowing down south." Boston, Halifax, St. John's – Liverpool. Twelve days. I'm sorry for people whose first trip abroad is flying over an ocean in a glorified aluminum cigar. I think it was Cunard who used to advertise "Getting there is half the fun," and it was – if you went by ship. The crew put on dances on the deck when we were in Halifax and although we were strictly forbidden to fraternize with the crew, the officers turned a blind eye. We bought cigarettes in boxes (how sensible!); learned to say, "A packet of Players, please." Talked until the wee hours with the other passengers, many of them students; survived the tail end of a hurricane. Our first sight of England was grey – Liverpool in the pouring rain.

How strange was the train from Liverpool to London with its small compartments you opened from the outside, its windows you let down by a leather strap. How strange to see porters with white faces. We walked all over London, and then we walked in the Cotswolds for five days, and then we took a train to Scotland.

If The Hill was the beginning of my social education, St. Andrew's gave me another great shove. At that time, only 5 per cent of British students went on to university (there weren't that many universities then) and if you gained a place,

you were there to study. You were also there to play, when you weren't studying, and the students at St. Andrew's knew how to do both. We lived in a co-ed
boarding house at 10 Hope Street, and because none of us had much money, we
would often choose a room and congregate, each person bringing sixpence
toward the gas metre. Sometimes we went en masse to the cinema ("Let's go
see how America won the war") or pooled our money for a round of drinks
and sandwiches at the bar of the Cross Keys Hotel. My parents didn't drink and
the only time I ever saw my grandfather drink was the day the war ended in the
Pacific. I never really drank back at college – you had to be twenty-one.

St. Andrew's is a very romantic old town with its ruined castle and cathedral, a cross marking the place where the first student martyr fell. Ghosts walk
the streets at night. We wore heavy woollen scarlet gowns; they helped against
the fierce winds coming off the North Sea.

A great many of the students I met were socialists; some were from emerging African countries or the Caribbean. I joined the Philosophical Society, the
Afro-Asian Society; I wished I could stay there forever.

In the breaks, we hitchhiked and took trains in Europe. Our parents didn't
seem suspicious that we kept "bumping into" old friends or the parents of old
friends, who gave us lifts from A to B. Anyway, letters took a while to reach
America; we were on to another adventure before they'd heard the bowdler-
ized version of the last one. I feel rather sorry for kids in this cyber-age, where
they feel they have to email back home all the time. Email can be a wonderful
thing, but I'm not sure if the new young travellers ever feel as free from paren-
tal ties as we did. I feel even sadder that letter-writing is a dying art form. I
may get a little picture of an envelope with the notice "You've got mail," but
there is no envelope, nothing to hold in your hand, no chance to marvel at the
other hands the letter must have passed through to get to the green mailbox
at the bottom of my path. No colourful stamps to examine.

I went back, reluctantly, to finish my degree in the States. I began to write
a novel called *Tomorrow We'll Be Sober*, taken from one of the drinking songs I
learned at St. Andrew's. By November of my graduating year – after a brief
stint as a copywriter for the same department store where I had missed the
chance to demonstrate hairbrushes – I was back in Britain. I tried hard to get
a job in London, but there was nothing doing – I was an alien, after all (I still

have my old Alien Certificate), and had to prove I could do the job better than a British person. Ha. A B.A. in English who couldn't type? I was offered a job selling Bibles door to door but decided against it as I had left the church – or thought I had. Finally, through a friend's advice, I got a job teaching school in Birmingham. Bishop Ryder's Church of England Infant and Junior School. It took me two buses and a walk to get there from where I was living and I had forty-eight six- and seven-year olds in my class, but once again, Fate was taking care of my education as a writer, throwing me into the deep end. Bishop Ryder's had been what was once called a "Ragged School," schools started in the nineteenth century for the purpose of teaching the poor to read. It was no longer classified as such, but it was in what we now call the inner city and most of the children were ragged enough, except the few whose parents worked at the fire hall or had some sort of steady work. They thought I was very peculiar: "Please, Miss, speak English." (I wrote about them recently in a piece called "Jammie Dodgers.") They lied, they stole, they could barely read. I hadn't a clue how to teach them anything, but I did my best. I also took them on field trips, thinking to enrich their little lives, but these always turned out to be disasters. At the Botanical Gardens and Zoo, three boys fed their pennies to the monkeys, which caused an uproar. Let me just say that whenever we went on one of these trips, we were asked not to come again.

Birmingham had a wonderful orchestra, a good library, a fantastic rep theatre. It also had the Bull Ring, which has long since been sanitized, but it was a great place to spend a Saturday afternoon, wandering round the market, eating cookies and winkles, listening to the patter of all the slippery dealers who were trying to convince you to buy a "genuine Spode" dinner service or three packets of the best nylon stockings for half a crown. I once did that and when I got home and opened the package, the stockings had no feet.

I fell in love, got married, had a child, and we immigrated to Canada, by ship of course: the old *Empress of France*. And then the amazing trip west on the train. I held the baby up to the window. "These are the lakes and these are the hills and these are the prairies, these are the prairies, these are the prairies." We settled first in Surrey, B.C., and then two years later moved into Vancouver. That was in 1961, and we thought we had finally settled down. We even bought a house.

Then in 1964, there was a chance to go to West Africa; we didn't hesitate.

We had two children by now and we took a train across Canada, had a brief visit in Binghamton, took a ship from New York to England, had a brief visit in England, sailed from Liverpool and out to Ghana.

Although I had been writing all this time, it was mostly stories or fragments of stories (I had long ago abandoned the St. Andrew's novel and I had been working on an M.A. at UBC). I rarely sent anything out; I don't think I was in any hurry. I was always a voracious reader, but life seemed more interesting, in itself, than writing about it. Ghana changed all that for many reasons, and in 1965 my first published story appeared as "An Atlantic First" in the June 1965 issue of the *Atlantic Monthly*. I no longer like that story – I think it far too *literary* – but it was written out of a great sense of pain and loss and I guess the editors could see beyond the pretentiousness. Two editors read it, one of them Edward Weeks, who was not only editor-in-chief of the *Atlantic Monthly* but connected to the Atlantic Monthly Press, and Robert Amussen, editor-in-chief of Bobbs-Merrill in New York. Both wrote me letters of praise; both wanted to know if I was working on a novel. Frankly, I could no longer imagine writing a novel, although there was one lurking in the depths of my mind, so I wrote back and said I was working on a book of stories. Bob Amussen said, "If you are willing to write a novel later, I will publish your book of stories when you finish it." I went with Bob (Atlantic Monthly Press also wanted to see my book of stories when it was finished) and I never looked back. I am now on my sixteenth and seventeenth books, but I doubt I would have continued at all (I was at a very low point in my life) if it hadn't been for that *Atlantic Monthly* story and for Bob Amussen.

So there we are. I think it's time for me to stop. Would I do it again – become a full-time obsessive writer? I'm not sure. Writers like to say, "I didn't have a choice," but I think you probably do. I think I would have liked to be a sound technician, or something to do with radio. From my first visit to Radio City, when we went on a tour and saw how sound effects were made – cellophane crumpled up close to the microphone for bacon frying, cornflakes falling for rain, blocks of wood for horses' hooves – I've always thought sound technicians probably had the most fun. Of course, it's all disc and digitalized now, I guess, so maybe it isn't so great. Anyway, I'm stuck with writing and it's stuck with me, like Br'er Rabbit and the Tar Baby. I've come to accept that this is what I do.

2005
RUDY WIEBE

Dear fellow writers, ladies and gentlemen:

June, 1973. Thirty-two years ago, when some eighty of us from across Canada came together at Neill-Wycik College just east of here across Yonge, to talk the Writers' Union of Canada into existence.

And you all still look so young.

Don't laugh at me when I say that — I'll have you know I'm younger than Leonard Cohen — by fourteen days.

—

We all know Margaret Laurence in her magnificent writing — but some of us were also privileged to know her in person, had the great pleasure of anticipating a new novel, or children's book, or essay from her, to read with eagerness, delight, and joy. Her bustling walk, her steady gaze out of those large, inquiring eyes, her raspy voice, her great bursting laughter. When she called you long distance on the telephone, as she sometimes did me — in those days of expensive tolls, rates were lowest after midnight, so calling Alberta from Lakefield was good; midnight for her was ten o'clock for me — called late at night to talk long and intensely, her voice instantly recognizable in all its warmth.

I first met Margaret when I travelled to her "cedar shack on the Otonabee River" in June, 1971. She then still lived at Elmcot in England, but found summers in Canada very good for working on what would become *The Diviners*; indeed, writing at "the shack" came to shape that entire novel, beginning with its unforgettable opening sentence: "The river flowed both ways."

After my visit, she wrote me, on "23 June '71," among other things:

> I have been working full blast, altho sometimes I feel this novel is getting out of hand and may be a bit crazy, but perhaps that is a good sign. It is going to be a longer haul than I thought, but it always is. I invariably think that *this* time it will be quick, painless, easy. But of course it never is.

She loved the many birds at the shack, especially the parent swallows whose babies had hatched, she wrote me, and who

> are incredibly nervous . . . have taken to dive-bombing me every time I go outside. I am trying to communicate the fact that I am no threat to their young. Seem to be a lot of aunt and uncle swallows zooming around, too . . . a really tribal society, I guess.

(*Addendum:* I can't resist this story: Two years later, Tena and I and our three kids visited her briefly on the river one day in August and she told us about her favourite bird, one that seemed so very concerned with her personal church life: all day long it sang, "Pres-Pres-Pres-Pres-Pres*by*terian!")

In June, 1973, the Writers' Union of Canada began to take shape when eighty writers met in Toronto; Margaret Laurence accepted being the "Interim Chair," and that fall, when she came to Edmonton to give public readings, she and I visited Horst Schmid, Alberta's Minister of Culture — in the twentieth-century governments, you still could use the word "culture," but now they can only mutter "heritage" or, worse, "community development" — and Margaret convinced Schmid that he should provide airfare for several Alberta writers to attend the founding meeting of the Union held in Ottawa on November 3. I was elected a vice-chair of the Union, and so there was also money for me to attend its first business meetings in December, 1973. That was Margaret Laurence, working for "the tribe."

She was the one who called us that, at our first meeting: "tribe." Perhaps a bit looser than "family," but clearly stronger "in the blood" than "community." After her death in 1987, the Union, in its wisdom — and I think it is that — established this annual lectureship in her name, and I find it very good, when we get together like this, that we remember a great writer in our midst, and tell the stories we experienced with her: her care and her anger and happiness and despair and hope and stubbornness and marvellous affirmation, to experience a bit of a fellow writer's life, for surely that is what we all are trying to live.

And there's the theme given me: "A Writer's Life." I take this to mean that I am expected to talk about my personal life as a writer, and I shall do that, and add as explanation the careful words of Groucho Marx when he spoke of his principles — not Karl Marx, Groucho — "Those are my principles; if you don't like them, I have others." Ergo, here's what I have to tell you: these are my experiences in the writing life; if you don't like them, I have others.

To say it straight: each of us has a particular name, a particular life; it is out of both that we write.

———

I see human beings as born into paradox and contradiction. In Western societies, we speak endlessly about human "freedom" — free, free, we must be free! Nevertheless, every one of us knows that much of our life is quite beyond our personal determination, leave alone control. The time and country and race of your birth, the two people who are your parents, the genetic programming you inherit, the food you are fed as an infant and the air you breathe — the size and shape of your nose, your legs, whatever, though nowadays some of that can be somewhat "corrected" — any personal detail can, at some moment, be of life-changing difference to you, and yet they are quite beyond your control.

Further, I understand ancestry, my "family," as being much more than merely a kind of necessary genetics. It is not an accident that in English we speak of a "family tree." Our life, our apprehensions, intuitions, imagining powers, are initiated and nourished for years by our connectedness to the humanity from which and within which we grow, as a tree branch is nourished by its leaves turning towards the light of the sun and its roots groping through the dark earth for water and nutrients. Each of us has this particularity of leaf and root which are the origins of our unique human existence: a personal name, a family name. Whether I recognize it or not, I am nonetheless a tiny branch on a family tree growing in the immense forests of all the earth's human beings. I am distinct; I may be solitary, but I can never be alone; light and air and earth, I am forever nourished and rooted.

That said, like most other Canadians, my personal family has been transplanted here from far away. Most recently from the Soviet Union, but earlier from the Russian Empire in Ukraine, and before that from Polish and Prussian Danzig back to sixteenth-century Netherlands, the town of Harlingen on the North Sea coast of Friesland. My parents and five older siblings arrived at Saint John, New Brunswick in February, 1930, fleeing Stalin's Communist "paradise," but over four centuries ago my blood ancestors were Frisians from the dyked polders of North Holland. They built windmills and dykes, dug ditches and drained land: they were engineers and farmers working with hands and feet and tools in the muddy earth to grow their daily food.

But here am I, born in the boreal forest of western Canada. In a log shack on a Saskatchewan bush homestead: "homestead," which is a Canadian legal description of land where people have lived for thousands of years as hunters and gatherers but now, by government decree, you are legally required to farm it. The trees and rocks are to be cleared away and the land ploughed to grow crops, to raise chickens and pigs and cattle. This northern, stony, glacier-haunted country so perfectly suited for hunting deer and moose, for trapping beaver, for picking cranberries and chokecherries and saskatoons, for swatting mosquitoes and black flies in the brief summer and for collecting poplar sap and listening to frogs in the brilliant green sloughs of spring – what are you trying to do here – farm? Go back to your muddy dykes in Holland and the Vistula delta, to your open steppe villages in Ukraine!

No, *this* is the land of my one and only birth. I love it – but I don't want to farm this stony land, nor squash whining insects all my life – I want to be a writer! So – sit around and do nothing all day but read and arrange and re-arrange words, toss them aside and grope obsessively for others – scribble, scribble, scribble! What's wrong with you? Do some real work like every Canadian, *earn* a living!

But I wanted to become a writer. And, as my mother would say if we could talk now, say in the Russian Mennonite Low German language we spoke to each other all our lives, say in astonishment and wonder: "By the grace of God, you have really become a writer." And I think, yes, I have become a writer. I am become one, many times.

Because, as writers know, every writing is the same and also always different. And the doubt always remains: "Yes, I have written before, but the question now is: can I write *this*?" Oh, years lengthen into experience and that can give you encouragement, give you ideas and maybe hope, perhaps even a dollop of confidence – I've done it before, I can do it again – but long experience will also reveal inevitable failures, failures you struggled to write but which never saw the light of publication, sweet failures you cannot forget at your sweet heart's core. And perhaps even now you regret some things you did write that were published: they may pain you as much as perhaps they pain others because they "have been made public" once and forever, they exist and cannot be changed. You can only write "stet" in the margin of that writing: as the proofreaders say, you must "let it stand."

(Most appropriate, the stained-glass window of Martin Luther behind me, with his indelible statement [I translate]: "Here I stand, God help me, I can do no other.")

Nevertheless, if a person wishes to create his or her life out of the daily and perpetual love of making things with language, it seems to me there can be very little "plan," but rather much more of hope, desire, obsession, perhaps prayer – which are never guides to you, but rather continuing apprehensions you can never quite avoid, never overcome, as perpetual as the beating of your blood. For it is not so simple to try and be a writer – I am not talking about writing occasionally, or writing memos, which are perfectly fine in their place – being a writer in Canada is never so straightforward as it is to be a doctor or teacher or carpenter or set designer or model or truck driver or cook.

But really, I don't mean to discuss the endless question all of us are always asked:

"How do you become a writer?" There is a far more basic question than that, which is: "If I dare to try to be a writer, what do I write?"

What do I write about?

Here I am, born and growing up in this cul-de-sac subsistence Canada bush community, not a writer in sight. 90 per cent of the families living here are like my family: either immigrants or refugees, all of them barely arrived here, without one bit of history in this place, or knowledge of it. In fact, this boreal forest is so strange and different from their former community life in their Russian steppe villages that for years all anyone can do is labour to learn how to stay alive here.

Born of a people that in nearly five centuries has scattered over four continents because they hold to Christian faith and pacifism: they will not obey a ruler who decides that now all citizens, for whatever reasons sufficient to him, must kill their fellow human beings. And so, to avoid such orders, they have to leave, migrate to some other part of the world that will accept them as they are: a people with clumsy peasant manners and certainly the wrong language. In my mother tongue of Mennonite Low German, not a book existed. It is an oral language only, so honed by centuries into the practical explication and gossip of farming and working peasants that to try and explain the concept of "novel" requires a long, circuitous sentence. In Low German, the words for "story" and "history" are the same word, *Jeschijcht*, and in such a spoken-only language words are like facts: either they *are*, and then they're true, or they are *not* and then they are lies. One or the other: that's all that's possible. With such a heavy linguistic, and moral, emphasis on *true*, why would anyone work a lifetime trying to write things that were not literally so?

So, with a language like that, how can you be a novelist? In fact, though I can speak it with complete fluency, and read it as well – there is today a Low German magazine published in Germany where some of my stories have been translated – I have never personally written in that language.

Fortunately, the traditional language of Mennonite school and church was classic High German, and the language of my Canadian school was of course English – so, without a single direct or difficult memory of having learned either, as a child I learned to speak and read both the languages of William Faulkner and Franz Kafka. That is one magnificent gift my dead-end bush community gave me.

Nevertheless, my dilemma remained: when I was growing up, I wanted to be a writer.

And of course I knew no writers, nor had ever met one; in the farm community where I was born and later the small Alberta town where I spent my teens, no writers existed. I read books endlessly, but I had no idea how you go about becoming a writer in Canada. Nevertheless, there is in the human imagination stirred by reading that which wants *more*. Not merely more of the same thing; the stimulated imagination always wants *more*, yes, and also *different*.

As I see it now, my verbal, literary imagination in *more* and *different* came both from the King James Bible and eventually William Shakespeare, and from Martin Luther's German Bible and Johann Wolfgang von Goethe.

I heard, and read, the Bible in both languages all my life. Then, in a senior English course at the University of Alberta, we read twenty of Shakespeare's plays, and my work in that class got me permission to take the same professor's university creative writing course a year later (a class of four students). But oddly, even that year of struggle with Shakespeare's work did not hit me imaginatively as it might have, in my own attempts at writing. Because Shakespeare was too venerated, too enormous; and though the course stressed his development from clumsy to superb, who could imagine any creative similarities with *him*?

But by the time I got to university, I understood the advantage of being able to read easily a second great world literature. And when I graduated, it was German that helped me win a Rotary Fellowship to travel in Europe and spend a year at the German University of Tuebingen. And it was in Germany that a Goethe drama performance literally showed me the personal possibilities of what Shakespeare had already revealed, though I had not yet recognized it. A performance of *Götz von Berlichingen mit der eisernen Hand* (". . . with the Iron Hand"), written by Goethe when he was twenty-three years old – exactly my age when I watched it.

Let me explain. Young Goethe wrote *Götz* because he loved Shakespeare's great, sprawling Elizabethan dramas, especially the early historical plays with their verbal richness of English kings and nobility, commoners and rabble, plays that in their powerful imagination ignored the classic hexameters of poetry, the rigid unity of time, place, and action. So Goethe was inspired to look for a unique person around whom to weave his own gigantic Shakespeare-like historical drama, and he found his subject in his home duchy of Franconia, a sixteenth-century knight named Gottfried von Berlichingen ("Goetz" is colloquial). Born of a noble family in 1480 in the Castle Jagsthausen, at age twenty-three (!) his right hand was destroyed by gunpowder in battle; when he recovered, he designed an iron hand which could immovably hold a sword or a lance. And one

July evening in 1958, at the end of my Tuebingen University year, I sat on temporary bleachers in the courtyard of medieval Castle Jagsthausen on its cliff above the Jagst River, facing the towers of the room where Goetz had been born, and I saw Goethe's great play being performed. No. I should rather say, I saw the life of Goetz von Berlichingen happen before my eyes. The turrets and towers of the castle blazed into light under the attack of the Holy Roman Emperor's army; cannonballs battered the massive walls, shook the seat under me. I was alive and terrified in the Peasants' War, the siege of Jagsthausen, 1525.

The action of Goethe's play really did not interest me; intrigue, war, hand-to-hand slaughter — God save us, who needs more brutality in the name of endless stupid honour, of power, especially killing in the cause of religion? Neither the compassionate figure of Elizabeth nor Goetz's tenderness with his children and servants can rescue that. But the subject itself — the local hero; the technique — that enormous, sprawling all-inclusiveness of ordinary peoples' lives, that was something else. An historical figure, from this particular and discrete place, this past, this people, living and loving and playing and fighting and dying in laughter and happiness and shame and stupidity and intrigue and pain and betrayal and speaking their own plain language with their own clumsy customs: Who needs the world snooty Empire of London? Of New York? Or even, may I be blessed, the Montreal and Toronto of *Two Solitudes*? Small as it may be, write your own place. Write your own people.

This is, of course, no earth-shaking, original insight. But for my understanding of myself, it was: a personal epiphany that gropes into your soul with an understanding that bends your uttermost thinking. All peoples, collectively and individually, have stories: every one, in the very life they live; and a true writer can make such story memorable. Somehow, I had to experience that: both in my head, the genius of actors telling this gentle/brutal story of Goetz, making me see it; and also had to experience it in my gut, the very stone walls of Jagsthausen pounding that story into the earth, into me. That brilliant summer night under the stars: I can still see Goetz and his men come riding their horses from out of the darkness into the castle courtyard — one side of which was simply the stage, the rest was filled with audience in raised tiers — see the reins of his massive grey warhorse in his iron hand as he swung down and embraced his running, shouting children with the other.

And then, the sudden explosion of cannon outside, the gunpowder flaring above the walls that were supposed to shelter us – though having just lived through the Second World War, everyone in that German audience knew that sixteenth-century gunpowder was already destroying, forever, the supposed safety of stone walls.

And destroying also the cowering safety of my largely unflexed and inhibited imagination. For beyond the curve of the globe, there was my home: the one and only place on earth where I was born and had my growing up. What stories had ever been told about my land? Nothing at all in English about my particular immigrant people, and not very much about my western Canada land, either. And if it had been, it was often written so badly I was ashamed to remember most of it: mostly silly, simple-mindedly stylized romances about Mounties, and weather, and fur traders, and dreadful, profoundly ignorant white patronizations of "the poor, vanishing savage," the "dark dwellers of the forest" who were pathologically incapable of becoming properly "White" and "civilized." Did I dare to try and tell my place, my people, different?

And the bigger question: Could I?

I returned to Canada in late summer, 1958, and within a year I was writing my first novel, *Peace Shall Destroy Many*, a story about Mennonite immigrants living in aspen parkland western Canada. That happened largely because of one man, and I want to pay tribute to him here: my Shakespeare and Creative Writing professor at the University of Alberta, Dr. Frederick M. Salter, a native of New Brunswick. When I discussed with him a possible M.A. thesis topic concerning Shakespeare and war, he stared off into space, saying "Yes, yes" until I was finished, and then he said, "Of course, Mr. Wiebe," (in those days professors and students conversed like that) "of course, I'm sure you can write a perfectly acceptable thesis on Shakespeare – a great many people can – but perhaps only you can write a fine novel about Mennonites."

That stunned me. It was Salter who in 1938 offered the first composition and writing course given at any Canadian university; W.O. Mitchell took that course in the early '40s, and so did I in 1955–56. Now, because of Salter the English Department accepted a "Creative Thesis" in its master's degree program, and here he was, in spring of 1959, as it were, daring me to write a novel. Out of the stories my people had lived. Leaking it into me, like poison.

Well, I was infected all right, for good. Or, if you like, I've been terminally ill with writing ever since. I finished the novel in nine months (I was too young to know that it should take years) and in August 1960, I received that most incredible letter any neophyte Canadian writer could get: a letter from Jack McClelland in Toronto telling me McClelland & Stewart would publish my novel if I'd work on it with his editors to our mutual satisfaction.

Another good person who helped me become a writer: Jack McClelland. And his editors, Claire Pratt and Joyce Marshall. No one ever becomes a writer alone; you need a tribe, with elders.

And in the process of imagining that first book, I discovered, quite unawares to me at the time, my own "Knight with the Iron Hand." He was a man of Cree-Ojibwa ancestry born one hundred and ten years before me near Jackfish Lake, within forty bush kilometres of where I myself was born. Mistahi-Muskwa – in English, Big Bear – circa 1825 to January 17, 1888. Fourteen years after I first read about him, I published my fourth novel, *The Temptations of Big Bear* (1973), and instead of the usual disclaimer that always appears before a novel: "Any resemblance to persons living or dead . . . etc., etc," it gave me great satisfaction to declare that "No name of any person, place, or thing, insofar as names are still discoverable, in this novel has been invented." Also, all the events and actions, dates and incidents, were historically documentable.

It was an approach to fiction which some Canadian reviewers thought cavalier, but of course it's been the way of writers since concocting stories was first invented, from Homer to – to pick a random contemporary – William Styron in *The Confessions of Nat Turner*.

Mistahi-Muskwa: that mysterious, spiritual Plains Cree man has haunted me for over forty years in fiction, film, biography. As have other people, the men and women of the past, of my particular spot where (through no decision of my own) I was born. Characters and events of history seen through fiction. More recently, the novel *A Discovery of Strangers* (1994), which tells of the historical encounter in 1820 between the Arctic Yellowknife Dene and the Englishmen of the first Franklin expedition. These are events that happened in my particular place on earth.

And *Sweeter Than All the World* (2001) is about historical people who lived throughout five centuries of Mennonite history, most personally about Adam

Wiebe, my direct ancestor who in 1644 invented the cable car to build up the earthen walls around Danzig to protect it from destruction during the dreadful Thirty Years' War. The stories never end.

Or Big Bear again, in *Stolen Life: The Journey of a Cree Woman*, a book which began in 1992 when Yvonne Johnson, who I did not know existed, wrote me a letter from the Kingston Penitentiary for Women telling me she had read *The Temptations of Big Bear* and wondered how it was I knew so much about her great-great-grandfather. Why had I chosen to write a novel about him?

Yvonne's disturbing letter, her long imprisonment and, when I met her, her powerful personality with her vivid telling of her life, reminded me more and more of Big Bear's unforgettable words when he faced Indian Treaty Commissioner Morris on the North Saskatchewan River in 1876. Big Bear said (I quote Morris's own written account):

> When I heard [the Governor] was to come, I said I will request him to save me from what I most dread – hanging; it was not given to us [by the Great Spirit] to have the rope about our necks.

Big Bear's doubled rhetorical image of destiny: the rope around the neck as the white instrument of legal execution, and also, the rope as the horseman's instrument of control: you put a rope around my neck with this treaty and you'll lead me wherever you want me to go, whether I want to go there or not.

Six years later, *The Edmonton Bulletin* (October 21, 1882) carried a long report with the headline "Big Bear and Others." Through expert translator Peter Erasmus, the newspaper quoted Big Bear, again speaking for his people, the Plains Cree:

> . . . There was a time when we had faith in the white man and believed his word, I am sorry to say it is far from being the case now. When the white man says anything to us [now] we listen, and in the meantime say in our hearts he is lying. . . . Often we recognize our horses that have been stolen [in] the white men's [herds] and [we] have tried to get them back, but never yet could manage to get the first one. Although we trusted the law [i.e., in

the North West Mounted Police] to help us, we never got the benefit of it, because our word is as the wind to the white man . . ."

"Our word is as the wind." In fifty years of writing, I believe it is Big Bear who has helped me most to understand the double meaning of that vivid phrase; wind not only as "vacant, empty, air vanishing into nothing" – which is what the white man sees in First Nations' words – but also wind as "animating spirit," the "living word" that moves over the formless void of all our mutual ignorance, to reveal itself in the numinous truth of story. Stories told continuously because we are human beings and our stories create meaning, create understanding between us. The longer I contemplated them, that is ever more clearly what Big Bear's words have come to mean to me.

For I would like to remind you of Canada's very recent social history. A mere forty years ago, the attitude of most Canadians towards the Aboriginal First Nations of our land was very different from what it is today, because at that time the attitudes of even thoughtful people were formed by books like George Stanley's *The Birth of Western Canada* – the standard western history text in my university days. Let me quote from a paragraph in Chapter 10:

The gravest problem presented to the Dominion of Canada by the acquisition and settlement of Rupert's Land and the North-West [1869], was the impact of a superior civilization upon the native Indian tribes. . . . The European, conscious of his material superiority, is only too contemptuous of the savage, intolerant of his helplessness, ignorant of his mental processes and impatient at his slow assimilation of civilization. *The savage, centuries behind in mental and economic development, cannot readily adapt himself to meet the new conditions* [my italics]. He is incapable of bridging the gap of centuries alone and unassisted. Although white penetration into native territories may be inspired by motives of self-interest, once there, the responsibility of "the white man's burden" is inevitable.

The "white man's burden" to take care of the "mentally incapable savages" he has overrun: with such an attitude among even the best educated, is it any wonder that, in the early 1970s, people asked me – and they thought it was a perceptive philosophic question – people actually asked me, "Six years of writing? Why do you bother writing a book about a dead Indian?" Of course, twenty-five years later, similarly "perceptive" people confronted me with, "How *dare* you write a book about an Indian!" – but that's a horse of a different colour, a different rope; I won't dissect that now. The fact is that, beginning with Maria Campbell's *Halfbreed* in 1973, and on to novelists like Haisla Eden Robinson (*Monkey Beach*) and Dogrib Richard Van Camp (*The Lesser Blessed*), dozens of First Nations writers have created for us all a previously unknown Canada with their powerful books: as they continue to live their writers' lives, their words become "as the wind" to us, the living wind of Canadian stories. To say it another way, their incisive words are cutting off the ropes of ignorance and prejudice from around all our necks.

—

To return to my original writer's question: What do I write about?

As I explained, when I was a teenager it seemed no stories had ever been written about my particular place, my small people. This was in part youthful ignorance, but only in part: in fact, almost nothing had been written. That lack was intimidating, but there were hundreds of books to act as models of how it might be done: for example, how Tolstoy wrote about Napoleon and General Kutuzov, how Hugo wrote about the French Revolution, how Dickens wrote about Mr. Pickwick perambulating around the English countryside. Prairie Canada had no such writers – all was silence – but what if you were, for example, a Greek and had Homer looking over your shoulder every time you wrote a Greek sentence, or you were Chinese and when you dared shape a Chinese word on paper, four thousand years of indelible Chinese classic literature settled down upon you? Wouldn't that intimidate you, too – perhaps a great deal more than silence?

When I consider this question, I feel my generation of Canadian writers – that is, those beginning to publish in the late '50s, early '60s – has been immensely fortunate. We were born into a time of growing general prosperity, of cultural awareness which gave us the opportunity to fill some of the gaps in our country's stories: with us began the enormous explosion of

Canada-wide, self-aware, multiracial literature. Since 1967, we have seen it grow exponentially larger, become truly worldwide during Canada's second century. So I think it proper that we here remind ourselves of those whose writing led us on, whose work we anticipated and enjoyed, our fellow writers who have now passed beyond us. I name them, not an exhaustive list nor in any particular order, but beginning with our "tribal mother":

Margaret Laurence
Sheila Watson
Robertson Davies
W.O. Mitchell
Marian Engel
Timothy Findley
Al Purdy
Mordecai Richler
Carol Shields
Earle Birney
Matt Cohen
Gwendolyn MacEwen

You might add others to this list of our fellow writers, as we remember them together in a moment of silence.

And I would say, to their memory:

> *Blessed indeed are the dead,*
> *who rest from their labour,*
> *for their works do follow them.*

—

One of the joys of the writing life in Canada today is the writers you meet, often at public readings or through the Writers' Union. You can easily become acquaintances, friends, even very good friends, and then enjoy even more reading their new books. Or, as can happen, if upon meeting you discover you can't endure someone, well, distances in Canada being what they are, you can easily avoid them for the rest of your life. When they do publish a new book, you need never even look at it on the bookstore shelf, nor read a review, just in case it's complimentary. And, if by some accident, you are forced to recognize that they have written a readable – perhaps even a very good – book, you can still avoid them with the thought that even unbearable dolts can, on rare occasions, produce something worth reading, *once*. So be it, that's a writing life.

I want to conclude with one more memory of Margaret Laurence, and a personal coda.

On October 6, 1986, Margaret called me on the telephone and we talked for a long time. I jotted down some of her words, and here are a few of them:

"I have been given my life's work to do and I've done it. . . . I've written fifteen books and raised two kids to maturity. . . . I am a kind of half-assed Christian person. . . . Rudy, I cannot believe in a personal immortality. . . . It seems bizarre that God will make some use of my life . . . Hang on a sec, I gotta get a Kleenex. . . . God is not just a Him, I believe in the female principle of the Holy Spirit. . . . I am overwhelmed by love."

That was Margaret Laurence; we remember her with love, and read her books once more.

My personal coda:

Years ago I read an essay by Albert Camus entitled "The Wind at Djemila." In it was a sentence which has been floating in my memory ever since (it's cast in the male language of the last century):

A man lives with a few familiar ideas, two or three at the most, and here and there, in contact with the world and men, they are polished, shaped, changed. It takes years for a man to evolve an idea that he can call his own, one that he can speak of with authority.

For my purposes here, I will take the term "a few familiar ideas" to mean the large concepts that have shaped my life's fiction: if you will, the great bones and spinal cord that hold the human shape of my novels erect in the factual and ideological profusion of contemporary life. When I consider fifty years of writing about my place and people, it seems to me I discern two such "familiar ideas":

One is the concept of First Encounter. How the Aboriginal people of this land, having lived here for hundreds of generations, first met Europeans, and their mutual reactions to each other. First Encounters.

The second is the Immigrant Experience. What happens when people leave their native, familiar world and come to a completely different place among, as it seems, totally different human beings? The Immigrant Experience in Canada.

I recognize these "familiar ideas" again and again in the millions of words I've written. Sometimes they seem rather limited; at other times they seem almost, perhaps even more than, sufficient. In any case, as it is, they are what they are: in large measure, my writing life. Here I must say "Stet." Let it stand.

For your considerate attention, I thank you.

You would not believe it. Well, I was born on the most beautiful day of my life.

It all began on a certain tenth of May, at noon, as the church bells were ringing to bring down the house so that my father, a school teacher, recited in Latin: "*Et Verbum caro factum est.*" *And the Word was made flesh.* But my father did not know that on that day with the Word, the whole sentence was made flesh. I was already chatty even before learning to talk. Very alive barely had I entered life, unquenchable at my very first suckling, curious before I had opened my eyes. Wrong start. Life would be much too short. I was short of existence to satisfy such an appetite, growing as quickly as the family tree which, as far as I'm concerned, reached Adam and Eve.

I learned very early that my only chance to survive, to escape choking in too small a space and too short a time, was to push back the boundaries of reality and to plunge into the parallel world. It happened in my third year. Don't panic, at three I did not go through all that analytic rubbish, I did not start an argument on reality and fiction. I just went to knock at my neighbour's house to relieve my mother from my boisterous existence . . . and, without realizing, to answer the call of Destiny. On that day I met Alice. Just like Alice in Wonderland, my neighbour led me on to the other side of the mirror and told me the story of the Three Bears.

I was three, there were three bears. I was Goldilocks. (If you have any doubts, just look at me.) There was I, heading to meet characters foreign to my home, living beyond the walls, inside the closets, between the leaves of firs, oaks, and elms, under the brushwood, in the folds of Time. The night that followed my entering the tales was far too long, I was anxious to reach the next morning, to return knocking at Alice's door, to go back to the Three Bears. Bit by bit, Alice got bored and suggested she tell me the tale of Tom Thumb. What? There was another one? And I immediately grabbed Tom Thumb's hand, far more amusing than Goldilocks. But most of all, if there were two tales, why not three, or seven or twelve? I couldn't count further, and was very far, as you can imagine, from the notion of the Infinite. Although I had just plunged into it. Head first into the Infinite! The unlimited possibilities. With Tom Thumb knocking at the Three Bears', accompanied by Puss in Boots, Cinderella, and the giant that eats small children, my whole life had toppled over. The giant had swallowed me. That day, or one of those days of my early childhood, I knew that I would spend my life listening to and reinventing stories.

That is the reason why at the age of five, when my eldest sister, who was already seven, suggested that I should begin to think of my future, I felt a cramp in my stomach. A future . . . ?

"You have three choices," she said.

"The Three Bears?"

"Three choices, stupid. For the boys, there are all kinds of futures: doctor, lawyer, priest, explorer, fireman . . . but a girl has three choices: mother, nun, old maid."

"I'll take the fourth."

"It doesn't exist."

"It does."

"It doesn't."

"It does."

"Name it."

Caught off guard, facing the bankruptcy of my life, I plunged.

"I'll be Cinderella."

In my own language of that age, I said, "*La petite Cendrillouse.*" I had chosen the parallel life, chosen to enter the world of tales and wonder. Without knowing it, I was entering Literature.

—

Many years later, I would understand that breathtaking plunge which I had risked at an age preceding the age of reason. Had I known on that very day, I would have felt the writer's cramp and been frozen dead for life. Very much later, when I truly came to writing, I measured the depth of water, the infinite ocean of subconsciousness.

I was born in the first third of the century, in the heart of Acadia, amongst a people just returning from exile and barely out of the woods. So . . . literature? How does one walk into it without credentials? Without past records, antecedents? On what grounds? No colleges, no academics, no literary lineage. But forefathers, oh yes! A lineage of storytellers, all, like me, born, at the sound of the church bells ringing that the Word was made flesh. All were bent under the weight of a memory so heavy that they needed desperately to throw it off.

Let yourself be led into History as one would enter Wonderland. Allow me to tell you a story.

Once upon a time, there was a people who could neither read nor write. So they began to tell stories. That was the right thing to do. During those years and along those shores, read what? And moreover, certain stories cannot be written. Even a cock-and-bull storyteller needs all his genius to clear the bush of a people's chronicle. So . . . write it? Go on! A century beating about the bush has no beginning nor end. By which leaf has the tree begun its foliage? No! One does not write the history of a people who invent stories as they go along.

One tells the stories.

So Acadia started to tell. But to tell so much and so well that the world began to look like its tales. And what tales! Noah's Ark seemed a dory in comparison with "*La Grande Boudeuse*" or "*La Défunte Flash*." And don't you dare compare La Corriveau to our cast-spelling, fortune-telling, toothless witch, carved in the memory of my people. Even le Père Gédéon, who figures he has a salty tongue and a spicy throat, is nothing compared to Tit-Louis, Don l'Orignal, Pierre a Tom, Calixte-à-Pissevite, or that old bitch Ozite, God save her soul!, who over a hundred years old kept on clearing her family tree, inside out, inside in, often beginning with the offspring. The Acadian storytellers piled up three centuries of verbal art, an art never exposed to the scrutinizing eye of the French Academy. Storytellers that passed on their knowledge from grandfather to father to son, who told in the perfect style and accent, a story which . . . a story, *voilà*!

History with a capital *H* is a character well known to me. So allow me to present it to you.

Thrice our History was on the verge of passing away. But at the very beginning, we thought it might never start. To be frank, it was quite its fault; it should have known better and chosen its hour. It was a bad idea to leave in fall anyway; winter caught up with it, still in its crib, drifting along the shores of Saint Croix Island, in the Baie Française or Baie du Fond, better known today as Bay of Fundy. But day by day and month after month, it yet managed to grow and reach the following summer. After which came the Deportation. Exile. Let's call this episode a rather gloomy moment. One can always fight against the winds and the high tides and drought and couch grass and stormy rains, as long as you go through it at home. But abroad? A Deportation is the toughest moment for History. Unless it can come out of it. If, by miracle, History survives exile, all of a piece, without having lost its wings . . . The worst would be to come home split in two. To bring back the Cormiers and the LeBlancs, leaving the Thibodeaux behind. To come back by night, late fall, without warning, neglecting to study the compass, and finally turning your head around to realize all of a sudden that half of your people remained in Louisiana and would never catch up with the others. I swear to God that without the dream of a lost Paradise, somewhere up North . . . no! So History started again. On foot. It climbed America barefooted, in the second half of the eighteenth century, alone, harness on its back. And when it finally reached the promised land, *eh bien*! The land had been promised in the meantime to somebody else and it was occupied. One has to be outrageously stubborn to start again for the second time, not knowing whether one is going to make it through the next winter.

A winter bound to last a hundred years.

A hundred years hiding in the woods. A hundred years not knowing who was whose brother; where the grandmother of your third kissing kin was hiding; where had gone the Babins, the Babineaus, the Bastaraches; in which island had landed the castaways of *la défunte* Espérance. A century of search, of loss, of rediscovering; of digging your hole in your own land, lumbering, planting, throwing your fishing nets and lobster pots into the sea. A century of grinning at Destiny. For don't you believe that we were going to beg on our knees. Who do you think we are! A heartless Destiny dead-set against the remains of a people coming back home gasping, stamping, breathing heavily, climbing an America that did not even notice its footprints in the muddy marshlands! . . . We have defied that Destiny! Setting the fallen stones upright, reinvigorating the rotten roots, reviving the dead. And on a bright spring morning, everyone puts his nose at the door to smell the air a bit, just to check the weather. The weather is fine, life can begin anew. So History starts again for the third time.

It was running late, one must admit, but today I have a whim that it caught up with Time.

Although at one point I was scared, afraid to see it lose its way, fall apart, quit fighting for survival. It was such a long journey! Especially, was I telling myself in 1880, how were we to catch up with the others already so well established on the continent, while we are still up to our knees in the marshlands of our islands? Which is the shortest road leading to le Chemin du Roy?

And now, fellow writers, I must reveal one of my writers' secrets. Paradoxically — but I belong to a race not short on paradoxes — I am about to unveil to an honourable literary society, the nasty tricks I played on literature. I came to writing through shortcuts; yes, in some way I caught up with you sideways. That was not quite fair play, I agree, but I had no choice. My father used to tell me, "If you don't know how to swim, dive and trust the sea, borrow its rhythm and it will carry you."

I tried it with the sea, then with life. And one day, when certain storytelling cousins of mine began to untangle the lineage of my people, I told myself, tongue-in-cheek: *What if I tried that with literature?* On that day I understood that I had just plunged into very deep water. I was about to risk nothing less than to rebuild my homeland with words. Moreover, with the words of my homeland. O father, what had you done to me! I felt as conceited as one of Molière's characters who planned to squeeze the whole Roman history into a single sonnet.

Allow me to say that my father is not solely responsible for my fancy. Before him came all those illiterates who night after night would pick up that exhausted History falling apart on the side of the road. They catch sight of it just in time, the breathless wretched thing, lift it, and lead it back home, limping and deaf. Once there, throwing logs on the hearth and spitting in the fire, they bring it back to life, the old bitch, and so History goes on.

Those storytellers were my sole true masters.

As a loyal daughter of the homeland, I must continue my lineage. I wish I could, as did those chroniclers and diggers of old roots, those peddlers of live, shocking, scary, and weird tales, I wish I could recreate the world in six days, then rest on the seventh. A world with its center in my own house and its circumference encircling the universe; with rays that go from my first neighbour to Mesopotamia; from my kissing kin to Charlemagne, Caesar, or the Queen of Sheba. I dream of filling the gap that we all feel in our hearts since the earthquake of the lost Paradise.

All that with words. More: with written words. For the oral tradition can at least rest on the accent, the intonation, the wave of the hands, the smile or grin, the blinking eyes, in some ways it can sprinkle the whole sentence with something of the overflowing soul. But writing! One disposes of twenty-six tiny and abstract signs to revive the past and to exorcise Destiny. It's very little to stop the passing of Time.

Yet the whole life is there, hidden within words. Like Michelangelo's David, according to the sculptor himself, was already hiding inside the stone. The artist's work is to discover it. To strip, scrape, chisel the marble, and unveil the hidden form that will reveal man's reflection of his own universe.

But Michelangelo, apart from the fact that he was Michelangelo, worked in marble which had very little slag. But the writer's raw material is life. It happens that life is crammed full of slag. It is up to him, therefore, to clear the earthy and crumbly scrap which covers the precious stone, the jewel buried in the heart of life. For one single Hamlet, how many dreamers juggling with *to be*s and *not to be*s; for one sole Don Quixote, how many braggarts fighting against windmills; for a single verse of Racine, "*La fille de Minos et de Pasiphaé*," how many mumblings, bawlings, bad *joual*, and cacophony!

Such is the writer's challenge . . . as you know, fellow writers. But what you probably don't know is how big the challenge is that faces the Acadian writer. Try to figure out the amount of scrap surrounding his History, the slag that weighs down his speech and denudes his style. And yet that is the raw material which he is asked to transform into beauty.

On a certain day of low tide, my head whipped by a northwester, feet wading in the marshlands, I was splashed by some kind of an inspiration: What if the sculptor began to search for his works directly in the slag? Why waste all that scrap? Why not try to change into beauty the slag as well?

Are the distorted and crooked characters less real for being slag? Is La Sainte less *sainte-nitouche* than La Sagouine is *sagouinarde*? And all those widows that haunt me and stand out as landmarks in my works, *La Veuve a Calixte, La Veuve Enragée, Ma-Tante-la-Veuve*, and finally the great widow of *Le Grand Dérangement*, are they less true or more ugly for being born on a stormy day? The ocean that smells of seaweeds and storms at the sandhills; the wrecks and the stumps which congest the shores and the woods; the shrunken witches bawling their curses; the snobbish, the intolerants, the oppressors, the critics . . . so much slag. But yet all that is life.

And therefore this is the sheer raw material for literature.

Now I am going to risk an ultimate sacrilege. I have a last statue to smash: that of an international French.

I mentioned my ambition to rebuild a homeland with my people's words. *La voilà. La vraie gageure.* The true pledge. The wager. Because our words are far from being the official words. It's hard to shout the cry, that kind of lump crammed in the throat for the past three centuries, to shout it in an international French. The international is so far from being personal and singular. For instance, how can one wish welcome to strangers in a universal language? In local or old French, in my hundred thousand words inherited from the Middle Ages, I am quite at ease and will say: *Y aurait-i' de quoi que je pourrions faire pour vous?* . . . No possible translation here. But trust me, it is limpid, warm, hospitable. But not very academic.

Yet it was to prepare for the birth of L'Académie Française that in the beginning of the seventeenth century, there appeared Malherbe and the great grammarians. To refine the language, codify it, squeeze it into strict rules . . . *enfin Malherbe vint*. Once and for all. But . . . *Malherbe vint pas chez nous*, he never reached our shores, I doubt if he had ever heard the name "Acadia"; in fact, the word *Acadien* took three centuries to be honoured by L'Académie Française. So the language, left to itself, entrusted to us alone, to our hearts and memories, drifted loose and free through the open fields, jumping over fences, dragging in the creeks, rubbing itself against the worst rabble of the land. It came out of it, soiled with filth and dirty words. A true little bitch of an outlaw tongue.

Outlaw, but also out of the ordinary. Because every misadventure has its good side. The trees that grow left and right, downward, upward, crooked, twisted, skinny . . . inspired by their own roots which draw the sap at the will of the sun and the winds, end up being quite harmonious. So does language that draws its sap from the roots of its homeland.

Let's acknowledge at once, and once and for all, that I am a *payse*. I wouldn't know how to translate that word. This is to say that I am different from the novelist and the playwright. I am a walking memory. A storyteller, peddler of imagination and old words. Antique words that I carry in my loins and throat, that we all pass along as a family gift from the ancestors coming out of Charente, Poitou, and Touraine, and that we would be happy to leave as a legacy to our offspring; words, *dragées de couleur*, as my master Rabelais would call them, frozen words which at the first thaw burst and begin to tell the epic of mankind.

For a long period of time, we have believed that culture was the exclusive right of cultured persons, wherefore the pleonasm. That was a meaning much too thin for the word *culture*, amputating it from its folk and live elements, which are both the founding of civilization and the inspiration of those that transmit it. The wildflower is no less flower than the garden rose; besides, without the fields, the gardens wouldn't know how and where to begin the flower.

If we have any doubt about that, let us just take a look at the cultures and civilizations that preceded us. Let us trace back History to its very beginnings. What tells us one of the oldest epics, that of Gilgamesh? The adventures of a young man that laughs, laments, fights, builds, hopes, flings stones, has a friend, and above all who tries to understand. That's all. But that's a lot. All the literatures put together from all civilizations do not tell more. *The Iliad* and

The Odyssey reveal the beliefs and the struggles of the Greeks; *Don Quixote* relives the daily life and impossible dreams of the Spanish people of the Renaissance; and Rabelais tells us, in a language that the most illiterate Acadian can still understand, that his fat, hair-raising, frightful giants were, deep down, good sorts of persons who wished mostly to drink, eat, sleep; eat, sleep, drink; drink, sleep, and eat. And to set out in search of the "*dive bouteille*," containing wisdom as well as good wine.

Literature tells us that. And we spend years in universities to learn it. We attend conferences and symposiums, and give ourselves grand airs to narrate the adventures of Don Quixote under the staring eyes of his valet Sancho who wets his pants.

No one will find that description of literature in school books; the scholars as well must also make a living and impose respect. They will say all that, but in profound words and complex sentences. If only one could read between the lines, one would probably understand better the meaning of literature. That is to say that the shortest fixed moment contains Eternity, and in the smallest bit of life is enclosed the whole world. I dream of the day when, with a large knife, I will cut a piece of existence surrounding me, isolate that scrap of life, put it under the microscope, or better yet, scrutinize it in slow motion. That might allow me to peek between the folds of life. We could be surprised to see under the microscope what goes on in a bowl of soup.

Eh bien, if my bowl contains the universe, what about my homeland? Do you doubt that one could discover in Acadia material to pass on to the generations to come? It's true that we could not, after the fashion of the great civilizations at their peak, indulge in the luxury of heroes such as Alexander the Great, Beowulf, or Charlemagne; but a Gilgamesh that throws stones at the Goddesses; a Don Quixote that strikes at the windmills; a Gargantua who wipes his nose on his sleeves, *mange son blé en herbe et se chatouille pour se faire rire* . . . oh yes! To live, we know something about that! With Dante, we know how foreign bread can be bitter and how hard it is to climb somebody else's stairs; with Antigone we have learned that the law of the mighty is not always right in the eyes of the dead; with Rabelais, we acknowledge that "*Mieux est de ri[re] que de larmes écrire / Pour ce que rire est le propre de l'homme*"; and after Hamlet, we can repeat: "*Crever ou pas crever, c'est là la grosse affaire.*" All that books narrate, we have known and lived. Like everybody else, we are familiar with the joys of life and the pain of injustice, familiar with fear in the eyes of Destiny and the anguish of being alive.

But it took us a long time to conquer the right to be heard. That's why the song of my homeland could sound to your ears like that of the swan.

If the Acadian hymn is to be the swan song, we have no time to lose. No time to take the side roads to reach literature in three or four centuries to come. We might not have them. We have them behind us. Today an Acadian must go straight ahead, cannot afford to learn slowly, stuttering, go through all the literary experiences from automatic writing, on to art for art's sake. He must find at once the absolute pitch. Take the bull by the horns, achieve the aim by the perpendicular.

A castaway does not learn to swim by easy stages, following the rules of the crawl, dogpaddle, backstroke, freestyle. No. He must be familiar with all the methods at that precise moment and choose by instinct the rules that the water on that day will decide for him. His life will depend upon his degree of trust in the sea. He who carries the sea within him will dare, swim, and survive.

The important question: Do we still have the instinct of the sea? Will we have the courage and the time to dive, leaving behind the buoy? Life is there, within reach, ready, generous, full of expectation. Acadia, for a long time, was pregnant with inspiration. Yes, that same Acadia, on the other hand, so virgin . . . A virginity as misleading as the wild woods. For nothing is more full of life and ready to give birth to a new world than the wilds, or a people isolated, forgotten, and reduced to silence. The longer its silence, the louder the scream that will come out of its mouth.

But he alone can shout it. For no one can be an Acadian but an Acadian. Let's say that's the only sphere where everyone is irreplaceable. In that, no one can replace anyone. The Acadian who wishes to reveal his homeland and his soul must do it himself. He must be the one to give his vision of the world.

Such is the defense of the writer who dares after Shakespeare, Homer, or Molière, pick up a pen and describe the world according to him. He dares because he knows that neither Molière, Homer, nor Shakespeare could describe at his place his vision of the world. After all, maybe Shakespeare did not have blue eyes; no doubt that Molière measured more than five feet; and for sure, Homer was not born on the Acadian shores. For those simple and obvious reasons, none of those could tell the world that I see and carry within me.

Il nous faut à nous aussi notre parole.

That speech, or that world, does not need to be great. Any artist knows that there is as much life in a breath as in deep respiration, that there is as much time in a second as in a century. The big and the small in literature are not that important. Maybe it's because the world is too small that we tend to enlarge it; because life is too short that we tend to immortalize it; because Paradise is hidden that we tend to recreate it. Well, who can best recreate life, reinvent Paradise, if not those who have not had their share? The small dream big. The have-nots will feel the need to sublimate the little they have so as to prove to themselves that they are alive and show the others their aspiration of being.

With such ambition, where do we start? Since we are deprived of ancestors – a background of writers, I mean, grammarians, academics – since we have no literary lineage, we have no choice but to hunt elsewhere, search further for our roots. And beyond writing is oral tradition. It is therefore in oral, primitive literature, transmitted from forefather to grandfather to father, that we will look for a lineage and a collective soul, and with that we shall dream of the universal.

I just used the big word, but the writer cannot afford to be modest. He must long for the universal, that is to say aim at speaking to others, to the universe, but speak of himself, of what is so essentially himself, that on that ground everybody feels at home. Man with a capital *M* does not exist for the writer. Especially for the Acadian writer. He knows that La Piroune or Pierre à Tom will have access to their capital *W* or *M* only after being deeply anchored as Pierre à Tom and Piroune. To become so, those characters have to be fully personified, strongly alive, of the type that you can meet anytime on the corner of the street. You must detect even the twitches of the characters you claim to bring to life, know them as your nearest neighbour before dreaming of making them so real that their reality will have the right to be written with a capital *R*.

When I am asked how I managed to write, at forty, the life of a woman of seventy-two, a washer-woman, a sailors' girl in her youth, when I am asked how I could deal with that, I smile in the Acadian way, that is, tongue-in-cheek: for I have not lived that kind of life. But that is not the main Sagouine: she is not first and foremost a whore, a charlady, an old woman. She's a woman of the sea who dreams of the homeland; a pauper who dreams of a just world where her children will have warm feet and eat each day their two meals of baked beans; a poet who dreams of spring, is afraid of death, and longs after a Paradise of store-made coconut pie. I can understand all that . . . except, of course, the coconut pie. I can feel the longing for spring, being also from Winterland; I can feel the trauma of unfairness, being from a bilingual country; I can feel the anguish of searching for my birthplace, a land that is part of me with a name in History books.

That is where dwells, let's say the word, the universal. But first, I had to find a woman in the flesh, real, alive, with character, a birthmark, a mentality, a physiognomy. Because the Woman with a capital *W* is never hungry nor has cold feet; was never horrified by injustice, never afraid of death. The real life that interests the writer is written with a small *r*. The Acadian reality as well.

How can we define that Acadian reality, the substance, *la matière d'Acadie*? First, one may say that the Acadian writer is just out of the woods. That is the greatest possible gift to the artist: the wilds. The virgin forest is the writer's Klondike.

Those hidden treasures, untapped, buried for many centuries in our sandhills and our memories, justify our actual craving for literature, literature which is writing as well as literary substance. Literature is an odd type of art, where words, metaphors, style go hand in hand with characters, ideas, adventures. In Acadian writing, everything is new, untouched, in its primeval state. Which makes it unique in the world. You may say that it is the specificity of all literature to be unique. Of course. Except that in the grand national literatures, odd is multiple and uniqueness, often repetitive. Not yet for us. We are not that lucky.

We have something like the notion, some kind of feeling that somewhere in our bare fields lies the Acadian spirit of an epic. Just like around King Arthur and his twelve knights was hidden asleep the epic of Brittany, and around Roland and Charlemagne, that of the Franks. Hence, could there be an Acadian heroic chronicle to be found, to be written? Admit that such a discovery is quite appealing to a newborn literature. Look at what lies before us:

a world springing out of the meeting of earth and saltwater which turns our soil into that kind of clay God used to create man; a world so often tossed from sea to sea, from shore to shore, with its olive branch between its teeth, that if Noah were to start anew his Flood, for sure he would introduce into the ark along with his pairs of animals an Acadian couple; a world so full of emotion and energy after three centuries of restrained silence, that only an explosion of words can release its soul. Words that will become literature.

It remains to be known whether we will have the heart, the courage, the resourcefulness to take up the challenge. Even whether we will have the time. There is no guarantee that we have much time left. In our case the urgency is now.

It is critical to express one's own universe, whether small or big. Maybe the greatest things will come out of the most deprived: a banished person who dreams of a homeland, such as Dante; a prisoner that longs for freedom . . . Cervantes; a blind man who recreates the epic of his people . . . Homer! An Acadian can understand the cry and lament of all the exploited, rejected, exiled of the earth. He can understand them and afterwards speak on his and their behalf.

Had I known at the age of three, when I entered the world of the Three Bears, hand in hand with Tom Thumb, or at five, entered the body and soul of Cinderella, that within a few decades I would have to enter by the main door into Literature, tell the story of a people and attempt the hazardous adventure to recreate the universe with words, harsh and rocky words, often for some obsolete, and in my own words translate my vision, my soul, my anguish, my hopes and dreams . . . had I known I would come to tell you all that in your language which is not mine — yet both just as beautiful — had I known what life was keeping in store for me, I wonder . . .

I wonder and I answer: even though the life of the writer is the most perilous and bold that one can imagine, yet it remains the greatest gift that the Creator has made to the Happy Few.

2 0 0 7

MARGARET ATWOOD

I'm very pleased to have been asked to give the Margaret Laurence Lecture for 2007.

I've divided it into two parts, which we could call Margaret One and Margaret Two.

I'll introduce both Margarets with a short quote from the writer William Gaddis: "If you're going to write a book, who asked you to do it? It is, in fact, quite an act of ego to sit down in a room while others are getting on trains and subways, and put one's vision on paper, and then ask others to pay to read it. Not only to pay, but to say, 'Isn't he brilliant?' It's an act of audacity."

On that note of audacity, I'll begin. Margaret One is of course Margaret Laurence herself. She was a founding member of the Union, as she was of the Writers' Trust, so I'd like to start by talking about her, about her own life as a writer, and about some of the various ways in which I knew her.

The Stone Angel was published in 1964. It wasn't Margaret Laurence's first work of fiction, but I think it's safe to say it was her breakthrough book, the one that brought her what was then a wide Canadian readership. I was twenty-four in that year; I was living in Vancouver, where I put together my first book of poetry to be officially published, *The Circle Game*, and where I wrote my first published novel, *The Edible Woman*. I was already engaged in the literary community of Canada; insofar as there was a community then, it consisted of poets. What few fiction writers there were in the country did not – as a rule – know one another, except through their books, which were few and far between.

In 1961, there were five novels published in English Canada by Canadian publishers. There were twenty or so books of poetry, but these included self-published mimeographed and hand-set pamphlets. The height of ambition as a poet was to get your book published officially, by a real publisher. Such poetry books might appear at the rate of one or two a year each, from Oxford, or Ryerson, or – oh bliss – from Contact Press, which was run by poets.

In 1964, I was earning my living by teaching at the University of British Columbia, where my courses included the whistle-stop undergrad course that went from Chaucer to T.S. Eliot at the speed of light, and a course for engineering students that took place at 8:30 in the morning in a Quonset hut left over from World War II. (I made the engineers read Kafka's fables, which they liked, since these contained problems and they could work on solutions to them.)

One day, Jane Rule, whom I knew through a friend, and who had kindly lent me a card table and some dishes for my sparsely furnished apartment, gave me *The Stone Angel*, by someone called Margaret Laurence. "You have to read this," said Jane.

She was right. I had to read that. I can still remember the excitement with which I did read it, crouched in my echoing apartment. *The Stone Angel* was one of those moments – like Mordecai Richler's *The Apprenticeship of Duddy Kravitz* – that were like beacons to young writers such as myself. It could be done, then. The impossible, dreamed-of thing could be done. You could write a novel about Canada – which at that time did not exist as a force in the international literary world, and pretty much did not exist as a force in Canada itself. You could write a novel about Canada that was real, and strong, and authentic, and smart, and moving. It was like watching an albatross take off from a cliff top for the first time, and spread its wings, and soar – yes! Flight is possible!

Let me take you back for a moment, just to enumerate all of those things that did not exist, in Canada, in 1964.

There were only a few publishers. The House of Anansi did not yet exist, nor did Coach House Press – the crowd of small publishers that sprang into being in the late '60s and the '70s was yet to come. There were some literary magazines – glossier ones like the *Tamarack Review* and *Canadian Literature*, respectable ones like the *Canadian Forum* and *Fiddlehead*, and unglossy ones like *Tish* and *The Sheet* – and we young poets bombarded them with submissions. There was – noteworthily – Robert Weaver's CBC program, *Anthology*, a lifeline and a vindication, because it actually paid money. By "money" I mean more than five dollars.

There were no cross-country book tours. There were no chain bookstores, except for Coles, which made a point of not selling Canadian books. There were some motley poetry readings in coffee houses, and sometimes at universities. There were no fiction readings. There were serious reviewers, however, in newspapers and magazines. There was no Writers' Union. There was no Writers' Trust. There were no agents to speak of. There was almost no way you could find out – as a writer – anything about contracts, or what would be fair in the way of pay, for you, as a writer. There was no Public Lending Right.

There were not many Canadian detective stories, or science fiction books, or children's books – not much Canadian genre fiction of any kind. I say "not much" and "not many" to cover my rear – in fact, it was probably more like "not any."

There were no paperback houses in Canada. Paperbacks came in from the States and England. Few paperback books were by Canadians. Again, I say "few" as a precaution, but I can't think of any.

There were almost no grants, though the Canada Council had come into existence in time to give Margaret Laurence some money. There were almost no prizes. There were no Writers-in-Residence. All of those things that might now go on a writer's CV – a CV such as one might submit in hope of yet another grant, prize, or writer-in-residency – what we might call the "career" aspect of writing – all of that, for good or ill, was in the future.

The lack of any need for an attractive CV meant that writers led more extravagantly disreputable lives than they seem to do now. They got drunk a lot, and made spectacles of themselves, and hit people, and fell backwards through plate-glass windows. This was mostly the poets – craziness was, and is, more tolerated in them than it is in novelists – but even the novelists were not expected to be nicely brushed and combed and showered at all times. Artists, being at that time an out-group, were expected to enact society's buttoned-down id. And enact that id they did.

I used to feel lacking in that respect — why couldn't I smoke without chok-ing or drink without puking? Why couldn't I be a real writer, and get TB or something, or at the very least, commit suicide? Readers used to ask me that. But as Margaret Laurence used to say, you have to be who you are.

People sometimes ask you — as a novel-writer, not as a poet — "Isn't it lonely, being a writer?" They mean sitting in your room by yourself, scribbling. But writers are happy to sit in their rooms scribbling as long as something good, or even anything at all, is coming out the other end of the pen, or — these days — onto the screen. There's another kind of loneliness, however: the feel-ing of being all alone in the enterprise you're committed to. Of not getting that much support from the society or community. That was the kind of lonely that Margaret Laurence was, early in her writing career.

What all of this meant was that anyone Canadian who had it in mind to write fiction didn't do such a thing lightly. You knew you might never get published, and if you did get published you might not have much of a reader-ship. A thousand copies sold for a work of fiction was very good, two hundred for a poetry book was normal. You couldn't count on making a living from your writing. Morley Callaghan did, but he was the great exception, and he'd got a good start in the States in the 1920s. Despite that, he had constant wor-ries about money — as did Margaret Laurence, even when she'd made some. Which she certainly hadn't in the early years.

Various historical factors account for some of the dearthiness we felt around us, as young writers, in the '50s and early '60s. Canada had once had best-selling authors — Ralph Connor, with five million books internationally; L.M. Montgomery, with the Anne books; Mazo de la Roche; Ernest Thompson Seton; and others. The Depression had wiped out some of that, and the advent of the cheap paperback — a business that was not controlled in Canada — had demolished the cheap Canadian hardback business that once existed. Then there was the War, and paper shortages; and then came the postwar period, and the decline of the British Empire, and the dominance of the United States as the new Last Man Standing superpower.

Canada, once a pillar of Empire, then an honest broker — Canada, which once had the most admired army and one of the three biggest merchant navies in the world — Canada, which had lost a large percentage of young men and lot of money in the First War, and then lost a lot more of both in the Second — was left a relatively impoverished, recently-colonial space, orphaned on the North American continent. Like most orphans, it was jeered at: No culture. No identity! Who was your father, anyway?

The other characteristic of that time — and it hasn't been much commented on — is that the postwar years — the late '40s, the '50s — were the most male-dominated period in international English-language literature since the eighteenth century. The same goes for publishers. Publishing was a gentleman's occupation. Women could be editors, sometimes; they could be secretaries; they could be publicists, and get chased around by the male authors — a standard practice. But they didn't call the shots. They didn't get to say who was to be graced with publication, and they didn't take the author out for the legendary four-martini lunch.

Here comes Margaret Laurence, then — determined to be a writer. This is the world she stepped into. A Depression childhood, a dead mother, then a dead father, then a war that wiped out a lot of the young men she knew; then a literary world in which it was commonplace to say that women couldn't write, and neither could Canadians, and any woman or any Canadian who tried was likely to meet more than one big slap-down. It's hard to imagine the sheer guts or perhaps obsessiveness that it must have taken to persevere in what must have seemed a futile and indeed a loony endeavour.

Writing — for Margaret Laurence — was not a hobby. Writing was not a hockey book on which you might spend fifteen minutes a day. Writing was a serious commitment. Writing was a life-and-death struggle. The metaphor she used most often about it was Jacob wrestling with the angel. Wounds were inflicted, in that fight. "I will not let thee go, except thou bless me," said Jacob. Or — he might have added — until one of us dies in the combat. And in human-angel fights, it's unlikely to be the angel who perishes.

Jacob got the blessing; Margaret Laurence got the blessing too.

Jacob's blessing was a mixed one. So was Margaret's.

What I'm leading up to is something rather delicate, but it's something everyone who knew Margaret — or has even read her biography — also knows: Margaret Laurence had a complex and difficult emotional life. And the result of it — and then a contributing factor to it — was her trouble with alcohol. She was not alone in this, especially in that generation. But she did everything intensely, and she was an intense drinker. Sometimes writers drink or take drugs to loosen up, or to overcome their fear: that blank page is a terrifying place. But the crutch can take over, and for a while – for quite a long time – in Margaret's life, it did.

Thus there were two Margarets – the warm, kindly, generous woman who helped young writers and spoke of other writers as "the tribe"; and the sad and angry and jealous one who came out at dusk, and then, as time passed, arrived earlier and earlier in the day, and railed and cursed and savaged people, and put their names on her official Shit List.

Which one was real? Both were real.

Anyway, just remember: as a writer, you don't have to be nice to be good.

—

I first met Margaret Laurence in the women's room at Rideau Hall, in Ottawa, in 1967. For *The Jest of God*, published in 1966 and read by me immediately, she'd won the Governor General's Award for fiction – the only big prize, then – and I, unaccountably – to myself, and indeed to others, some of whom never forgave me for it – had won it for poetry. I'd had to borrow a suitable dress and earrings from my Harvard graduate school roommates, who incinerated my Hush Puppies when I was away, on the grounds that such footgear was too disreputable for a figure of my now-august standing. I'd blown some of my prize money on contact lenses, and though I could get them in, I had trouble getting them out, and couldn't do it without a mirror; and as I couldn't wear these lenses for more than two hours without crying, I'd rushed into the women's room – like Cinderella at the stroke of midnight – to pry the offending bits of plastic off my watering eyeballs. Margaret Laurence was in there, pulling herself together and shaking like a leaf: public appearances of any kind made her very nervous.

On that occasion, she couldn't have been kinder. As for me, I admired her so much it was like meeting – well, Simone de Beauvoir – the only difference being that Simone de Beauvoir scared the pants off me, and Margaret Laurence did not, or not at that time. She got scarier towards me later, but that's another story.

At her best as a writer, Margaret Laurence was amazing; as a participant in the emerging Canadian literary life of the '60s and '70s, she was crucial. I would like to add here that much of what she and others worked so hard to achieve in the area of public support for the arts is now in danger. What would Margaret say about the present climate – the present political climate – the present destructive federal political climate, as it relates to the arts? I believe she would say, "If you want something, fight for it." I believe she would say, "Give 'em hell." No – she would say, "Give 'em hell, kiddo."

And about that, I have nothing better to add.

—

Now I have come to Margaret Two.

My own journey as a writer began in a different time – not in the '20s, before the Depression, but in 1939, at the end of it, and also two and a half months after the onset of the Second World War. I was thus two years old during the most dire part of that war – when it was by no means certain Britain would not go down in flames – and five when it ended – I can remember V-E Day – and six, seven, eight, and nine when we were living in the still-constrained postwar years. That darkness some readers may have glimpsed between the lines or at the edges of my otherwise sunny pages may well have its origins then.

Don't worry – I'm not going to give you a year-by-year biography of myself. Instead, I'll get right down to the crux of the matter: Why do I do this? This writing thing?

Every time I start a new novel, I find myself saying, *This is too hard!* As a monk from the middle ages wrote in the margin of the manuscript he was copying, "Writing is boring." He meant the physical act, but he might as well have been describing the whole ball of wax.

Why on earth does *anyone* do it? I ask myself. It's such a useless pursuit – who cares what a bunch of made-up people or rabbits or talking mushrooms on Planet X are thinking and saying? Why am I wasting my time, only to go through the depressing and cannibalistic ordeal of publication? Not only do you find yourself disappointed by your own book – it's never quite what you hoped – but also someone is sure to heave a few rotten eggs at you for being so puffed up as to think that anything you can set down on paper would ever be worth reading by a serious-minded person.

And so it goes, this inner monologue, until I either give up on the book I'm writing or reach a place where I'm enjoying it.

But for times of need — such as radio interviews, or today — I've developed a cover story about writing. It sounds like this:

We are our stories. Without them, we can't remember who we are, because we can't remember how we got here. Without our narratives we're lost in the present. People have always understood themselves and their cultures through the stories they've told, and individuals do the same. The art of storytelling is an intensification of something every human being does, because doing it is essential to what makes us human. Where did we come from? Why are we here? Where are we going? We all know some variations of this group of questions, because it's not possible for us to ignore them.

I can go on like this for hours; most of the time it's pretty convincing, even to me. But it doesn't answer the only inevitable question that faces a writer every day, and that is: What comes next? Or, in another version: Why should the reader turn the page?

How did I get into it? I ask myself. This writing caper. Is it too late to take up some other pursuit? Maybe I could be a golfer, or a forger of some kind, or — I know! — a lifestyles coach! That sounds like fun! I could give people wise but annoying advice, and make them eat sardines and do push-ups.

But it's too late for that. My own personal ship left the harbour a long time ago. I'm out on the open sea. There's no turning back.

—

It all started on the planet of Neptune, inhabited by the eight-foot-high flesh-eating Alfels and the raft-dwelling Mineracs, and their pets, the yellow and green and explosive ten-legged Spintles . . .

But no. I must restrain myself. It all started sixty-odd years ago, as I am at present sixty-seven, and I began writing at the age of four. (Yes, the evidence exists.) So those black-and-white films about World War II that you see on the History Channel coincide with the beginning of my writing life.

I used up a good many pencils between the onset of my early writing and the pause that took place in it between age nine and age sixteen, when I started up again with serious writerly ambitions. During my younger writing period, my family spent a lot of time in the northern Canadian woods, where there were no movie theatres, no TV, no plays or musicals, and no radio. When it rained, you could read, or you could write and draw. I did all three of these.

I had an older brother who was an avid and prolific writer; so he was my first role model. He was a good deal more interesting than me, as a writer, at that age. He had already grasped the main elements of the narrative art. Charles Dickens said, "Make 'em laugh, make 'em cry, make 'em wait," but my brother would have added, "Make 'em shoot off guns."

This was the war era, but it was also the comic book era, featuring Dick Tracy and Flash Gordon and similar heroes, so wars and noir criminals and other planets are never far from my brother's plots. He always used up the red and yellow and orange pencils before any of his other pencils, on the explosions and fires and bombs. This enabled me to make some gratifying trades involving the silver and gold pencils – he didn't have much use for these, but I did, as I was a monarchist, and liked to add crowns to my characters.

I learned a lot about writing from the writing done by my brother. Here, for instance, is the opening of *Alfred's Youth*, the first in a series. It is a useful study in narrative precision.

"Chapter One: *Born*." (You see, he nails down the basics, right away.)

"Alfred's mother had three twins. One Alfred, one John, one Ben. They played with and liked each other. Their father had been to war and had died. He had been a million Air and a great champion." (Here is another good hint: bump off any potentially overly protective parent, or your characters will not have much scope for adventure.)

To continue: "He had a great many things. He left five thousand million dollars for his wife. She kept them hidden in a secret vault. She kept loaded revolvers everywhere, even under the bed. She didn't care to be robbed. 'If any robbers come, I'll fill 'em with lead,' she said."

You can see that my brother had nothing against a strong female character. You will also have immediately grasped the theme of this book. Note that, as early as page two, the promise for conflict and indeed for prolonged firefights is deftly suggested – a promise that is amply fulfilled in the chapters that follow. My brother drew many pictures of bullets and their trajectories, criss-crossing in mid-air. This is a pleasing way of covering the pages while maintaining the necessary tension.

Whenever my brother got tired of gunfights, he had his characters do one of two things: a) have a nap, or b) eat something. This has been a major influence on my own work. Some authors provide no food or drink of any kind for their characters, and no downtime in the form of sleep, but I feel remiss if I don't allow them both.

My brother seems to have written the Cast of Characters and the chapter headings for his books first, and then filled in from there. He was also prone to supplying maps and diagrams – showing the locations of the fights – and after a while, the maps and diagrams seem to have more or less taken over. Once he started detailing the bone structures and respiratory systems of his characters, a corner had been turned, and he was headed non-stop for biology. Ever since that fatal moment when "What are they thinking?" was replaced by "*How* are they thinking?" he was fingered for neuroscience, which was indeed where he ended up.

Most of my brother's books take place on other planets. Some are works of fiction, others works of natural history. *What's on Neptune?* combines the two, being a fictional treatise on the animals, plants, and loathsome bacteria to be found on Neptune. (Neptune is where the eight-foot-high flesh-eating Alfels, the raft-dwelling Mineracs, and the explosive ten-legged Spintles live, for those who have been paying close attention.) If you've ever wondered why you haven't wanted to visit Neptune, this book has the answer. The bacteria are, if anything, even worse than the other wildlife, causing everything from weakness and dizziness to madness, starvation, rashes, and death.

It's not very far from my brother's 1946 version of Neptune to my own 2003 novel, *Oryx and Crake*, except that, in my admittedly somewhat longer work, Earth takes the place of Neptune, and the bacteria and unpleasant scavengers have been created not by Nature, but by us. However, it's the same general idea: don't go out for walks, because you might never make it back from them.

What's on Neptune? begins with a standard disclaimer that all novelists might well emulate: "This story is not true. Of course, there is a planet called Neptune, but its inhabitation is unknown. I have made up a number of things that will be used in the next two volumes." I think that's pretty straightforward, and would also stand up in court.

Then it says, "Read on." As a writer's advice to a reader, this cannot be bettered.

In comparison with my brother's voluminous oeuvre, my own production was skimpy and pedestrian. Although I too had some characters who lived on other planets, they were pale imitations, and did not have nearly so many weapons. I also wrote a novel about an ant, which stands as a testament to modernist minimalism. The fact is that ants don't do very much, but I — as narrator — managed to make much of the not very much that they do. The egg stage, the larval stage, the pupal stage, the emergence as a full-fledged worker ant — all are described. Eating, crawling, and biting are each given their due. There's even a happy ending, not a thing I have managed a lot since. But I do keep trying.

It seems that my brother got fiction-writing out of his system as a child. I, however, must have felt that I had a lot of unfulfilled promise reserved for . . . later.

—

Next chapter: *Later*.

I'll skip the subsequent sixteen or so years — eventful though they were — and place myself in 1964, the very same year, you'll remember, in which I first read *The Stone Angel*. In the previous year I'd taken time out from graduate school to write. (The bare-naked truth: I was afraid of my graduate-school Latin reading exam.) I lived in a run-down Toronto rooming house and completed a luckily still-unpublished novel, while working days at a market research company. I also got engaged, a grim business that rendered me almost catatonic — the response, I expect, to yet another rejection by a publishing house of yet another manuscript of poems. Actually, it was worse than that — first the book was accepted, and then, *after I'd told all my friends*, it was rejected, by the third member of the editorial team. Well, who wouldn't get engaged after that?

But a fortune teller told me it wouldn't work out, and he was right. I borrowed six hundred dollars and ran away to England, and then to France; and after that I went to Vancouver and wrote *The Edible Woman*, subsisting on Kraft Dinner and Smitty's Pancake House pancakes. I drank so much instant coffee to keep myself awake that I can't tolerate it to this day. I also drank a kind of wine called Kelowna Red that dyed your tongue a permanent vermillion. But young people have a tolerance for that kind of life.

The Edible Woman didn't actually get published until 1969, because the publisher lost the manuscript, so it appeared just as the women's movement was making its debut. It got two kinds of reviews – those written by people who hadn't noticed the movement yet, and who thought I was a young person who would get more mature later on – true enough, I did, the alternative being death – and those who had noticed the movement, and had decided that I was one of the dreadful Them.

—

I've now told you about my first writing, my first role model, my first poetry book, and my first published novel. What came next? Alas – once they begin to be successful, people's lives become less interesting, at least to those observing them. Inside one of his early books, my brother wrote, "By Harold L. Atwood, author of *Tim the House Mouse*, *Adventure in Smell-Fish Bay*, *Caller Kingbird*, etc." It's the "etc." that says it all.

I am now in the "etc." period, and whatever its productions may be, their appearance is no longer greeted with the dramatic howls of rage or shouts of welcome that once heralded their arrival. True, there's always some grudge-bearer waiting to poke you in the eye and thus get briefly onto the Internet, but such efforts lack the flair they once had, and begin to border on the mugging of old ladies, an activity lacking in heroism. Let's face it: suspense is more possible when a person is younger – when a really spectacular failure or a coma-inducing drug addiction or a messy domestic break-up or sluttish affair are all still within reach.

Nevertheless, despite the fact that I am in the "etc." period, you might want to hear a few bits of juicy inside info about that most portentous of subjects: "How I Write."

"With a pencil" is the short answer, but it is also the cheap answer. You deserve more. So I'll jump to the time of my 2000 novel, *The Blind Assassin*. I began this book with some vague ideas about an orphan of sorts in search of her vanished parents — ideas that soon evaporated almost completely. What remained was the setting — a town in Southern Ontario, sort of like Paris, Ontario, with its harbour, and sort of like St. Mary's, with its quarry, and sort of like Elora, with its old mills now turned into tourist attractions.

Attached to this town was an elderly woman who'd lived through the same decades that my mother and my grandmother had — that is, the entire twentieth century. Both of those real people were far too nice to appear in a novel by me, so the old woman was neither of them. She was a nastier creature, and one who knew she was nearing the end of her life.

In fact, she'd toppled over the edge — she was dead, and her secret life was being discovered by a younger relative, via some letters found in a hat box. But this didn't work out, so I had to throw away the hat box and start again.

This time the old woman was still alive, and her secret life was being discovered — against her will — by two nosy younger people, who had wormed their way into a suitcase in which there was a photograph album. But these two folks started having an affair, and the man was married and had just had twins, and this situation began to hog the centre stage. I had to shut the adulterous couple up in a drawer, where they still remain. I took away the suitcase, but kept a couple of the photographs.

Then, after the usual bouts of pessimism and despair — was it too late to go into some other line of work that might require a talent for productive lying, such as accountancy? — the old woman began speaking in the first person, and this time I was able to proceed. The old woman still had a secret life, and she still had a container with some giveaway evidence in it. The container was a steamer trunk — it got bigger with every one of my attempts — and the things in it were the very same things that are to be found there to this day, in the chapter called . . . "The Steamer Trunk." And that is how you know I always tell the truth.

What else can I say about writing? Well — I usually draw a birthday chart for the characters in my books, so I know what age they are in relation to one another. Sometimes, like the Portuguese writer Fernando Pessoa, I even draw up their horoscopes. I always research as I go along, rather than beforehand. For *The Blind Assassin*, old newspapers and magazines — the ads and the gossip columns and society weddings and write-ups of charity balls — were especially useful to me, as were — for the Golden Age lizard-man sci-fi tale within the tale within the tale — the science fiction magazines from the '30s and '40s: *Weird Tales*, and the like.

But of course everything you write has deep roots, invisible sometimes to the reader, but also to the writer as well. Until I found a bundle of child-era writing in the cellar of my mother's house, put away in — yes — a steamer trunk, I'd forgotten the extent to which *The Blind Assassin* has its origins in my early writing, and also in the parallel universe of the writing my brother was producing. I was his primary reader, as he was — to a lesser extent — mine. The menacing bioforms on the Planet of Neptune — dangerous though they were — existed absolutely for me, on their own imaginative terms. And I could visit Neptune, and observe them, and return safely. That is one of the great virtues of fiction: the characters may not get out of it alive, but the reader does.

So, to refer to a question I asked earlier — Why on earth does anyone do it, this writing thing? — I suppose that's the answer: to create a living world whose doors stand open for anyone who desires to enter.

Thank you.

2008

JOSEF ŠKVORECKÝ

My first novel was set in the Canadian North and its heroes were Canadian trappers. Although I am speaking to a Canadian audience, this is not an attempt at *captatio benevolentiae*. Rather, it is a statement of fact. The manuscript is deposited at the Thomas Fisher Rare Book Library of the University of Toronto. I wrote it when I was ten years old, all sixteen handwritten pages of it.

As works go, this one was not entirely original. As soon as I learned how to read, it became an obsession of mine. One of the first authors who captured my imagination was James Oliver Curwood, then very popular in Bohemia. His novels illuminated the darkness of my bedroom as I drifted off to sleep, replaying themselves in my mind like so many wonderful action movies. I didn't realize at the time that he was American, as his stories were most often placed in Canada; indeed, so many of them were as to make it worthwhile for Pierre Berton to write *Hollywood's Canada*.

Early in his career Curwood wrote two parts of a planned trilogy, *The Wolf Hunters* and *The Gold Hunters*, which were eventually translated into Czech. Set in the Canadian northern wilderness, the books' characters were hunters, Mounties, and Indian beauties. The public eagerly awaited the translation of the final part, but it never arrived. For reasons which remain unexplained, Curwood never wrote it, choosing instead to write almost thirty other works, before dying suddenly in 1927. The disappointed public was left only with the title of the unwritten work: *The Mysterious Cave*. At the suggestion of my father,

I decided to write my own conclusion to the trilogy and borrowed Curwood's title to name my first artifact. Only later did I discover that I wasn't the only one to do so. A Polish translator of Curwood's works, Maria Boghuszynska-Borowikova, who used the pen name of Jerzy Marlicz, eventually wrote the concluding part. But by then I was lying in bed at my parents' main-street flat in our hometown of Náchod, fighting for my life.

———

I had contracted pneumonia. At that time, before the discovery of penicillin, it was a very serious illness, especially in children. I mostly remember the nights; the shining bald pate of Dr. Kraus, his cold ear on my back, listening to my breathing; my teary-eyed mother and ashen father in the background. I was their only child and in the end it was Dr. Kraus who saved my life. I don't know whether he did it by his constant care – he came to see me three times a day, often in the middle of the night – or because he had brought back from a medical congress in London a new medicine that he administered by injection, after getting my father's permission to do so. For many years I was convinced that the medicine he had brought from London was penicillin. But that was most likely nothing more than wishful thinking, which generated the idea intended to celebrate that soft-spoken small-town doctor in my mind.

Indeed, he lived in a small town, but he was wealthy and he used his wealth to keep up with the scientific advances in his field; thus the journey to London. He was Jewish and eventually, with his wife and young son, he went on another journey; that journey brought them, together with millions of others, to Auschwitz. Miraculously, he and his son survived their stay in that incredible twentieth-century domicile of death, and upon liberation at the end of the war, hoping against hope to be reunited with his wife, they set out on yet another journey, this time walking back home to Náchod. He almost made it, but near the once-famous spa of Chudoba, no more than twenty kilometres from home, he stepped on a landmine. I often remembered him and he appears in my stories. A few years ago I received one final memento of that dear man from his son, now an architect living in Boston. It was a letter from the Health Ministry of the Protectorate government, icily giving the doctor permission to continue the treatment of a few of his old patients, but forbidding him to accept any new ones, and ordering him to discontinue his medical practice altogether by a certain date.

—

I returned to my books during the interminable period of post-pneumonia convalescence, and I wrote another novel. This one was a bit longer and it wasn't about Canadian North. I called it *Men of Steel Hearts*; it was set during the Anglo-French wars in colonial North America.

When I was finally back on my feet, my parents sent me to spend the summer at the *pension* of Onkel Otto and Tante Blanka, where various summer sports were practiced, only German was spoken, and Czech was forbidden. My parents wanted to kill two birds with one stone, in a manner of speaking: to turn me into the young athlete that I was before I got sick, and to allow me to practice my German, which I studied with the cantor of the synagogue in Náchod, Mr. Adolf Neu. He was another in the gallery of Jewish people from my youth who were dear to my heart. In a stroke of merciful irony, Mr. Neu never made it to Auschwitz. He was diabetic and, because Jews were not allowed to purchase insulin, he died soon after arriving at the Terezín ghetto.

Onkel Otto and his wife Blanka were also Jewish, and most of the boys and girls at that brief moment of earthly paradise in the corner of Northern Bohemia known as the Teplice Rocks were also of that religion, nationality, race, or whatever it was. Many years after the war, at some congress in Canada, I met one of the few so-called Aryan members of our troupe, a passionate soccer player during the day and a Monopoly addict at night. He was the only one I ever met.

Most often I remembered Paul Pollak and Alex Karpeles, especially the latter; I even dreamt of him on occasion. For a long time I wasn't sure whether I met him in his British Army uniform in reality or in a dream. But it was only in a dream. The last reminder of him I discovered recently among some old correspondence. It was a postcard Alex and Paul sent me in the fall of 1938, after Munich; they wrote, with unintended irony, that we had almost become citizens of the Third Reich and that their English professors — Alex and Paul both attended the English Secondary School in Prague — who during the Munich crisis went home to England, were slowly getting ready to return.

Another memento of the paradise in the Teplice Rocks, I no longer have —
my first "published" novel. Paul and Alex published their own mimeographed
magazine in which they may have published, but possibly only promised to
publish — my memory fails me in this instance — my novel *Men of Steel Hearts*.
Both Alex and Paul belonged to some Zionist youth group, of which I knew
virtually nothing, and the magazine, if my opus actually appeared in it, disappeared from this world, together with its publishers and their friends. They
survive only in my book of short stories, *The Menorah*.

—

But I am getting ahead of myself. After my pneumonia I went back to the
books that my father would buy me on the advice of old Mr. Reimann, a book-
seller in Náchod. My father was great at bowling, he sang in the local choir and
was a passionate amateur actor, but of literature he knew nothing. Once he
brought me an American adventure novel which Mr. Reimann had emphatically recommended to him as highly appropriate for children. After supper
that night, I went to bed and started to read it. The book was illustrated and
so I first looked at the pictures. They petrified me — and, naturally, drew me
to the text. I stared at them over and over, at apparitions with bulging eyes,
leaning over the gunnels of a schooner, skeletal figures clinging to the upside-
down keel of a ship. The book's title was *The Narrative of Arthur Gordon Pym*.
Soon Mother came in and made me turn off the light. But the book was magical and I had a long time ago mastered the trick of reading under the covers
with a flashlight. And I read, on and on, in that sight-destroying light, until I
fell asleep, and slipped into a classical child's nightmare. I cried out for help;
my terrified mother ran in from her bedroom and stuck a thermometer under
my arm. I had thirty-nine degrees Celsius.

The book and its author, his Pym and then Berenice, Ligeia, Morella — that
whole terrifying throng followed me throughout my life. Many years later that
distant nightmare resulted in a film, *Poe and the Murder of a Beautiful Girl*. That
film I had to write, just as I had to write the novel *An Inexplicable Story, or, The
Narrative of Questus Firmus Siculus*. It was an overdue tribute to the man who,
in a peculiar way, as it were, set a frame around my life.

As I met Poe so early in life, I didn't read the brothers Grimm; nor did I read any fairy tales. Their horror seemed laughable to me in comparison to the terror that happened on deck of the *Grampus*. Instead, I kept on consuming books for young readers from a distant country of which I knew nothing. Ernest Thompson Seton's *Two Little Savages* brought me back from Tsalal to the kinder world of wisdom in the wild woods of America. I had no idea where I was; maybe the text of these books was not sufficiently localized for their pre-teen readers. Not until I went into exile did I discover that the deep woods where Yan built his shack lay in the Don Valley, adjacent nowadays to downtown Toronto. I read about the mysterious *Rolf in the Woods* and about the sad song of a dying Indian; this is what remained with me from a story that I didn't entirely understand. I read my way to *The Preacher of Cedar Mountain*, and there I foundered. There was a certain magic to all of it, which I didn't understand well enough, yet it charmed me.

At that age, I didn't really read the books — I let them enchant me.

Soon I had fallen victim to the mysteries of Tarzan, to the permanently un-requited love of the high priestess La from the City of Opar towards the Lord of the Apes. She impressed me far more than did Jane, later the wife of Lord Greystoke. Of the adventures of the American John Carter on Mars, one illustration from *A Princess of Mars* remained with me: it showed the hero embracing the Martian Princess, Dejah Thoris, above a cradle containing what looked like an ostrich egg. The caption under the picture read: "Many hours were spent standing above the fruit of our love . . ." Of all the adventures of the intrepid American on the Red Planet, I remembered only the scene of the lovers above the egg. It found its way into my only work of science fiction, *Pulchra, the Story of a Beautiful Planet*.

God only knows why I fell under a lifelong spell of Anglo-American litera-ture. My father had some leather-bound and gilded Collected Works of a cer-tain Czech classic, but I never saw him open any of the volumes. Mother had some distant French roots and when she read, it was usually French poetry, masterfully translated by the author of *R.U.R.* and *The Makropulos Case*, Karel Čapek. I moved on from the Lord of the Apes to Arthur Ransome's *Swallows and Amazons*, to those comfortable adventures of boys and girls at a calm lake somewhere in England; then on to the trickeries of Mrs. Richmal Crompton's William, whose Czech equivalent had the expressive moniker *The Family Menace*. By unchartered back roads of youthful reading, I finally arrived at Sinclair Lewis and American literature.

—

I read it in poor, frequently actually appalling translations – yet it still fascinated me. My book of books, *A Farewell to Arms,* I discovered during the war in a prewar translation by the quisling-to-be, Emanuel Vajtauer. After the war he vanished without a trace, leaving behind a text, in which up until the moment of Catherine's tragic death during the delivery of her stillborn baby, the two lovers address each other politely, using the formal *thou*, or as the French would say, *vouvoyer*, and in which Frederic Henry, dead tired from rowing through the night across Lago Maggiore, complains that he "got drunk drinking grog," although the only alcohol on the boat is a bottle of brandy. Regardless, the book fascinated me, although the discovery of style came only after the war, when I got hold of Hemingway's original. Apparently, a good writer is indestructible, even if assailed by a war criminal.

Then, sometimes before the United States entered the war, I added music to literature; and *that* really was a revelation.

Father gave me a wind-up gramophone and I used some saved-up pocket money to buy a few Brunswick 78s. I removed the first record from its ripped paper jacket, placed it on the turntable, applied the needle, and in that instant it seemed to me I was listening to music of the spheres. I didn't know what it was, but that's what it felt like. Harmony of the saxophones, gliding from tone to tone; the rhythm of swing, previously unheard; Chick Webb, followed by a woman's voice identified on the label only as "vocal chorus." Only years later did I find out it was seventeen-year-old Ella Fitzgerald. I must have played that record at least a hundred times, desperately trying to understand the words of the swinging singer. *I've got a guy, he don't dress me in sable* – this much I understood; but then came *He looks nothing like gable* . . . My pocket-sized English dictionary – I couldn't find a better one – translated the noun "gable" as "the front part of the house, the façade." What sort of a monster was that girl dating? The problem

irked me, but I couldn't solve it until years later, when two liberated English
POWs, Herbert Percy Siddell and Edward Martin, helped me out in May of
1945. After listening for a few times to my well-worn disk, they guessed correctly that the boyfriend in the song was a Gable with a capital G.

—

This new interest in music, which reminded my father of screaming monkeys,
didn't appeal to my parents. After many appeals for a musical instrument, they
bought me – a xylophone. One could play swing music on it, but I didn't know
how, and at that time I hadn't heard of Red Norvo. Meanwhile, Sláva Zachoval
put together his large swing band in Náchod, with five saxophones, one of which
was actually a baritone, which at that time I only knew about from the one and
only, ill-informed, prewar book on jazz that was available. The instrument was
owned by a youngster from a village near Black Mountain, a wooded hill overlooking Náchod; the fellow never penetrated the mystery of black syncopation,
but he owned a baritone. After another prolonged campaign of appellations, my
father finally bought me a tenor saxophone, but by then it was too late to join
Zachoval's big band. It already had two tenors and so I had console myself by
playing in a very amateur band, for which I actually provided the name: Red
Music. The name wasn't reflective of any sympathies for communism; rather, it
showed my ignorance at the time. In Prague there was a famous band called Blue
Music, and so I gave our band this rather unfortunate misnomer. (Incidentally,
Blue Music's excellent piano player, Jiří [later George] Traxler, eventually set-
tled in Canada; he is still going strong at ninety-five.)

I played and played, but not well enough. I had the love, but not the talent.
Years later, I wrote *The Bass Saxophone*, which was in effect the ultimate confir-
mation of the veracity of Faulkner's statement in the chapter "An Odor of
Verbena" from the novel *The Unvanquished*: ". . . those who can, do, those who
cannot and suffer enough because they cant [sic], write about it." But at that time
I wrote and I wrote, one unfinished novel after another about a small-town tenor
saxophone player on a victorious journey with a final destination of Hollywood.

—

Father happened to be the unpaid manager of a cinema, owned by the athletic club Sokol. I drew slides for the cinema that introduced the Coming Attractions and was rewarded by a nightly pass to the movies. Náchod had two movie houses, which traded free passes with each other. The programs changed three times weekly – there was no television – and on Sundays matinees were added. Consequently, I had certain special privileges that made me the envy of all my schoolmates: every day I would see a different film. The United States had not yet entered the war, with the result that I first fell in love with a young lad whose name was Freddie Bartholomew, followed by Judy Garland and finally Canadian Deanna Durbin. Of course, I wanted to become a film director, although I soon forgot about the Hollywood stars and replaced them with local beauties. Two in particular emerged from the crowd: Marie Dresslerová and Irena, the town councillor's daughter. They both ended up in *The Swell Season*, from whose pages they managed to charm, in quick succession, two Irish musicians: first Anthony Thistlethwaite, who wrote the song "Marie Dresslerova" about one of them; and then the better known Glen Hansard, who received the English translation of my book from a fourteen-year-old Moravian student, Markéta Irglová. That encounter resulted in a CD called *The Swell Season*, and this past February in an Oscar for Glen and Markéta for the best song of the year; they sang it in their film called *Once*.

—

After a series of unfinished novels about the triumphs of a Czech tenor saxophone player in the land of jazz, I finally stopped daydreaming and, shortly after the war, I wrote my first attempt at so-called serious prose: a novel, *The Cowards*. Until then I suffered from a shortcoming that probably afflicts all young neophyte authors: the lyrical prose passages, the descriptive and atmospheric parts I could write, but my dialogues came across like conversations between puppets at a village fair. Eventually I improved, with help from two sources. After the war I finally bought an English copy of *A Farewell to Arms*, and then, as a student at Charles University in Prague, I started to date a girl, whom I called Maggie. She worked as a sales girl in a department store. In Hemingway, I discovered dialogues that neither preached nor informed. Maggie, on the other hand, didn't know how to speak other than in dialogue — and she spoke almost non-stop. *I says — he says.* The dialogues were expressive: *I says go to hell! — He says go screw yourself!* Suddenly I got the hang of it: first in the short stories "Spectator on a February Night" (about the Communist putsch in 1948), "Laws of the Jungle" (about my experiences in the border regions after the postwar deportation of the local German population), followed by "Filthy Cruel World" (about a Jewish girl to whom I was engaged before I met my future wife); and, finally, in *The Cowards.*

By then I was already going out with Zdena, whom I married in 1958. Almost immediately, she helped me live through the bizarre affair around the publication of *The Cowards*, which was my first encounter with the Communist censorship. After a few generally positive reviews, the whole thing blew up. For two full weeks, day after day, a succession of critics, using almost similar verbiage, condemned the novel, through which I entered into the world of published literature. From simply cursing me as a "mangy pussycat," to observations hardly drawn from the book's pages, which compared *The Cowards* to "penny dreadfuls," to the "despicable" Radio Free Europe broadcast, with all sorts of other "praise" thrown in for good measure. There were too many for me to quote here; anyone interested in the matter can find all of them in the detailed and exhaustive essay by my friend and colleague Michal Schonberg from the University of Toronto, called, aptly, "The Case of the Mangy Pussycat," published in *World Literature Today*, Volume 54, Number 4, Autumn 1980.

This introductory salvo of so-called "literary criticism" was followed by the largest purge in film and literature prior to the Soviet ambush of Czechoslovakia in August of 1968. I was dismissed from my position at the journal *World Literature,* but the courageous and well-connected editor-in-chief of the publishing house that produced the journal simply transferred me to the department that published translations of Anglo-American books. All in all, I came through better than many others. The careers of several editors and film dramaturges were either interrupted, or permanently ended, in conjunction with the *Cowards* affair.

Subsequently, I had a few more similar encounters. One involved a story based on Zdena's childhood experiences, called "Me and My Dad, the Show-Off," which opened with the lines: "My problem is that I come from bourgeois background. Once upon a time that used to be a blessing, but in those days my background wasn't the least bit bourgeois." A very patient censor spent two hours trying to explain to me, as I was being particularly stupid, that each comrade could only have one background, which rendered my introductory sentence illogical; finally, frustrated, he put the kibosh on it altogether. The novel *The End of the Nylon Age* was banned for being pornographic: the lady protagonist reclined on a sofa in a glittery evening gown, her breasts heaving up and down as she drew deeply on a cigarette. In addition to that, Elsa Triolet, the wife of the French communist author Louis Aragon, threatened to sue me for copyright infringement of her novel *The Age of Nylon*, after my book was eventually published several years later. I managed to persuade her that she gained priority to the title by virtue of my opus being confiscated for gross indecency by the Communist censors a few years before her novel appeared.

—

Those of you who have read *The Cowards* might find it hard to understand what all the fuss was about. In order to understand, you would have to be familiar with the theory of socialist realism. That is difficult to do unless you read the particular works, but to do that you would need to know one of the languages of the colonial evil empire; the one that used to refer to itself by the Orwellian expression "the Peace Camp." In actual fact, the critics never really arrived at the *theory* of socialist realism. However, in practice, the products of the zenith of Stalinism could be compared to cheap westerns of years gone by. These were written according to the following formula: A stranger arrives in town, which is riddled with corruption and crime. He shoots all the criminals, redeems the redeemable, and either marries the local school teacher and settles down, or, if she turns him down, he rides off into the sunset. You find an analogous formula in the products of socialist realism. A young Party Secretary from the capital arrives in a small town, which is full of corrupt officials and American spies, running rampant. The Party Secretary from the capital arrests all of the spies, redeems the redeemable, and marries either the local doctor or the school teacher, or, if he is turned down, he rides out of town, likely back to the capital.

—

Soon after the affair of *The Cowards,* I ended up at the infectious ward of one of Prague's hospitals with a case of hepatitis. It was known at the time as serum hepatitis and I contracted it from a contaminated syringe. It happened before the days of disposable syringes; the glass ones that were used were sterilized by boiling, but that didn't kill the hepatitis viruses. Other patients usually left the hospital, cured, after three weeks, but I stayed on and on, four months altogether. Other than worrying that I might come to a bad end, there wasn't much else to do, and I was bored out of my mind. Czechoslovakia didn't have public television, and the hospital library contained only the Collected Works of Marx, Engels, Lenin, and Stalin, and the abovementioned literary products of triumphant Stalinism. Friends were allowed to bring me books to the hospital, but they had to leave them there so that hepatitis wouldn't infect others. For the most part, they were only willing to part with murder mysteries, which often arrived without the title page, or, what was worse, without the last pages.

Murder mysteries were a genre that I scorned; I was, after all, an aspiring *serious* young writer. But during my hospital confinement, I discovered their value. In my situation – being young, newly married, and seriously ill – few people would reach for Dostoevsky. I read the stories about murders and detectives, the so-called Great Ones, at first reluctantly, but then with growing enthusiasm; and I still believe that they contributed significantly to my cure. When I returned home and began to recover, I actually started to write them. The result was *The Mournful Demeanor of Lieutenant Borůvka*, followed later by many others.

In the end, they also helped to cure my wife.

—

What ailed her was not hepatitis, but deep, suicidal depression. After the fall of communism in Czechoslovakia, the agents of the disbanded National Secret Police provided a former dissident journalist with a list of their so-called "volunteer" collaborators, or, to use a neo-Orwellian term, of snitches. The dissident published them and Zdena discovered her name on the list. Needless to say, she never was a snitch and never signed any so-called "binding agreement," to quote Orwell one more time. Despite that, her name was included on the list, as were the names of many other innocent people. The real agents used to receive bonuses for every living soul that they managed to snare, and often even for dead ones. Their supposedly "volunteer" collaborators were very frequently victims of shameful blackmail — other than murder, regarded as the most despicable crime in the jurisprudence of civilized countries. I wrote a novel about all of that, *Two Murders in My Double Life*. It was published in Canada a few years ago. I am sure anyone interested can get it at the library. As I saw my wife crying, desperate and hopeless, I suggested to her that we start to write murder mysteries together.

—

As it happens, Zdena started her successful literary career in the old country with a book of three novellas, *Pánská jízda* (*The Gentlemen's Outing*). Once in exile, she continued her success with the novel *Honzlová,* which was published in English by Harper & Row in the United States, Great Britain, and several other countries under the title *Summer in Prague*; unfortunately, it didn't come out in Canada, her new homeland. The book received a number of excellent reviews, and subsequently Zdena conceived the idea of establishing a publishing house. Over time it grew into the largest exile publishing house of Czech literature, issuing books that were forbidden in Czechoslovakia. The price she paid was that she now had very little time for her own writing. Nonetheless, the works that she published proved that she knew her craft; or rather, that it was far more than mere craft.

And so we wrote whodunits. To date, we have completed six, and we are halfway through the seventh. One of them is currently being made in Prague into a feature film.

—

I too was subjected to all manner of accusations. One of the more pernicious ones purported that I "stole" the translation of the American novel *The Cool World* by Warren Miller — the Czech title was *Prezydent Krokadýlů* — from my deceased best friend. When I was forbidden to publish, he submitted my translation under his name, in other words, he covered for me; but then he suddenly died, and, many years later, when the issue of who translated the book arose, he couldn't confirm my authorship. That same friend, Jan Zábrana, also signed his name to three murder mysteries that we wrote together at the time, when my name couldn't appear on any publications. Fortunately, on that occasion we decided to play a little trick on the authorities: if you were to read the first letters of the first word in each chapter in one of the books, you would discover a Latin acrostic: "*Škvorecký et Zábrana fecerunt ioculum*," or "Škvorecký and Zábrana committed a prank." Or, from another perspective, "Škvorecký and Zábrana flipped the censors a finger." Thus I managed to ward off the accusations that, as an author, I was a thief of the most unsavoury kind.

———

In thirty-nine years of living in Canada, I have written many more books than in the almost thirty years of my adult life in Czechoslovakia. Why is that? The answer to that question is rather simple, although some people who are lucky enough to be born in this country might not give much credence to it. In Canada, I found the one thing that I didn't have in all of my earlier adult life in Bohemia. That thing was freedom.

In Canada, I didn't have to factor censorship into my writing; I simply wrote. If I remember correctly, I managed thirty books – novels, collections of short stories, as well as non-fiction. Five of the best-known works, written in this country, are *The Swell Season, The Miracle Game, The Engineer of Human Souls, The Bride of Texas,* and *Dvořák in Love*.

———

You may want to ask why I did it, and, why am I still at it?

Like every individual, I had many things and experiences on my mind, which I wanted to share with others. Some of these I wanted to relive by committing them to paper, and surprisingly, they had more magic when written down than when I actually lived them. As Nathaniel Hawthorne tells us, memories are often like that: "Sublime and beautiful facts are best understood when etherealized by distance." Also, the clowns, whom I loved since I was very young, sitting on my mother's lap in my father's movie theatre, watching *Fido to the Rescue*, those serious clowns like Chaplin, Keaton, Arbuckle, Lloyd, and so many others, taught me that one first has to entertain one's audience, and after that, with a bit of luck, one might also be able to say something meaningful about life. But one has to write it well. Then, as I learned from Hemingway, one's writing might take on additional meanings.

In fact, I wanted to be an entertainer. I hope that in some of my books, at least, I managed that.

Translated by Michal Schonberg

2009
ELSPETH CAMERON

The library was my favourite place, and books my favourite present, in my hometown of Barrie, Ontario. I loved the feel and smell of books as well as the worlds they contained. My father catalogued my "library" when I was three. I gave my first book review on the local radio station when I was eleven, thanks to Molly Brown, the wonderful librarian who guided my reading.

It was the following year, when I was in grade seven, that I had an experience that was the basis for my fascination with the interplay between life and literature. We studied Alfred Noyes's nineteenth-century poem "The Highwayman" – a romantic ballad about the risks a dashing highwayman took to see his sweetheart Bess, the daughter of an innkeeper whose establishment is frequented by rowdy soldiers intent on capturing the highwayman. To complete the love triangle, Tim, the inn's ostler, who also loves the beautiful black-haired Bess, sees the highwayman kiss his beloved and betrays him to the soldiers inside. Using Bess as a lure, the soldiers shoot the highwayman "down like a dog on the highway" when he returns to see her.

The poem opens:

> The wind was a torrent of darkness among the gusty trees,
> The moon was a ghostly galleon tossed upon cloudy seas,
> The road was a ribbon of moonlight over the purple moor,
> And the highwayman came riding –

Riding – riding –
The highwayman came riding, up to the old inn door.

This melodramatic description was far from the ordinary life of an adolescent girl in the small Victorian town that resembled Stephen Leacock's Mariposa, but I loved it.

That year, our class filed into the hall, where we sat on book covers bearing a map of Canada to see a presentation. This time it was a movie – a silent black-and-white film of "The Highwayman." In the dim light, our stout, middle-aged teacher Mrs. Cameron (no relation) read the poem in her stentorian voice as the film proceeded jerkily. Today, I would find it hilarious, but in those days before television, I was enraptured. I was in another world, until Tim the ostler appeared, shaking his fist from the stable door at the highwayman rising up in his stirrups to kiss Bess who was leaning out a courtyard window. I recognized Tim the ostler. He was Mr. Etherington, our school janitor, a small meek man who scattered Paris Green on the floors before sweeping them. How could this be? How could he be both the janitor *and* Tim the ostler?

I pondered this overlapping of life and art for months. I stared at Mr. Etherington whenever I saw him. I would like to have asked him about it, but I was timid and he never spoke to anyone. It has remained a vivid memory, like the odour of Paris Green.

In 1961, I left Barrie – following a man – to study English at the University of Toronto. Though I knew nothing of it, Margaret Atwood and Dennis Lee were in their last year there – in fact, Atwood published her first book of poems, *Double Persephone*, that year. E.J. Pratt and Northrop Frye and Jay Macpherson all taught there.

But Canadian literature was very much on my mind. The course I looked forward to most was "American and Canadian Literature." I was curious about Canadian literature. I had no idea I had already read some: *Anne of Green Gables*, for instance, and the animal stories of Ernest Thompson Seton, especially *Monarch, The Big Bear of Tallac*. I had also studied Hugh MacLennan's *Barometer Rising* in grade eleven. It escaped me that it was set in Canada. Probably I didn't know that Halifax was in Canada, since my family never travelled. Or perhaps I had not understood the novel because sections referring to the illegitimate child had been censored in the interests of sound moral development. We all knew of girls who had "gone to visit an aunt," or dropped out of school altogether, but no connection was to be drawn between literature and life.

The course that I expected would introduce me to Canadian literature was a disappointment. We studied Hemingway, James, Dickinson, Thoreau, Emerson, Fitzgerald, and Whitman. In the last class we were given a short list of Canadian writers and told that there would be an optional question about them on the exam. That was it.

This made me think. How could *all* the writers of one country be inferior to *all* the writers in another country? The professor was from England. He should know. Yet I was unsure – and even more curious about Canadian literature.

I found one of the very few courses in Canadian literature taught in 1962 at UBC, where I transferred – following a man. Here it was at last: Roberts, Carman, the Scotts, Pratt, Wiseman, MacLennan, Callaghan, and Earle Birney – whom I saw loping along the halls between his classes in creative writing. I recall a reading by Phyllis Webb from her new book of poems *The Sea is Also a Garden*. One of my assignments was on the elegant homosexual poet Daryl Hine. My professor suggested I interview someone called Jane Rule. She invited me to her house, where I also met Helen Sonthoff, her partner (though I did not grasp it at the time). I remember talking to Helen in the living room when Jane came bounding down the stairs in old jeans shouting, "They've taken it! They've taken it!" She was referring to her manuscript *Desert of the Heart*, just accepted for publication. That was my first of almost two thousand interviews to date with people who personally knew a writer I was studying or were writers themselves.

That year, it became clear that there *were* Canadian writers, that many thought they *were* important, and that they were accessible, part of a living tradition. It was a tradition I wanted to honour. I wrote my final year's honours essay on Adele Wiseman's *The Sacrifice*.

In 1964 – following a man – I transferred to UNB to study with Desmond Pacey and with Fred Cogswell, who had been editing *The Fiddlehead* for twelve years. Fredericton, they assured me, was the "cradle of Canadian literature." I wanted to write my M.A. thesis on Robertson Davies. "Robertson Davies: Canadian Moralist" is an embarrassment today. It was never published – with good reason. Yet I had dug deep in my research, tracking all his newspaper columns, essays, speeches, and writings.

I transferred back to the University of Toronto for my Ph.D. – following a man. There I was told that I could not do a Ph.D. in Canadian literature because there wasn't enough literature of sufficient merit to warrant serious study. Reluctantly, I did work in Victorian fiction, mainly because I knew it had influenced Canadian writers, but also because I thought it might help me understand my parents.

By the end of that year, having drifted far from the Canadian literature I wanted to study, it took little to persuade me to leave the program and go to San Francisco – following a man. That was the Summer of Love, and I was in Golden Gate Park with the rest of the hippies when Timothy Leary urged everyone to "Turn on! Tune in! Drop out!" I danced in the strobe-lit Fillmore Auditorium to the live music of The Grateful Dead and Jefferson Airplane, joined anti-war protests, worked odd jobs, and did not read a book all year.

I returned to Canada in July 1967 – following the same man. Driving into Montreal, where I had transferred my Ph.D. program from U of T, I heard Charles de Gaulle on the car radio declaring, "*Vive Québec libre!*" The significance of this moment in history was lost on me then, but it triggered an interest in French-Canadian literature, which I would pursue later.

That was the summer of Expo '67 in Montreal and I remember hearing many readings by international writers. Yet there was one poet, introduced by Phyllis Webb (who by then was a radio personality at CBC), who was Canadian. He was "that unlikeliest of poets," Al Purdy. He was described as "a high-school dropout, rider of the rails, farm labourer, demoted RCAF sergeant, and retired mattress-factory worker." Two years before, he had won a Governor General's award for *The Cariboo Horses*. I read it at once.

At McGill, Hugh MacLennan and Louis Dudek were both faculty members and Frank Scott was dean of the law school. Yet by then, I had half finished my program in Victorian Fiction and had no time to pursue anything but that. I finished my thesis "The Double Personality in Victorian Fiction" on the 17th of July, 1970. The following day, my daughter was born. She was three weeks late, a triumph of mind over matter.

A month later, I took up my first position at Concordia University (then

Loyola College) in a department of thirteen, all but one of whom were American or British. I was to teach courses in Canadian literature and direct a new program in Canadian Studies – one of the first in Canada. The Writer-in-Residence program also began around that time, and Loyola hosted writers like Al Purdy, John Newlove, and John Metcalf. I was asked to organize a reading series of Canadian writers for 1972 and 1973.

In retrospect, it was a remarkable line-up: Margaret Atwood, who had just published *Surfacing* and *Survival*; Earle Birney, whose selected poems had been published in 1969; Michael Ondaatje, who read from *Billy the Kid*; Marian Engel, who had to be roused from sleep on my office floor to read from her work-in-progress *Bear*, which shocked everyone; Al Purdy, whose current poems were about his experiences up north; P.K. Page, who spoke of the mystic experiences to be had in orgone boxes and read from her Brazil journals; John Newlove, whose collection *Lies* had just won the Governor General's award; Susan Musgrave, who read enigmatic poems about strawberries that would later appear as *Selected Strawberries*. Suddenly, Canadian literature was blossoming. Now, instead of being asked, "Is there any?" I was being asked, "Did you *really* meet Margaret Atwood?"

I took up biography because of poet Frank Davey in 1974. At a conference that year, he gave an incisive talk about Canadian literary criticism. It was mainly thematic to its detriment, he said. He was referring not only to Atwood's *Survival*, which had legitimized Canadian literature, but also to D.G. Jones's *Butterfly on Rock* (1970) and John Moss's *Patterns of Isolation in English-Canadian Fiction* (1974). Davey pointed out that in other countries, thematic criticism had been built on the foundation works of bibliography and biography. In Canada, these were missing. I knew at once that this was what I wanted to do.

I wanted to write a biography of a Canadian writer. *Which* writer was not of much importance to me. They all needed biographies. Robertson Davies seemed likely, since I had written a short critique of his work in 1971 for a series edited by Bill French of the *Globe and Mail*. I thought that series shortchanged Canadian writers, but it was a start. Because I was a single mother of two by then, I could not imagine commuting to Toronto to interview Davies extensively. So I chose Hugh MacLennan, who agreed to cooperate. Location, location, location.

I thus stumbled upon a theory of biography which has puzzled many: Do not approach biography because of the subject. Approach it instead with an engagement in biography itself.

It took six years to research and write *Hugh MacLennan: A Writer's Life*. The whole process was immensely exciting. I felt like an explorer in undiscovered territory, and to some extent, I was. MacLennan lent me the letters he wrote home from camp when he was eleven, and many of his school essays. (As an aside, I have noted that almost all my subjects had mothers who saved things in the expectation that their child would become famous.) The University of Calgary library had a huge collection of MacLennan materials, including six letters MacLennan had written to his father *after* his father died. McGill – where MacLennan was underrated – had not catalogued his materials. I found them heaped into cardboard boxes in no order at all. They included manuscripts of two novels written before *Barometer Rising* – still unpublished. The discoveries went on and on. I went down a mine in Cape Breton, visited his room at Oriel College in Oxford, saw the cottage at North Hatley where he spent happy summers writing with his wife Dorothy Duncan – a writer herself, who won a Governor General's award before he did. I interviewed everyone I could find who knew MacLennan, saw a video of the ballet that inspired MacLennan's novel *The Precipice* at the New York Public Library for the Performing Arts, and interviewed the ballet's choreographer, Antony Tudor, a Buddhist with shaved head and orange robes, at his shrine-like home, furnished only with cushions, in New York. I spoke with Lord C.P. Snow and his wife, Pamela Hansford-Johnson, both novelists, in their apartment in London, England. This was my real education. I was exhilarated living life by proxy.

I thought of my MacLennan biography as strictly academic, mainly because it was published by the University of Toronto Press. When it won awards and was a public success, I was astonished. Maybe, just maybe, I was a writer.

I was immediately asked by various popular journals to write profiles of Canadian cultural figures: first by *Saturday Night*, then by *Chatelaine, Toronto Life, Equinox,* and *Leisureways*, among others. My first subject was Peter Newman. I was warned that he might be difficult, but I was surprised to notice a microphone in the pine cone centrepiece on the table where I interviewed him, in case I misquoted him. I was recording our interview, but so was he!

Jack McClelland, Veronica Tennant, Timothy Findley, Laura Legge (secretary of the Law Society of Upper Canada), Pierre Berton, Vicki Miller (head of the Toronto SPCA and animal rights activist), B.J. Birdie (mascot for the Toronto Blue Jays), Marlene Nourbese Philip, Neil Bissoondath, Howard Engel, Andrée Ruffo (Quebec Youth Court Judge), and singer Anne Murray.

For many of these assignments, I was sent off to do interviews. *Chatelaine* sent me to Las Vegas to see Anne Murray's show and accompany her to the recording studio. She hated her work, she told me, hated the glitz and the high heels and sequined dresses – one of which she gave me, since we were the same size. My interviews – held mainly in the homes of those I talked to – were an education in life. One stands out: my interview in the kitchen of Timothy Findley's actress ex-wife, a small, childlike woman who climbed around the shelves, counters, and appliances as she spoke. The only assignment I regret turning down was a trip to Hugh Hefner's Playboy Mansion to interview him and his new Canadian wife.

I often interviewed as many as forty people for my profiles, some of which won national awards. And during this time I was trying to live my own life. I moved from Montreal back to Toronto in 1977 – following another man – had a third child, and began the long and difficult process of starting up the academic ladder again. It took ten years of renewed contracts and an open competition before I was a tenured professor at U of T, the rank I had left in Montreal. Academic colleagues were prepared to accept a biography, even profiles for *Saturday Night*, in the publish-or-perish fray, but they were appalled that I was publishing in "lesser" magazines. I was delighted, because somehow I had reached a far wider audience than the academic one. My research training mattered, I knew, but I had begun to think of myself as a writer more than a professor.

I think my five years of journalistic profiles helped me with my next biography, of Irving Layton. He was Writer-in-Residence at U of T when I began. I remember well the lunch at the Faculty Club when he asked me to write his biography (he later denied this).

If interviews for MacLennan were an adventure, interviews for Layton were even more so. Living *this* life by proxy was entirely unpredictable. I remember visiting Layton's second wife Betty (Boschka) at her run-down studio-home in the woods north of San Francisco. Lying across the sidewalk was a naked couple sunbathing who were not at all bothered when I stepped over them. I interviewed a young poet in a halfway house who believed he *was* Irving Layton. He had thrown himself off an overpass in Montreal but survived. I took the precaution of asking his psychiatrist to make sure an interview about Layton would not trigger something I might not be able to deal with.

A pivotal point suddenly occurred about three years into my research. Layton looked intently at me in the middle of an interview and announced he was beginning his own memoirs. I knew it was a challenge. Fortunately, by then, I had realized that no two people using the same materials would write the same biography. In my preface to *MacLennan*, I had said so, and went on to say that even I – at a different age or time – would have written a different book. There was no such thing as a "definitive biography." After a split second, I encouraged Layton to write his memoir and went on.

In fact, by that time, I wished I could rewrite my biography of MacLennan. Through thinking about Layton's life, I had developed a concept I thought of as "set point": a point (probably one of many) at which a person's essential character was formed – or revealed – which could be useful as an opening chapter. No doubt this idea came from the necessity in journalistic profiles to catch the attention of the reader in the first paragraph or two. Such an opening chapter would be something like the opening chord or phrase in a piece of music that sets the tone or pace for the whole work.

For MacLennan, that "set point" seemed to me to be the explosion in Halifax when he was nine. Not the famous Halifax Explosion that occurred when he was ten, but the one a year before when his feared and loved authoritarian doctor father descended the basement stairs with a lighted match to investigate the odour of gas. He blew up the entire house. Now, I would start with a dramatic description of that explosion, followed in my second chapter by the even more destructive Halifax Explosion, which left young Hugh with a lifetime fear of disruption, in a permanent struggle to keep everything stable, and espousing linear development in his life and writings. His first novel was set in the Halifax Explosion. His last, *Voices in Time*, not surprisingly, concerned life on earth after a nuclear holocaust.

For Layton, the "set point" seemed to me to be his strong childhood relationship with his angry, vocal mother, whose rhyming Yiddish curses filled the house. Israel Lazarovitch (his given name) – whom she nicknamed "Flamplatz" ("exploding fire") – was her favourite, the youngest of twelve, the one she believed was a "Messiah," the one most like her, the one who helped her with her front-parlour grocery and slept in her bed, because of their cramped apartment, until he was thirteen. I began *Layton* with a short dramatic chapter depicting this as vividly as I could, using as my model the chaotic opening scene of the film *Amadeus*.

By sheer coincidence, the continuous narrative of twelve chapters of equal length suited MacLennan himself: a respectable, steady, conservative, responsible citizen – an intellectual and serious patriot with the high ideals and work ethic of his professional class and Calvinist background. Layton could not have been more different. He loved disruption and chaos, was unpredictable, shrewd, sensual, culturally Jewish, working-class – characteristics that served his poetry well, but made his life chaotic. Readers felt they had met MacLennan. Even MacLennan wrote me that I knew him better than he knew himself. If readers were to feel they had met Layton, I had to change entirely the way I presented him.

Beginning with a "set point" helped. I then used fifty-five chapters of wildly varying lengths and a variety of points of view and a variety of tones to keep the reader off balance. Sometimes I saw chapters in terms of colours. "Romania" was pink, for example, whereas "Flamplatz" was red. I juxtaposed chapters in which Layton seemed to be one thing, then contradicted himself immediately. In other words, I used *discontinuous* narrative and startling variations in point of view from the different players in events – those of Layton's wives, for example, as opposed to his own. Inevitably, this led to humour, and I deliberately used flippancy in my writing, chapter titles, and photo captions. I called the chapter about Layton's first wife, Faye Lynch, "Lynched." Others were "Backflips" and "Sceneshifter." Because the end result was a series of glimpses or broad brushstrokes of Layton, I called my biography a "portrait." No matter how ridiculous, mischievous, disreputable Layton was, I never lost sight of the fact that the best of his poems were magnificent, not in spite of but *because of* these characteristics.

I was overwhelmed by Layton's long and virulent attack on me. Over five hundred hate-mail letters came to my home and office, some with obscene names for return addresses. One contained a sketch of me with a noose around my neck. He wrote letters to everyone who might influence my career: the president of U of T (telling him to fire me); granting agencies (telling them to stop giving me grants); magazine editors; and people significant in my personal life, including my parents in Barrie, who were terrified. He wrote to newspapers calling me an anti-Semite and listing the "bloopers" in my book – a few of them valid, but most of them quotes from people I'd interviewed, or misinterpretations. He did his best to sue me. I remember the day the bailiff came to the door with a suit against my use of the photo of Layton on the cover. It was easy to produce the permission to use all his materials, signed by Layton, but it was not so easy to withstand the onslaught. He encouraged people I had interviewed to sue me, and each time I had to produce tapes or notes to prove them wrong. It seemed that year that I spent more time at the lawyer's office than anywhere else. Finally, one of his friends – a woman who had made a record of him reading in Sault Ste. Marie – sued me for defamation of character and damages. After reading what she told me, Layton had refused to sell the record. That day and a half in court was terrifying. Even more terrifying were the three months that followed, during which the judge made up her mind. I did not yet have tenure at U of T and knew that I would not get it if my research was shown to be unreliable. When I won the case, it was a relief, but no triumph for me. I never had a chance to enjoy the positive reception my book enjoyed elsewhere.

At the time, I thought it was significant that Layton's unfinished memoir – now labelled "Volume One" – was published the same day as my biography. I believed that there would be no second volume, and there was not. What upset me most was the widespread rumour that Layton and I had dreamed up the whole debacle as a publicity stunt for both books.

With hindsight, I now think that Layton's tempestuous reaction was fundamentally the same as MacLennan's. They were both reactions – in characteristically opposite styles – to abandonment. I came to see at this point that a living subject for biography enjoys the intense attention of the biographer. The biographer comes to know more than anyone else about his family and friends, about his life in general. MacLennan comforted himself by prolonging his contact with me beyond publication. For a year or two, he phoned me late at night to talk over his life in a maudlin, slurred voice. Layton reacted like a child in the "terrible twos" and never spoke to me again. Even when we were both interviewed back-to-back by Peter Gzowski for CBC's *Morningside*, Layton entered and left by the front door. I was instructed to use the back door. With hindsight too, I now understood the dangers of writing about a living subject. When Oxford Press showed interest in a biography of Leonard Cohen, I declined.

Instead, I accepted the request of Penguin Books to write a biography of Earle Birney, with the cooperation of his partner Wailan Low. Birney was under full-time care in the hospital for dementia and, though he could read aloud, understood nothing of what he read. He did not recognize me. I'm not sure he recognized Wailan Low. I had met Birney on a few occasions – notably as one of the readers in my Loyola series, and also when I interviewed him about Layton. Occasionally our paths crossed in Toronto. I had a good idea of his physical presence, one of the advantages of writing about a living subject.

The research challenge was enormous. MacLennan and Layton had taken me five years each, but Birney would take much longer. Birney's mother had started saving everything from the beginning. Even his first baby shoes and a lock of hair from his first haircut can be found in the archives. The U of T – only one of several collections – had over twenty thousand files (he sold them in 1966 for twenty thousand dollars), hundreds of photos, and many sound and video recordings. Birney's first wife Esther used to joke that he even sent his toenail clippings to the archives. Later in my research, I discovered that there were duplicates in the collections, a fact that helped me understand Birney's duplicity.

Partly because of the sheer weight of this material, *Earle Birney: A Life* is too long. He was so active, travelled so much, wrote so easily and quickly, had such a full academic life as well as a complicated personal and political life, I could not include everything. The book is too heavy to do justice to the nimble Birney.

I found the red-haired Birney a sort of cross between MacLennan and Layton. He reminded me of Loki, the Norse god representing the principle of change. Dynamic and unpredictable, the red-haired Loki was a trickster and a cultural hero, providing man with sunlight as well as fire. He was like a more dynamic MacLennan or a more cerebral Layton. The difference with Layton can be seen in their language. Layton exaggerates broadly, but Birney had a fondness for needle-sharp puns. It can also be seen in their army experiences. Layton rebelled against authority, dragged his loaded rifle around dangerously, flaunted what he called his "conspicuous incompetence," and was discharged within the year. Birney *was* an authority, becoming a major and serving as one of the first to administer psychological tests to soldiers.

After, and even before, my biography of Birney was published, friends and interviewers asked me: first, why I didn't write a novel (since, they said, my biographies read like novels); and second, why I hadn't written a biography of a woman; and third, why I didn't write about my own life. This gave me much to think about. Had I followed men around in my writing as I had in my life? Who was I, anyway, apart from these biographical subjects whose lives had absorbed mine for almost two decades? Had I been living mainly by proxy?

When I stopped to take stock, I became a feminist – much later than other women in my generation. I had been too busy *living* a feminist life, my reading entirely taken up with research and teaching – not to mention raising three children – to engage with feminist theory. I had never had a room of my own, had never thought to ask.

I saw that during the writing of *Birney*, my own life was in chaos. The year after my biography was published, I moved to Calgary – this time following a woman. This personal blurring of gender boundaries certainly went against the grain – as had so much else in my career to date. Because I could find nothing written about a situation like mine, I decided to try a different kind of life writing, a memoir documenting the turbulent past four years. I had written warts-and-all biographies. It would have been less than honest to write anything but a warts-and-all memoir. *No Previous Experience* upset my family and shocked many people. Yet there were others – all strangers, all women – from many walks of life and several different countries who wrote to thank me for putting into words what they too had lived through in some form or other. I received hundreds of letters and emails – some as recently as two months ago (one from the Netherlands and one from New York). Now when I meet people, they think of my memoir, not my biographies.

When I left Calgary in the fall of 2001, driving back to Ontario – following no one – I began writing poetry. Just outside of Calgary, I got out of the pickup truck I had set up so I could sleep in the back, and threw my house key as far as I could into a field, got back in and drafted this poem, "The Last Time I Saw Our Housekey":

> *It was describing a brassy arc*
> *above a field of over-ripe wheat*
>
> *At one end my hand*
> *circling down now*
> *its own wheel of fortune*
> *separate from the familiar burnishing*
> *of cold metal in warm palm*
> *that signaled home*
>
> *At the other end*
> *who knows*
> *a flurried dismay of ants slipping*
> *across the unbearable intruder*
> *crushing their anthill*
>
> *the click of metal against a semi-circle of steel*
> *the momentary twist of a hoof*
>
> *a puzzled farmer squinting*
> *wondering whether this was the key*
> *to something he had forgotten*

It was a declaration of independence. I arrived in Toronto on 9/11 to be dragged to the television by friends to see and feel that apocalyptic destruction at the very time the foundation of my own life was in ruins.

I settled in St. Catharines, where my feminist contribution to a local magazine took me to my next biographical subject: sculptors Frances Loring and Florence Wyle. They had done several works at the Rainbow Bridge. In teaching Canadian Studies all these years, I had been especially dissatisfied with art history works. They seemed like expanded encyclopedia entries that offered little about the way art was created and less about the emotional impact of art and the kind of people who created it. I had the same feeling I'd had when I began *MacLennan*. The field seemed to cry out for a substantial biography to honour a Canadian artist – in this case, a couple of women who had lived and worked together for fifty-five years. Loring and Wyle – The Girls, as they were known – had managed to support themselves through sculpture alone in art-deprived Toronto from 1911 to the late '60s. Although they had between them created over five hundred sculptures – many of them in prominent public spaces, like the statue of Sir Robert Borden on Parliament Hill – they were in danger of being forgotten. Once more I was going against the current, against the unspoken rule that only art historians write about art, against the precedent I had unwittingly set of writing about famous men; against the notion, too, that joint biographies were especially difficult.

To begin with, I spent two years reading and reading and reading about sculptors and sculpture. My research launched me into a whole new set of adventures: to the Art Institute of Chicago, where Loring and Wyle had met when they took classes together, into today's sculpture classrooms, into the home-studio on Glenrose Avenue that is almost unchanged from the days in which they lived there; to a brass foundry in Georgetown, where I watched the process by which plaster casts are turned into bronze statues.

The book's "set point" came to me in a dream from which I awoke with the strong impression that the key to the biography was Frances Loring. A short dramatic scene of her striding into the Art Institute in Chicago, about to meet Florence – an encounter in which they claimed they "clicked at once." I ended the book with Frances's initials, F.L., which she had painted sloppily in red on the modeling stand she used that was still in the old studio. To me, those initials suggested the ghostlike absence of The Girls from the Canadian scene after modernism replaced the neoclassical tradition in which they worked. For the first time, I had to describe the decline and death of my subjects – an experience that deeply upset me and lent an elegiac tone to the last section of *And Beauty Answers*.

Living life by proxy has been an unparalleled series of adventures for me: adventures in life and in the craft of writing. At first, I wanted to be invisible, immerse myself so thoroughly in the lives of my subjects that I could voyage into them and return, like the Ancient Mariner, to tell their tale. To empathize effectively, I had to learn the things they cared about: an obscure Egyptian province under the Romans — Oxyrhynchus — which MacLennan studied for his Ph.D.; communism in 1930s Montreal as Layton — briefly a Party member — understood it; the more complex Trotskyism that inspired Birney to meet Trotsky in Norway; and the kind of training in neoclassical sculpture that Loring and Wyle underwent.

I still think that the biographer must be invisible. How many biographers can you name? Biographies are known by their subjects, not their authors. In the end, the research dominates. If you don't have material, you must ingeniously distract readers from gaps in information. It is having too much information that is the greatest danger.

In *The Artist's Way*, Julia Cameron (no relation) cautions new writers to stop reading biographies, to stop living through other people. My immersion in what I saw as the undervalued lives and works of my subjects, I now see, not only postponed my feminism, but ironically caused me to neglect my own life. If my curiosity about Canadian literature had not been whetted in 1961, and if I had still been drawn to biography, I would probably have chosen a British or American subject. But I was drawn to the underdog, to Canadian writers who were dismissed or derided.

Now, as a result of this process, I have stopped living for or through others. Stopped favouring male subjects over females, discovered feminism and with it my own voice. I have just published my first collection of poetry, *Sirens & Sailors*. Life writing now includes my own life. The interplay between my life and the lives of others has become manageable, not all-absorbing. I have a room of my own. I now see the power of the biographer. Though invisible, the biographer plays a major role in establishing the canon.

At the time I wrote about MacLennan and Layton and Birney, I could not have imagined standing here speaking to you about the ways in which my life and the lives of my subjects are intertwined. I would not have thought it important enough. Now I see that leaving a record, bearing witness as a life writer really matters.

2010

MARIE-CLAIRE BLAIS

I'd like to speak about the very close and mystical connection between a writer and her characters – penetrating and intuitive, practically visceral as an extension of her own life, certainly embodied in the real world. Not enough is said about this miraculous fusion of character and author that books can catalyze, almost as though the reader barely even senses it, lives it, or considers its importance. Yet the strength of this cognitive link is what makes the characters so true, so approachably human for some readers or even all.

Faulkner knew his rebellious student Temple in *Sanctuary* well enough to describe her in all her spellbinding complexity, and he clearly had a fully and intimately drawn Temple in mind well before writing her into the book, as with all the characters around her, each one ready to corrupt the naive innocence in this spoiled child of an aging judge, brought up in a Memphis crushed under the weight of its prejudices and Puritanism: a chorus of contradictory values and passions that are the characters of Horace, Goodwin, Popeye, Red, and so many others. Never could he have done this without a living confrontation with all of his creations in every guise, whether brutal or appealing, nor without direct contact with these souls in all their heaviness and grace, nor without descending into the private hell, the unexpressed misery, the slender hopes and hidden yearnings of each one. So unrelentingly sharp is his observation and his analysis, far outstripping any frontier of judgement – an analysis made up only of impregnation and immense empathy – that the author not only realized that he, in fact, *was* Temple, Popeye, and every one of them, but he became Temple, emerging from the Letters Club Ball, at the student gala, in the dazzle of music, and he knew exactly who Temple was at that moment in her life, the pure child arm-in-arm with the student, already forewarning us in the chill gaze of her eyes, in the painted lips and simmering fervour so like voracity, warning us of the fragile destiny coming to her and those around her in the violent drama that awaited.

This drama is everyone's, really, one in which we all will lose our innocence and our lives, driven by uncontrollable impulses, energy, and compulsions into becoming their playthings, just as the student Gowan toys with Temple by leaving her in the hands of those who will rape her in a barn, or play with the life of a black man as hanging judges do. All this is premonitory in Faulkner, all is foretold in the ritual of disaster, Temple's helplessness in the face of her attackers, repeating to herself, "I knew something would happen to me," helpless and alone with her torn body. The author feels and listens to all of it, allowing us to hear the song of the condemned killer in prison, while others down by the fence in their worn coveralls join in singing with the black man, as Faulkner says with an irony steeped in pain, the tiredness of the earth and the joy of heaven, experienced in their poverty. Still, this last song of the convict at his window, surely Faulkner had heard it before, and the coveralls of those poor people come to sing with him, bathed in sweat, surely he had touched them with his eyes before ever describing their texture. This is the intimacy of deepest pain, Temple's, the condemned man's at his window, born in Faulkner and alive in us.

As writers, of course, we have tried to unravel the mystery of humanity set upon by all kinds of madness, tried to understand, even internalize who exactly these people are that commit such crimes, and who, in their innocence, are the victims of such murders, whether individual or collective. For Faulkner, whether it be Red's vengeance or Goodwin's, any single murder quickly becomes a matter for all. This puzzle of guilt, of joint responsibility, is what we as writers have tried to describe.

In *The Execution*, a stage play of mine,* we are in a boarding school where two schoolboys plot the murder of one of their classmates, then enact the crime. The play is a study in innocence, evil, and complicity. Thus Kent becomes

---

* First performed on March 18, 1968 at Théâtre de Rideau Vert, Montreal, directed by Yvette Brind'Amour.

the invisible author of the crime against the wholly innocent Eric, and draws Stéphane into the murder with him. And not only Stéphane, but their whole class with him: one monstrous act of collective guilt, of which Kent himself will simply wash his hands and leave no incriminating evidence.

"Take it easy," Kent says to Stéphane.

Let me explain. At 7:15, I'll take up the watch in the corridor, I'll see to it that no one observes the three of you as you leave for your morning walk, you and Christian Ambre holding Eric by the arms and dragging him toward the stairway, as if he were drunk or slightly ill. You'll go down to the yard, I'll be waiting for you there. Then you'll walk towards the woods, with Eric between you. He won't be heavy, he is only a child. You'll wait for me under the tree where we usually meet. I'll join you there. Then, we'll walk to the centre of the woods and bury Eric beneath the trees. We must be back here before noon, in time for the midday meal. We'll come in at the sound of the bell, as usual. We must think of everything. We may be questioned about our absence from chapel. We'll say that we were here in my room, studying for the exams. Tomorrow morning, Christian Ambre will be the first to speak to the superior about Eric's disappearance. That will establish our innocence . . .

Who now would deny after all these years that these murders of innocent students on campuses in the United States, Canada, and Europe go on and on and on, as though Kent were more than a character dreamed up by a writer, but a true and self-perpetuating malevolence without end? Yet this young man, however perverse and malicious, must surely be a child of our times, like those of Columbine, and surely the writer – through him and through them – must look for the origin of all this violence, even to the point of identifying with their despair at having to endure the pain of living in our world, itself perverse and violent, and apparently leaving them no way out but murder . . . total, collective, and suicidal murder.

In *Sanctuary*, Faulkner describes Temple's rape as a chain of collaboration and conspiracy involving a number of people, and which little by little leads the whole town into bloodshed and fire. Red, witness and party to the rape, and the object of Temple's love later on – so handsome, and so much the

plaything of impotent Popeye – Red will die in a casino at the very instant he
wants to get closer to Temple and to love her for herself in selfless redemption; Goodwin will burn alive in a park or vacant lot at the hands of a hateful,
vengeful mob on a pyre of treacherous hatred, his life gone up in a column of
smoke; Popeye will be hanged for his crimes; when the compassionate judge,
Horace, is unable to save all these lives, in a fit of guilt born from moral pow-
erlessness, he himself turns to crime.

After young Eric is killed, Stéphane, Kent's silent partner in these invisible,
remote-controlled murders, and guilty by association, says:

> Eric? Eric? So you were only our first victim then? How many more will be
> there after you? The annihilation of your innocence has only just begun!
> Lancelot and d'Argenteuil will be charged in my place. Kent will find some-
> one else to replace me. You will die again, Eric! I can still hear the voices of
> those students who killed with joy, their laughter penetrates the walls of the
> prison. "Applaud!" says Kent, and together they raise their childish voices in
> noisy applause. [*We hear the distant cheers of the chorus. They grow in intensity,*
> *then abruptly cease.*] How many more victims will there be after you, Eric?

Through him, the author questions herself as to the purpose of so much
violence, intervening from afar, though not absent, moulding herself to their
thoughts, first of one, then the other, whether in a novel or a play, often after
having known them, met them somewhere before setting them down in
the book, which then becomes a life-act of enormous vitality, linked as it is
to living beings caught suddenly in the middle of their journey, however
clouded with mistakes. It's as though the author is there as well to describe
how it is possible to make a mistake, to give in to fateful mistakes, like for
instance Temple's actions in leaving the well-advised safety of her university
on a night-time escapade that will turn her fate to tragedy. In *The Execution*,
Stéphane, a boy who is sensitive to others, might not have given in to the
diabolical pressure of Kent, but he does, a little like the hero of *Crime and
Punishment*, out of defiance against moral convention, and because he allows
himself the illusion of his own intellectual superiority and obeys a poorly
grasped Nietzschean principle.

It was in the '60s, and I remember some young people were actually charged with murder in a college, but this victim was an adult, one of their teachers, not another child. Of course they were there and perhaps guilty too, but what evidence was there to indicate murder? They were seventeen, and one of them came through it unscathed, then fled to another country, the charges still vague and uncertain. A second would be imprisoned for a different offence: shoplifting. The gravest suspicions rested on the seventeen-year-old, and the author began writing to him and sending him books in prison. When he did confess, it was mere adolescent bluster at a time when his delirious words could not be taken at face value by the jury. He, of course, was to become Kent in the play, just as many other people did in many other books, though he always struck me as more like Stéphane than Kent. The true Kent might more likely be the one that had fled, gone, never to be seen again. Surely an intimate knowledge of one or the other was needed to talk about it; who otherwise could even remotely connect the attractive, well-brought-up, middle-class faces in the papers with the perfect murder? No clues left behind but a concealed blow to the back of the head or neck of their unfortunate victim. What motivation could there be for these angelic-looking teenagers to resort to such cruelty?

Writing to the real-life model for Kent or Stéphane, or reading his letters from prison, wouldn't have had anything essential to reveal to the writer, except his abundant intelligence, his vivacity, and his failure to be understood by anybody; perhaps one of the two boys was a genius, bored with his ridiculously fruitless and simplistic studies, rebelling against the all-enveloping power of the church, whether Catholic or any other, rejecting absolutely everything, as Rimbaud had done at that age, and killing any victim at random as though there were nothing else for it, in a kind of indolence of heart and spirit.

Philippe l'Heureux, the imprisoned young writer in the triptych *The Manuscripts of Pauline Archange*, describes his prison life in a book of his own, *Prison Chronicles*: "The condemned occasionally heard the bells ringing on the distant deserted plain." These lyrical words worthy of, say, a Jean Genet in *The Thief's Journal*, might just as well have issued from the mouth of a boy murderer, someone who's taken a wrong turn, someone who nevertheless knew how to write and think so clearly and so young. To his words, the author adds:

Nothing seemed more dismal to him than the walls of his cell, but as he sought his *raisons de vivre* in the interior world of his captivity, was it not necessary for him to exalt courage, even crime, in the only human community he had come to know? Like the choir of madmen when their dreams expired, he felt intensely the burden of his oppression and the humiliation of his almost animal existence in that prison. What troubled him most . . . was "the boundless energy" of imprisoned men, "the monstrous sacrifice of their lives," as he expressed it, even so far as to wonder if the true community of assassins was not that class "which legislated the laws of expiation and sacrifice, returning to the very act which he had wanted to accomplish with his first murder the trial of his father, a just man, a good man, who was nonetheless responsible for the execution of a fellow man." According to [Philippe]: "All judges [Philippe's father is a judge] live in a very fragile citadel, where they wrongly imagine themselves to be protected from the horde of criminals whose energies and desires they have confined, but who are already prowling as restlessly as wild beasts about their shaky dwelling, awaiting the hour of justice . . ."

Philippe, like Stéphane or Kent, has a gift for self-expression, extending even to the reasons for their crimes, eloquently and seeming to do justice to themselves through the punishment exacted by society, and urged on by the nihilistic feeling that life is absurd, and that no life is worthy of respect – not their own, not anyone else's. Rather than commit suicide, they appear to be saying, why not pass that vengeance and apocalyptic destruction on to someone else, someone weaker, like Eric the schoolboy, their defenceless sacrificial lamb . . . or in Philippe's case, the murder of an elderly father, judged like a killer by his own son, because he himself once had that right legally, when allowing a man to hang.

If the author listens to them too closely, without disentangling their ambiguities, the characters' exuberant and clouded philosophical language might seem rational, because they themselves feel so intellectually secure, and she could thus blind herself to their criminal guilt, wondering whether they should not be defended, no matter how guilty, by virtue of their tender age. One can only recall Truman Capote's tears on the day the two killers portrayed in *In Cold Blood* were executed. How he would have wished for the end of the death penalty before it cut short the beneficial changes that his contact with them had begun to produce. All he had wanted was to do a journalistic report, as neutral as possible, on them and their scandalous actions, but he was carried away by his own romantic and poetic testimonial and found himself no longer capable of judging them and their heavy sentence. Now he sought only to find out who they were, where they came from, what kind of childhoods they'd had, who their parents were — just the facts — but he became a reporter, then a confidant, and increasingly human himself in this world of crime which was so new to him. He sought out its cause and its origins, like some incurable illness.

The "*enfant terrible* of American literature," so rich and sumptuous, the author of *The Grass Harp* and the initial stories of a childhood so soon drawn to the powers of writing, became, through the spare, sober writing of *In Cold Blood* — a crystal-clear style almost devoid of images, tracing the confessions of the two young killers as though he'd always known them in their least significant past acts right up to the day before the carnage, rendering the world of greyness and disenchantment in which the two young men had lived, failed lives as delinquents, two lives unlit and devoid of affection or love — the writer concentrating more and more on their troubled childhoods, abandoned and abused. Be they maltreated, abused, or just totally forgotten in the dreary world that had been their childhoods and youth, could all this really explain the horror of their actions as adults, or is there simply no explanation at all?

During his visits to them in prison, Truman Capote began to notice changes in them, an attempt to rehabilitate themselves, a gradual awakening of conscience, some form of return to humanity. He knew that even if they'd been spoken and written about as cold-blooded killers, monsters (and he himself knew it after visiting them in prison), they took drugs and perhaps suffered from mental handicaps, and they regretted what they had done in the suffering they now underwent and in the knowledge they would be put to death; yet these were two young people living, and soon dying, in total hopelessness. How then would the writer himself survive the recounting of such darkness? He would have to be the last slender link between them and the world of the living. Doubtless these words came back to haunt him: before these killers were killers, they were youths, children like any others, perhaps untracked by the abuse they had known, now men breaking out into the freedom of crime and death, like Miles in Henry James's *The Turn of the Screw*, surely the only way out, possibly even a triumph for these two murderers, themselves prisoners of a delinquent milieu: dying, killing themselves through the murders of others.

No doubt, Truman Capote in his vulnerability plunged headfirst into this painful tale without ever letting go of his characters, too real, too human (even humanized by himself), unable to let go of them: two death-row inmates whose deaths he knew would be an even greater atrocity than what they had done, execution simply aggravating the murders that had gone before, however much they were approved by all. Life itself being a writer's raw material, it was the little of what was left for these two killers that inspired Capote, and just as life can be endangered, so can a writer's mind, spirit, and body — Kafka, Artaud, and so many others remind us of that. Why should it be astonishing to see a writer's commitment so immediate and so complete that it translates everything around one, including malleable humanity, which we put on, and the pitfalls that lie in wait? The trap laid for Truman Capote, from the opening pages and his first acquaintance with the murders, was to recruit him as an accomplice who would chronicle the bloody history without ever intending to. So soon he would be consumed by his heroes, defeated by so much cruelty, the cruelty of getting too close to this forbidden world of the criminal. A writer, of course, is curious about everything, wants to know about everything involved with being human, and the less he can control this new conspiracy, the more it frightens him. Nothing about this can be generalized; the crimes are singular, double, each one unique to its perpetrator, regardless of whether they worked alone or as partners.

In this desire to know all, to assimilate through writing all that is best and worst in us, beauty as well as ugliness, Dostoevsky in *Crime and Punishment* must have felt in his bones the pride and freedom of his hero Raskolnikov, young and ardent, inventing his own philosophy of crime, just as Kent will do, and possibly Capote's young murderers as well. Surely the essence is this: total independence without any thought of others. Raskolnikov exercises free will through killing, just as Kent does, and this becomes a philosophical gesture, however stamped with terror. The vertigo must be left behind as one reaches for the inconceivable, and this Raskolnikov will do; yet, even as he does so, he will change and repent. Possibly the love of Sonia will save him yet, the love Dostoevsky must himself have felt for his hero, comparing the two of them in every throe of conscience, for the love of Sonia will lead him to the Gospel.

What surprises us, this about-face, must surely have been the awakening of the writer to the metamorphosis of love, for so often his characters are transformed by an encounter such as this, some divine force driving them onward, even in solitude sometimes and deciding all at once to turn themselves in, seek out the punishment, accept it, consent to it like the holy Alyosha, for during his exile to Siberia, Dostoevsky had only the Bible to read. He lived through his own trial of religious doubt and was deeply marked by it: "The main problem to which the entire book [*The Brothers Karamazov*] is directed is the same one that tormented me all my days: the existence of God." These words are also spoken by Alyosha and again by Raskolnikov upon his conversion by Sonia; thus the author and the family he gave birth to can so completely be fused and lost in one another — though not without rigour and craft — in one another, towards one another, in a constant exchange of identities.

He also shows a noticeable and distinct attraction to each of the brothers Karamazov. Ivan the intellectual is perhaps closest, though an atheist, in his constant state of doubt and metaphysical anxiety, often very destructive to those whose affection he enjoys. Dostoevsky describes himself in his personal diary as a very imperfect being, tormented and unhappy with his failings, like Ivan, destructive of what he loves, of the object of his tenderness, a pure feeling that is part of him, the simple, gentle, and generous Alyosha. If Alysoha is a mystic, he is unaware of it, like Francis of Assisi looking after his animals. He is all love and sweetness, but still Ivan's criminal spirit, working through Smerdyakov, the cursed bastard son, to kill his father, and for that Ivan will turn mad, Smerdyakov will kill himself — Smerdyakov, the soul poisoned by Ivan, might also corrupt Alyosha's purity, Alyosha so steeped in abjectness by his brothers, though without his knowledge. Here again, one can easily imagine the author switching to and fro among his heroes, whether perverse like Smerdyakov, underhanded like Dimitri, or vengeful like Ivan. Each of them struts his hour and tells his sad tale, but always with a thousand and one shadings and subtleties, each of them complicated, each needing his chance at redemption, a door opening to let in the pain of humanity in search of some sort of consolation or redemption. For Dostoevsky, there is always this unexpected encounter with love, here incarnated in all its simplicity by Alyosha: Alyosha, who believes he can redeem the crimes of his brothers by humility and prayer – perhaps no more than a childish delusion, Ivan being responsible for his acts all along and bearing alone the responsibility for his extremes of madness. He it was who incited the weak Smerdyakov to kill their father and thence to commit suicide, and how could the ineffable love of Alyosha save his brothers, who are already lost? This question Dostoevsky puts to us, seeming to say, "Just how far are we responsible for others?"

Through this question, Dostoevsky makes us feel the attachment he has for his characters, almost indivisible, each of them questioning, and being questioned by, the author. There is no definition or judgment of them in terms of evil or, for example, the dissimilarity between Alyosha's candour and Smerdyakov's propensity to domination and abuse by his brother Ivan. Where, then, is the boundary between innocence and criminality? In Dostoevsky's tenderness, the holy figure of Alyosha perhaps shows an increasing affinity for the idiot.

Prince Myshkin, like Alyosha, is an innocent martyr to the cruelty and mockery of others. Upbraided, spurned, and banished for his sincerity, an epileptic like Dostoevsky himself, he is the target of sarcasm from his peers, blood brothers with the author, both of them searching for that bright, burning ideal: one a prince, often compared with Christ the innovator, who could in a single act understand and pardon, as the prince feels compassion for Nastasia and even for the horrendous Rogozhin. Even this mad criminal benefits from the charitable vision of the prince and of Dostoevsky, the latter drawing on his deep knowledge and broad experience of the world he knows and lives in to portray his heroes, whether valorous or despicable. Who better to describe Prince Myshkin's visionary comas born of his epileptic attacks than Dostoevsky himself, and who better to describe the imprisonment and deportation of his heroes to Siberia than this author condemned to exile and near-execution, escaping only by a miracle? This unspeakable brush with death is a moment that will imprint itself on his entire body of work and on the lives of his heroes, all of whom will denounce the death penalty at some moment: the terror and horror of being seconds from the firing squad, then being pardoned by the Tsar. Dostoevsky's oppressed are everyone's oppressed, everywhere and in all times; in this, his work could not be more transparent. Had he not himself experienced this great pity for the complete helplessness of others, the physical and psychological deprivation of Prince Myshkin during his fits, falling down in the street, abandoned and despised by all?

Faulkner's emotion, likewise, is very strong indeed, when describing those characters who are dearest to him: little Lena sitting by the side of the road, alone and pregnant in *Light in August*, before setting out on foot to meet her seducer in the sawmill, thinking about how far she's already come from Alabama, poor and desolate, wearing a homemade dress and staring at a cart approaching her and thinking she's already in Mississippi, little Lena wrapping her shoes up in paper to keep them safe. With what affectionate attention to detail he portrays what Maurice-Edgar Coindreau called "the savage fresco" of Faulkner's world, Lena being just one among so many equally powerful depictions in this turbulent fresco that includes the mulatto Christmas in *Light in August*, perhaps sharing the same innocence with Prince Myshkin, though violent and rebellious — Christmas, who assassinates his tyrannical white mistress and burns the house down in a lack of understanding between races that so overflows with hatred and contempt that even Miss Burden, come from the North and having lost her own parents in the anti-segregationist cause, someone who could be Joe Christmas's liberation, gets caught up in the fierce vengeance and bitterness that he cannot put behind him. So consumed by vengeance is he that he himself must die of it. The fury and vigour with which Faulkner throws himself into this fresco, this stifling milieu in which his characters find themselves, reflects out of shadows in the worn and suffering face of Joe Christmas and his victim, Miss Burden, soon to be burnt. A single sentence serves to define the latent hatred and racial conflict in this book; Miss Burden lives in a luxurious mansion where Christmas comes to visit her in order to satisfy his lascivious desires, he who lives in a pathetic hut in the woods, and very few words are needed to express the hatred or injustice.

In our literature, the connections between authors and their characters, their heroes, are clear and precise, for it could hardly be otherwise in the work we do. We are indivisible. In *Surfacing*, a haunting, powerful novel, the central character's whole past and non-past are unfolded during her search for her missing father and her re-examination of her childhood in the vast and desolate bush of Northern Quebec. The author, with her deep, unique insight, her sensitivity to her characters, shows us the truth about the life surface, or the lives' surfaces, of her characters. Reading this tense and strong book, the "I" who is the narrator recounting the story of David, Anna, and herself, three young people apparently going off in an old car for a swim in the country, is also the hallucinatory "I" of Margaret Atwood the author, searching out what lies hidden beneath the surface appearance of these young people, their lives, their seemingly placid and provincial pasts, when the isolated voice of the narrator notes the absence of a being that haunts them all. This is the question for Anna the palm reader, and it is the brutal return of the past for this narrator as well.

"Do you have a twin?" asked Anna. I said No. "Are you positive," she said, "because some of your lines are double." Her index finger traced me: "You had a good childhood but then there's this funny break." She puckered her forehead and I said I just wanted to know how long I was going to live, she could skip the rest. After that she told us Joe's hands were dependable but not sensitive and I laughed, which was a mistake.

Right away, the writer's control pulls us into their intimacy, all three: the narrator, who tells us David is "dependable but not sensitive"; Anna, who possesses a mysterious knowledge of the others' secrets; the narrator, who, though refusing to hear Anna's revelations, knows she herself hides a hurtful truth even from herself, a searing memory, almost shameful. We are witness to the decomposition of a lie and will remain haunted by it ourselves. "I feel deprived of something" (says the narrator), "as though I can't really get here unless I've suffered; as though the first view of the lake, which we can see now, blue and cool as redemption, should be through tears . . ." And around the narrator, there is also an entire story.

Throughout, there is a personal climate of unease and disquiet belonging to the narrator, a surrounding political atmosphere, not just the separation that creates "two solitudes" and the frontiers between them, their languages and their ideas, but also a cloud of threatened war, the approaching Vietnam War, and at the same time the narrator's memory. And herein lies the author's finesse in knowing just how to connect the inner unease that is the narrator's, and the political and social malaise also in the air, the disturbance of an entire epoch, which is also spelled out by the three characters. Suddenly, through these childhood recollections, though before her birth, the drama having been implanted in her, the birth and death of the little brother, is a ghost emerging from the lake, as in a nightmare:

> My brother was under the water, face upturned, eyes open and unconscious, sinking gently; air was coming out of his mouth.
>
> It was before I was born but I can remember it as clearly as I saw it, and perhaps I did see it: I believe that an unborn baby has its eyes open and can look out through the walls of the mother's stomach, like a frog in a jar.

Through these lines, we can feel the almost complete fusion between author and narrator, as in her poems — fusion as poetic vision, both prophetic and backward-glancing, to the time of birth or before that. A child able to sense what its future life will be can already feel guilt for the other child drowned, the eternal little brother destined to haunt the author of *Surfacing* forever.

Like Kafka or Hubert Aquin, the author can be so fully subsumed in the narrator that they are one and fully in harmony. Thus, in *The Trial*, Kafka causes us to share his sense of being closed in, his suspended state while awaiting a sentence that we too will undergo. In *Les Sables mouvants / Shifting Sands*, one of Hubert Aquin's novels, we are reminded of Kafka's tribulations, "with his obsessive interior monologue," in the opening lines of the story: "I'm caught between the four walls of memory, in a damp low room. I don't dare look through this window. It gives me the feeling of being in a cellar." Thus is the inner prison named, the author the captive within the four walls of his memory, "trapped in a kind of grave," and we can no longer be sure if it is the author or the narrator who is speaking, so impossible is it to tell them apart. Here we are, says Joseph Jones, with "the young Aquin turn[ing] away from ordinary narrative toward the signature qualities of his later writing." Such frankness on the part of the young writer captivates us and sweeps us up "into an obsessive mélange of recollection and speculation," in which the beauty of a loved one is suddenly transformed into ugliness when François, the narrator, yields to apprehension at seeing the one he loves again in a Naples hotel room. When she is so close to him in this room, will he imagine her unfaithful: "So little did we look directly at each other. A kind of certainty assured me that Hélène was no longer the same. What might be the cause of this sudden change of direction on her part." From this certainty will come his nightmare, his tumble into the byways of a love that will gradually turn to hatred. In the writing, it also becomes the author's "private apocalypse," as though we penetrate the conscious memory directly without stopping at the narrator, forgetting he is really François, an imaginary narrator in any case, just as K. in Kafka is fated by the absurdity of his sentencing as a mortal — and ourselves with him, every bit as much as the writer.

This is Kafka's real outcry, practically audible, at the injustice of being born to die: *Do you see the injustice of mortality looming over every single being? How can we live serene and healthy knowing this inevitability? How can you? Is there any sense?* K. wonders. Surely this is how Kafka's anguish must be interpreted by us the closer we come to his characters. Whether in *The Trial* or in *Metamorphosis*, we know that beneath the symbols, these books enlighten and deliver us from these questions that face us in the finitude of our fate. Of course, the author's irony is always there beside us, running through the grotesque figure of the cockroach: a victim both human and animal, utterly and desperately turned inwards on himself.

Again like Kafka, Aquin feels a complete affection for his characters, however sombre and discouraged they be from their condition, and shares their integrity and sincerity to the end, bearing witness to their knowledge of the abyss within us, no hand outstretched in an offer of support. In his *Letter to His Father*, the young Kafka, as a writer humiliated by his despotic father, already shows his wellspring of precocious experience for the humiliation and rejection the victim in *Metamorphosis* will face.

Similarly, Gabrielle Roy also expresses her affection and oneness with her characters, as in *The Tin Flute* (1945), in which the characters immersed in the working class are true portraits of this particular world, as recognizable as in Zola, where each must fight misery in his own way for a purpose which is often lofty and mystical. It is as though this purpose were actually the author's, her characters embodying lost treasures waiting to be discovered, like an artistic gift, however inaccessible. For instance, there is the vigorous portrait of her hero Alexandre Chenevert (1954) — of all her characters, perhaps the dearest to her heart, whose hopes will be misunderstood and disappointed: hopes of getting out of this pitiful life as a bank teller and becoming someone else, an active man, saviour of humanity. This man, crushed by the servility of his day-to-day life at a drab job he hates in a drab life he hates equally, this man will die without attaining his dream, squashed and abased, dying without even being able to express even one of his hopes for a better life, one he has nevertheless earned. Here indeed we sense the care the writer has for this poor man, a hero's life betrayed by a failed life, a false life he never believed to be his own, he with such noble hopes of living differently, and who never stopped looking for a meaning to his ludicrous existence. We and the author both appear to wonder: *Had Alexandre Chenevert's soul always been filled with huge desires, only to be smothered in pettiness?* This very real description of solitude, in which the author and character commune so closely, is what reveals the author at work, always listening and watching her characters in their precise milieu, all the Cheneverts of this world, unable to surmount a reality that engulfs all their dreams. The author, of course, sympathizes with the defeat of this little bank employee, his failed marriage as baleful as his job, the failure of a man to reach his ideal of brotherhood and humanity because of the difficulty he has communicating with others, a life wasted in all of its vague desperation.

The works of Chekhov, too, are so often a reflection on injustice and inhumanity, in plays like *Uncle Vanya* (1897) or *Three Sisters* (1901), where the daily oppression of life, of boredom, snaps all impulses toward freedom – just as Gabrielle Roy carries on the same reflection on fates and hopes cut short. One may not know how it happens, whether by wear and tear, time, or the stagnation of monotony, but all of a sudden, the characters are forced to face this drama of quiet decline with lucidity and an absolute lack of self-pity, but impressed with the sterility of their existence, once so promising, like the three young women in *Three Sisters* or the winning heroine in *The Seagull* (1896). Chekhov's respect for human pain derives perhaps from his profession as a doctor, but certainly from his deeply felt and lived experience as a writer, as he cared for the sick in and around Moscow, in some forgotten neighbourhood where the entire population was ravaged by famine and cholera. Such suffering nurtured the memory of the writer every bit as much as he needed to appease that suffering through writing and to comfort those subjected to it, defenceless, poor peasants. This inexhaustible spring of others' pain would yield other portraits, including *Uncle Vanya* and *The Seagull*.

Reading the works of Gabrielle Roy, Margaret Laurence, Morley Callaghan, and so many others who comfort and console us like angels along our path, we can feel only gratitude and lightness of spirit at the raising of their voices in poetic song, at the transformation of basest reality into the fine crystal of their words and inspiration. But let us not forget that it is the sensibility and consciousness of these writers, constantly on the move, that carries these books, which in turn deliver them to us. All this has its price; every one of these authors pays it, for in searching beneath the surface into other people's lives and their own, they must first absorb it into their very skin and their own spirit before telling it in the form of stories. This, for many authors, is torturously painful, and often the most ordinary stories are the hardest to relate, even tragic. A case in point is the women in flight portrayed by Alice Munro in her *Runaway* stories: women leave, run away to change their lives for the better, turning their lives inside-out for nothing and, like so many women, disappear without a trace. These lives, though banal in appearance, are chased down with unforgettable sensitivity to what these women are lacking, whether courage, determination, or just a missed opportunity. They have, of course, left behind home, family, and husband, gone, fled, and yet unable to break the chains they have worn for so long and perhaps forged the indolent habit of wearing. The perspicacity with which these lives of women are observed from the inside is evidence of how intimate they have become and how assiduous and solid is the analysis in making us readers the witnesses to these lives in turmoil.

We are deeply shaken by the works of Mavis Gallant and Timothy Findley, two great writers touched by the violence of war, its effects on ordinary people, the displaced, the disoriented, the uprooted. The impression we are given is of actually being present, in the middle of disaster, following the exodus, the wanderings through prewar and postwar Europe, whether ruined or rebuilding, the emotion and the awakening of fear that these horrors could be repeated. For these writings are premonitory in tone, stemming precisely from the sensibilities of these writers' having invested their spirits in the description of this world, which is nakedly also our own. Or is it the one that awaits? Fearlessly, they have tackled subjects we would often rather avoid: violence and war and their future impact; displacement and the sorrow of wandering; the solitude of those who have nothing. Yet before writing such serious books, they too suffered these things, at least in their minds, the tension of concentrating on their weight and abrasiveness, just as I did myself when writing about Kent as he led his school friends to murder, knowing full well that his was a true story, however demonic, and that it would be repeated again and again in our schools and universities, as we have recently seen.

Sometimes, though, the attachment an author feels for the characters, the heroes-to-be of our novels, stories, or plays, is a happier, more enchanting one, perhaps surprising, even disconcerting, fascinating, all at once. For here we are at the edge of a life story — several, in fact — and if they spin away from tradition or conformity, so much the better. How can the world be complete without its fringe groups, its exiles, or its bereft and lonely, in a world off to the side not governed and hemmed in by conservative morality? Doubtless, it was in this temptation to pay tribute to a man condemned by all that Faulkner wrote in *Light in August* about Joe Christmas, the black assassin, as homage to the precariousness of a life already at a disadvantage from birth.

Translated by Nigel Spencer

2 0 1 0
GRAEME GIBSON

Truth is like the sun, its value depends wholly upon our being at a correct distance away from it.

— Hjalmar Söderberg

... it is a fallacy that those who were present can be trusted to know what happened.

— Max Hastings

Rummaging in memory, which I've been doing rather a lot of recently, I found no sign before 1956 that I considered writing to be a way out. When the notion did surface, I was in my second year at the University of Western Ontario – after having failed out of military college – and it had become clear that I was not going to distinguish myself as an honours student in English and Philosophy. Indeed, I'd begun to suspect I wouldn't survive another semester at Western. Fortunately, I was on the threshold of my third year and managed to avoid a "life" decision by escaping to the University of Edinburgh.

At the time, I was joined at the hip with a young man in one of Mavis Gallant's *Paris Stories*, who "after numerous false starts was looking for an open road." In such states of mind, the possibility of being a writer – without too much awkward thought about actually becoming one – often looks like an open road. I dimly recall bits and pieces of crushingly bad writing from that time. However, I did do one useful thing: I started a journal and beavered away at it for five years, actually growing up somewhat in the process.

My Edinburgh evasion was enhanced by the events unfolding in 1956 and 1957. We were deep in the Cold War, and one among many of its unsettling dramas was President Nasser's decision to nationalize the Suez Canal – in response to a significant provocation, it must be said – which he did two months before I arrived in Southampton aboard the S.S. *Columbia*. Once I had settled into an Edinburgh boarding house, the Hungarian revolt erupted. Six days later, with support from both France and the U.K., Israel invaded Egypt. Everything was so highly charged, so much more dramatic than my life in southwestern Ontario, that it occurred to me that I should be a journalist. If I'd had the money, I'd have bought a trench coat like Humphrey Bogart's, and tied the belt around my waist instead of using the buckle.

Fortunately I didn't do that, but I began scribbling outraged rubbish when Soviet tanks entered Budapest to subdue the uprising. The BBC carried desperate appeals from beleaguered Hungarians, and almost every day there were protests and demonstrations at the university and in the streets of Edinburgh. Tartan Tories, Marxists and Trots, Scottish Labour, Liberals, and Scottish Nationalists all joined in the ferment.

The dark agitation of that time, and the sense that God knows what would happen, was an emotional and cultural revelation for me. And at least partially as a result, I began churning out personal impressionistic stuff in earnest.

Edinburgh itself, with its statues and monuments to writers such as Scott, Burns, and Robert Louis Stevenson, contributed to that scribbling. The city had suffered very little modernization in the mid-'50s, and the Old Town seemed its original self at night, when sharp winds from Scandinavia burst all around us. My street was still lit by gaslight, and in the yellow fogs that drifted through the lanes and closes, I imagined Burke and Hare, Mr. Hyde, even the tapping stick of the terrible Blind Pew. I was haunted by a piper in ragged Highland dress who played for drink on bitter evenings outside the pubs in Rose Street. And I became friends with a complex musician, an organist who entertained us by playing triumphantly in an empty church after the pubs had closed. He once said to me, "Gibson, you have an untidy mind." As a gesture of appreciation for that observation, I gave his name to a character in one of my novels.

On January 13, 1957, after another supper of haggis and neeps in the basement dining room of Mrs. Adam's boarding house, the BBC broadcast a mesmerizing radio drama. It was Samuel Beckett's *All That Fall*, which begins with a chorus of farmyard animal voices and the footsteps and then talk of old Maddy Rooney as she walks to the railway station to meet her husband Dan. Most other boarders drifted away, but I was captivated. I had never encountered a voice that was anything like Beckett's, nor had I read one, either.

When I boarded the S.S. *Fairsea* for my return to Canada, I was carrying two large British Post Office envelopes stuffed with my bits of prose. Late on a wild evening in the middle of the Atlantic, I went alone to the pitching stern of the ship, and grabbing handfuls of paper from the envelopes, I hurled them into a black sea churning with froth from the ship's propellers. That gesture was such a release that I like to think it was my first editorial decision. Perhaps it was, because I held back several pages that were written soon after hearing Beckett's *All That Fall*. Oddly enough, these survivors would probably have slipped nicely into either of my first two books, *Five Legs* or *Communion*.

In November 1959, after failing my M.A. at Western, I arrived once again in Southampton, but this time with Shirley Warrington, who would become Shirley Gibson once her divorce was finalized. We knew it would proceed because I was the co-respondent.

It had been a confused and largely unproductive two years since I'd boarded the S.S. *Fairsea* for my return to Canada. I'd not written a word, except in the journal, and it was clear the time had come to set some psychic records straight, both for myself and others. I had to tell my own side of the story, but I couldn't know what that story might be until I wrote the book I'd begun desperately dreaming about.

Before starting this somewhat alarming task, I had to get a job and find somewhere for us to live. We were, as the saying goes, in the family way.

My younger brother, Alan, who was an unemployed actor, offered to put us up until we found our own place. His room was in a small row house crouching beneath the Battersea Power Station. I had been assured there'd be little trouble finding work as a supply teacher in London, so we all expected our stay with him to be short-lived.

I applied by post to various regional education officers, as instructed, but received no response. It eventually began to look dire. Alan's room had been a small parlour facing onto the sidewalk; behind the sliding door separating us from what had been the dining room, a desolate Indian coughed cavernously; it went on and on and in time began to sound like death. Soon it was December, the house was cold and the kitchen full of bicycles: when I rubbed grease off a small notice by the kitchen sink, where we washed and brushed our teeth, I saw that it said, PLEASE LEAVE THIS KITCHEN AS YOU FOUND IT.

Alan finally moved in with his girlfriend, but our neighbour kept on coughing. We found ourselves relying on friends for courage and occasional loans. Bemoaning my fate over supper in *Diogenes*, a friend's rented houseboat moored at Cheyne Walk, I was asked if I posted my letters from Battersea, which of course I did. "Well, that's it," he said. "You don't think they're going to hire people who live in Battersea? You've got to send them all again, but from Kensington or Chelsea." And he was right. I did as suggested, and was soon employed at a secondary modern school with nine hundred boys in Ladbroke Grove, and we moved into a garden flat (read: basement) in Barons Court.

It was a tough school, one that had suffered the ugly race riots that shook Notting Hill the previous year. The boys had all failed their 11-plus, which meant that most were waiting for the law to free them from school. Serious tensions and discipline problems remained: it became clear that I'd been hired not only because I was a big young man, and a dispensable Colonial, but I had recently earned my commission at the Royal Canadian School of Infantry.

The first time I turned my back on one class (and I'd avoided doing that for a couple of weeks), three kids threw something at me. I learned that the teacher I'd replaced had been driven from the school by boys throwing stones at him from ambush. When he got police protection, the attacks stopped; once the protection left, the attacks resumed. He quit.

I came closest to trouble when I first entered a class of older boys, all of whom were shouting and leaping, utterly out of control. When reasonable orders for quiet failed, I bellowed "SHUT UP!" in my most authoritarian Parade Square voice. Few noticed, so I strategically threw one of the bigger miscreants against the wall. In the silence that followed, one boy, obviously the barrack-room lawyer, said I could be fired for that. I agreed; then, getting the boy's name, I wrote a note saying what I'd done, and that he appeared no worse off for the experience. After dating and signing it, I gave it to him and said he could do with it as he wished because I'd rather dig a big hole in the ground for a living than put up with their crap.

Those boys – including the one I'd pushed against the wall – became my most enjoyable class. They'd long been bored silly, and humiliated, but they weren't stupid. We once discussed Frost's "Stopping by Woods on a Snowy Eve" as a death wish.

It was the despair and frustration in the teachers' common room that unsettled me most; what if I turned out like that? I volunteered for all recess and lunchtime supervision and nobody objected. Outside, I got to know the kids and consequently avoided most of the confrontations other teachers endured.

Although the work was physically demanding and emotionally exhausting, we were enjoying London and our child, and I found myself beginning to write seriously for the first time in my life.

By early spring, I was teaching a group of thoroughly rewarding nine- or ten year-olds in Kensington. When our son was born, they sent me home with bundles of cards and gifts for baby. By that time, I had written enough to want someone to look at it, someone I could trust. The logical choice was Eugene Benson. We'd been close friends at university, and he was the only person I knew who had written a novel. It wasn't publishable as it stood, but it was genuinely interesting. Anyway, he'd offered to look at what I was doing.

A month after I'd watched my eighty-some pages vanish into the Royal Mail, the term ended, whereupon Shirley took Matthew back to Canada in an attempt to mollify his grandparents. London was expensive, so I moved to a modest boarding house in Oxford and resumed my struggle with the book. A Swiss girl, who appeared from somewhere, was so impressed to discover that I was a novelist that she persuaded her aunt in Zurich to let me and the family move – rent-free – into a villa on the Cap d'Antibes. "My aunt is paranoid about Arabs," she told me. This was an unbelievable piece of luck because, what with an inheritance Shirley had just received, we would escape winter and I could work full-time on the book.

Eventually, a registered package with my manuscript and Eugene's notes arrived. There were ten pages of the latter, each with writing on both sides. I recall he'd used a ballpoint pen with blood-red ink, but that may be retrospective melodrama. It was a tough but remarkable and very courageous gift. In the midst of all kinds of encouragement and helpful suggestions, Gene said I'd clearly been working very hard; however, he couldn't find anything on the page that revealed why I was doing it. If you don't find it important, he asked, who will? He also said he could only find a handful of sentences that suggested I had any talent whatsoever. Much later, I assured him that there were at least fifteen.

Despite dismay and spasms of self-pity, I was oddly comforted to discover that Eugene's judgments hadn't surprised me, that – not for the first or the last time – I'd been fooling myself. In the event, I returned earnestly to his letter. I soon bundled up the eighty-some pages and hid them in a trunk. Years later, I pulled out his letter and that first desperate text and confirmed how fair and constructive Eugene had been. To this day, I consider his among the most courageous and valuable gifts I have received as a writer.

Once we'd settled into the villa's servants' quarters on the Cap d'Antibes, it became clear that I'd have to write outside the house, perhaps in a local sidewalk café like Ernest Hemingway. Which is what I did. Drinking coffee in spectacular weather until eleven or so, then moving on to beer or pastis, I began to learn how to write.

I had accepted all of Eugene's suggestions, except his conviction that stream-of-consciousness was too ambitious for a beginner like myself. Without underestimating the difficulties, I knew that my characters, and the dramatic events in their lives, would have to be rendered through the atmosphere of their minds. It just wouldn't work otherwise.

In order to take control of my prose, I began by making the first sentence work exactly as I wanted, and then continued one sentence at a time until I had fashioned the first paragraph. I hovered over each paragraph until I knew that it served its purpose and I could do no more. I'd then write the first sentence in my next paragraph. And so it went, one page after the other, and very slowly indeed. In the evenings, I'd make whatever small changes seemed necessary, and then compose a rough version of the sentence I planned to start with the next day.

Eugene had been right, of course; the absence of a conventional story line led me into numerous blind alleys. But I plugged away. Quite unexpectedly, one of the few decent essays I'd written at Western, "The Structure and Imagery of Milton's *Lycidas*," came back to reward me. Marrying what I'd learned from it with my pleasure in the way characters and situations offstage can be evoked by snatches of a theme in opera, especially Mimi's in *La Bohème*, I gradually began to recognize and then more fully exploit the logic of what I'd been doing.

It was a slow and often frustrating business. By the time we left France, I'd only managed twenty-five or thirty pages of what would become *Five Legs* almost eight years later. While there was significant editing done to the final manuscript, those early pages remain largely as written.

Having mentioned my first literary admirer – the Swiss girl who fortunately hadn't read a word of my dreadful manuscript – I will recount my first public appearance as an author. After beavering away for several months at the café, I was approached by a fussy-looking woman in her forties who had taken to nodding and smiling at me. After awkward pleasantries, she asked if I'd attend one of her literary soirées. I thanked her but declined. She urged me to change my mind. I thanked her with regrets. She went away, but returned frequently with the same request. In desperation, I agreed to join her group on a specified date when we were sure to have left town.

By the time we unexpectedly extended our stay, I'd forgotten the dreaded soirée. One night, the telephone rang. It was not a good moment. Shirley and I were having an old-fashioned argument and I had developed a fierce headache. It was the woman calling urgently about her soirée – where was I? I had to come immediately. Quick-quick. Everyone was waiting. For some inexplicable reason, I didn't plead mortal illness or the recent death of a family member. Weakened by the argument and my headache, I set out into the night. As I followed her directions into the centre of town, I began to fear that this escapade would be worse than sherry and biscuits in somebody's parlour. On top of that, I discovered I was still wearing my woolly slippers.

As I turned a corner into an ancient square, I saw her gesticulating at the end of a promenade beneath formidable arches. Almost before I'd arrived she seized my arm, dragged me up stone stairs, yanked open a door and propelled me onstage. Blinding lights transformed my headache into a major event. "*Maintenant*," she cried with evident relief, "*de Canada, l'auteur Graeme Gibson.*" I was dumbfounded. There was a smattering of applause. Staring wildly into darkness behind the lights, I heard my voice saying, "*Bonsoir, Mesdames et Messieurs!*" and then, after a long pause, "*Mesdames et Messieurs, bonsoir! Bonsoir. . .*" I then darted off stage, rushed down the stone staircase, and trudged home. By the time I got there, I was pleased with myself. It had been a narrow escape.

In *Communion*, a young man finds himself in a kitchen with a group of women who are languorously flushed with drink and rather intimidating. One asks him what he does best. He thinks for a moment, and then, pointing to the back door, says: "When the time comes, when it's absolutely essential, I can walk from here to there. To the back door there." One of the women says "Good. Not everybody knows that." Obviously my experience in that blinding auditorium lies behind my young protagonist's response.

When we returned to Toronto in the Spring of 1961, a university friend – one who had already purchased a Bentley – hired me as a market researcher, one of those folk who went from door to door with questionnaires containing hidden agendas about soap or tinned vegetables. It was intriguing for a while, if only because an occasional housewife, as they were then known, would behave in unexpectedly provocative ways.

My next piece of luck was to find a teaching job in the Ryerson Polytechnical Institute's English department. I was hired by Eric Wright, who twenty years later would have great success with his engaging Charlie Salter novels. While he didn't appear to be writing at the time, he'd had stories in *The New Yorker* and *Punch*, which made him the first published prose writer I'd met.

The early '60s were busy, melodramatic, and ominous: newspapers maintained their circulation with the Bay of Pigs invasion and the Berlin Wall, with the Cuban Missile Crisis and the Space Race, which was parading national egos and gobbling money. Nuclear bomb tests blossomed on every side, and even Vietnam raised its head, with Kennedy sending in his first group of "advisors." It isn't surprising that many people I knew at the time had had at least one nuclear war dream.

Obviously there were other kinds of news stories as well, but most of us paid little attention to them. Some dealt with an alarming series of wildlife die-offs resulting from the commonplace spraying of chemicals such as DDT. In 1962, Rachel Carson's iconic *Silent Spring* propelled these concerns to the surface. Symptomatically, I was scarcely aware of its publication. Deep in a hard and seemingly endless struggle with my novel, I was dreaming of another kind of apocalypse and picketing the American and Soviet Consuls after each new testing of the Bomb. My imagination was seized by another book published that year, Günter Grass's *The Tin Drum*.

Ryerson was a fine place to teach, but with seventeen class hours a week I had little energy left for writing. By the end of 1963, I had asked for and received a year's absence – without pay – so I could finish the book in Mexico. As Shirley and I set off for Oaxaca in July, with two children now, I swore that if I hadn't finished the book by the time we returned, I'd chuck it. That rash vow caused me considerable stress as the months and then years rolled by.

Once in Oaxaca, we moved into a flat on the second floor of a large house with a garden through which two dangerous German police dogs roamed at night. From one window we saw the town, and from another the mountains. Apparently, Frieda and D.H. Lawrence lived there while he was writing *Mornings in Mexico*. This struck me as a promising sign. On the other hand, Malcolm Lowry had his most terrifying visions in Oaxaca. I thought of him empathetically one night while a pack of feral dogs savagely attacked a burro. They were just out of sight around the corner, and confronted with their terrible wild voices and the despairing cries of the burro, even the dogs in our garden fell silent.

The novel was far from finished when we returned to Toronto. I'd accomplished a great deal, but far too much remained and I knew that a return to full-time teaching would cripple my always precarious momentum.

Arnold Edinburgh suggested I try for a Canada Council grant. He also persuaded Jack McClelland and Charles Israel, a fine film and radio dramatist, to support the application. It was successful, and by 1966, although back at Ryerson half-time, I was slowly writing my way towards the end.

On August 12, 1967, seven years after my obsessive sentence-by-sentence struggle began in the sidewalk café on the Cap d'Antibes, I wrote the last sentence of *Five Legs*. I don't recall making changes before giving the manuscript to McClelland & Stewart, and I certainly didn't re-read the text. Each type-written page remained in the chronological sequence in which it was written. It had been a long haul, and Shirley's encouragement and faith throughout had been unswerving and essential.

Apart from Eric, I'd still only met unpublished writers. There were a surprising number of us in haunts such as the King Cole Room (beer at fifteen cents a glass) or the Pilot Tavern. The most convincing among them was Juan Butler, who went on to publish three novels before killing himself. However, when M&S began to include me in their legendary book launches, I found myself in the heady world of real writers like Farley Mowat, Pierre Berton, and June Callwood. I began to feel I was on my way, especially since my second novel, *Communion*, was beginning to take shape.

After almost five months had passed without a word from M&S, I began to fret. When I complained to Farley one afternoon in the Park Plaza bar, he pointed across the room and said, "There's Jack. Go get him." Unwisely, I did ask McClelland about my manuscript. I even pointed out that he'd had it for five months. He stared at me with his pale blue eyes and said I'd hear from them on Monday. The fellow sitting with him, who listened intently to this exchange, turned out to be a feature writer doing a profile of McClelland for *Time* magazine. I wasn't surprised on the Monday to learn that M&S would not be publishing my book.

In January, I submitted it to Macmillan Canada, who kept it for only two months. Early in the wait, my editor — whose office kept shrinking, which I did not take to be a good sign — told me in an elevator taking us to the same roof bar of the Park Plaza that I'd have to marry the daughter of a French-Canadian lumber baron so there would be enough paper for my book.

With refusals from a Canadian and an English publisher, I turned to Doubleday. David Manuel and a young Doug Gibson did such a decent job of turning my book down that I experienced a spasm of triumph. "Graeme," explained David Manuel over a fine lunch, "we'd love to publish your book but New York won't let us. Branch plants don't do research." It was almost as if they'd accepted the novel.

I recounted these stories in the Pilot Tavern, in the Embassy beer hall, and around countless kitchen tables. Perhaps to shut me up, Kildare Dobbs and George Jonas independently – and within a week of each other – suggested trying the House of Anansi, a publisher I'd not heard of before.

By the time I met Dennis Lee, I must have been wild-eyed. We neither said much. I undoubtedly conveyed relief that he'd read the book, and hope that he'd like it. Perhaps I explained that it was my only copy and I'd once spent several horrible days in a gigantic lost-luggage warehouse at the airport in Mexico City before finding my suitcase with the novel inside. Leaving him, I wandered off, mustering the old, almost reliable daydreams the best I could.

Many people, including me, have written about Dennis Lee's quite remarkable role as an editor, so I won't dwell on it here. It is enough to say that I discovered later that he'd feared *Five Legs* would bankrupt Anansi: not only was it a complicated stream-of-consciousness work, and their first novel, it was too long. The expense of publishing it meant they'd have to charge at least $2.50 for the paperback, and $6.50 for the cloth. Despite this, Dennis went ahead, and the book appeared in April 1969. I don't think any of us were prepared for what then happened.

I went out Friday at midnight for Bill French's column in the Saturday *Globe and Mail*. Fumbling with the pages under a streetlight's brownish glow, I found the review's title: "A Glowing Anti-Puritanism in Sorrow." It was a remarkable review: French had somehow caught and conveyed what I'd been trying to do. I almost wept with relief.

The first run of two thousand copies sold out within weeks and a second printing of twenty-five hundred appeared shortly after. I have no idea how many people actually read *Five Legs*; I have certainly come across copies in second-hand stores that are suspiciously pristine. Be that as it may, the novel's unexpected and unusual success undoubtedly contributed to Anansi's growing publishing program.

Before *Five Legs*, Anansi's only fiction was Dave Godfrey's intriguing *Death Goes Better with Coca-Cola*. In the two following years, they produced two collections of stories and fifteen novels that included work by Austin Clarke, Matt Cohen, Marian Engel, and Roch Carrier. Two-thirds of the seventeen titles were by new writers. According to the *Canadian Encyclopedia* (online), in 1969 Anansi produced a third of all novels published in English Canada.

Between 1968 and 1971, Anansi's list acquired poets such as Allen Ginsberg, George Bowering, Joe Rosenblatt, and Michael Ondaatje. They published George Grant's *Technology and Empire* and Northrop Frye's *The Bush Garden*. Published in 1968, Mark Satin's *Manual for Draft-Age Immigrants to Canada* sold sixty-five thousand copies, mostly by mail. That success highlighted the desperation of draft-age Americans.

Anansi was only one among many small presses that appeared in the late '60s. Notable among others were Quarry and Coach House in 1965, and Oberon in the following year; then came Anansi and Mel Hurtig in 1967, Sono Nis in 1968, and New Press in 1970. On the whole, these were avant-garde and/or nationalist houses that produced a remarkable range of significant, often challenging writing.

Much has been said about the renaissance, the enthusiasm and optimism that Anansi and other small publishers encouraged and represented. Most of it is true, or true enough, but there's another, darker side to it. The fact is, it was often a hard, even torturous, and imperfect energy that we shared. Looking back at the injury of silence, the breakdown in egos and in marriages, the violence of suicide and Sonny Ladoo's murder, and the often terrible but sometimes comic intensities, it is clear that much of what we collectively achieved was done at cost.

Nor did any of it happen in a vacuum. Anti–Vietnam War protests were fed by what we now call troop surges, by napalm and the bombing of Hanoi. Severe race riots broke out in Watts, Detroit, Cleveland, and Newark. Martin Luther King and Robert Kennedy were murdered, and in 1970 the Ohio National Guard's massacre at Kent State University led to a nation-wide students' strike in the U.S.

In Canada, the Front de Libération du Québec kidnapped Richard Cross and murdered Pierre Laporte. This prompted Pierre Trudeau's government to impose the War Measures Act in response to what was called a state of "apprehended insurrection." The military was deployed in Quebec and a largely indiscriminate "rounding up" of Francophone Quebec intellectuals and artists followed. Few were charged with anything at all. Many of us felt that our generation lost its political innocence at that time.

Two months later, the sale of Ryerson Press to an American publisher caused a modest but transformative Canadian revolution. Canadian publishers quickly formed an emergency committee to protest the sale, and a mixed group instigated by publisher James Lorimer marshalled a protest in front of the Ryerson Polytechnic Institute, which is now a university.

We arrived with a large American flag, a ladder, and prepared speeches of fiery outrage; to our astonishment, the press awaited us. I clambered up the ladder, which leaned against the breast of Egerton Ryerson's imposing statue, and draped Old Glory about his shoulders. We then sang "I'm a Yankee Doodle Dandy" and rushed home to watch ourselves on television.

To its credit, the Ontario Progressive Conservative government (and I emphasize the "Progressive") struck a Royal Commission on Book Publishing, and appointed the inspired trio of Marsh Jeanneret, Dalton Camp, and Major-General Richard Rohmer as Commissioners. One of them told writer and playwright Max Braithwaite that they needed prose writers at their hearings. Max got a bunch of us together in his apartment, where we agreed to try and be sensible.

Those present on stage at the hearings included June Callwood, Ian Adams, Marian Engel, Farley Mowat, Margaret Atwood, Gwen MacEwen, Fred Bodsworth, Dave Godfrey, and Max Braithwaite. There weren't many in the audience, so it didn't take long to discover that Hugh Garner was sitting at the back of the hall. A self-proclaimed "One Man Trade Union," Garner was a real writer, who had won a Governor General's Award in 1963. He could, however, be difficult. And he was. After condescending to the women, he declared that writers didn't need anyone else helping them out. Our presentation quickly turned into a melee.

Some of retreated to lick our wounds in a beer parlour beneath the Park Plaza Hotel, where the idea of a prose writers' organization took hold. A few of us began to talk, to plan, and eventually test the idea with others across the country.

Initial discussions took place in Marian Engel's house in Toronto's Annex. As Andreas Schroeder puts it, "We had some meetings on Marian Engel's back porch. We did get a little tanked, it helped the optimism."

Our first public step was to invite a group of writers to a planning meeting in December 1972. The Ontario Arts Council's visionary Ron Evans bankrolled that first conference. Ron had already provided money to retain Alma Lee, who joined us from Anansi on the tacit understanding she would become the Union's Executive Director.

Six months later came a more formal conference at Neill-Wycik College in Toronto. About eighty of the one hundred and fifty writers we invited managed to attend. After two days of discussions (chaired by poet and leading constitutional expert Frank R. Scott), we agreed that a writers' union should be officially formed. Margaret Laurence was unanimously elected Interim Chair — albeit against her better judgment.[*]

The Writers' Union of Canada was founded November 3 in Ottawa's National Arts Centre, with Marian Engel taking the Chair. Frank Scott again supervised the proceedings elegantly and with great patience. One of the reasons we weathered the Union's more bizarre and unpleasant confrontations is that Frank Scott was our constitutional mentor, and Harold Horwood our *Robert's Rules of Order* martinet.

An additional benefit from Frank Scott was his clear-eyed sense of what the Writers' Union should *not* be.

THE CANADIAN AUTHORS MEET

Expansive puppets percolate self-unction
Beneath a portrait of the Prince of Wales.
Miss Crotchet's muse has somehow failed to function,
Yet she's a poetess. Beaming, she sails

From group to chattering group, with such a dear
Victorian saintliness, as is her fashion,
Greeting the other unknowns with a cheer—
Virgins of sixty who still write of passion.

The air is heavy with Canadian topics,
And Carman, Lampman, Roberts, Campbell, Scott,
Are measured for their faith and philanthropics,
Their zeal for God and King, their earnest thought.

---

[*] *Canada Writes*, Union Members' Book, 1977.

The cakes are sweet, but sweeter is the feeling
That one is mixing with the literati;
It warms the old, and melts the most congealing.
Really, it is a most delightful party.

Shall we go round the mulberry bush, or shall
We gather at the river, or shall we
Appoint a Poet Laureate this fall,
Or shall we have another cup of tea?

O Canada, O Canada, O can
A day go by without new authors springing
To paint the native maple, and to plan
More ways to set the selfsame welkin ringing?

After Marian's stint, I became Chair in 1975. Our professional concerns were Public Lending Right, the development of a standard minimum contract, the almost complete absence of Canadian writing in the schools, and a policy of vigorously lobbying governments about the specific problems facing writers and readers in Canada. However, since few writers in the early '70s knew more than a handful of their peers, our first substantial accomplishment was the focusing of a country-wide community of professional Anglophone book writers – what Margaret Laurence called "the tribe."

During a National Council meeting in Vancouver, the Province's curriculum development officer told us that he'd love to see CanLit taught in the schools, but there wasn't any. Flabbergasted, National Council decided to establish a "Teachers and Writers Education Project." Union members involved in the work agreed that our own books would not be included.

Five working groups were formed, one each in British Columbia, the Prairies, Ontario, Quebec, and the Atlantic Provinces. The teachers, all of whom had taught Canadian Literature in high schools, represented different areas within their regions. Union members Andreas Schroeder, Terrence Heath, and Barry Dickson, along with translator Sheila Fischman and Geraldine Gaskin, each acted as a co-ordinator of a working group. Eve Zaremba, who joined the Union later, managed what soon became a complicated and expensive business.

Collectively, they produced ten guidebooks with titles such as *The North/ Native Peoples*; *Coming of Age in Canada*; *Quebec Literature in Translation*; and *Women in Canadian Literature*. Funds came from foundations, the Ontario Ministry of Education, teachers' unions, and other government agencies.

When we reported to the AGM, there was an impassioned revolt because not all members had been included in the guides. A heated confrontation forced me to relinquish the Chair in order to argue the case on behalf of Council. We lost, as perhaps we should have, and were instructed to take the project elsewhere. This created a problem. We had raised and spent much money, and thirty-five teachers, along with various members of the Union, had donated months of their time to the project.

Under the circumstances, we couldn't simply hand the guides to a commercial outfit, so a few of us, notably David Young, Alma Lee, and myself, set out to establish the Writers' Development Trust.

Had we not done so, none of us would be here this evening.

Because David had a small trust of his own, he probably embodied the idea and had a sense of how we should proceed. Alma controlled us and the process with a solid hand, and I, well, I think I did a lot of enthusiastic talking about what fantastic things a trust could do for writers: accommodation and/or support for indigent writers, for example, or translation funds, free beer, and the Good Lord knows what else. We all did what we could to raise money. The guides themselves eventually contributed; nobody seems to know how many were sold, but it was certainly over forty thousand copies, with most of them going to high school English teachers.

When David and I recently reminisced over a glass, he characterized the whole process as a cloud of smoke and mirrors, and it was all coming out of my mouth. This is flattering, but at best only partly true. There were a lot of mouths involved, far too many to mention here, and a lot of words. Perhaps none were more significant than a quotation from André Malraux that we used to inform and promote the resource guides: "The mind suggests the idea of a nation," he said, "but what gives this idea its sentimental force is a community of dreams."

We are still collectively working on those dreams, and also on that country.

ACKNOWLEDGMENTS

The opening lines quoted on pages 36–37 are from, respectively: *The Wind in the Willows* by Kenneth Grahame (1908); *Alice's Adventures in Wonderland* by Lewis Carroll (1865); "The Lady with the Dog" by Anton Chekhov (1899), translated by Constance Garnett; *Pride and Prejudice* by Jane Austen (1813); and *A Tale of Two Cities* by Charles Dickens (1859).

The lines on page 53 are from Adele Wiseman's *Memoirs of a Book Molesting Childhood and Other Essays*. Toronto: Oxford University Press, 1987.

"The Nineteen Thirties are Over" (pages 54–55) is from Miriam Waddington's *Collected Poems*. Toronto: Oxford University Press, 1986.

The lines on page 59 are from *Enchantment and Sorrow* by Gabrielle Roy. Toronto: Lester & Orpen Dennys, 1987.

"Brown Sister" by Emma LaRocque (page 78) was published in *Writing the Circle: Native Women of Western Canada*, edited by Jeanne Perreault and Sylvia Vance. Edmonton: NeWest Press, 1990. Reprinted by permission of the publisher.

The quote on page 104 is taken from Margaret Atwood's address to the American Booksellers Association Convention in Miami, Florida, June 1, 1993.

W.O. Mitchell's lecture was originally titled "'The Poetry of Life'" and previously published in *An Evening with W.O. Mitchell*. Toronto: McClelland & Stewart, 1997.

The lines on pages 171–72 are from Edna Staebler's *Cape Breton Harbour*. Toronto: McClelland & Stewart, 1972.

P.K. Page's lecture was previously published in *The Filled Pen: Selected Non-Fiction* (University of Toronto Press, 2007). The lines from "Waiting to Be Dreamed" (pages 188–89) are from *The Hidden Room: Collected Poems* by P.K. Page. Erin, ON: The Porcupine's Quill Press, 1997. The lines from "Truce" (page 199), "Another Space" (pages 199–200), "Address at Simon Fraser (Excerpt)" (page 200), and "Poor Bird" (page 202) are from *Kaleidoscope: Selected Poems* by P.K. Page. Erin, ON: The Porcupine's Quill Press, 2010. Reprinted by permission of the publisher.

The quotation by P.K. Page of F.R. Scott's poem "Is" (page 198) has been approved by William Toye, literary executor for the estate of F.R. Scott.

The lines from Eldon Grier on page 198 are from his poem "Ecstasy" in *Collected Poems: 1955–2000*. Victoria, B.C.: Ekstasis Editions, 2001. Reprinted by permission of the publisher.

The lines on pages 209–10 were published in slightly different form in Peter C. Newman's *The Distemper of Our Times: Canadian Politics in Transition: 1963–1968*. Toronto: McClelland & Stewart, 1968.

The lines on pages 242–43 are from Ernest R. Hilgard and Richard C. Atkinson, *Introduction to Psychology*, 4th Edition. New York: Harcourt, Brace & World, 1967.

The lines on page 296 are from Alexander Morris's *The Treaties of Canada with the Indians of Manitoba and the North-West Territories Including the Negotiations on Which They Were Based, and Other Information Relating Thereto* (1880).

The line from Nathaniel Hawthorne on page 341 is from *Our Old Home: A Series of English Sketches* (1863).

The quotations from Marie-Claire Blais's *The Execution* (pages 360 and 361) are from the translation by David Lobdell. Vancouver: Talonbooks, 1976.

The lines on page 363 are from Marie-Claire Blais's *The Manuscripts of Pauline Archange*, translated by Derek Coltman and David Lobdell. Toronto: Exile Editions, 2010.

The lines on pages 369 and 370 are from *Surfacing* by Margaret Atwood. Toronto: McClelland & Stewart, 1972.

The lines on pages 370–71 from Hubert Aquin's *Les Sables mouvants / Shifting Sands* were translated by Joseph Jones. Vancouver: Ronsdale Press, 2009.

The quotation from Andreas Schroeder on page 387 is from Mark A.

Schaan's *Voices of Fire: The Writers' Union of Canada and its Impact on Canadian Cultural Policy*, University of Waterloo, April 2002. Readers: Dr. Robert Williams and Dr. Hildi Froese Tiessen.

The quotation by Graeme Gibson of F.R. Scott's "The Canadian Authors Meet" (pages 388–89) has been approved by William Toye, literary executor for the estate of F.R. Scott.

Author Photo Credits

Hugh MacLennan (page 9): © Yousuf Karsh / Library and Archives Canada; Mavis Gallant (page 23): © Alison Harris; Dorothy Livesay (page 52): © Suzanne Ahearne; Roch Carrier (page 64): © John Deniseger; Maria Campbell (page 76): McMaster University Library, Historical Perspectives on Canadian Publishing (http://hpcanpub.mcmaster.ca); Timothy Findley (page 86): © Elisabeth Feryn; Pierre Berton (page 112): © Elsa Franklin; Farley Mowat (page 130): © Peter Bregg; Peter C. Newman (page 203): © C Lantinga; Rudy Wiebe (page 286): © Danielle Schaub; Antonine Maillet (page 302): © Paul Labelle; Margaret Atwood (page 315): © Graeme Gibson; Elspeth Cameron (page 343): © Robert Lansdale; Graeme Gibson (page 375): © Lutz Dille

ABOUT THE CONTRIBUTORS

MARGARET ATWOOD

Margaret Atwood is the author of more than forty books of fiction, poetry, and critical essays. Her newest novel, *The Year of the Flood* (2009), is the follow-up to her 2003 Giller Prize finalist, *Oryx and Crake*. Other recent publications include *Moral Disorder* (2006), a collection of interconnected short stories; *The Door* (2007), a volume of poetry; and *Payback: Debt and the Shadow Side of Wealth* (2008). Additional titles include the 2000 Booker Prize—winning *The Blind Assassin*; *Alias Grace*, which won the Giller Prize in Canada and the Premio Mondello in Italy; *The Robber Bride*; *Cat's Eye*; *The Handmaid's Tale*; *The Penelopiad*; and *The Tent*. Margaret Atwood lives in Toronto with writer Graeme Gibson.

PIERRE BERTON

Pierre Berton is a Canadian icon. He authored fifty books and worked as a journalist and broadcaster. He is best known for his works of narrative history, such as *Klondike: The Last Great Gold Rush* and his two-part history of the Canadian Pacific Railway, *The National Dream* and *The Last Spike*. He received numerous honorary degrees and over thirty literary awards, including the Governor General's Award for Non-Fiction, which he was awarded three times. A founder of the Writers' Trust of Canada and a long-time serving director, Berton was at the head of the decision to create the Margaret Laurence Lecture series. He maintained a keen interest in the project, helping to select the speakers each year. He died on November 30, 2004.

MARIE-CLAIRE BLAIS

Marie-Claire Blais wrote her first novel, *La belle bête*, at the age of seventeen. It instantly became a classic of Québécoise literature and was translated into many languages. Since that auspicious debut, she has published more than thirty books, including *Une saison dans la vie d'Emmanuel*, which won the Prix Médicis, and *Naissance de Rebecca à l'ère des tourments*, which won her a third Governor General's Literary Award in 2008. In 2006, Blais received the Writers' Trust of Canada's Matt Cohen Award: In Celebration of a Writing Life. She divides her time between Key West, Florida, and Montreal.

JUNE CALLWOOD

June Callwood was a writer, journalist, broadcaster, and social activist. She worked energetically to investigate and promote the causes of social justice and humanitarianism, especially on issues affecting children and women. Starting out as an eighteen-year-old reporter at the *Globe and Mail*, she published more than twenty books, including *The Law is Not for Women* and *Jim: A Life with AIDS*. She founded or co-founded over fifty Canadian social action organizations, including youth and women's hostels; Casey House, a Toronto hospice for people with AIDS; PEN Canada; and the Canadian Civil Liberties Foundation. In recognition of her tireless volunteerism to support writers, Callwood received the Writers' Trust Distinguished Contribution Award a month before she died on April 14, 2007.

ELSPETH CAMERON

Elspeth Cameron has written biographies of Canadian literary giants Hugh MacLennan, Irving Layton, and Earle Birney. *Hugh MacLennan: A Writer's Life* was hailed as the first full-length biography of a Canadian writer, was shortlisted for the Governor General's Award, and won the UBC Canadian Biography Award. Cameron has also written several other books, including the memoir *No Previous Experience*. She headed one of the first Canadian Studies programs in Canada at Loyola College (Concordia) in 1970. "No one would let me write a Ph.D. thesis on a Canadian writer at U of T in 1965," she says. "They told me that there wasn't enough Canadian writing of any importance and that I would not get a job in that field." She currently teaches English Literature at Brock University. Her most recent book, *And Beauty Answers: The Life of Frances Loring and Florence Wyle*, was published in 2007. She lives in St. Catharines, Ontario.

MARIA CAMPBELL

Maria Campbell is a Métis author, playwright, and teacher. She started her career in 1973 when she published her first book, the memoir *Halfbreed*. That book has since become a literary classic and continues to be one of the most widely taught texts in Canadian literature. She has also written four children's books and translated oral stories into print. Her first professionally produced play, *Flight*, was the first all-Aboriginal theatre production in Canada. She has received numerous awards, including the Chalmers Award for Best New Play and the Dora Mavor Moore Award for playwriting. Campbell recently retired from the University of Saskatchewan, where she taught Native Studies, Creative Writing, and Drama. In 2010, the Pierre Elliot Trudeau Foundation selected her to be a Mentor.

ROCH CARRIER

Roch Carrier is one of the most widely read Québécois authors both in English and French. Born in Sainte-Justine, Quebec, he studied in Montreal and Paris and taught literature before becoming a full-time writer. A quote from his short story "*Le chandail de hockey*" ("The Hockey Sweater"), an allegory about the linguistic and cultural tensions between English and French Canadians, can be found on the back of Canada's five-dollar bill. His 1964 collection of stories, *Jolis deuils*, was awarded that year's Prix de la Province du Québec. He is best known for his early *Trilogie de l'âge sombre*, in particular his first novel, *La guerre, yes sir!* (1968), which remains his most widely studied literary work. He has been director of the Canada Council of the Arts and the National Librarian of Canada. Carrier lives in Montreal.

WILLIAM DEVERELL

William Deverell was a journalist for seven years and while working his way through law school. As a lawyer, he was counsel in more than one thousand criminal cases, including thirty murder trials, either as defender or prosecutor. His first novel, *Needles*, won the fifty-thousand-dollar Seal Prize in 1979. His subsequent fifteen books include *Trial of Passion*, which launched the Arthur Beauchamp crime series and won the 1997 Arthur Ellis Award for best Canadian crime novel and the Dashiell Hammett Prize for literary excellence in crime writing in North America. *April Fool* also won the Ellis Award, and his last two novels were shortlisted for the Stephen Leacock Medal for Humour. The creator of CBC-TV's long-running drama series *Street Legal*, Deverell lives on Pender Island, British Columbia, and in Costa Rica.

TIMOTHY FINDLEY

Timothy Findley was a novelist and playwright. Born in Toronto, Ontario, he had success as an actor before turning to writing. His first two novels, *The Last of the Crazy People* (1967) and *The Butterfly Plague* (1969), were rejected by Canadian publishers and were eventually published in Britain. In 1977, his third novel, *The Wars*, won the Governor General's Literary Award and established Findley as one of the country's most compelling and best-loved writers. He was a founding member and chair of the Writers' Union of Canada, and a director of the Writers' Trust of Canada. He resided in Stratford, Ontario and the south of France with his partner, William Whitehead. He died on June 20, 2002.

MAVIS GALLANT

Born in Montreal in 1922, Mavis Gallant left a career as a leading journalist in that city to move to Paris in 1950 to write short stories for a living. Since that time she has been publishing stories on a regular basis in the *New Yorker*, many of which have been anthologized. Her world-wide reputation has been established by books such as *From the Fifteenth District* and *Home Truths*, which won the Governor General's Award in 1982. In 1996, *The Selected Stories of Mavis Gallant* was published to universal acclaim. She has received several honorary degrees from Canadian universities and was made a Companion of the Order of Canada in 1993. In 2001, she became the first winner of the Writers' Trust of Canada's Matt Cohen Award: In Celebration of a Writing Life. She continues to live in Paris.

GRAEME GIBSON

Graeme Gibson was born in London, Ontario, in 1934. He published his first novel, *Five Legs*, in 1969. He is also the author of *Perpetual Motion*, *Gentleman Death*, and, most recently, *The Bedside Book of Beasts*. A long-time cultural activist, he co-founded both the Writers' Trust of Canada and the Writers' Union of Canada. Gibson is a recipient of the Harbourfront Festival Prize, the Toronto Arts Award, and the Writers' Trust Distinguished Contribution Award, and is a Member of the Order of Canada. A dedicated conservationist, Gibson is chairman of the Pelee Island Bird Observatory and is Joint Honorary President, with Margaret Atwood, of BirdLife International's Rare Bird Club. He lives in Toronto.

DOROTHY LIVESAY

Dorothy Livesay was born in Winnipeg in 1909 and educated at the Universities of Toronto and British Columbia and the Sorbonne. She married and lived in Vancouver from the late 1930s until 1958. She worked for UNESCO in Paris and Northern Rhodesia (Zambia) from 1959 to 1963. She returned to Canada as a Writer-in-Residence at several universities until the late 1980s, while continuing her own work. Her first collection, *Green Pitcher*, was published in 1928 when she was nineteen. In 1944, Livesay won the Governor General's Award for her book of poetry *Day and Night*. In 1947, her most critically acclaimed work, *Poems for People*, captured a second Governor General's Award and the Lorne Pierce Medal for Literature. A major figure in the rise of modernist poetry in Canada, Livesay mentored generations of Canadian poets. Her literary career spanned seventy years; she wrote more than two dozen books and received eight honorary degrees as well as the Orders of Canada and B.C. Livesay died in Victoria on December 29, 1996.

JANET LUNN

Janet Lunn was born in Dallas, Texas, in 1928, and came to Canada in 1946 to attend Queen's University in Kingston, where she met and later married fellow student Richard Lunn. A beloved children's author, she published her first novel, *Double Spell*, in 1968. She has also published non-fiction and picture books for young readers and received the Governor General's Literary Award for Children's Literature (text) in 1998 for her fifth novel, *The Hollow Tree*. She received the Writers' Trust of Canada's Matt Cohen Award: In Celebration of a Writing Life in 2005. She says that "I have lived through the flowering of literature and the arts in Canada, and I think I have been here in the best time Canada has ever had." Lunn lives in Ottawa.

HUGH MACLENNAN

Hugh MacLennan was born in Glace Bay, Nova Scotia, in 1907. When he was seven years old, his family moved to Halifax. MacLennan was ten years old when two ships collided in the harbour. The resulting blast, known as the Halifax Explosion, was the greatest man-made explosion in human history prior to the atomic bomb. His first published novel, *Barometer Rising* (1941), chronicles this event. His next novel and probably his most famous work, *Two Solitudes* (1945), won him the first of five Governor General's Awards. In 1951, Hugh MacLennan moved to Montreal and joined McGill University's Department of English, where he continued to write and publish. Montreal remained his home until he died on November 7, 1990.

ALISTAIR MACLEOD

Alistair MacLeod was born in North Battleford, Saskatchewan, in 1936 and raised among an extended family in Cape Breton, Nova Scotia. He still spends his summers in Inverness County, writing in a clifftop cabin looking west towards Prince Edward Island. In his early years, to finance his education he worked as a logger, a miner, and a fisherman, and he writes vividly and sympathetically about such work. He has published two internationally acclaimed collections of short stories: *The Lost Salt Gift of Blood* (1976) and *As Birds Bring Forth the Sun* (1986). In 1999, MacLeod's first novel, *No Great Mischief*, was published and later won the International IMPAC Dublin Literary Award. In the spring of 2000, MacLeod retired from the University of Windsor, Ontario, where he was a professor of English. He lives in Windsor.

ANTONINE MAILLET

Born in Bouctouche, New Brunswick, in the heart of Acadia, Antonine Maillet received her Ph.D. in literature in 1970 from the Université de Laval. In addition to her seventeen plays and monologues and many translations, she is the author of over twenty novels. While writing and lecturing are Maillet's main occupations, she is also often called upon to represent Acadia both in North America and internationally. She has received over fifteen literary prizes, including the prestigious Prix Goncourt for her novel *Pélagie-la-Charrette* (1979), and has been awarded thirty-one honorary doctorates. Among other titles and honours, Antonine Maillet is a member of the Royal Society of Canada, a Companion of the Order of Canada, and an officer of the Ordre de la Légion d'Honneur de France. She lives in Montreal.

W.O. MITCHELL

W.O. Mitchell (1914–1998) is best known for his novel *Who Has Seen the Wind*, a Canadian classic that has sold over three-quarters of a million copies since its publication in 1947, and for his "Jake and the Kid" stories, dramatized in CBC's radio series in the 1950s and 1960s. Over his sixty-year writing career, he wrote ten novels, two collections of short stories, about two hundred and fifty radio and screen plays, and five stage plays. His work won numerous awards, including two Stephen Leacock awards, three ACTRA awards, and the Chalmers Canadian Play Award. Through his radio, television, and live reading performances, he earned a reputation as one of Canada's favourite storytellers. Perhaps no other Canadian writer has been so versatile, not only in art form, but in audience appeal. He was made an Officer of the Order of Canada in 1973 and named to the Queen's Privy Council in 1993. He will be remembered as the writer who put the Saskatchewan prairies and Alberta foothills on the literary map of Canada.

FARLEY MOWAT

Farley Mowat was born in Belleville, Ontario, in 1921. He served in World War II from 1940 until 1945, entering the army as a private and emerging with the rank of captain. He began writing for a living in 1949 after spending two years in the Arctic. He remains an inveterate traveller with a passion for remote places and peoples. He has forty-four books to his name, which have been published in over twenty languages in more than sixty countries, including *Never Cry Wolf*, *Owls in the Family*, and *Lost in the Barrens*. He lives in Port Hope, Ontario.

PETER C. NEWMAN

Peter C. Newman was born in Vienna, Austria, and emigrated to Canada from Nazi-occupied Czechoslovakia in 1940 as a Jewish refugee. He has been writing about Canadian politics and business for nearly half a century. His *Renegade in Power: The Diefenbaker Years* (1963) revolutionized Canadian political reporting with its controversial "insiders-tell-all" approach. His autobiography, *Here Be Dragons: Telling Tales of People, Passion and Power*, won the Writers' Trust of Canada's Drainie-Taylor Biography Prize in 2004. A former editor-in-chief of the *Toronto Star* and *Maclean's*, Newman has been recognized with seven honorary doctorates, a National Newspaper Award, and election to the News Hall of Fame, and he has earned the informal title of Canada's "most cussed and discussed" commentator.

P.K. PAGE

P.K. Page was born in England in 1916 and moved to Canada at the age of three. Raised in the prairies, she first came to the attention of readers in the 1940s through her regular appearances in *Preview*, a Montreal-based literary magazine. Her collection *The Metal and the Flower* won the Governor General's Award for Poetry in 1954. Twice shortlisted for the Griffin Poetry Prize, Page received the B.C. Lieutenant Governor's Award for Literary Excellence in 2004. A new collection of her work, *Kaleidoscope*, was published in 2010 and is the first in a series of volumes to be published over the next ten years intended to complement a scholarly project that will collect all of the poet's work online. Page was a visual artist (under the name P.K. Irwin) and her work is represented in the permanent collection of the National Gallery of Canada. Page died on January 14, 2010.

AL PURDY

Al Purdy was born on December 30, 1918, in Wooler, Ontario. He served a long apprenticeship as a poet, finally breaking through with *The Cariboo Horses*, which won the Governor General's Literary Award in 1965. From that time forward he was able to support himself full-time by writing. He and his wife Eurithe travelled widely while alternating their permanent residence between British Columbia and Ontario. Purdy published thirty-three books of poetry, a novel, an autobiography, and nine collections of essays and correspondence. His *Collected Poems* won him a second Governor General's Award in 1986. He died on April 21, 2000, in Sidney, British Columbia. The Al Purdy A-frame Project is currently raising funds to purchase and establish a Poet-in-Residence program in the house Purdy built in Ameliasburg, Ontario.

JOSEF ŠKVORECKÝ

Josef Škvorecký is a Czech émigré. He grew up under two dictatorships, was involved in the underground of 1950s Prague, and published fiction which was later, for political reasons, seized by Czech authorities. After the Prague Spring of 1968, Škvorecký came to Canada and taught at the University of Toronto. He continued to publish novels, including the 1982 Governor General's Award—winning novel *The Engineer of Human Souls*. He also, along with his wife, Zdena Salivarová, founded 68 Publishers, which brought books by writers such as Václav Havel, Milan Kundera, and Bohumil Hrabal into print for the Czech community in the Western world. He lives in Toronto.

EDNA STAEBLER

Edna Staebler was born in Berlin (now Kitchener), Ontario in 1906. She began her career as a teacher and later became a well-respected freelance writer in the 1940s and '50s, writing articles for *Maclean's*, *Chatelaine*, and *Saturday Night*, among others. She became an early innovator in creative non-fiction with *Cape Breton Harbour* (1972), an account of her stay in the Maritimes. Later in her life, Staebler was widely known for her series of popular cookbooks, *Food that Really Schmecks*, based on Mennonite home cooking. In 1991, she established the Edna Staebler Award for Creative Non-Fiction. She died on September 12, 2006 at the age of one hundred.

AUDREY THOMAS

Audrey Thomas was born in Binghamton, New York, and emigrated to Canada in 1959. She is the author of a number of highly praised novels, including *Intertidal Life*, an obsessive introspection of a failed marriage, which was published in 1984 and nominated for the Governor General's Award for Fiction. Thomas has received three honours from the Writers' Trust of Canada: the Marian Engel Award, the W.O. Mitchell Literary Prize, and the Matt Cohen Award: In Celebration of a Writing Life. She has been a tireless contributor to the development of the Canadian literary landscape, having served on the Arts Advisory Board, the Canada Council, and on the national executive of the Writers' Union of Canada. Thomas splits her time between Galiano Island, British Columbia, and Victoria.

Rudy Wiebe was born in 1934 on an isolated homestead near Fairholme, Saskatchewan. He is the author of nine novels, five short-story collections, and ten non-fiction books; his novels *The Temptations of Big Bear* and *A Discovery of Strangers* both won the Governor General's Award for Fiction. In 2007, he received the Charles Taylor Prize for Literary Non-Fiction for his memoir *Of This Earth: A Mennonite Boyhood in the Boreal Forest*. *Rudy Wiebe: Collected Stories, 1955–2010* was published in 2010. He has been a professor emeritus at the University of Alberta since 1992, and he lives in Edmonton.